A Rendezvous With Destiny

The Roosevelts of the White House

by

Elliott Roosevelt
and James Brough

G. P. Putnam's Sons, New York

B
973
Rooseve
1975

DATE DUE

A Rendezvous With Destiny

The Roosevelts of the White House

Also by the Authors:

AN UNTOLD STORY:
The Roosevelts of Hyde Park

For our children and grandchildren in the hope that time remains for peace and a good life to be built on earth for them and their generations of all mankind:

William, Ruth, Elliott Jr., David Boynton, James, Ford, Gretchen, David Macaulay, Christopher, Stephanie, Emilie;

Dana, Nicholas, Christopher, Ruth, Hays, Chandler, Laura, Elliott III, Elizabeth, David, Matthew, Melinda, Melissa, Tasha.

Contents

*Illustrations will be found
following page 224*

ACKNOWLEDGMENTS

The personal reminiscences and interpretations contained in these pages have been augmented from a number of sources, both published and unpublished, notably the files of the Franklin D. Roosevelt Library, Hyde Park, New York, whose director, William R. Emerson, and staff are most sincerely thanked. Of the published works, the most heavily drawn on are *F.D.R. His Personal Letters 1928–1945*, edited by Elliott Roosevelt (New York, Duell, Sloan & Pearce, 1950) and *As He Saw It*, by Elliott Roosevelt (New York, Duell, Sloan & Pearce, 1946).

Grateful acknowledgment is made to James MacGregor Burns, the preeminent biographer of Father to date, whose *Roosevelt: The Lion and the Fox* (New York, Harcourt Brace Jovanovich, 1967) and *Roosevelt: The Soldier of Freedom* (New York, Harcourt Brace Jovanovich, 1970) were frequently employed to check the accuracy of memory and confirm some speculations.

Much of the London background in the second part of this present volume derives from *English History 1914–1945*, by

A. J. P. Taylor (New York, Oxford University Press, 1965). Deep appreciation is extended.

Other works whose contribution proved to be significant include: *This Is My Story,* by Eleanor Roosevelt (New York, Harper & Brothers, 1937), *This I Remember,* by Eleanor Roosevelt (New York, Harper & Brothers, 1949), *Speaking Frankly,* by James F. Byrnes (New York, Harper & Brothers, 1947), *Triumph and Tragedy,* by Winston S. Churchill (Boston, Houghton Mifflin, 1953), *Memoirs,* by Cordell Hull (New York, The Macmillan Company, 1948), *The Forrestal Diaries,* edited by Walter Millis (New York, The Viking Press, 1951), *The Secret Diary of Harold L. Ickes* (New York, Simon & Schuster, 1953), *Eleanor and Franklin,* by Joseph P. Lash (New York, W. W. Norton, 1971), *I Was There,* by William D. Leahy (New York, Whittlesey House, 1950), *White House Diary,* by Henrietta Nesbitt (New York, Doubleday, 1948), *The Roosevelt I Knew,* by Frances Perkins (New York, The Viking Press, 1946), *The Public Papers and Addresses of Franklin D. Roosevelt,* edited by Samuel I. Rosenman, Volumes for 1928 to 1936 (New York, Random House, 1938), Volumes for 1937 to 1940 (New York, The Macmillan Company, 1941), Volumes for 1941 to 1945 (New York, Harper & Brothers, 1950), *Working With Roosevelt,* by Samuel I. Rosenman (New York, Harper & Brothers, 1952), *Roosevelt and Hopkins,* by Robert E. Sherwood (New York, Harper & Brothers, 1948), *Roosevelt and the Russians—The Yalta Conference,* by Edward R. Stettinius, Jr. (New York, Doubleday & Company, 1949), *On Active Service in Peace and War,* by Henry L. Stimson and McGeorge Bundy (New York, Harper & Brothers, 1948), *Memoirs,* by Harry S. Truman (New York, Doubleday & Company, 1955), *Years of Trial and Hope,* by Harry S. Truman (New York, Doubleday & Company, 1956), *Correspondence Between the Chairman of the Council of Ministers of the U.S.S.R. and the Presidents of the U.S.A. and the Prime Ministers of Great Britain During the Great Patriotic War of 1941–1945* (Moscow, Foreign Languages Publishing House, 1957), *Roosevelt in Retrospect,* by John Gunther (New York, Harper & Row, 1950).

Of the men and women who gave their help, special thanks are due to Dr. Howard Bruenn for use of his clinical notes, Janet Aston for her skills and enthusiasm at a typewriter, and Fred Renshaw of Polydor, who at a time of crisis rescued tapes chewed up by a hostile recorder.

Preface

Ever since I was a young man, I have been reading books about my father. They fill half my library shelves, and more are added every season. I suspect that records have been set by the number of authors who, with varying degrees of accuracy, have tackled the subject of Franklin Delano Roosevelt and the rare speed, historically speaking, at which those millions of words have been rushed into print.

He has been depicted on one hand as a combination of Machiavelli and Judas Iscariot, on the other as George Washington, Thomas Jefferson, and St. Augustine reincarnated. Lately, it has become fashionable to picture him as an aging Lothario, taken up with a secret love affair, while he let the Soviets bamboozle him. Regrettably, the man as he was in full dimension is almost lost to view.

It is my conviction that, in these times of trouble for the United States, he should be seen again for what he truly was, a leader of his countrymen through years which parallel our own. When he came to office, Depression darkened the land, just as it looms again today, and within twenty-four hours, he made the first move to dispel the darkness. Morale had reached rock bottom then; he set out immediately to restore hope to Americans. He found the Presidency remote from the people and power dangerously concentrated in high places, a situation not entirely unfamiliar in 1975.

From the moment of his death, there has been no dearth of celebrants eager to dance on his grave. The effort to discredit him enlists those forces which have contrived to control the United States since the era of Andrew Jackson. When they faltered in 1933, he saved them. In return, they tried to destroy his Presidency. No President since then has challenged their power.

It is time to reassert the truth about FDR and his achievements—and equally important, for completeness of understanding, to spell out the deeds of the men who deliberately distorted the facts as they brushed aside his vision of a world freed from war and ever-present hunger.

Every one of us pays for the consequences. We are held to ransom by oil-rich nations hitting out to adjust the imbalance of international wealth, which Father planned on rectifying thirty years ago. Though we live under threat of nuclear devastation, the piling up of hydrogen bombs continues, flint and fuel to the fires of inflation. Distrust divides the world, which under Father's ultimate design would be united in a common campaign to improve life for all.

To try to whitewash my parents would be a disservice to their memory. My father was a complex human being but no seeker after glory; he left that to one of his celebrated contemporaries and to some successors in the White House. Historians of the future deserve to be acquainted with all facets of his nature, as his family knew them.

History must record that he led the greatest social revolution the free world has ever known. He inaugurated a system of governmental responsibility for every citizen that has been accepted by each succeeding Administration. He built a military machine with an incredible productive capacity. He was the progenitor of the United Nations, who served his country fearlessly and with remarkable compassion. There have been differences in the character of Presidents and the Presidency in recent years, but few improvements.

The growth of Mother's personality and the expansion of her relationship with Father began during the White House years. All five of us children reached maturity in that rarefied atmosphere. We were left with scars and some anguish as an inheritance that influenced the course of our lives. For myself, I have no excuses to offer.

I believe that April 12, 1945, when Father died, marked the day when morality in government began to pass from the picture. The downhill road carried us into Vietnam and the abyss identified as Watergate. These remembrances of promised glory are written in the equal belief that it is not yet too late to start the climb back uphill once more.

These pages tell the story of what he accomplished, how he did it, and what he might do were he faced with the problems of today. My father was convinced to the end that he was destined to clinch victory in war and to forge the peace to follow. That his life ended too soon for those purposes to be achieved can be regarded as his one significant defeat.

E. R.

We that had loved him so, followed him, honored him,
Lived in his mild and magnificent eye,
Learned his great language, caught his clear accents,
Made him our pattern to live and to die!

—ROBERT BROWNING

A nation must believe in three things.
It must believe in the past.
It must believe in the future.
It must, above all, believe in the capacity of its people so to learn from the past that they can gain in judgment for the creation of the future.

—FRANKLIN DELANO ROOSEVELT
June 30, 1941

I

THE MIGHTIEST GIFT

1

I T would have suited everyone in the family better, I think,
if the guests could have shown up late. But the hidebound
rules of Washington society demanded unconditional punctu-
ality in meeting the President, and the invitations were for dinner at seven forty-five. Now time was getting short, and only
Mother had found more than a minute or two to acquire a general idea of where all the rooms were situated upstairs or down
on the four floors. Our luggage had been hurried over a few
hours beforehand from the Mayflower Hotel on Connecticut
Avenue, where Father, Mother, Granny, and the rest of us had
stayed overnight on the eve of this Inauguration Day in rented
rooms of no particular splendor.

There was nothing fancy either about the looks of our well-
worn furniture that had been set in place in the White House,
with Mother applying a helping hand to lift or push. The creaking wicker chairs that had seen long service in Hyde Park
scarcely spoke of Presidential grandeur now that they stood in
some of the sitting rooms. Nothing we owned could match the
plushy elegance of the furnishings that the outgoing tenants
had taken with them. Out of Herbert Hoover's self-made millions as "the Great Engineer," he and his wife could well afford

to dress up the mansion, as Mother had noted after silver-haired Lou Hoover took her on an inspection tour from attic to basement a few days earlier.

Mother also suspected—rightly, as it turned out—that the ancient wood-paneled kitchen and the dismal cellars were plagued with descendants of the same roaches and rodents that Uncle Ted and his family had found there when he became the first of the Roosevelts in the Presidency thirty-two years ago. In its outward appearance the house seemed to embody the distinction and simple dignity of the Constitution itself. Inside, the living quarters were as graceless and uncomfortable as some of the deals that had been settled within their walls in the years since Uncle Ted's departure.

She had already gone through what she would have to call a *trying* day. It had been a challenge to make small talk with Mrs. Hoover in the limousine that took the two of them from the White House to the Capitol in the wake of the Presidential car. Nonetheless, she had an easier task than Father, who could not coax a civil word from the man he had defeated last November by a popular vote of 22,809,638 to 15,758,901. Father disliked being disagreeable to anybody as much as he disliked disagreeableness in other people. But Hoover clearly regarded Franklin Delano Roosevelt as a traitor to his class, whose victory would mean that "grass will grow in the streets of a hundred cities." Father contented himself with waving his top hat to the crowds that lined Pennsylvania Avenue and flashing them the smile that was to become a symbol of his Presidency.

A limousine had sped Mother back early from the inaugural stand, where she had found the waves of cheering "a little terrifying." The cold wind there had pulled wisps of hair out from under her hat and chilled her in the two-piece, pinstriped wool costume with the fur piece draped around her shoulders. She had to be back by five fifteen to supervise the serving of tea and tiny sandwiches to the multitude that swarmed through the State Dining Room and the East Room, and she was already concerned over how the budget could ever be stretched to cover such expenditures. At that moment in time, the Roosevelts were short of ready cash. Granny could always be relied to dip once again into her own fortune to bankroll her only son, but neither of my parents cared to resort to the well more often than was strictly necessary.

"I never was really carefree," Mother acknowledged when she looked back on her White House years, and today, Saturday, March 4, 1933, was surely one of the least joyful days among them. Seventy-five dinner guests would be presenting themselves very shortly. The long-suffering housekeeper, Mrs. Henrietta Nesbitt, was not installed on the premises until the following Tuesday. This evening's gathering would be like holding a family party in a strange hotel into which the Roosevelts had just been registered, with grave reservations about room service and the capabilities of the kitchen. Father would not be back for almost another hour.

Where Mother was nervous, Granny was jubilant. She had anticipated this day, she convinced herself, for more than half a century, from the moment her incomparable son was born. If her daughter-in-law remained a trifle too *gauche* to carry off the occasion in the style it deserved, Sara Delano Roosevelt would set a model for her to copy, if she could. In her seventies, her spine was as straight, her jaw as strong, and her commanding hazel eyes as bright as ever. She took special pains with her *toilette* this evening, with every gleaming hair arranged in place in her pompadour, resplendent in a long gown fitted snugly to her majestic frame, with her magnificent pearls looped on the pale skin of her imposing bosom.

Granny had been largely responsible for the guest list. The basic idea was to make it a purely family celebration, limited in genealogical distance to first cousins on either side. As it turned out, there was a marked preponderance of Delanos, which was only fitting in Granny's view when *her* ancestry could be traced as far back as William the Conqueror.

It could only have been through some oversight of hers that a man she despised as much as anyone in the world was included, though his right to be there certainly equaled hers and his mood for rejoicing probably soared higher. Louis McHenry Howe gave twenty years of his life to making Father the elected leader of the American people. More than anyone else—and that included Mother and Granny—he nursed Father back to political life after polio crippled him in 1921. In Louis' opinion, the White House was the only worthwhile goal for the man he regarded as the greatest human being that civilization had produced, whom he served as manager, goad, and inspiration.

But Louis invariably looked like a wizened gnome in his

crumpled clothes gray with ash from a nonstop supply of
drooping Sweet Caporals. The hacking cough caused by em-
physema punctuated everything he said. His attitude toward
Father was never better expressed than in a pep talk Louis gave
to campaign workers in the previous fall's election: "You're
nothing. Your face means nothing. Your name means nothing. . . . I don't want to catch you or anybody else trying to
crowd into a photograph. . . . All you have to worry about,
night and day, day and night, is this man Roosevelt and get him
to the White House no matter what." Though that was Granny's point of view exactly, Louis could not be rated *couth,* and
couthness weighed heavily in her judgments of everyone, not
excluding the Oyster Bay, Long Island, branch of the Roosevelt
family, which produced President Theodore but in all other respects was singularly lacking in couthness as she defined it.

For today's ceremonies Louis might well have been outfitted
by Brooks Brothers in person. We could scarcely recognize him
in his rented finery—silk hat, immaculate morning coat, gray
trousers with knife-edge creases reaching to the sparkling
shoes. Above his standup shirt colar and dark cravat, a rare
smile added even more wrinkles to his sunken, pockmarked
cheeks. On the Capitol steps as he took the oath of office, Father, whose interest in clothes was nonexistent, did not rank in
the same sartorial class as Louis.

"This great Nation will endure as it has endured, will revive
and prosper," said the new President. "So, first of all, let me as-
sert my firm belief that the only thing we have to fear is fear itself—nameless, unreasoning, unjustified terror which para-
lyzes needed efforts. . . ." There, the original text read "to
bring about prosperity once more." That was too tame for Father. He amended the phrase shortly before he spoke it: "to
convert retreat into advance."

Six months previously, in a campaign speech, he had spelled
out the philosophy that he brought to his latest task. Six hundred corporations controlled two-thirds of American industry.
"Existing economic organizations" must be adapted to "the
service of the people." "I do not believe," he said, his voice soaring, "that in the name of that sacred word, individualism, a few
powerful interests should be permitted to make industrial cannon fodder of the lives of half the population of the United
States."

Those rightists like Hoover who proclaimed that Father was prescribing Communism as a cure for whatever ailed America could convince themselves that their suspicions were well founded as they had heard him address the country today. He promised action to make jobs for the hungry, to bring back life to the farmlands, to restore the people's buying power. He would lead a disciplined attack on "our common problems." He would strive to maintain a balance between executive and legislative authority, but if that did not work, he would ask Congress for emergency power "as great as the power that would be given me if we were in fact invaded by a foreign foe."

Conversation at dinner between Father and his guests promised to be interesting. Apart from our immediate family, the vast majority of our relatives were dyed-in-the-wool Republicans.

At six o'clock he was wheeled back into the house, jubilant after watching the marchers parading on Pennsylvania Avenue in honor of the thirty-second President. The parade was the only feature of his next three Inaugurals that he really enjoyed. The rest of the ceremonials struck him as being decidedly overdone, and he never ventured to repeat anything like this impending dinner.

He was suntanned and fighting fit from the fresh air and sunshine he had enjoyed for two weeks in the waters of the Bahamas aboard the *Nourmahal,* the yacht of his friend and neighbor in Dutchess County, New York, Vincent Astor, "a dear and perfect host." Astor was one of the handful of maverick millionaires who were especially close to Father. My parent, the champion of the common man, delighted in the company of the sympathetic rich. As a member of his finance committee, Vincent had donated $25,000 toward Father's election. And when Hoover had attempted to smear Father with an accusation that he was devoted to a "philosophy of government which has poisoned Europe," Astor denounced that charge as a lie.

It was during the fishing trip only eighteen days ago that the President-elect came close to being assassinated. He had gone ashore at Bay Front Park, Miami, Florida, to attend a reception when an out-of-work bricklayer, Giuseppe Zangara, aimed a fusillade of bullets at him, denouncing "all officials and everybody who is rich." Five men in Father's party were hit; Mayor Anton Cermak of Chicago died of his wounds. Such was the climate of the times. Among the black-tied men and long-gowned women on their way to join us this evening there were some who, like hundreds of thousands of other well-to-do Americans, would ask themselves whether the country was on the brink of violent revolution. They fancied that it was not too far-fetched to draw parallels to the plight of Czar Alexander holed up in his St. Petersburg palace when anarchy spread throughout Russia. But Father was no czar, and he derided the efforts of the Secret Service to provide him with protection for which he saw absolutely no need, though, in his wheelchair or hoisting himself along on his steel-braced legs with the help of someone's friendly arm, he made an easy target for any assassin.

At five minutes past six he was hauled up in the creaking little elevator to the second-floor study for the swearing in of his Cabinet. All but one of them had been picked well in advance, almost without exception for political reasons. "Cactus Jack" Garner of Uvalde, Texas, Speaker of the House of Representatives until he was elected Vice President, was there only because of a deal swung at the Chicago convention of the Democratic Party the previous June. Balloting to select the candidate to run against Hoover threatened to end in deadlock. Garner had nourished Presidential dreams of his own until a telephone call from William Randolph Hearst in his California mountaintop aerie of San Simeon persuaded him to throw the votes of the Texas and California delegates behind Father. Jack's consolation prize was second place on the ticket, a place he considered "not worth a pitcher of warm piss."

Big Jim Farley's appointment was preordained, too. His vital role had been to clinch the bargain with Hearst and round up the 945 delegate votes that made Father the Democrats' choice for the White House. Farley's reward was to be named Postmaster General, the traditional post for political boondoggling.

Cordell Hull, former Senator from Tennessee, was the gray-haired eminence who was now Secretary of State because he wielded great power within the party. Father also had great respect for the astuteness and knowledge of foreign affairs he had shown in his career in both Houses of Congress.

The new Secretary of the Treasury was a converted Republican, Bill Woodin, of the American Car and Foundry Company, one of whose qualifications was the $10,000 he contributed to

Father's campaigning. While the country staggered on through a banking crisis which posed the biggest immediate threat to its future, Woodin wore himself out as a loyal lieutenant to Father, who was really his own Treasury Secretary, and devil-may-care in his approach to the job.

Governor George Dern of Utah was sworn in as Secretary of War principally as a result of Father's having met and liked him at a number of governors' conferences when he was Governor Roosevelt of New York. George had proved to be among his strongest backers for the Presidency.

There was nothing novel, rare, or reprehensible in the process by which these people were chosen. Father singled out the ten men and one woman who ostensibly would be the senior executives of his first administration in line with a tradition that dated back to George Washington. Political debts must be paid in political coin. Fences must be mended, regional and bloc interests respected, friendships remembered, firm relations established with Congress.

Old Claude Swanson, Senator from Virginia, who dressed in an antebellum frock coat and wing collar, had been chairman of the Senate Committee on Naval Affairs during World War I, when Father worked in Washington as a belligerently ambitious Assistant Navy Secretary. Swanson's health was none too robust, but Father appointed him his first Secretary of the Navy, rating him "a delightful man."

As Secretary of Commerce, Dan Roper represented a token of Father's gratitude to William McAdoo, himself a loser in the deadlocked 1924 Democratic convention which named John W. Davis as its Presidential candidate, to be trounced by Calvin Coolidge. In last summer's hassle in Chicago, McAdoo had joined Garner in swinging the precious delegate votes to Father, and Roper was a leader of McAdoo's men in the Democratic Party. In his day, Dan had been an Assistant Postmaster General. Father thought that "he knows the government and has courage." Later experiences with his starchy Commerce Secretary persuaded him that Roper was "as funny as a crutch."

Both the prickly Harold Ickes and the visionary Henry Wallace were one-time Republicans. Now Harold was Secretary of the Interior, and Henry of Agriculture. Father relished Harold's slam-bang campaigning for him, and he respected Wal-

lace as a farm leader in the Corn Belt and his thinking in looking for ways to allay the present plight of agriculture. He could
smell trouble in their future relationships with each other, but
he felt certain that he could handle them, as he could handle
virtually everyone who came within his orbit.

The one precedent-breaking woman in the Cabinet, Frances
Perkins, owed her appointment more to Mother than to anyone
else. She had been extolling the abilities of Frances from the
day Father was first elected Governor of New York in 1928.
Mother was hesitant about pressing her protégés on him at that
time. "These are suggestions which I'm passing on," she told
him, "not my opinions, for I don't mean to butt in." Frances,
known not always fondly as "Ma" Perkins, had proved her skills
after he made her his Labor Commissioner in New York State.
Now she was United States Secretary of Labor and, as her Cabinet colleagues were to find, an incorrigible chatterbox who
could seldom resist the temptation to pour a few more Bostoni-
an-accented words into his ear.

Where Mother had played a part in getting Frances where
she was today, Homer Cummings of Connecticut owed his job
as Attorney General largely to Missy LeHand, the calm, bright-
eyed Catholic who carried the title of secretary and served Father with her heart and soul. The appointment had been earmarked for Senator Tom Walsh of Montana, celebrated for his
fearlessness and integrity in laying bare the scandals surrounding the sale of Teapot Dome oil leases in Warren Harding's administration. Father had counted on having Tom beside him in
formulating the new legislation that would be needed to set the
country on course through the hurricane of the Depression.
But Tom died just before the Inauguration, en route to Washington after his second honeymoon. It was Missy who suggested that Father should consider Cummings to fill Tom's shoes.

On this Saturday evening, Missy had not yet moved upstairs
into the third-floor apartment that was to be her permanent
home.

As soon as the new Cabinet had been sworn in, Father sat
them down for their first formal meeting, to give them a taste
of his initial tactics for tackling the crisis, which had deepened
in the four-month lull between November and now. The count
of unemployed stood somewhere between fourteen and sixteen

millions. In the past three years, more than five thousand banks had failed, wiping out the savings of whole towns at a go. Investors on the New York Stock Exchange alone had seen an incredible $74 billion loss on their shareholdings, which amounted to $616 a head for every man, woman, and child in the country.

He barely had time to change into dinner clothes before our guests began to present themselves. Mother waited to greet them at the door, while Granny was satisfied to wait for them to approach her to observe more formal social niceties. Father sat close to her in one of his handmade wheelchairs, which consisted essentially of a narrow, hard-seated dining-room chair with double-rimmed wheels and a bracket for holding an ashtray to receive the tapping of his ever-present cigarette in a long holder.

The Delanos were out in full force, as was inevitable, led by the gentle head of the clan, Granny's brother Fred, railroad director, regional planner, and man of many parts. He was a great favorite of Father's, whom he had helped and succored in a hundred different ways, including the provision of a private railroad car to take him home to Manhattan after the polio attack on Campobello Island, New Brunswick, where we had our summer home. Uncle Fred was a widower; he came tonight with his two daughters and their husbands.

Sharp-tongued Laura Delano, whom we called Aunt Polly, was there, curbing her habit of needling Mother, and so was her sister Louise, with her banker husband, Fred Adams. Here came Mrs. Price Collier—she was another of Granny's sisters, Aunt Kassie—who lived in high style on an estate at Tuxedo Park, New York. Lyman Delano, board chairman of the Atlantic Coast Line, came to pay his respects. Long ago, when Granny was trying to block Father's desire to marry Mother by packing him off on a Caribbean cruise, Lyman had taken pity on the lonely girl and asked her to a dance.

I believe that Kermit Roosevelt, Theodore's second son, who had horrified the Oyster Bay branch by turning Democrat, was there in the throng with his wife Belle, whose father had been ambassador in Madrid. Kermit, a friend and partner of Vincent Astor, had been a shipmate of Father's aboard the *Nourmahal* two weeks ago.

The Roosevelt family's predilection for matrimony between cousins, like Father's and Mother's own marriage, made half the people here some kind of kin to each other. Theodore's younger sister Corinne, still sprightly at seventy-two and always cordial to both my parents, was especially welcome. His older sister, Aunt Bye, was sadly missed. This grand old lady, who had taken Mother under her wing when she was a guilt-tormented child, was too tortured by arthritis to leave her Connecticut home. But Helen Robinson, daughter of Father's older half-brother, "Rosy" Roosevelt, made a dutiful appearance with her husband, Teddy, arriving from the mansion known as Henderson, some miles west of Rochester, New York. Her stepmother, our Aunt Betty, who was Granny's neighbor at Hyde Park, brought her customary Cockney cheeriness to this bizarre occasion.

And, of course, Alice Roosevelt Longworth, Uncle Ted's firstborn daughter, was with us. Almost two years of widowhood had done nothing to curb her style or her irresistible compulsion to lord it over Mother. Cousin Alice breezed in as if the White House were still her natural home, as it had been for the seven years of Uncle Ted's tenancy, which encompassed the marriage there of "Princess Alice" to Nick Longworth. Yet I heard no mention of Theodore's name from her or anyone else either before or after dinner.

We gathered initially in the small drawing room, notably subdued and far from exultant. The only exception was Granny, who was also the only one in the company with the strength of mind to patronize Alice. All four of us Roosevelt sons and our one sister mixed with the crowd. Franklin Jr. and Johnny had come down from school in Groton for the weekend. Sister Anna and her first husband, stockbroker Curtis Dall, would stay upstairs overnight with their two children, Sistie, aged six, and Buzz, three. There was no doubt within the family that this seven-year-old marriage was running into rough weather.

Jimmy, too, was a houseguest, along with his first wife, formerly Betsy Cushing, a charming girl who loved to tease and be teased by Father. I would spend my own first night in the White House along with the first girl to whom I was married, Betty Donner, whose father founded the Donner Steel Company of Pennsylvania. Our only child, two-month-old Bill, remained behind in a nurse's care in Manhattan. Let it be said that our marriage was in a similar state to that of the Dalls'.

In the drawing room, Alice sought out Mother, who seemed forever to humble herself in her cousin's presence. "You'll be able to learn after a while how to handle affairs like this," said Alice. "I'll help you if you like." Mother expressed her thanks, her nervousness mounting under her cousin's patronage. She wondered, I am sure, just how long it would take before she could establish her own interior calm and personality.

It was a singularly joyless evening. Smiles were restrained, voices hushed. A sense of near-imminent disaster dominated everyone. The congratulations offered to Father were often little more than perfunctory. The question foremost in the minds of some of his guests was not hard to guess: Was Sara's often spoiled son, the "feather duster" as he was described in Oyster Bay, equal to the job? His responsive smile was sincere enough, but his own thoughts were obviously elsewhere, on the enormous obligation that he had undertaken and must tackle first thing in the morning: the revitalization of America by way of the New Deal he had promised its people when he flew to Chicago last summer to accept the nomination.

Dinner was served buffet style, an austere meal without trimmings or so much as a glass of wine. Repeal of Prohibition was one plank of the Democratic platform, but another month was to pass before even the sale of beer began. Watching these self-assured relatives of ours chatting together, it was impossible to suppress the idea that as a class their very existence was in hazard.

The progenitor of the American Delanos, Philippe de la Noye, was a Pilgrim who landed at Plymouth in 1621, and the family fortune began to grow almost immediately. Their roots were always in New England. "My eyes just naturally turn to the East," Granny used to declare; never in her life had she traveled west of Buffalo.

Delano ships sailing out of New Bedford made the family rich and cosmopolitan in its outlook. The China trade accelerated the piling up of money, some of it undoubtedly earned from the sale of opium in an era when opium and its derivatives could be bought openly in virtually any city in the world. One of Granny's uncles, Franklin Hughes Delano, of

The Homestead, Fairhaven, Massachusetts, augmented the fortune by marrying Laura Astor and promptly retired from commercial business. Ties with the Astors did not end there. Helen Schermerhorn Astor, a niece of Laura's, was Rosy's first wife and the mother of Helen Robinson, who was with us tonight. The Franklin Delanos had no children, so a share of their wealth fell into Granny's hands; she showed her gratitude by naming Father for her beneficent uncle.

"You know," Granny would say, "I have always been a great believer in heredity, and Franklin's wanderlust can be attributed directly to my own love of ships and distant horizons."

When her father, Warren Delano II, died, he left her $1,338,000 of the funds he had accumulated in China after his original fortune had been wiped out in the crash of 1857. Granny was nine years old when he sent for her, his wife, Catherine, and their six other children to cross the Pacific in the square-rigged clipper ship *Surprise* to join him. They lived for a year in Hong Kong, then on the island of Macao across the bay. A picture of the Macao house was one of Father's souvenirs, hoarded along with literally hundreds of thousands of other mementos of the past.

"I was brought up on the story of how the Delano family's principal competitors were the British," Father once recalled. He never forgot that the British would drive a hard bargain if they could.

Some of his Roosevelt ancestors had had trouble with the British, too. In the West Indies sugar business, they had trade rivals among the British and French—"and that," Father liked to point out, "is what made them revolutionists rather than Tories in 1776."

By the time of the American Revolution, the New World Roosevelts had enjoyed well over one hundred years of steadily expanding prosperity since pioneering Claes Martenszen van Rosenvelt stepped ashore at Nieuw Amsterdam some time in the 1640's from Holland. Father, steeped in family history, thought of himself quite seriously as a Dutchman. His sympathies for the Dutch lay close to the bone. He started delving into genealogy as an undergraduate at Harvard. He could reel off the names and circumstances of every known forebear, beginning with old Claes's son Nicholas, who went to Kingston, New

York, and established the first Roosevelt link with the Hudson Valley.

"Steady" was the key word for the respectable, industrious men who, for six generations, preceded Father. None of them made anything approaching Delano money, but they bought land, thousands of acres of it, along the Hudson to qualify as landed gentry along with the Van Wycks, the Stoutenburghs, the Beekmans, and the rest. Not until the railroad boom came along in the nineteenth century did any of our Roosevelt ancestors amass a few million dollars. Even then they clung to being country squires instead of tycoons of industry in Manhattan.

Granny was not really impressed with the Roosevelts at all. "My son Franklin," she would confide to her friends, "is a *Delano.*"

Now Delanos, Roosevelts, Astors, and every other family watching its financial worth eroded by the Depression that refused to end were all close to panic. The profit system itself, the very source of their capital and income, had failed, in the judgment of more and more frustrated Americans. If that were true, what would replace it? Anarchy? Fascism? Communism?

The country had just suffered through its worst winter of hardship in living memory, with hunger the only, ever-present reality for millions. While Hoover had tried in vain to mousetrap Father as President-elect into a joint declaration rejecting public works projects as a remedy, the Great Engineer set up the Reconstruction Finance Corporation with equally pathetic results. The RFC had authority to lend $300,000,000 to state governments for relief; it had put a mere tenth of that inconspicuous sum into circulation.

The supply of the ingredient essential for the working of our civilization—money—had started drying up after the October, 1929, collapse of the stock market. Factories were closed and furnace fires banked. Wages were cut for those with jobs. Part-time work was the rule everywhere. The whole country was spiraling downward toward unimaginable chaos.

Thirty cents for a ton of coal he had dug was a miner's average pay. He could dig perhaps ten tons a day and work three days a week. Oil in the East Texas fields fetched four cents a barrel. It stayed in the ground, because there was little demand for gasoline at any price.

Farmers, poorer every year since 1920, could make no more than a dime on a bushel of oats, so chattel mortgages and fore-closures were the order of the day. In the fields and orchards, vegetable and fruit crops had rotted away. Their market price did not pay for the harvesting, yet hunger was nationwide. Cotton pickers were paid thirty-five cents for 100 pounds, and at that rate a man could not feed himself, much less his family. Cotton, too, went to waste in the fields of Texas, Oklahoma, Louisiana, and Arkansas.

When tax payments could not be met, schools by the thou-sands were shut. Teachers who were not fired out of hand went to work sometimes without pay. To many people, and Mother was counted among them, the fate of the educational system promised to jeopardize the standards of an entire generation to follow.

Countless families found that they simply had too little to live on and nowhere to turn except to their neighbors or to local welfare agencies. Landlords were in much the same plight. When rents went unpaid because of stark inability to pay them, only a vengeful man would evict his tenants, since his chances of reletting were slim.

It was not too farfetched a fancy to foresee the extinction of the entire middle class unless something like a miracle was achieved in a hurry. Nobody had been prepared for what was happening. The business community as a whole had tried to bury the truth of the disaster. The booster spirit that pervaded every chamber of commerce led businessmen to pretend that hard times would disappear if you simply ignored them, and most newspapers across the land fell in line with that thinking. "Don't borrow trouble" became something of a watchword.

When the harsh facts could no longer be ignored, morale took a nosedive. This was America, the land of unlimited op-portunity. Poverty on this scale was impossible here, yet poverty prevailed from coast to coast. I was exceedingly familiar with the consequences as I had seen them in New York.

Out-of-work bond salesmen, executives, managers, and office staff joined the swollen ranks of shoeshine boys, making five cents a shine. Nineteen of them could be counted on a single block off Times Square. Others worked as street salesmen, ped-dling cheap neckties, rubber balls, roasted chestnuts, hot dogs. Or they would set up orange-box stands to sell sandwiches at a nickel apiece outside the labor exchanges, where the lines stretched longer every day.

Men who had lost both their job and the will to bootstrap themselves back to self-respecting employment pleaded for dimes on the street corners or went begging from door to door. The homeless slept huddled in topcoats and newspapers in the city parks.

It had been a Christmas as bitter as winter at Valley Forge. Most besieged communities had scraped together the resources to provide baskets of food or handouts of groceries for the poor among them. There were so many in need that the effort was no more than a straw set up to stem a flood. And in any event, uncounted hosts of people were out of reach of any communal charity.

The highways teemed with nomads, displaced from farms and factories. They wandered, helpless and demoralized, looking for work that did not exist, dreaming of finding it over the horizon, if only they could hitch a ride there. Alongside the railroad tracks at nightfall, their campfires flickered as they put together a day's meal to share—Mulligan stew, perhaps, or stale bread at three and a half cents a loaf. Riding the rods under a freight train or sneaking into a boxcar promised a fast trip, provided a man was not killed or crippled on his journey, as hundreds were every year. In one twelve-month period, a single railroad counted 186,000 "trespassers" on its runs.

A similar wave of homeless swirling across the land had been an accompaniment to the Soviet revolution. There, 3,000,000 young *bezprizorni* had terrorized towns and villages. Knowledgeable Americans pointed out the parallel situation. There were equally ugly omens. Farmers in Arkansas had taken to sacking grocery stores to put food on their tables. Others blocked highways to protest the collapse of a market for their harvests. Last May, jobless veterans of World War I had marched in a ragged army on Washington to demand the immediate payment of cash bonuses. One of Hoover's most callous deeds in office had been to order General MacArthur to burn out and uproot the Bonus Expeditionary Force from the shacks the marchers built across the Anacostia River from Washington. Sheer fear of revolution drove him to that action, which appalled Mother.

Conservative fears of revolution were linked with fears of the

Soviet Union. That faraway land remained an enigma, yet its sheer size as the largest country in the world exercised a kind of gravitational force in the United States. Ever since the Bolsheviks overturned the provisional, reformist government of the Socialist Premier, Alexander Kerensky, and seized power in November, 1917, the United States had had no normal diplomatic ties with the new rulers of Russia. News dispatches from such discerning reporters as Walter Duranty in Moscow were filtered through strict censorship. Just what conditions were really like in the "workers' state" was impossible to determine when Communist propagandists in the *New Masses* and elsewhere pictured a paradise where poverty was eradicated and the right-wing press talked exclusively in terms of slave labor camps and starvation.

Yet more and more harassed Americans were taking to wondering whether life under Stalin's dictatorship might not be as forbidding as it was held to be. One hundred thousand of them applied for jobs there, which escalated the fears of the conservatives that the present national mood of discontent could change overnight into revolutionary fever.

Over dinner, none of us dwelt on such things. On the surface, all was calm if not especially bright. The man closest to the reality of the country's dilemma was absent. Louis Howe, who kept himself in touch through an intelligence network of local political workers and volunteer newspapermen, had begged off. He had no compulsions to change his relationship with Father, who remained "Boss" to Louis, never "Mr. President," and Louis usually did as he pleased. He would feel out of place among all these rich cousins. He needed to go home to Poughkeepsie and clear up his affairs there before he came back next Tuesday to make the White House his permanent address.

Time was drawing near for the family party to be over. Just before ten o'clock, Father, Mother, and we five offspring must be off to the Washington Auditorium for the Inaugural Ball. It fell to Uncle Fred to make the evening something more than a dull gathering of people with not too much in common except accumulated wealth and present fears.

The toast, if I remember correctly, was drunk more appropriately than in sweet cider. On signal from Uncle Fred, all of us rose and raised our glasses. "To the President of the United

States," he said, and that was it. Father responded with his beaming smile, then it was time to leave. The black-coated usher outside at the front door carefully noted the hour of nine fifty-five.

We were back again at precisely one A.M. on Sunday, the second day of Father's Presidency. He had a final, cheerful word for us before he was wheeled to his bedroom. We had heard him say the same thing many times before at Hyde Park, at Campobello, and in the narrow, red brick townhouse on East Sixty-fifth Street, New York, where he first fought the good fight against the paralysis of his legs: "Good night. Sleep tight. I'll see you children in the morning."

In the morning, it was church for us all at St. Thomas', while Bill Woodin went into preliminary conference with some giants of the banking world. The United States was afflicted with its own national paralysis in finances, for which the bankers could find no remedy. Charlie Mitchell, chairman of National City; Albert Wiggin of Chase National; William Potter of Guaranty Trust; Seward Prosser of Bankers Trust; Tom Lamont, senior partner of J. P. Morgan & Company, who once rented from us on East Sixty-fifth Street—none of them as yet had agreed on a united course of action to restore public confidence in banks in general. A run, starting in February, had reduced cash and gold reserves to a perilously low level. By March 1, twenty-one states had declared total or partial bank holidays, barring their doors to their customers. That particular element in the overall crisis, the stark lack of dollars in circulation, had top priority on Father's mental agenda.

He tackled it after lunch and resolved it before supper. The bankers themselves, he found, were "much at sea as to what to do." He reported as much to the Cabinet, summoned for a two-thirty afternoon session. There was no way the problem could be handled, he concluded, so long as each state had a different method for coping with it. *Ergo,* it must be dealt with on a national basis. Some of his Treasury advisers, like some of the bankers, doubted whether he had the legal power for that. Homer Cummings came up with the answer. He cited a 1917 law designed to regulate the hoarding of gold or cash. Father decided that it gave him authority to proclaim that every bank in the land would be closed for four days, beginning this mid-

night, to provide breathing space for the preparation of new
legislation to reopen sound institutions and reorganize the
weaklings. He set seventy-two hours as the deadline for drafting this Emergency Banking Bill. At noon next Thursday, the
Seventy-third Congress would convene in special session to
consider it.

He ate a quick supper with us before Franklin Jr. and Johnny
went back to Groton, then returned to work until after midnight. First, he heard out a Cornell professor, George Warren,
who had a theory, fascinating to Father, that the price levels in
the country could be manipulated by changes in the price of
gold. Then he had a call sent out to bring reporters from the
wire services to the White House, to explain in advance why all
banks were to be shuttered. He gave a five-minute radio address to the American Legion Convention; he had a visit from
Cordell Hull; finally, he went to his bedroom—and started
another diary, which petered out two days later.

I was itching to leave Washington. In a strictly nonsuffering
sense, I was one more victim of hard times. In partnership with
Jack Kelly and Jim Nason, I worked in a New York advertising
agency, which still exists under their names. My major contribution to the firm of Kelly, Nason, Roosevelt had been to
bring in some Democratic Party accounts, but the business was
scraping bottom. Most advertisers were paring their budgets to
the bone or abolishing them altogether. The company was not
earning enough to support three men and their families.

I decided it was time to pull out and head West again, to
country I had known and loved since I was fifteen years old,
working in rodeos and coming home to Hyde Park with a tattoo
on my left arm that Granny denounced as a "mutilation." I had
an introduction from Mother to Isabella Greenway, a New
York society belle of 1904 who married one of Uncle Ted's
Roughriders and went with him to Arizona. She owned a ranch
there and was a Washington Congresswoman besides.

I stayed in the White House long enough to see Louis move
in, then set out by way of New York in a maroon Plymouth
coupé with a fellow *voyageur* and friend, Ralph Hitchcock, who
also worked at our agency. My wife was reluctant to leave New
York. I was more reluctant to accept a job in his steel company
which my father-in-law offered me, though at twenty-two years

old I felt in no way qualified for it. Betty spent a few more days with my parents.

The company of two in the Plymouth suffered from a cash-flow problem from the start. Putting together some traveling money was a considerable undertaking when there was no-where to cash a check. The sooner we could touch base in Arizona and avoid ruinous overnight hotel stops, the better off we should be.

We took a southerly route through Little Rock, Arkansas. Despite scrimping on funds, our cash balance had sagged below the danger line. The banks remained closed. In our hotel room, I picked up the telephone and asked the operator to put in a call to the White House, National 1414. Very shortly, Father was on the line.

"How are you, Bunny? How's the trip going?"

"Just fine, Pop. Only I have a problem."

"What's that?"

"I've gotten this far, but now we've only thirty-two dollars left between us. I don't think we can stretch it to get all the way to Arizona. You've got the banks shut tight. There's no place around to cash a check."

"That's too bad, Bunny, but I can't send you any money. You'll just have to use your ingenuity and do the best you can. Find a place along the way and stay there until things clear up. I'm sorry for you, but all I've got is eight dollars."

I fervently wished him the best of luck in getting the banks breathing again and hung up, wondering how much closer to our destination thirty-two dollars would take us. As it turned out, there was no need for concern and no call for ingenuity. The next twenty-four hours provided a foretaste of the lures and enticements that surround the children of the Presidency.

Ralph and I thought we should make for Dallas, Texas. Before we left, the local Little Rock newspapers judged that the presence of a President's child deserved a story. The published interview reported that I was heading West in a maroon coupé. We were rolling along the highway on the outskirts of Dallas when a Texas state trooper on a motorcycle overtook us and flagged us down.

"Pull over," he said, "and identify yourself." That done, he told us to follow him into town. "There are some people who'd like to see you." For a moment or two, I fancied that one of them might be a judge with a mind to pin a fine on us for speeding.

The trooper escorted us into the Baker Hotel in downtown Dallas, where a delegation of businessmen waited to welcome us open-armed. One of them was part-owner of the place, Fenton Baker. Another was C. R. Smith, vice-president of what was then known as American Airways.

We were ushered up to the Presidential Suite. The refreshments set out on a table there gave no sign that repeal of Prohibition lay in the future, on December 5. Would we care to be the guests of honor at dinner that night? In our present financial circumstances, that sounded like the answer to prayer. Soon afterward, another delegation came to call, this one from Fort Worth, where a fatstock show and rodeo was a current attraction. How would we like to make a public appearance there the following day? We said that we would be only too happy.

In Fort Worth, I was presented with a beautiful pearl-handled revolver and asked to lead the grand march in the rodeo, mounted on a magnificent gelding. Similar glad-handed treatment carried us through three more days at a total cost to ourselves of not one nickel.

El Paso was the next stop. The Plymouth would be driven there to await us, we were told, while we would be flown there at no expense by American Airways. The highlight of El Paso hospitality was a plane trip across the border into Mexico. The feasting there included an escorted visit to a huge distillery which was busily producing Kentucky bourbon by the barrel load.

After two more days in El Paso, we finally said good-bye to our hosts, climbed into the Plymouth, whose tank had been filled with gas, and departed on the last lap of our journey to Tucson and Mrs. Greenway. We still had sixteen dollars left of our nest egg.

A number of genial people were introduced during that stay in Texas. C. R. Smith became a close friend as time went by. He was an intimate of the big operators of the oil industry, which at that moment of its history was dying on its feet. The greatest natural resource of Texas could not command enough of a market price to make it worth pumping from the wells. The producers were going broke and looking to the federal government to save them.

I met Charles Roesser, whose wells were earning him some money, and Sid Richardson, who had none, since the holes he was drilling seemed fated to be dry. Both men, along with another, Clint Murchison, whom I met later, were to show a certain interest in my career while Father was in the White House. I was vaguely aware that I was being sized up as a prospect. A real courtship was due to follow.

2

There was no detectable trace of fatigue in Father's voice on the line between Washington and Little Rock, yet he had reason to be feeling the pressure. On the Thursday when Congress convened, he worked until two in the morning, which was not exceptional for him. That meant an eighteen-hour day, starting almost as soon as he opened his eyes at eight A.M. and reached for his daily pile of newspapers, brought in with his breakfast tray. On those March mornings, when the house was chilly because Mother preferred it that way, he would knot the sleeves of an old sweater around his shoulders while he learned what the papers were saying about his achievements to date. Putting on a dressing gown singlehandedly presented difficulties for a man who could not stand unaided.

On many mornings, conferences with members of his Cabinet, staff, and advisers began while he was still propped up against the pillows or sitting at the hand basin in his bathroom shaving with a straight-edged razor, while the particular male visitor squatted on the lid of the toilet seat. Father drove himself harder than ever before and took it for granted that everyone in his circle would follow suit. The pace was too much for some of them. Before the summer was over, Bill Woodin, always frail, had been worked close to death, which did, in fact, take him early the following year.

The results of those labors into the small hours of Thursday morning represented a glorious triumph for the team. Beginning at noon, the House of Representatives spent three hours in the procedure of organizing itself. At four o'clock, it passed Father's first bill by acclamation. Three more hours of debate in the Senate saw it approved there, 73 for, 7 against. At eight thirty-seven P.M., Father signed it into the law that enabled the banks to reopen within ninety-six hours, relieved of fears that they would be drained dry by their depositors.

"I have a little time to turn around to consider the implementing of the new Administration," he wrote that day to Jim Cox in Dayton, Ohio—Cox had been the Democrats' candidate for President and Father his running mate in the 1920 election that swept Warren Harding into the White House.

"I regard Berlin as of special importance at this time, for many reasons which you will understand." He aimed to appoint Cox as ambassador to Germany, but Cox begged off, pleading that his chain of newspapers and other business enterprises demanded his attention.

The importance of Berlin lay in the fact that a new leader had risen to power there on January 30, which was Father's fifty-first birthday. Adolf Hitler was bent on making Germany a force to be reckoned with again. As yet, he was only "Chancellor" and nominally subordinate to President von Hindenburg; "Führer" was the title he chose for himself when Hindenburg died in August, 1934, and the two offices were merged in a unified dictatorship.

In Father's thinking, the emergence of Hitler was a manifestation of the Depression, which engulfed the world. His brownshirted Nazis of the National Socialist German Workers' Party might well have been held in check within the postwar Republic of Germany if trade between nations had expanded, not contracted, after 1929 and German living standards had gone up, not down. Much the same was true of Japan. The impact of the Depression aggravated that country's endemic problem of too many people occupying too little land. It excused the demands of the dominating industrial cartels for overseas territory to be seized and new markets opened up. It was no coincidence that

Japanese aggression had begun with the seizure of Manchuria in the crucial year of 1931, then escalated into war with China a year later.

Closer to home, a calamitous drop in commodity prices was breeding unrest throughout Latin America. Something would have to be done to stabilize conditions down there, but right now the home front commanded priority attention. As the Republican floor leader, Congressman Bertrand Snell said on Thursday, "The house is burning down. . . ."

Father applied one of his favorite maxims: "Strike while the iron is hot." On Friday, twenty-four hours after passage of his banking bill, he struck again. He rattled Congress with a warning that the federal government was hell-bent for bankruptcy with an expected deficit in excess of $1 billion in the coming fiscal year, beginning July 1. His remedy was an economy bill, empowering him to slash every government employee's salary by 15 percent and cut the pensions of war veterans "in a spirit of justice to all."

Howls of protest from the American Legion and other organized veterans echoed around Capitol Hill. In the past, Congress had bowed to such outcries. Even now, the habit died hard. Ninety Democrats refused to go along with Father, but sixty-nine Republicans gave him their votes. A divided Senate fell into line after he had surprised Congress with another sudden shot. As the Senators began their debate, he asked for authority to make beer and light wines legal again after sixteen parched years of Prohibition. That was sure to alleviate some of the pain of pay and pension cuts. Congress voted a resounding yes to beer and wine.

On Sunday, at the start of his second week, he established himself overnight as a master in the art of communicating heart-to-heart with the people—he broadcast his first "fireside chat." The subject was the financial crisis, what it meant in everyday terms, and what he was doing about it. The first draft of the talk was put together by economists of the Treasury Department. After he read it, he tossed it aside and picked up a yellow scratch pad to begin over again. His final reading copy, typed in oversized letters, disappeared minutes before he faced the three microphones. He unhurriedly picked up a mimeographed copy prepared as a handout for the press, took a sip of water, extracted and tamped out his cigarette from its holder, and waited for the signal to begin at ten thirty P.M. "I want to talk for a few minutes with the people of the United States about banking. . . . Confidence and courage are the essentials of success in carrying out our plan. . . . Together we cannot fail." Off in Tucson, I felt the same glow that suddenly warmed the souls of the millions of others who listened to him. When he had finished, he had a sandwich and a drink.

Except for the radio technicians, he sat alone in his oval study, where a pastel portrait of Mother gazed down on him from above the door leading into the hallway. He had it hung there as soon as he moved in. It was a combined present from all us children on his past birthday and he was overjoyed with it. Not so Mother, who had no idea that it was in the works.

The artist I commissioned made surreptitious sketches of her at various meetings she attended in New York, in church at Hyde Park, and elsewhere. The finished portrait was unveiled at the party we gave Father at Hyde Park, after the birthday candles had been blown out and the cake cut and served. At the sight of it, Mother burst into instant, angry tears. "It's hateful!" she sobbed as she fled from the dining room to hide away upstairs. But Father kept it above his study door to the end.

The results of that first fireside chat were the determining factor that kept Congress in session for one hundred epic days. His original thought had been to get only a handful of the most desperately needed emergency measures approved, then let the lawmakers go home until a whole portfolio of permanent legislation was ready for them. But starting on the Monday morning, the newspapers he read at breakfast could not find words ringing enough to sing his praises. The telegrams pouring by the thousands into the White House echoed those sentiments. Within seventy-two hours, 4,507 national banks opened their doors again, with no panicky lines waiting outside. Hope was replacing the mood of despair. Roosevelt, the editorialists agreed, appeared to know what he was doing, and he was doing plenty.

He immediately capitalized on his advantage. Leaders of the House and Senate would be happy to keep Congress at work. Congress, sensing the spirit of the people, was ready to hand Father whatever powers he asked for, so long as he could achieve results like this. "We seem to be off to a good start" was as much as he would acknowledge.

All over Washington, squeezed into hotel rooms and make-shift offices, the men he had gathered around himself for the task of saving America labored day and night to draft the laws to bring about that end. Louis, installed in an upstairs suite along with a shelfful of medicine bottles and a mysterious safe that only he ever opened, jeered at these newcomers as "the brain trust." The name stuck as soon as one newspaperman got wind of it.

It was made up of all manner of men. Five of them were Columbia University professors—Ray Moley, the thin-lipped, narrow-eyed economist; acid-tongued Adolf Berle; Rex Tugwell, with his breezy talk of "doing America over"; Joseph McGoldrick and Lindsay Rogers, both of whose memberships were short-lived. Sam Rosenman, the agile attorney who helped write Father's speeches, acted as recruiting agent for this group, which Father preferred to call his "Privy Council."

Basil O'Connor, once a law partner of Father's and still his personal attorney, active with him in promoting the polio treatment facilities of the Warm Springs Foundation, had to be reckoned a member. General Hugh Johnson, a leather-cheeked West Point cavalry officer and onetime adjutant of financier Bernard Baruch, was enlisted within a matter of weeks.

On the fringes of the "trust" were people such as Lew Douglas, who looked like a plainsman and served as Father's iron-handed Director of the Budget. Charlie Taussig of the American Molasses Company; Joe Eastman of the Interstate Commerce Commission; railroads expert Don Richberg—they and a dozen more made up the team employed by Father. They came from a variety of backgrounds, bringing as many viewpoints to his attention. What he looked for in all of them was ideas and information, no matter whether or not they agreed with him. He listened and he learned from them, but he invariably made up his own flexible mind.

In the course of the next three weeks, he urged Congress to put more money into farmers' pockets and relieve them of some of their fears of foreclosure of farm mortgages, which had driven men to threaten deputy sheriffs with loaded shotguns.

He sought to set up 2,600 camps in a Civilian Conservation Corps to provide immediate work for 250,000 young men in building dams to drain marshland, reforest blighted landscapes, and fight forest fires. On the same day, March 21, he proposed making government grants to the states for unemployment relief, the largest such program then known to history, devised to ensure that victims of hard times need no longer starve.

There were not enough hours in a day for more than a few minutes, usually at dinner, to be shared with his family. As soon as he was dressed, he would swing himself into his wheelchair for the ride down by elevator to basement level as signal bells rang three times to give notice that the President was on his way. Then he was wheeled out through an exit door of the residence along the covered walk past the rose garden that led to the executive offices. The pace was always brisk. He would draw on a cigarette, clutching an armful of homework reading, while a messenger trailed behind carrying a wire basket piled high with more manila folders.

Lunch was customarily served on a tray at his massive mahogany office desk wherever room could be found on its top among the clutter of littered ashtrays, a vase of fresh flowers, mountains of paper, an onyx inkstand with two steel-nibbed pens, a ship's clock, a chromium-plated water pitcher, an assortment of Democratic donkey models of all sizes, and a sentimental scattering of other knickknacks.

Conferences filled every working hour of his day. His advisers, members of the Cabinet, visitors with opinions that interested him, well-wishers and self-seekers—the demands on his time were endless. Missy protected him. Her closeness to Father, dating back now for thirteen years, gave her unique knowledge of his strengths and weaknesses. She took it as her personal responsibility to keep obstacles from his path, manage his schedule, and supervise his immediate secretarial staff. He kept his office chilly, so Missy and the other girls wore sweaters at this season. In the evenings, after dinner, the working relationship continued in his study when Missy and Father wound up one day together and prepared for the next.

Mother saw less of him than the handsome, prematurely graying Missy. She gave no voice to her resentment until sixteen years afterward, when she wrote: "Missy was young and

pretty and loved a good time, and occasionally her social contacts got mixed with her work and made it hard for her and
others." But in those days she often invited Missy to go horseback riding before breakfast in Rock Creek Park with her and
her dear friend, Elinor Morgenthau, who lived in Fishkill, a few
miles down the Hudson from Hyde Park, with her husband
Henry.

On March 17, the twenty-eighth anniversary of their marriage, Father had seen so little of Mother during the days just
passed that he scribbled her a note and enclosed a modest
check with it for "dearest Babs."

"After a fruitless week of thinking and lying awake to find
whether you need or want undies, dresses, hats, shoes, sheets,
towels, rouge, soup plates, candy, flowers, lamps, laxation pills,
whisky, beer, etchings or caviar I GIVE IT UP! And yet I know
you lack some necessity of life—so go to it with my love and
many happy returns of the day—F.D.R."

Intended or not, there was a cutting edge under his banter,
which must have hurt. The "necessity of life" which she lacked
most was a manifestation of deeply felt love from Father or any
one of her children.

He left her to "work out my own salvation," in her own
phrase. She was a devoted Democrat and therefore more than
satisfied to have helped elect a Democratic President. But a
First Lady's role was even more shadowy than that of a Vice
President, who at least had his Congressional duties to occupy
him. Her immediate predecessors in the White House had
shunned any part in public affairs: Lou Hoover, so retiring as
to be almost invisible: Grace Coolidge, excluded by Cal even
from social functions: Flo Harding, an effusive Mrs. Babbitt.

A social conscience as sensitive as a seismograph compelled
Mother to make more of herself than these. At the same time,
she had to avoid the course chosen by Mrs. Jack Garner, who
worked for years as her husband's office secretary, cooked his
lunch on an electric broiler—and forbade the serving of liquor
at home, so that Cactus Jack resorted to a cubbyhole in the Capitol, where he and Nick Longworth used to play poker most
evenings as they sipped bourbon from the keg.

Father was too busy to pay much attention when my mother
rummaged through the furniture stored away by previous oc-

cupants. She had the help of Nancy Cook, her boon companion and partner in Val-Kill Industries, which on a modest scale produced handmade furniture, fabrics, and pewter in a little stone-built factory a mile or two away from Granny's house at Hyde Park. Making over the interior of the White House was fine by him so long as it cost nothing and his own personal quarters were not disturbed. After all the efforts of Mother and Nan, the place did not compare in style with Granny's tastes, and the guest beds at 1600 Pennsylvania Avenue remained notoriously uncomfortable.

He conferred with Louis, and they could see no objection to Mother holding her own press conferences, provided she stuck to her announced intention of staying clear of politics in her answers to reporters' questions. That aroused her enthusiasm to the point where she jumped in ahead of Father and called in thirty-five newspaperwomen on her first work day as First Lady, forty-eight hours before Father talked to the press. On occasion, her enthusiasm carried her away. One day, the news broke that Mother had served a White House luncheon of stuffed eggs, mashed potatoes, prune pudding, and coffee at a minimal cost of seven cents a head. The capabilities of Mother and her housekeeper, Henrietta Nesbitt, fast became a wonder in the land.

On that score, Father's opinions were in a strict minority. The operations of Mrs. Nesbitt were one of the crosses he chose to bear. This stolid lady of German stock had previously managed her sister's farm at Staatsburg, a few miles upstream from Hyde Park. Mr. Nesbitt was either dead or disposed of by divorce—I never heard her mention him. Laura Delano first recommended her to Mother as a good hand at baking pies and strudels for catering large affairs at the Executive Mansion in Albany. One regular commission Mrs. Nesbitt had from Mother was the shelling and salting of peanuts, fifty pounds at a time, for Father to nibble on at Hyde Park. Mother hired her largely out of pity. Mrs. Nesbitt had very little money.

As White House chatelaine, she supervised an initial staff of thirty-two—a chief butler and his assistants, all blacks, who served at table; ladies' maids, chambermaids, and the rest. Economizing on the number of help employed soon cut the total by half a dozen. When she arrived, she complained that

there were not enough utensils in the kitchen for cooking a respectable family meal on the ancient gas range, not a cookbook
to be found, and nowhere near enough sheets and towels.

In a neat, dark dress, she reported to Mother for instructions
every morning, to plan menus for the day. Mother's prowess as
a cook was limited to scrambling eggs. She cared nothing about
fine food and refused to allow that Father or the rest of us
could be any more concerned than she. Father, who would
have been an epicure if he had been given the opportunity, began grumbling about the meals served under Mrs. Nesbitt's su-
pervision within a week of her reporting for duty. Restricted in
his wheelchair from dining out except on ceremonial occasions,
he was at the mercy of Mrs. Nesbitt's kitchen.

Breakfast was a particular bugbear. At Hyde Park, we were
brought up on a diet of homelaid eggs and bacon from the
farm, delicious fresh fruit, and lashings of cream. Father's
breakfast tray was pitiful by comparison, with a meager strip or
two of bacon and an overcooked egg. Early on in the game, Father would have liked to see Henrietta given her marching orders and replaced by someone better acquainted with the
meaning of haute cuisine. But he could not bring himself to fire
anyone; "I'm a complete softy," he confessed. Mother was more
than loyal to her housekeeper. She ignored his grumbling just
as she ignored her children when we added our complaints
about the food, which truly was noninspiring. Mrs. Nesbitt
stayed through to the end.

In fairness to that much maligned lady, it must be said that
the budget set for her by my parents was as tight as a drum. It
was doubtful whether any one of Father's predecessors had
ever counted housekeeping dollars so carefully. Mrs. Nesbitt
prided herself on scouring the town for food bargains and
spending even less than she was allotted. She would cater a
mammoth reception—sandwiches by the thousands, cake, ice
cream, and coffee—at thirty cents a head. She supervised the
serving of sixty meals on an average day at a cost of eighty cents
per person, but so far as Father was concerned, she could not
provide him with a drinkable cup of coffee.

He was especially fond of quail, pheasant, and other game
birds, preferably hung until they were ready to fall from the
hook, then barely warmed before serving. Henrietta's ways

with these delicacies left him in despair. Men like Baruch would play up to his fancy by shipping him a brace or so of his favorite fowl, which Mrs. Nesbitt's department would promptly ruin. Now and then, his irritation would get the better of him, and a rocket would be fired at her head: "Feathered game should never be plucked until just before it is eaten. Taking off the feathers dries up the meat. F.D.R."

In those less grandiose days, the Presidency was run on a shoestring by contrast with the inflated costs which the taxpayers tolerate in 1975. Father's salary was $75,000 a year, to which was added an expense allowance of $25,000. Out of that, he had to feed his family, staff, and guests. Secret Servicemen on the premises were supposedly provided for from a different budget, but he was wise to the fact that they often ate in his kitchen.

With the best will in the world, making ends meet was impossible. In the first ten-month calendar year of his Presidency, his net taxable income was $59,520.29. He paid $11,364.33 of that to the Internal Revenue Service. Of his $70,403.51 net the following year, $16,139.29 went in federal taxes.

No custom or law in 1933 required a President to divest himself of his shareholdings. Father, however, was a firm believer in purity in investments—no President should have stock in a company with self-seeking requests to make of the government. He felt that Granny must abide by the same rule. He combed their portfolios before entering office, sold all his mining shares, and instructed her to dispose of hers. He wanted no part of his income to be derived from sweated labor underground. Coal owners were notorious slavedrivers, using lockouts and blacklists as their weapons. His remaining holdings were not substantial by rich men's standards, and dividends were rare after the bottom fell out of the stock market. He kept his head above water financially only through Granny's largesse. She subsidized his Presidency to the extent of $100,000 every year, which she regarded as her duty to him and to her country.

After one month in office, he was thrilled by "the fine temper of the country," but he did not for a moment delude himself into thinking that the corner was anywhere near turned. "Things look superficially rosy," he said, but that had been achieved by deliberate deflation of the economy—$4 billion locked up in the shuttered banks, another billion to be taken out of circulation by the Economy Act. What had to be prescribed next for the ailing United States was a measured dose of inflation, "though my banker friends may be horrified."

Money had to be pumped in somehow so that market prices would pick themselves up from the floor as an essential step toward restoring profitability in trade and manufacturing. This thought stemmed from an English economist, John Maynard Keynes, a Cambridge University professor who, practicing what he preached, made—and lost—fortunes buying and selling on the commodities market.

He was brought to Father's attention by William Waldorf Astor, married to a firebrand Member of Parliament in London, Nancy Astor, both of whom were good friends of Granny. Keynes held the audacious view that the cure for the Depression lay in deliberately unbalancing a nation's budget by massive spending and minimal taxation. Conservative thinking, on the other hand, postulated that only wage cuts, price cuts, high taxes, and a budget of black ink could put a nation on the road to recovery.

A brain as nimble as Father's found Keynes' unorthodoxy fascinating, much more so than the staider views of most American economists. My parent regarded the Wall Street crash as the inevitable finale to an era of history. In April, 1933, he had no clear-cut idea of what the next chapter might be, but he was already feeling his way to the maxim that "recovery is not enough." He cast around for practical means of restoring economic health to the patient without pretending to himself or the people that he had yet found the answers. He went on the air in May for a second fireside chat, to make that abundantly clear. "I do not deny that we may make mistakes of procedure," he said. "I have no expectation of making a hit every time I come to bat. . . . We cannot ballyhoo ourselves back to prosperity."

But inflation was worth a try; it might work like a shot of adrenalin to stimulate the heartbeat of the economy. A surefire method of forcing up prices would be to devalue the dollar. How to manage that? By abandoning the so-called gold standard, which set a fixed value for the magical metal that served on world markets as a measure of worth for every nation's currency. Father obtained a joint resolution of Congress to take the United States off the gold standard. Lew Douglas snorted that "this means the end of Western civilization." More enlightened opinion considered that, in the words of the House of Morgan, he had "saved the country from complete collapse." Stocks on Wall Street showed signs of life. Sales of American-made goods overseas could be made at more competitive prices. The draining away of gold from United States banks into the financial institutions of Europe was heavily reduced.

Starting in the fall, he would authorize the Reconstruction Finance Corporation to buy gold newly mined in the United States at floating prices. He was out to test George Warren's theory that higher-priced gold would boost the price of everything else, while federal money was pumped out to expand consumer's buying power.

Applause from Keynes echoed across the Atlantic. "Mr. Roosevelt," said the Cambridge sage, "has made himself the trustee for those in every country who seek to mend the evils of our condition by reasoned experiment within the framework of the existing system. If he fails, rational change will be gravely prejudiced throughout the world, leaving orthodoxy and revolution to fight it out. But if he succeeds, new and bolder methods will be tried everywhere."

Father's plan called for the price of gold to be set by a committee of three, made up of Jesse Jones, the wily Texas banker who headed the Reconstruction Finance Corporation; Dean Acheson from Groton, Yale, and Harvard Law School, a young pillar of the Eastern Establishment and now Undersecretary of the Treasury substituting for ailing Bill Woodin; and Henry Morgenthau, the Fishkill neighbor currently working as governor of the Farm Credit Administration, known to Louis as "Henry the Morgue."

Father's voice was raised in the counsels of these three. He could no more resist having a say in their pricing deliberations than he could give up smoking, which he ventured to try now and then. He was totally lacking in the reverence for gold that colored the thinking of his "banker friends," Jesse Jones among them. The first price established was $31.36 an ounce, equivalent to a 66-cent dollar in gold value. At one conference some-

where along the line, Father decided to add a further 21 cents
an ounce to the price of silver, principally because, as he said,
"That's a lucky number—three times seven." Three months after the manipulation began, the government was buying gold at
$35. The dollar, as a result, had been devalued to 59.06 cents,
and there it stayed pegged for forty years.

   To most people, apart from Father and Louis, Jones was an
intimidating presence, an archconservative in finance, who
played his own game and swung great weight in Congress—by
Louis's tally, 10 Senate votes and 40 in the House of Representatives. For the benefit of the Boss, Louis turned his hand to
puncturing Jesse, who bridled at Father's cavalier approach to
gold, which Jones held to be the very foundation of the profit
system. Louis wrote a poem, formally entitled, "The President
Pays His Respects to the Secretary of the Treasury and to the
Chairman of the Board of the R.F.C."

> Shiver me Timbers
> Over the Stones,
> I, too, having a tale
> 'Bout Jesse Jones.
>
> One morning drear
> I had a cold,
> And all I needed
> Was just more gold.
>
> "O Jones, O Jones,
> Give me some gold,"
> And all I got
> Was just more cold.
>
> Just then Bill Woodin
> Came along,
> And joined to mine
> His beauteous song.
>
> "O Jones, O Jones
> Give us some gold,
> Or else we'll give you
> Back your cold."

As one we sneezed
At Jesse Jones—
He handed out his gold
With groans.

So now we hold
This lovely gold,
We got with groans
From Jesse Jones.

Woodin, in fact, was already too ill to continue working. In November, Father persuaded him to take a leave of absence rather than resign. He filled his place in the Cabinet by designating Henry the Morgue as Acting Treasury Secretary. In Louis's biased judgment, Henry was little more than the Boss' errand boy.

Meanwhile, before the hundred-day session wound up, Father had pushed one crisis measure after another through Congress. Sometimes, there was balky debate, but never a defeat for any proposal. He was handed what was in effect a blank check, along with dictatorial power to conduct the affairs of the country as he saw fit.

Looking back eleven years afterward, he said: "If there ever was a time in which the spiritual strength of our people was put to the test, that time was in the terrible Depression of 1929 to 1933. Then our people might have turned to alien ideologies— like Communism or Fascism. But—our democratic faith was too sturdy. What the American people demanded in 1933 was not less democracy—but more democracy—and that is what they got."

They received it through a multitude of channels, all devised to ease the soul-destroying fear of the future that spelled death to democracy. The new Agricultural Adjustment Administration paid farmers to limit their crops and their herds so that the market would no longer be glutted with produce that they lost money on. Young hogs slaughtered in the cutback were frozen and given away to families on relief.

The Tennessee Valley Authority came into being to team manpower and natural resources together in rehabilitating 40,000 square miles of the river's watershed in seven states and develop the valley for all its people with cheap hydroelectric power, flood control, the planting of new forests, and the intensive development of new industry. In 1950, the late John Gunther checked off two of the major consequences of this monumental project: average income in the valley had risen by 495 percent, and "the atomic bomb could never have been produced when it was except by virtue of the enormous supplies of electricity made available by TVA." If public ownership and control on this scale constituted a species of Socialism, Congress showed no alarm. The legislation won approval by big majorities in both Houses. The TVA was as close to Socialism as Father ever went.

He created the Home Owners Loan Corporation to refinance costly mortgages for householders at lower interest rates and lend them money for real-estate taxes and repairs. Congress voted aye to that within a month and showed the same speed when he came up with a plan, the Railway Reorganization Act, to streamline railroad transportation as part of the next chapter for America, which was rapidly taking shape.

But the Senate had reservations about the next bill he submitted on Capitol Hill. It was labeled "The National Industrial Recovery Act." It called for "a great cooperative movement throughout all industry in order to obtain wide reemployment, to shorten the working week, to pay a decent wage for the shorter week, and to prevent unfair competition and disastrous overproduction." On anybody's terms that was an exceedingly tall order, but essential in Father's view.

It represented a gargantuan experiment in making over the life of the American working man and the freedom of those he worked for to write the rules under which he was employed. The age of laissez-faire died with the passage of this bill, which established yet another agency, the National Recovery Administration, with peppery Hugh Johnson in charge. The new law covered every aspect of employer-employee relationships.

It was responsible for establishing a five-day, forty-hour week as a standard in United States industry.

It gave labor the right "to bargain with employers through representatives of their own choosing," which put power squarely into the hands of the union organizers and opened up almost limitless horizons for a generation of activists like John L. Lewis and his followers in the Congress of Industrial Organization, created as a rival to the more docile American Federation of Labor in 1935.

NRA enrolled 90 percent of American industry under its codes. The Blue Eagle emblem, a kind of membership badge, blanketed the land. Rumblings of criticism sounded on the left. Weren't there dangerous parallels between the whole operation and the patterns of a Fascist corporate state? Didn't it encourage monopoly in business and the fixing of prices? Father did not see it that way at all.

For investors large and small, the New Deal brought the Truth-in-Securities Act, which spelled the end of jungle law on Wall Street. Sworn facts about securities offered for sale or sold across state lines must now be filed with the Federal Trade Commission. Out of this came the Securities and Exchange Commission, to which Father appointed one of his stalwart campaign fund-raisers, Joseph P. Kennedy.

"That," said Louis Howe, "is like putting a cat to guard the pigeons."

Joe Kennedy was one of the group known as "Roosevelt-Before-Chicago" men, like the brain trusters originally assembled by Father to supply ideas and write speeches for his run for the Presidency. Kennedy had made his fortune as a financier in any number of ventures, including a Hollywood motion-picture studio, which brought the perennially seductive Gloria Swanson under his wing. Flattery of Father was part of Joe's stock-in-trade. A few days after this first term began, a congratulatory message from Joe mentioned a visit he had just paid to a convent: "The nuns were praying for you."

Joe was susceptible to the charms of a variety of ladies as well as Gloria and his patient wife Rose, the mother of his children. After lunching with him one afternoon in the Ritz-Carlton Hotel on Madison Avenue, New York, my sister Anna discovered that she, too, was on the list. She eluded his embraces by running around his suite, dodging behind the sofas, scuttling around the grand piano, with Joe in amorous pursuit until he lost his breath. Anna regaled us with the story, but Father tolerated his old companion's fleshly weaknesses. In January, 1938, when war loomed in Europe, he did not hesitate to send up to the Senate the nomination of Kennedy as United States ambassador to the Court of St. James's.

For the hungry, the greatest measure of New Deal democracy came in the form of the Federal Emergency Relief Act, with an immediate grant of $500,000,000—subsequently raised to $5 billion—made available through a brand-new agency, the Federal Emergency Relief Administration. Onto the scene came the gaunt-cheeked, sickly Iowan who was due to outrank Father as the ultimate target for the hatred of the New Deal's enemies.

On May 22, Harry Hopkins, who had worked for Governor Roosevelt in a similar New York State relief job for two previous years, was made administrator of the new agency. During his first morning in office, he disposed of $5,000,000. "I'm not going to last six months here, so I'll do as I please," he said. His own salary stood at $8,000 a year. He had not apparently been the original choice for the post. He was so inconspicuous in those days that he scarcely rated a mention in Washington newspapermen's tabulations of the key figures in the Administration.

He received a simple instruction from Father: Get relief to those who need it and forget about politics. Harry interpreted that as meaning cash payments, not grocery slips, for impoverished families, along with clothing, medical care, and shelter in rented rooms. So one more precedent was set for the shape of future society.

The remedies Father had contemplated in the course of the past twelve months were being accepted by Congress. Factory wheels were turning again, with production up, according to one index, from a March low of 56, heading toward a June high of 93. The economy was stirring, and people were eating again. His rule-of-thumb approach had saved the profit system in the United States at least for the time being.

"It is commonsense," he said, "to take a method and try it. If it fails, admit it frankly and try another."

What was emerging was far removed from pure capitalism as capitalists had known it in the irretrievable past. Father was quizzed on the subject by an old friend, Senator George Norris of Nebraska: "What are you going to say when they ask you the political philosophy behind TVA?"

"I'll tell them it's neither fish nor fowl," was his lighthearted reply, "but, whatever it is, it will taste awfully good to the people of the Tennessee Valley."

New Deal America, a hybrid of private enterprise and massive federal spending, was alive and kicking. The principal grievance of more than a few industrialists was that he would not go farther and apply taxpayers' money toward running their businesses for them.

The coal operators pestered Harold Ickes to get a federal dictator appointed to run the mines. The biggest men in the oil industry—Seubert of Standard of Indiana, Farish of New Jersey Standard, Skelly of the company that bore his name, Pew of Sun Oil—were all engaged in buttering up Harold, looking for a minimum price per barrel to be established by the government. Even Harry Sinclair, one of the plotters in the Teapot Dome leases scandal, showed up in Ickes' office before the summer was over. But they got nowhere with Harold, whose sympathies lay with underdogs, not fat cats. Father's insistence on a skin-tight federal budget to underpin the outpouring of relief dollars did not provide rescue funds for coal or oil.

It would have been easier all around for him if he could have heeded his brain trust, which almost to a man urged him to concentrate his efforts on the domestic front and tackle internal questions first. But the ramifications of worldwide Depression compelled him into action overseas.

Cuba, which had been a ward of the United States since the Spanish-American War of 1898, was on the verge of revolution that spring. Desperate poverty prevailed as a consequence of prohibitive American tariffs on imported Cuban sugar. The brutal Machado dictatorship could not last much longer. Riots were erupting in the streets of Havana. The army was approaching the point of mutiny. The American owners of sugar plantations, gambling casinos, and other interests were terrified of a takeover by the peasants.

Father sent Sumner Welles, his erudite, patrician Assistant Secretary of State, to Havana with the rank of ambassador to determine whether an orderly change of government could be brought about. Both my parents had a high regard for the abilities of Sumner Welles, though Mother knew more about him than Father. His mother had been a close friend of hers, and Sumner had been a schoolmate at Groton of her only brother, Hall Roosevelt. Welles seemingly had all the necessary qualifications for a distinguished diplomatic career: brains, the right Eastern Establishment background, a rich wife in the former

Mathilde Peake. There was, however, a flaw in his character
which Mother could not recognize and Father ignored. Sumner
Welles was bi-sexual.

From Cuba, he sent an SOS to Washington, urging that the
crippling American sugar tariff be cut somehow. "Absolutely
impossible at this session," Father replied. "The important
thing is to have Congress adjourn as quickly as possible." He
would be trying his luck and risking their resentment if he refused to allow the legislators to return home when the heat and
humidity of Washington were rising every day.

Neither would he agree to Welles' suggestion for "strictly limited intervention." The last thing Father wanted was to land
troops on Cuba when his thinking was already leading him toward a "good neighbor" relationship with Latin America. But
he saw "no reason whatever why we cannot start immediate
conversations for a trade treaty with Cuba." He would have enthusiastic support on that from Cordell Hull, who had been
battling for tariff cuts from the day of his maiden speech as a
young Congressman.

Results showed within twelve months in the Reciprocal
Trade Act. The first agreement signed under its terms was with
Cuba. Sugar duties were slashed by 40 percent. Americans pursuing happiness at any price could find it in peace again at the
casinos and brothels of Havana, where the Yankee dollar was
official currency and the cash flow was fantastic. The Bay of
Pigs was no more than a point on a map.

With Father's blessing, the ogre Machado was supplanted by
Fulgencio Batista, the shrewd "Little Corporal," a swarthy,
square-faced part-Indian, who made a habit of promising Cuba
a new deal modeled on that of FDR, one of his two avowed
heroes. The other was Abraham Lincoln. Portraits of both
Presidents hung in the library of Batista's hacienda. Father was
not flattered.

"I know he's a bastard," my parent would say, "but he's *my*
bastard."

He might have wished he could say the same about the Japanese diplomat, Yosuke Matsuoka, who bowed his way into Father's office on his return journey to Tokyo from Geneva, but
Matsuoka was far from being swayed by any American. He had
just led his country's walkout of the League of Nations because

the peace organization had dared to condemn the Japanese seizure of Manchuria. En route to Washington, he issued a public
statement deploring Claude Swanson's announcement that the
United States fleet would remain in the Pacific. That, said Matsuoka, would only add fuel to Japanese resentment of America.

Perhaps ingenuously, Father wondered "if he said this in order to ingratiate himself against assassination by the Junker
crowd when he gets home." Protests by the thousand poured
into the White House.

The reception he gave Matsuoka was icy. There was absolutely no point in letting his visitor know that as early as at his second Cabinet meeting, Father had raised the possibility that
sooner or later the United States might have to wage war
against Japan. It was permissible to speculate that those few
minutes in the Presidential office raised the temperature of the
diplomat's anti-American hostility by another degree or two.
Back in Tokyo, his sentiments grew increasingly violent. As
Foreign Minister before Pearl Harbor, he helped to forge the
Berlin-Rome-Tokyo Axis, which attempted to conquer the
world.

As yet, of course, no battle lines had been drawn. On the contrary, the question foremost in the minds of Europe's political
leaders, always excepting Hitler and Mussolini, was how to disarm and make sure that the holocaust of 1914–18 would prove
to be what politicians had promised the Allied fighting men,
"the war to end wars." The cost of armaments, not pacifism,
was the driving force.

For the past year, contingents of diplomats meeting in Geneva had been searching in vain for formulas that would scale
down the size and expense of every country's armed forces
without risk of attack from a neighbor. France and Germany, in
particular, could not come to terms. The Germans sought
equality, the French demanded guaranteed security from
another invasion by *les Boches*. Chances of making progress
were even slimmer now that Hitler ruled in Berlin. Would his
delegation stay around the conference table or desert it? When
he summoned the Reichstag to assemble on May 17, the decisive moment appeared to have arrived. On the eve of that
meeting, Father issued a personal appeal to the leaders of fifty-
four nations, urging them to remain in conference, sign a com-

mon nonagression pact, and cut back their armies and their armaments.

His plea went unheard. In the eyes of jaded European diplomats, the new President of the United States might be working wonders at home, but he carried doubtful credentials as an
international statesman. In the wooing of Hearst and the California delegates which preceded the Chicago convention, Father had reversed himself in his attitude toward the League of
Nations. He had been advocating American entry into the
League for a dozen years before that. But because Hearst detested the idea, Father vowed that now he, too, was against
United States membership. Mother, a Wilsonian Democrat who
stuck to her beliefs, was so appalled by the switch that she
would not speak to him for three days. The flood of letters piling up on his desk on that occasion showed she was not alone in
her revulsion.

Father made one more attempt to gain the respect of the
country's old wartime allies at the Geneva conference. Through
his chief delegate there, Norman Davis, who had worked for
Wilson, he made a tentative gesture toward internationalism.
Provided that the rest of the world could agree on disarmament, he declared, the United States would walk in step with
any collective action against an aggressor. The second pro-
nouncement made no more impact than the first. If this was a
token of Father's revised thinking about involving America in
other nations' problems, the Senate Foreign Relations Committee concluded that it did not care for that one bit.

What interested Congress far more than the deadlock in
Geneva was the question of how America was going to collect
the astronomical sum of $12,195,087,279 and ninety-two cents
which had been lent to the Allies during World War I. At
the top of the list of borrowers stood Britain, owing
$4,802,181,641.56, closely followed by France, due to repay
$4,089,689,588.18. Scraping together even interest payments
was a well-nigh insuperable problem for both countries when
3,500,000 Britons were out of work and France floundered in
similar straits. The pound was shaky in London and the franc
was frail on the Bourse. Clearly, another world conference, to
tackle the whole question of international finance, was long
overdue.

Preparations for that provided Mother with her first experience of playing hostess to dignitaries from overseas. She would have felt less fluttery if Father had given her more advance notice. White House guestrooms were usually filled at weekends. Granny came down regularly to keep an eye on Father's progress, begging him to take a few days off and go back to Hyde Park—and making sure that space was provided on his appointments calendar for anyone, such as her New York banker friends, that she wanted him to see.

Franklin Jr. and Johnny would visit from Groton. Anna and her two children were soon to become permanent guests. Hall Roosevelt dropped in from Detroit, an exuberant giant of a man with a taste for martinis that frightened Mother. All of us boys were happy to see Hall and roughhouse with him in the second-floor hallway. One Christmas, both Franklin Jr. and John suffered twisted knees in the scuffling, and at Val-Kill one day Hall's son Danny finished with a broken arm.

Father asked how many guests were expected over an April weekend. Perhaps some of them should be deferred, he said, because "a few Prime Ministers" might be staying with us. The total, however, was only two—Ramsay MacDonald, the harassed leader of Britain's National Government, with his daughter Ishbel, and Premier Edouard Herriot of France. Father wanted exploratory talks with them before the World Economic Conference opened in London. Mother apologized to the family because pride of place at the dinner table must be given to the guests. Louis scored a social hit that weekend with Ishbel MacDonald, who made a farewell present to him of a halibut for his breakfast.

If the British Prime Minister fancied that he could win over his affable host, he was disappointed. In the British view, the forthcoming London conference would fail unless the crushing war debts could be renegotiated. Father was adamant that the subject had no place on the agenda. Face-to-face talks in Washington between the United States and any country that owed it money was the only approach he would consider.

The honeymoon with Congress was too precious for him to show any appearance of being soft with debtors overseas. He wished to prove himself tougher in this than Hoover, who had permitted the British to forgo one payment under the moratorium on international debts which he promoted for a year beginning in 1931. Now the dollar's convalescent strength must not be jeopardized. The inflow of cash must be resumed. The thank-you note which Ramsey MacDonald sent from 10 Downing Street reported that he and Ishbel had felt "so much at home at the White House," which could be only a compliment to Mother's hospitality, not to any discussions he had with Father.

King George V in person opened the conference which met, not unappropriately, in the Geological Museum at South Kensington, where it proceeded to fossilize the principles of low tariffs and stable currencies to which every government represented there paid lip service. MacDonald occupied the chair. Though he could count on few favors from Father, he had received a letter from him offering an ingenious solution by which Britain could avoid being stigmatized as a defaulter.

If the British could not come up with the entire sum due on June 15, why not a part payment, and that in silver "as has been authorized by Congress"? "This feeling," the letter said, "is based on the thought that it would make clear in both countries that there has not been a default. It avoids a debate on terminology." This was a typical FDR approach—bland, inventive, with a gentle hint of pressure.

But he was adamant that war debts must not be debated at the London sessions. "That stays with Poppa—right here" were his parting words to the American delegation, led by Cordell Hull, that set off for London, supposedly to help solve the economic troubles of the world before they came back.

Within a day or so of the opening, reports reached Father that the American delegates were at loggerheads, while the conferees were pressing for stabilization of all currencies, including the dollar. This was the last thing Father wanted to happen until the American greenback had increased its strength against the pound, the franc, and everyone else's money. If that was what was going on, it had to be stopped. He ordered Ray Moley off to England and sent with him an odd choice as companion, Herbert Bayard Swope, once executive editor of the old New York *World,* a sharp wit and an influential Democrat.

In spite of trouble in London, however, Father had won his

way over the British debt payment. Twenty-four hours previously, they had deposited with the United States Treasury $7,000,000 in silver to meet a $10,000,000 installment. Father was satisfied, but Congress subsequently declared the British were defaulters nevertheless. After that, Britain quit. No further payments were forthcoming.

June 16 was also the day when Congress finally adjourned; when the Banking Act was born, to insure depositors' funds up to $5,000 by the Federal Deposit Insurance Corporation; when Father signed the National Industrial Recovery Act into law. It was his turn to sing the praises of the lawmakers for their cooperation, which he told them, "has proven that our form of government can rise to an emergency and can carry through a broad program in record time."

With that said, he took off with the zest of a schoolboy playing hooky for a vacation aboard *Amberjack II,* a little auxiliary schooner he had chartered, to be piloted by himself. It was four months since he had recharged his energies with fresh air and salt spray. He could scarcely wait to get away. There would be one or two cockpit conferences with men such as Lew Douglas and Colonel Edward House, the busy little Texan who had been Woodrow Wilson's one-time intimate and now proffered advice to Father. Otherwise, my parent was as free as a sea gull. During the One Hundred Days, he had obtained fourteen acts of Congress, granting him more power than he wanted or asked for. The foundation stones of a different America had been laid fair and square.

First, he went to Groton to see Franklin Jr. graduate. Then he was driven to Marion, on Cape Cod, to put on his old slacks, frayed sweater, and the floppy panama hat that always looked as though it had been slept in, as it sometimes was. He would have been the despair of a wife who paid more attention to her husband's clothes than Mother did. Jimmy and a crew of two boarded *Amberjack II* with him. He charted a course for Gloucester by way of Martha's Vineyard, Nantucket, and Provincetown.

He kept the Secret Servicemen assigned to guard him in a continual state of alarm. Since he had no intention of having his vacation spoiled by their dogging him, he would change course and make landfall at unheralded locations, while they debated

whether they should sound the first alarm with the Navy or the
Coast Guard.

From Gloucester, he headed for Portland, Maine, to pick up
Franklin Jr. and Johnny, then up skirting the craggy coastline
to the tiny island where he had walked unaided for the last time
in his life. He had never returned before to Campobello since
the August day when Louis managed to get the Boss' stretcher
loaded onto a luggage cart, then through the window of the
railroad car provided by Uncle Fred.

Father, by now, had reconciled himself to the fact that he
would not walk again. He had surrendered that hope when he
chose politics as his life's work. As for being crippled, he disre-
garded that completely, driving from his mind any thought
that he was less than a normal man. Taking risks was a compulsion, to prove to himself that he was no invalid. Memories of
Campobello had been too painful, I believe, until this day. He
decided that this was the time to exorcise the memory, now that
he had satisfied himself that he was an effective President of his
countrymen. But if all this was true, he did not admit it to any
one of us.

Early in July, his vacation over, he was rowed out from the island and hoisted aboard the cruiser *Indianapolis* to take up the
work load again. On Campobello, he had picked up a cold, just
as he had thirteen years ago when he took a cold dip in the
ocean and was permanently paralyzed twenty-four hours later.
He had six of his Cabinet come out in a submarine chaser for
luncheon when the *Indianapolis* anchored off Annapolis. He
congratulated them on their sturdy constitutions in surviving a
choppy trip.

Cablegrams waiting for him spoke of the London conference
breaking up in confusion. Moley and Hull were feuding. Foreign delegates had interpreted the sudden arrival of the Columbia professor as a sign that Father was having second
thoughts about stabilizing the dollar; Moley was recognizable as
a traditionalist in his outlook on "sound" money. Hull needed
to correct that false impression. On the day of the luncheon
afloat, Father torpedoed the conference.

Moley had forwarded to him, with approval, a plan for stabilization, which Father totally rejected. The American dollar
must be allowed to float upward. The London conferees knew

it was useless to go on. Only Hull's skill as a statesman deterred them from adjourning on the spot. The experience soured Moley, who quit government service two months afterward to edit *Today*, a magazine financed by Vincent Astor, Averell Harriman, and Mary Rumsey Harriman. He remained in Father's good book and helped out as a speech writer for one more year. Then, in an angry quarrel between them, he broke with the New Deal and joined in the chorus of its critics.

Father took his departure philosophically. It was clear to him that Moley spoke with the voice of big business and the New York bankers. They deserved a hearing, but they were not going to be allowed to manipulate policy. Hull's ruffled feathers had to be smoothed when he returned three weeks later. But Keynes, at least, was convinced that Father had been one hundred percent correct in his action.

3

That summer, Father encountered a family situation that had to be dealt with, and unfortunately I was responsible for it. While I was in Arizona, Betty and I agreed that we had come to a parting of the ways. I became the first White House child in history to seek a divorce. A shock wave of righteous indignation rolled across the land.

Father showed great understanding. I was 2,000 miles away, too far for him to break away from his desk and come out to talk with me himself, but he sent Mother off on her first transcontinental flight to meet me in Los Angeles. With every member of the family regarded as "hot" copy by the city desks, that trip itself made news headlines. My new friend, C. R. Smith, flew with her from Texas to California. Commercial flying was still an arduous business for passengers, bounced around for a day and a night, with stops for refueling along the route.

Mother enjoyed it, immune as usual to discomfort, grateful for an opportunity to be useful and serve her family in a time of stress. I like to think that her journey to Los Angeles gave her a glimpse of a pattern of living she might create for herself. Reporters and photographers were waiting every time the plane touched down. She refused none of them.

The message she brought from Father amounted to this: "Why not try waiting a while? Don't get an immediate divorce. Let things cool off before you go any further." Being inexperienced and extremely headstrong, I refused to listen. I insisted on going ahead. Mother could not believe that, with no job in view, I could be thinking of finding a new wife.

The divorce was granted in Nevada. From there, I went to Chicago, where Anna joined me, again on the instruction of Father. He wished her to accompany me to my second wedding, which took place in Iowa in July, a matter of days after I left Reno. There was no question yet of Father making difficulties for any one of his children in a domestic upheaval.

My second wife was Ruth Googins, whom I had met during the providential March visit to Dallas and Fort Worth with Ralph. We stayed briefly in Fort Worth again before we drove back to Los Angeles and a job for me with William Randolph Hearst as aviation editor of the Los Angeles *Express*.

The next disturbance within the family that my parents had to cope with involved Anna. When her marriage to Curtis Dall finally was brought to its end, she moved into the White House with Sistie and Buzz, to stay there until John Boettiger, a Washington correspondent for Bertie McCormick's vociferously right-wing Chicago *Tribune*, caught her fancy and made her his wife.

Mother's ingrained sense of inadequacy made it inevitable that she blamed only herself for her children's failings. The two broken marriages, and the others that followed, saddened her more than it did any one of us who went through the divorce courts. She felt that the guilt was all hers because she had been unable to extend to us in our nursery days the warmth of love that the young find as necessary as food and drink.

Just as she refused to pass judgment on us, so she would not condemn the marriage partners we left behind. She showed remarkable kindness toward Betty and Curtis and all the rest of the rejected spouses later. To the new spouses whom we introduced to her, she gave her friendship, wholehearted and impartial.

Her grandchildren—first Sistie and Buzz, then Jimmy's offspring and mine—could depend on receiving the affection which she was belatedly learning how to demonstrate. Her innate austerity made it impossible for her to gush over them, but they knew how much she cared. She was too busy to take them off on typical grandmotherly excursions to downtown stores, the circus, or a play. Babysitting was out of the question—there were too many calls on her time for that. But she was proud of her grandchildren, and she made that abundantly clear when she had them in for tea and a sweet homemade cake prepared under the direction of Mrs. Nesbitt. Their turn with Grandfather came at breakfasttime, when he encouraged them up onto his bed, to hug them as he had once hugged each one of us as children.

She had little cause to shoulder the blame for her children's derelictions. The fault, of course, lay mainly with us, not Mother, in our instability as adults when we should have known better. The fact of the matter is that the five of us were catapulted into a heady atmosphere of reflected power and glory at an impressionable age. When we were exposed to temptations, romantic or commercial, we proved ourselves to be easy marks.

We lacked the training that would have enabled us to keep our feet on the ground. We were too inflated with our own importance to appreciate that in most cases the business opportunities that came our way owed everything to Father's being in office. We children had ready access to him. He made time to listen to us. That was why we had our pick of jobs when there were still 10,000,000 unemployed. And similar considerations would hold true for Margaret Truman, John Eisenhower, Lynda Bird and Luci Baines Johnson, Julie and Tricia Nixon, Michael, John, Steven, and Susan Ford, and every future child of the White House so long as influence peddling was condoned in America.

Jimmy was a notable example of an enthusiastic young man being used as a conduit to Father. My eldest brother was still at Harvard Law School in 1930 when a Boston insurance broker, Victor De Gerard, gave him a part-time job at fifty dollars a week. Possibly he figured that to be a modest bet on a likely winner, when Father was already being strongly tipped as a candidate for the White House.

When Father became President, the Boston broker established close agency connections with some of the biggest insurance companies in the United States. De Gerard, with Jimmy's help, became a pioneer in the planning of what is known today as group insurance, covering millions in the work forces of major corporations. My brother's tax returns, which he published in order to defend himself against a later storm of public criticism, disclosed that in 1933 his income had risen to $21,714.

After severing his alliance with De Gerard, Jimmy joined another Bostonian, John Sargent, in setting up the firm of Roosevelt and Sargent, insurance brokers. In not too long a time, they had a highly profitable business with a nationwide reputation. Father promised both Jimmy and myself that one day, when there was a moment to spare, he would try to explain "the great willingness of some people to be awfully nice to you." He had no personal illusions on that score, yet he felt duty-bound to be awfully nice to us if we wanted to introduce a caller into the White House.

The seed of another ambition began to sprout in Granny's mind. Jimmy, her first grandson, had been named for her husband, James Roosevelt, a paragon among men, in her judgment, whom she held in respect while he lived and revered after his death in 1900, when Father was eighteen. So Jimmy had a special place in the dynasty as she saw it. Her only child had fulfilled to the hilt her expectations of him. His eldest son should be trained to follow in his footsteps. She believed that Jimmy should waste no time in embarking on a political career.

She suffered from loneliness in the comfortable old house at Hyde Park, which saw very little of Father these days. He could spare her fewer of the attentions which had been her principal source of joy for most of her life. The letters he wrote were scribbled in haste: "Thanks so much for your two notes. . . . The news you have by the papers. . . . Lots of love." Sometimes on the telephone he was brusque to her because he was so preoccupied. She felt neglected.

The expanding generosity of Mother's heart led her to find pity for the matriarch, who had shown her daughter-in-law precious little pity in years gone by. She made a point of visiting Granny whenever she could in the house which Mother had not been allowed to have a hand in running. She kept Granny up to date on events in the family and took her out in New York and Washington. Most of the roots of Mother's resentment were changed now. In the White House, she had something of a home of her own, which Granny had no hope of taking over.

Mother had her own private retreat and escape valve in the rambling stucco cottage at the bottom of the hill at Val-kill, and she was rapidly acquiring a national reputation for herself as a result of reams of newspaper stories. Our retiring, middle-aged mother, much to everyone's surprise, was enjoying herself as First Lady. She would reach her forty-ninth birthday on October 11.

Her biggest problem was lack of time to fit in all the things that she felt she ought to be doing. Todhunter School for girls in New York City, which she owned in partnership with Marion Dickerman and Nancy Cook, could not be dropped altogether, but she cut down responsibilities there to the limit of teaching a class in current events and invited every graduating class to a weekend in the White House. She kept a finger in the operation of Val-Kill Industries—and made up losses from her own pocket.

Louis was well satisfied with the results of the years he had spent coaxing and coaching her, originally to save the Boss from being harassed by her and then out of sympathy for Mother's need to find channels for her energies. When the war veterans of the bonus army marched to Washington again in May and Father had them housed and fed in old army huts on the other side of the Potomac, it was Louis who brought Mother to meet them. He would not permit the presence of any Secret Serviceman to spoil the effect of his masterstroke in public relations. Before she left the camp, she joined in a chorus of a bittersweet song they brought back from the war: "There's a long, long trail a-winding, To the land of my dreams. . . ." They sent her off with cheers. Only three months ago, Zangara had tried to assassinate Father in Miami.

Colonel Edward Starling, charged with protecting the lives of my parents, was perpetually frustrated by Mother. She would not dream of allowing any of his agents to follow her around. On all her travels, she never took a maid and seldom a secretary. At his insistence, she agreed for a while to carry a small revolver in her capacious handbag. "It's really quite *useless*," she objected, "because I could never bring myself to *shoot*." She hadn't the least idea of aiming and firing and no intention of learning.

In desperation, the Secret Service presented her with a little gas gun, the size of a fountain pen, to pack in her pocketbook. With that, they told her, she could momentarily disable an attacker. "I am sure that nobody would *attempt* such a thing," she exclaimed. She did not bother to be taught how to use that, either.

In the first year of the Presidency, Mother traveled 40,000 miles, and her mileage increased after that. The Washington *Star,* which delighted in sniping at all of us, rated as news on one occasion the fact that, in the headline's words, *Mrs. Roosevelt Spends Night at White House.*

Her journeys as "my will-o'-the-wisp wife"—Father's description—were prompted by himself in the first instance. Since he was limited in his own ability to tour the country to see the practical effects of his programs, Mother could fill the role for him. The feeling that at last she could prove her usefulness was the vital catalyst of change in her character. He was her instructor in what to look for: "Watch the people's faces. Look at the condition of their clothes on the washline. . . . Notice their cars."

She packed her own bag, which was done in a matter of moments. A nightgown, a change of underwear, her blue bedroom slippers, a little toilet bag—that was about the extent of it. She took along a separate bag for her knitting, which went everywhere that she did, and a carryall that served as a pocketbook, crammed with letters to be answered, a notebook, and the rest of the working equipment for her journey. She toted all three pieces herself. No porter was ever necessary, except when she left on an overseas trip, which might call for one small extra valise.

By train or plane, she traveled as an ordinary, ticket-buying passenger. She kept her eyes, her ears, and her heart open. The scope of the contribution she made was borne home to me on the countless occasions when someone would come up to say, "I sat next to your mother one day, and we talked all the way to —." Their destination might have been Los Angeles, Chicago, New York, or just about anywhere in the country. "We had a fascinating time. She's a wonderful woman." I heard few contrary opinions.

She wrote meticulous reports on her observations, on which Father came to set great value. For the first time since we children could remember with real clarity, he appreciated these abilities of Mother's. The newspaper interviews she gave and the personal contacts she made brought a mountain of mail—300,000 letters in that first year—to be tackled with the help of her brisk secretary, Malvina Thompson, who shared a second-floor cubbyhole with Mother's social secretary, stately Mrs. Edith Benham Helm, back with the same duties she had performed for Mrs. Woodrow Wilson.

By no means all of the letters were answered with a stock response. Those which Mother concluded deserved more attention were forwarded with a note from her to the government officer or department concerned. She laid her pipelines with great care and deliberation. Where her relations with a Cabinet member were close, as with Henry Wallace or Frances Perkins, the letter went straight to that individual. If cordiality was lacking, as in the case of Harold Ickes, Mother cultivated an assistant secretary in that department as the target for her memos and her source of information.

She had a terrier's tenacity in keeping after a question once she raised it. It was impossible to fob her off with an evasive reply, as a long list of bureaucrats discovered to their regret. She wanted a copy of every reply they sent. She tolerated evasiveness only in Father, and not always in him. As a last irritated recourse, she would sometimes dump a problem unearthed in the mail right on his desk. Mother quite consciously exercised the power of mystification to obtain results. Did a note from "AER" reflect the thinking of the President? Puzzled departmental officers had no means of knowing, so they were seldom ready to take chances. They did what they imagined he expected of them on the strength of her instructions.

Using much the same technique, she had no hesitation in trying to find jobs within the government for men and women whom she regarded as deserving and qualified. If she ran into obdurate opposition from the like of the "old curmudgeon," Ickes, she would "hit the ceiling," as he ruefully noted in his secret diary after one encounter with her. Harold had little time for any Roosevelt with the exception of Father, and he had decidedly mixed feelings about him.

None of the family riled Ickes like Mother. Nothing she did sat well with Harold, from the "undrinkable champagne"—one glass apiece—that she served at Cabinet dinners, to the appointees she managed to introduce into various departments. He accused her in private of loose talk about Cabinet officers, which he said, embarrassed Father. She was, in Ickes's vinegarish judgment, "altogether too active in public affairs . . . harmful rather than helpful."

Less egocentric men than Harold found it enormously helpful to make an ally of Mother, whose loyalty to anybody, once it was given, was unshakable. Her regard for Wallace, for example, was heightened by his willingness to sit and listen patiently to her accounts of the hardships she found among farmers on her tours of the Corn Belt. He showed a compassion that matched hers; Ickes and others brushed her aside whenever they could. A bond of tenderness shared grew between the Secretary of Agriculture and herself.

When Father created the Civil Works Administration that fall and put Hopkins in charge, Harry enlisted Mother on his side. The vehement idealism of this shrewd, hard-driving man appealed strongly to her. With his wife Barbara and baby daughter Diana, he lived in a Washington apartment on $250 a month in order to make support payments for three sons of a former marriage.

He would like to be able to make some money for clothes and food, he told one reporter. "Mrs. Hopkins is yelling for a winter coat." But Harry was incorruptible. A different Mrs. Hopkins was offered a magnificent fur coat when he took her with him to Moscow after Father's death, but the only gifts Harry would allow his wife to accept from the Russians were a few low-priced trinkets.

Like Wallace, Harry relied on Mother to echo his viewpoint with the force of her own convictions when she talked with Father and so underline whatever Hopkins advocated as a matter of policy. Father had reason to rate CWA as "an enormous success . . . putting four million people to work with real wages." Within four months, 180,000 public-works projects were started up and close to a billion dollars spent, to the wrath of Harold Ickes—CWA money was lopped off his budgets.

Harold thought that CWA should be in his charge. He was every bit as cost-conscious as Lew Douglas, whereas Hopkins did not care a hoot about the taxpayers' money, only about the speed at which wages could be paid. "People don't eat in the long run—they eat every day," he insisted, which was Mother's opinion precisely.

CWA did away with the "means test," which, as it was currently being enforced in England, was threatening to overthrow the government there in a storm of public indignation. The means test meant the denial of relief to a man if he had money saved or if other members of his family were employed. Father judged that to be as iniquitous—and politically inflammatory—as the idea of handing out money as a dole to anybody capable of work. What is loftily described nowadays as the "work ethic" colored every New Deal relief program of the Public Works Administration, the TVA, the Works Progress Administration that came along in 1935, and the rest.

Handouts, in his philosophy, were debilitating. They would destroy a man's pride in himself, in feeling that he had earned what he received. If that happened, an able-bodied workingman would be reduced to a zombie, and the whole country would run downhill again. "Welfare" as we know it today remained for his successors in the Presidency to invent and perpetuate like an endemic plague of our times. Louis Howe pushed ahead with his personal plan of making Mother the administration's symbol of sympathy. She would be seen everywhere in the country as living proof that care for *people* was the foundation of the New Deal. She was willing, tireless, and indestructible so far as her physical health was concerned. The Boss must be shielded by a code of honor on the part of press and newsreel photographers. Falling in line with Louis' wishes, they were persuaded to refrain from shooting pictures that revealed the fact that Father could not walk or stand without support.

Louis involved Mother in a project which, in one of its side effects, gave evidence of the Boss' wisdom in entering office with his hands clean of the grime of owning stock in the coal mines of West Virginia. For years Father had toyed with the thought of resettling impoverished families into brand-new, self-supporting communities, built by the Government, where they would be provided with housing and all social services, along with employment in the factories that were an integral part of the scheme. Louis, too, enthused over this new-style homesteading as an effective means of combating decay in the cities and opening up job opportunities in areas where the Depression had hit hardest. He went on the air to say as much in one of the talks he gave for the National Broadcasting Company. Louis earned $900 for nine minutes, the best rate of pay he had ever known. Harry Hopkins was another New Dealer who made a few hundred extra from time to time, in his case by writing articles for magazines. The most vicious Roosevelt-haters could not bring themselves to brand this as corruption within the Administration.

Appalachia struck Father as an ideal place for launching the first experiment in homesteading on modern lines. Strikes, lockouts, and blacklisting had kept some miners there unemployed for eight uninterrupted years. Ragged families lived close to starvation in broken-down company houses in a landscape as devastated as the battlefields of France after the last German shells were fired. Communist Party organizers had moved in to foment more trouble. Relief workers on the spot sensed a race against time in the making. Violence would flare unless living conditions improved.

Mother was sent down to make a prelimiary report. Seated in her customary place at the middle of the table across from Father, she told the dinner guests one night after her return about a boy she saw there clutching his pet rabbit, which his sister had told him was all there was left to eat. One of the guests was William Bullitt, who was actively inveigling himself into grace and favor. A breezy letter from the Yale Club in 1932 enclosed $1,000 for Father's campaign fund with thanks "from the bottom of my heart for being so kind to me." He followed up in the course of the next few years with gifts of champagne, brandy, fishing rods, and a dressing gown. At dinner that night, he promised Mother $100 to save the rabbit's life.

Father gave Mother an overseer's responsibilities in the Appalachia resettlement project, with Louis backing up her efforts. The first decision of consequence was to buy a 1,200-acre farm and the house that stood on it fifteen miles from Morgantown, West Virginia. In one month, three dozen miners' families were quartered in the old mansion at Arthur Farm, which gave the whole Arthurdale project its name, and 164 more were alerted for moving into the fifty prefabricated Cape Cod houses which Louis ordered by telephone at a price of

$1,000 each. At the same time, the PWA allocated $525,000 for building a furniture factory at Arthurdale, which was to make post-office equipment and provide the community with a cash crop to repay Washington the $1,500,000 put up for the operation. At the pace Mother and Louis were setting, it seemed likely that Arthurdale would be a going concern by early next year, with some of its new tenants in their prefabs this Thanksgiving.

None of that would be too soon. The rosy glow of Father's first four months had faded already. Unemployment was a long way from being cured. "There aren't nearly enough people back at work," he said. Wages and spending were rising extremely sluggishly. Prices were falling, if anything. Local relief programs were so disorganized that he wanted Army kitchens put on call to feed the hungry in the worst black spots.

"On the whole," he wrote Granny hastily, "the situation is not good because so many people are getting their toes stepped on. . . ."

He felt certain that the trouble could be traced back to the very business interests he had saved and those New York bankers who clung to the concept of "sound money" and denounced his scuttling of the London Economic Conference. "The real truth of the matter is," he thought, "that a financial element in the larger centers has owned the government ever since the days of Andrew Jackson," who came into office in 1829 with a slogan of "Let the people rule" and found himself landed into conflict with the Bank of the United States. "The country is going through a repetition of Jackson's fight . . . only on a far bigger and broader basis," said Father.

4

He was given a hint of trouble on the day he took the United States off the gold standard. The necessary order needed the signature of Dean Acheson, acting for Bill Woodin. Undersecretary Acheson balked at signing without an opinion on the legality of the move from Homer Cummings.

"Don't you take my word for it that it will be all right?" Father demanded, in a rare rage.

Acheson coolly replied that it was he, not Father, whose signature was called for. "That will do!" Father snapped. He got his way, but he was of a mind to throw Acheson out of the administration. He had a habit of whistling tunelessly to himself to cool down after such encounters. I am positive that he had recourse to that on that afternoon.

John Gunther related the aftermath. A few days later, Woodin sent for his Undersecretary. "Look here, son, you're in terrible trouble. The President has a paper on his desk, firing you. If he does, I've told him that I'll resign. You'd better resign gracefully yourself. Write him a nice letter in longhand, and you are not to keep a copy."

Acheson would not be dictated to. He was prepared to quit, he said, but it was for him to decide whether or not to copy his own letter. On the day that Morgenthau was sworn in as Woodin's successor, the departing Treasury Secretary brought Acheson into the room with him unannounced. Father's face clouded, then cleared again.

"I'm mad as hell at you," he told Acheson, "but for you to come here today is the best act of sportsmanship I've ever seen." It must be added that he was sometimes prone to overstatement.

Woodin and Father parted good friends. When the first formal reception of the year was held in the White House early in December, Father wore pearl dress-studs that were a gift from Bill. "Much gold lace and thousands of frills," said his note of thanks, "but the sensation of the evening was the 'boozum' of the President."

The American dollar had just survived three weeks of intense pressure, designed to restabilize its value in gold and put a stop to Father's policy of controlled inflation. The Bank of England was fighting to hold the worth of a dollar down in order to make a British pound note equivalent to $3.90 instead of the going rate of $4.60. Father scoffed at that as "unsound from the American point of view. . . . I should hope to see the dollar go to $5.00 or more in relation to the pound."

Stock prices dipped on Wall Street following the breakup of the London conference. He blamed the speculators for that: "Everybody got to speculating, and things went too fast." Rumors spread on the stock market that four or five billion dollars in American capital had been whisked out of the country for investment overseas. He had that checked out privately. The truth was that the flight amounted to no more than $700,000,000.

There was more evidence of a concerted, clandestine effort to discredit Roosevelt. The American Legion and the American Federation of Labor joined in an unlikely coalition to hire Carnegie Hall for a thinly attended rally protesting Father's policy on inflation. His ancient, unforgiving rival for the Presidency, Al Smith, released a letter to the New York Chamber of Commerce, proclaiming: "I am for gold dollars as against baloney dollars." A senior Treasury Department adviser, O.W.M. Sprague, made a great show of resigning after playing an undercover role in stirring up public discontent.

Sprague, who had formerly served in the Bank of England, had been one of the American delegates at the London stabilization talks. Since his return, Father had spoken with him at length on several occasions to try to obtain some constructive counsel. All he received was the familiar line about fixing the dollar's value *vis à vis* the pound.

Sprague attempted to bulldoze Father by claiming that if he resigned from the Treasury Department, United States bonds would inevitably fall five points. "Sprague," my parent concluded, "is a nuisance. He carries no real weight except with the Bank of England crowd and some of our New York City bankers." He would not accept a "silly" letter of resignation from the disgruntled economist, who published it, anyway, as a call to arms against Father.

Other resignations followed as the rift over "reflation" grew among his advisory team. Douglas quit as Director of the Budget. George Peek walked out as head of the Agricultural Adjustment Administration. Dean Acheson went off to practice law again, to come back to Washington in 1941 as Assistant Secretary of State. The conservatives were abandoning Father. So long as they adhered to what he derided as the "old fetishes of so-called international bankers," he was not sorry to see them go, but he had no animosity.

The core of the opposition, he believed, lay in something he referred to as "the Mellon-Mills influence in banking and certain controlling industries." Andrew Mellon of Philadelphia had amassed an enormous fortune in association with the J. P. Morgan interests in public utilities and power. Ogden Mills was a New York banker, with an estate at Hyde Park not far from Granny's, who succeeded Mellon as Secretary of the Treasury under Hoover. This was Father's first test of strength with the forces that, in his belief, had always until now held the whip hand in America. An infinitely greater struggle awaited him four years later, after his attackers had come out into the open and organized to pull him down.

Right now, the primary cause of hostility among big business was the National Recovery Administration and its flamboyant chieftain, Hugh Johnson. The general, drunk or sober, ran his operation like a circus. When he was not standing stage center in Washington, joking, cajoling, and badgering businesssmen and labor leaders, he was crisscrossing the land in an army plane, making headlines at every stop. Most of his publicity techniques were borrowed from World War I devices to drum up enthusiasm for the draft and sell Liberty Loan bonds— badges, billboards, mass rallies, and a parade that blocked New York's Fifth Avenue for half a day. The Blue Eagle adorned factory walls and chorus girls' panties alike. In the public mind, the leather-faced general and the Blue Eagle became twin symbols of the New Deal.

Postmaster General Farley contributed an NRA postage stamp to help the cause. Father, whose personal stamp collection contained well over a million specimens, had some reservations about it. "The honest farmer, who looks like me; and honest businessman, who looks like Grover T. Whalen; and the honest blacksmith, who looks like Lionel Barrymore, are magnificent. But Oh Heavens what a girl! She is wearing a No. 11 shoe, also a bustle, and if recovery is dependent on women like that I am agin recovery." He also had some reservations about Hugh, whose essential mission was to coax industry leaders to agree among themselves on codes of fair competition and improved working conditions. Signed by the President, these hastily concocted agreements carried the weight of law. His most eminent biographer, James MacGregor Burns, has an anecdote about a Cabinet meeting where Father reported how Johnson had marched into the Presidential office one day, carrying three more codes for signature. The ink of "Franklin D. Roosevelt" was scarcely dry on the last of them when Hugh glanced at his watch, stuffed them into his pocket, and rushed out the door, muttering that he had only five minutes to catch his plane.

"He hasn't been seen since," Father chuckled.

Johnson had anticipated that he would be in charge of the millions of dollars in public-works spending envisaged in one section of the National Industrial Recovery Act. When Father handed that to Ickes, Hugh raved that he would quit there and then. Father commissioned Frances Perkins: "Stick with Hugh. Keep him sweet for me." She took him for a tour of Washington, driving for hours until he cooled down.

Old-line industrialists resented Government intervention in their businesses by way of NRA. Even more, they detested that section of the NRA act giving unions the right to collective bargaining, breathing life into organized labor, which had been laid low by the Depression and men's need to take a job at any price. Workingmen by the millions sought to be enrolled as union members, convinced that Father was wholeheartedly on their side. ROOSEVELT WANTS YOU TO JOIN THE UNION said the not entirely accurate message plastered at the mineheads by order of John L. Lewis, the bushy-browed Welshman with a taste for Shakespeare who controlled the United Mine Workers. He repaid the debt that he felt he owed Father by contributing $469,870 to his campaign fund in 1936. Other titans of labor, like Dave Dubinsky of the International Ladies Garment Workers and Dave Beck of the Teamsters, dug into union funds for the same purpose.

Union leaders tested their newfound strength, and a rash of strikes erupted. More workers walked out of their jobs in the first summer of Father's Administration than in the twenty-four months of 1930 and 1931 combined. So the National Labor Board, empowered to investigate and mediate disputes, had to be set up in a hurry. Almost unanimously, the big corporations complained that it was stacked against employers as a group. I happened to agree with them.

Protests against NRA were not confined to the right of the political spectrum. The initials of Johnson's whirlwind agency stood for "Nuts Running America," according to Senator Huey P. Long of Louisiana, who had taken to goading Father on the Senate floor. The pulpy, pockmarked "Kingfish" had showered him with gratuitous and often derisive advice from the day he took office. The two of them had known each other as governors—Governor Long entered the Senate in 1930. Father entertained him just once at Hyde Park, when Granny delivered herself of one of her most celebrated comments: "Who is that dreadful person sitting next to my son?" She classified him with another group of politicians who gathered on the porch another day. Taking care not to lower her resonant voice, she exclaimed, "Why, they look like a lot of gangsters!"

But Long, unbelievably, had stood up for Father in the Chicago convention skirmishing. In the early months of the first term, the Kingfish walked into the White House office looking for his payoff in the form of federal patronage. He wore a straw

hat, which his insolence demanded he keep on his head unless
it was in use to whack Father's knees by way of emphasizing a
point. Father kept on smiling, as pleasant and noncommittal as
only he could be. The Kingfish made his departure when he
realized he was getting nowhere. "What the hell is the use of
coming down to see this fellow?" he asked Jim Farley outside. "I
can't win a decision over him."

"That," Father said to me afterward, "is a man totally without
principle." Ickes went further. Long, he snapped, suffered
from "halitosis of the intellect."

The Kingfish ruled Louisiana like a feudal baron—and joked
about it. "Most of the people would rather laugh than weep," he
insisted, so he read recipes for frying oysters into the Congressional Record and introduced a bill containing instructions for
playing the jaw harp. After his rebuff by Father, the two of
them never met again, but Long's response was to deliver ha-
rangues on the Senate floor against "Prince Franklin, Knight of
the *Nourmahal*," "Lord Corn Wallace" and "Chicago Cinch Bug
Harold Ickes."

In his barony of Louisiana, he pictured himself as a champion of the poor, a drawling demogogue who hammered at
"the interests," the big corporations who secretly supported
him. "Every man a king!" was his battle cry in 1932. Out of that
arose his Share Our Wealth plan, promising a minimum
$2,000-a-year income, which he promoted as a replacement for
Father's more rational programs.

The Kingfish was no joke to my parent. To his keen eyes,
Huey Long had much in common with Mussolini, who by
promising the impossible had made over Italy into a Fascist
state. Long boasted that he would be in the White House after
1936. It was evident that he had no scruples about the route he
would choose to get there. Not long after their encounter in the
Presidential office, Father began to look for means of unhors-
ing Long and and his cronies, who ran Louisiana.

An inquiry made of Guy Helvering, Commissioner of Internal Revenue, brought to light some useful ammunition in September, 1933. Following the Kingfish's election as governor five
years earlier, $100,000,000 was spent on new roads, a new capi-
tol in Baton Rouge, and other civic enterprises in the state. The
IRS had received a flurry of complaints that a large proportion

of those funds had been paid as "commissions" to state officers, who had neglected to report them as taxable income. It was a situation worth pursuing.

That winter, when temperatures in the capital fell to a record 6 below, saw renewed hardship in many areas in spite of everything that was being done to alleviate distress. At Arthurdale, fifty families shivered in tents because Louis' Cape Cod prefabs arrived too small to fit the concrete foundations that had been poured in advance for them. The cost of resettlement, originally estimated at $2,000 a family, was already running above $10,000. Mother's insistence that corners must not be cut in providing decent accommodations drew fire from Ickes, who resented her "interference." The expense was "shocking" to him. "I don't see how we can possibly defend ourselves on this project."

He quoted Father as telling him, "My Missus, unlike most women, hasn't any sense about money at all." She felt that no house would be complete without a bathroom. Father wanted to leave it up to each homesteader to install every bit of plumbing for himself as soon as he could afford it.

As Ickes forecast, Arthurdale proved indefensible against attack. Congress barred the Post Office from buying any of the equipment turned out by the new factory there. Comptroller General J. Raymond McCarl, a Republican holdover from Harding's regime who delighted in spiking New Deal schemes, ruled that no federal funds could be spent to underwrite any other manufacturing on the site.

Magazines and newspapers jeered at Mother's languishing enterprise as a classic example of the fate that would befall America if the sacred principles of private enterprise were subverted. The Republican Party, making its first attempt at a political comeback, pretended that Arthurdale was part of a Communist plot for the takeover of the country. Perhaps a red scare would destroy Father's astounding popularity. A Labor government had been tricked out of office in England by the dangling of the Bolshevik bogey a decade earlier, when a letter, purportedly from Zinoviev, president of the Communist International, spurring British Communists to sedition had been published in Conservative newspapers just before election day.

The vessel of hoped-for wrath that the Republicans came up

with was Dr. William A. Wirt, superintendent of schools in
Gary, Indiana. On March 24, 1934, banner headlines reported
a brain trust plot to revolutionize the United States. The authority for this revelation was Dr. Wirt. In a letter read to a
committee of Congress, he claimed that unnamed brain trusters had personally informed him that Father was only an
American Kerensky, due to be supplanted by a Stalin—
presumably Rex Tugwell. Wirt cited Arthurdale as a telltale
straw in the wind.

On both sides of the House, there was no shortage of Congressmen eager, as always, to get ther names into print. Republican John Taber of New York had already denounced Arthurdale's stripling factory as "a proposition to further the Socialist-
ic programs launched by this adminstration." Democrat George
Terrell of Texas vowed that "the Constitution is being violated
here every day because there isn't a line in the Constitution that
authorized the expenditure of federal money for other than
federal purposes." He foretold that Hopkins' CWA was "going
to start civil war and revolution."

What the situation demanded was a special committee to investigate the truth or falsehood of Wirt's charges. Representative Alfred Bulwinkle of North Carolina was named its chairman. It turned out that Dr. Wirt had been a guest at a dinner
party with some minor officials of the government, but made a
mistake in identifying the source of his information. It was not
a member of the brain trust he had talked with but a correspondent of Tass, the Soviet news agency, who was speculating
on what *might* happen next in America. Wirt's off-duty interests
extended beyond scholastics. Ickes reported that he consorted
with the silver-shirted comrades of the American Fascist Party
in Gary. Being compared with a Russian political failure
amused Father to the point where he once signed a memorandum to a certain Foreign Minister with a flourishing "A Kerensky Roosevelt."

The plot to discredit him fizzled out, but his opponents
would try again. It was not his way to berate Congress, no matter what it did. He sent off a note to Bulwinkle: "You have been
fair and dignified and I am confident that the country appreci-
ates it." The reporting of the hullaballoo that he read in his
breakfast newspapers clinched his conviction that four out of

five proprietors of the press were rockbound in their bias against him. But while his enemies commanded the printed word, he had the radio and his fireside chats to more than even the score.

His final word on Arthurdale, which ultimately had to be written off as a well-intentioned mistake, and the close to one hundred similar communities ultimately built by the New Deal, made no excuses. "These projects represent something new," he said, "and because we in America had little or no experience along these lines, there were some failures. . . ."

He could probably justify his feeling that homesteaders should pay for their own plumbing because the work that went into installing an indoor swimming pool in the White House cost not a cent in tax money. Extensive remodeling of the whole structure was begun that summer to make more room in the executive offices for the expanding staff, to install seven new bathrooms and a dazzling, stainless steel, all-electric kitchen for Mrs. Nesbitt. "Working here," Father grumbled, "is much like working in a boiler factory!"

It was agreed that a pool should be added in which he could take the only regular exercise available to him. It was paid for by the dollars and dimes in public donations that descended on Washington, to be collected in a special fund for the purpose. He accepted this tribute with good grace, though he was adamantly opposed to being memorialized in other ways. Admirers in and out of government constantly urged him to allow some new bridge, park, or highway to be named for him.

"But I am still alive," he would explain. "I wouldn't dream of such a thing."

Possibly there lurked somewhere in his mind the ancient Greeks' idea of *hubris,* the penalty the gods exacted for overweening pride. He applied the same standard to other men. The giant hydroelectric generating complex straddling the Colorado River was no longer to be called "Hoover Dam" but "Boulder Dam." In 1947, Harry Truman restored its original title.

Father broke his rule for the sake of the charity that meant the most to him. He sanctioned the minting of the Roosevelt dime because it was linked with the National Infantile Paralysis Foundation. He had set up the Warm Springs property—the bubbling spring itself, a derelict hotel and cottages, and 12,000 acres of Georgia hills—as a nonprofit foundation in 1929, which was the year after he bought it and the start of his first term as governor of New York. Basil O'Connor took on the task of raising donations to develop Warm Springs as a treatment center for polio victims.

Then O'Connor served as president of the foundation and seized on the surge of public sympathy for poliomyelitis sufferers aroused by knowledge of Father's handicap. The annual March of Dimes piled up millions of dollars for treatment and research, which was to be crowned by discovery of Dr. Jonas Salk's vaccine. Gala balls organized in every state to celebrate Father's birthday added to the gross. Mother, however, withheld her approval of Basil. She questioned the size of the salary he drew from the foundation. Fund-raising expenses and overheads accounted for fifteen cents of every March of Dimes dollar, which struck her as an exorbitant percentage. And with Basil simultaneously making more money as president of the American Red Cross—her sensibilities could see no justice in that.

Father was embarrassed by the adulation he received, no matter what the source. A crowd's shouts of "God bless you, Mr. President" or individual cries of "You saved my home" or "You made a job for me" alarmed him. He considered himself no god. He intended simply to do his best, try anything to see whether it worked, and keep slogging on in the conviction that in the end he would inevitably succeed.

The pool turned out to be more important in keeping him fit than his spring fishing trips or the autumn days he spent at Warm Springs. Most days, when he left the Executive office wing, he was wheeled along the colonnade that took him past the pool en route to the White House proper. He would go in for a swim to relax for the evening ahead. In the water, he could swim like a seal, his massive shoulders flexing, or stand unaided, recapturing for a few moments the fancy that he might walk again.

After he had dried off, he was eased in his terry-towel robe back into the wheelchair, to be pushed to the elevator and then into his second-floor bedroom for a rubdown by a Navy yeoman skilled in the art of massage. On the same level as the pool, along the interior basement corridor, was another place of almost daily call, which meant pain instead of pleasure. Two cubbyholes there provided quarters for Captain Ross McIntire and a Navy medic, who administered remedies for Father's chronic sinus problem.

McIntire was posted from the Naval Hospital, Bethesda, Maryland, as Father's personal physician on the recommendation of Admiral Cary T. Grayson, who had functioned in a similar role for Woodrow Wilson. A good word in the right places carried great weight in any Presidential entourage. Grayson was an adept of politics as well as medicine. Convinced that Wilson had suffered serious brain damage in 1919, he worked with Edith Wilson and Joe Tumulty, the President's secretary, for seven months to keep the truth a secret from Congress and the people.

Dr. McIntire was a nose and throat specialist. He appeared to be just the man for Father. Head cold miseries plagued him in spring and fall, sometimes developing into influenza and putting him to bed for days on end. He would sit reluctantly in McIntire's cramped office while the Navy doctor ran wire probes up through his nostrils to drain all accessible sinuses. No kind of local anesthetic could be given. It was one time of day when there was no trace of the radiant smile. He had a physical checkup once or twice a year. So far as I know, Mother had none.

For his colds, he treated himself with Vick's VapoRub. To do anything more would mean coddling himself, which he flatly refused to do. He presented problems as a patient for chunky, easygoing Captain McIntire, whose Navy training made it difficult for him to give orders to his Commander in Chief. That became frighteningly clear toward the end of Father's life.

A stuffed-up nose did not spoil his normal good humor. He slept soundly, no matter what, and woke in the best of spirits, reaching for a cigarette and a cup of coffee from his bedside table. Almost as soon as his eyes were open, he could expect a call from Louis, who claimed the right to talk with him at any hour of the day or night. He spent as much as two hours a day on the telephone, instantly accessible to around one hundred men and women who knew that the switchboard would put them directly on to him without going through Missy or her Irish Catholic assistant, Grace G. Tully.

The thought of surrounding himself with a defensive screen

of functionaries never crossed his mind. He had to identify with the *people,* in whose courage and decency he never ceased to believe. The way to do that was to keep himself available to them. Presidents before and after Coolidge employed the tight-lipped technique of getting rid of visitors by saying as little as possible to them. Father had a different approach. He drew out anyone who interested him by letting them see that in most instances he had broad preliminary knowledge of the subject to be discussed. He silenced those who bored him by keeping up such a flow of one-sided conversation that they had little chance to say a word.

Mother did not understand how he could behave in this fashion. She accused him of being compulsively indiscreet. It was not until years later that she realized this was one method of testing a visitor's own powers of discretion. She complained that "often people have told me that they were misled by Franklin." Harold Ickes was one such person. To his diary, he confided that it "hurts to say" that Father's word could not be trusted.

Ideas gushed from my parent's brain like water from a hose. He had the same knack as Uncle Ted for going through newspapers, the pages of a book, or the sheets of a memorandum at a hard gallop, retaining the essence of what he read permanently in his memory. Verbosity irked him as much as deception in any government document. "Boil it down," he would order. "Get rid of the weasel words."

"It leaves me cold" was a condemnation; "I'm tickled pink with it" was high praise.

He went through a working day like a huntsman riding an obstacle course, taking things fast, never sparing himself. He was perhaps unique among the heads of state of the great powers in that he relied almost exclusively on his memory of any conversation, seldom making a note or dictating a memorandum of what had transpired. If he did scribble a word or two, it was likely to be on a scrap of paper slipped into his pocket.

Around four in the afternoon, it was time to tackle the mail, preferably with Missy, who by then would have taken care of much of it herself after the eight or nine thousand letters which came in most days had been winnowed and distributed for action by other staff. The wire baskets deposited on his desk were filled to overflowing, since he insisted on missing nothing of importance or anything touching on his incredible range of personal interests. He handled a staggering volume of correspondence, by letter, telegram, or handwritten note, though he was known to shuffle some particularly thorny documents down to the bottom of the pile to give himself more time to brood over his reply.

I leave myself open to charges of bias and say that he used words like a master of the English language, plain words, written or spoken, free of gobblydegook and incapable of misinterpretation. In his manner of thinking, his meaning had to be crystal clear, because only by communication could he exercise leadership and explain the cogent reasons for his policies.

He corresponded in the same amiable style with a miner on relief as with a reigning monarch. After he selected his law partner of a dozen years ago, Grenville Emmet of the defunct firm of Emmet, Marvin and Roosevelt, as Minister to the Netherlands, Father picked up a pen to write to Queen Wilhelmina:

> YOUR MAJESTY:
> . . . As you may know, the Netherlands is the land of the forebears of my family and I have cherished a sentiment of affection for and deep interests in your nation. I am therefore glad indeed that I am able to entrust the relationships between The Netherlands and the United States to Mr. Emmet, who is one of my oldest personal friends. I am certain that you will find him a delightful gentleman who will further the many mutual interests of our countries. . . .

He maintained a healthy respect for Congress and expected a similar response so long as he was frank with the leadership in both Houses. He was against paying veterans their long-fought-for bonus in 1934 and authorized Henry Rainey, Speaker of the House, to say so. When advocates of the bonus took this to be a political ploy, indicating that Father would let the bill in question become law without signing it, another memo was whisked off to Rainey:

"Naturally when I suggested to you that I could not approve the bill for the payment of the bonus certificate I did not mean that I might let it become law without my signature. I don't do things that way. What I meant was that I would veto the bill,

and I don't care who you tell this to." Father, in fact, set records
in the number of times he used the prerogative of veto in his
seesaw relations with the lawmakers.

His preoccupation with economizing showed itself in a hundred ways. A Hyde Park neighbor, James Plane, evidently fancied that it would be easy to solicit a fellow taxpayer's support,
even though he was President, for channeling in CWA funds to
improve and extend the local water supply. Father responded
with a telegram:

FRANKLY I CANNOT SEE ANY GOOD OBJECT SERVED IN EXTEND-
ING WATER MAIN SOUTH OF MRS. ROGERS' NORTH BOUNDARY. ALL
HOUSES FROM THERE SOUTH HAVE ADEQUATE WATER SUPPLY. THIS
KIND OF A PROJECT WILL MERELY COST THE TAXPAYERS A LOT OF
EXTRA MONEY IN THE FUTURE.

He loved words and any opportunity to add to his vocabu-
lary. After Prohibition was repealed, an army of politicians,
perpetually campaigning for reelection, claimed credit for it.
Herbert Bayard Swope addressed a playful letter to the New
York *Times* with a reference to this "euhemeristic" tendency.
The *Times* changed that to "euphemistic," then printed an
apology for its error after Herbert protested. In his breakfast
reading, Father followed the fracas with glee and twitted Swope
on the outcome:

> Sir: The Typographical Union has lodged complaint under
> their code against you for submitting copy to the New York
> Times containing the word "euhemeristic." A hearing will be
> held by me at your convenience. It is respectfully suggested
> that a jail sentence can be avoided by you if hereafter you will
> provide a dictionary of your own copy to all typesetters. P.S.
> By the way—what does the darn word mean anyway?

Learned Herbert filled him in. Euhemerus was a scholar of
Attic Greece who speculated about where the myths surrounding Greek gods had their origin.

Fun had to be largely of Father's own making in the White
House. It obliterated *angst,* as the psychologists term the gnawing anxiety which reduces a man's ability to act under pressure.
Part of his prescription for effectiveness demanded that he free
his mind of worry in order to concentrate on the job in hand.

The shield he raised for self-protection was composed of laughter, created and shared.

A sense of fun was probably more important than any other single quality in gaining admission to his innermost circle. Banter, joshing, and horseplay were his favorite forms of relaxation, preferably over a few drinks or a poker game which, to Mother's disgust, might last until six in the morning on vacations. Colonel Edwin M. Watson, nicknamed "Pa" from the time he reported for duty as military aide, was as dear a friend as any Father had. Florid-faced Pa was a crack shot in the hunting field and an expert deep-water fisherman, with a habit of talking to his catch as he reeled it in.

He starred as the hero of one anecdote that Father never tired of telling. Pa went to Bernie Baruch's South Carolina plantation, Hobcaw Barony, for some quail and wild turkey shooting along with Admiral Grayson, by now retired and heading the American Red Cross. One morning, Pa tethered a tame bird in the brush. At his first glimpse of it, the admiral started pumping shells, ten in all, before he killed the decoy. On hearing of this, Father dispatched a memorandum jointly to them:

> From Commander in Chief U.S. Forces
>
> To Hospital Apprentice Third Class Cary T. Grayson and Gunner Third Class E. M. Watson
>
> Subject: The efficiency record in artillery defense in severe engagement in Old Quail War
>
> 1. Field Marshal Baruch reports that in repelling the enemy's landing party on the coast of South Carolina more corpses were found in front of your gun than in any other sector.
> 2. The C. in C. has in person dissected sufficient samples of said corpses to certify that many of them perished from shell fire—only a minority showing the effects of death from sheer fright.
> 3. You are, therefore, presented with the Order of the Red Cross First Class, with sago palms.
> 4. You are from this date detailed to serve in the Tear Gas Squad of the President's personal bodyguard.

A few months later, another tale concerning Pa was added to Father's lexicon. From the Woodmont Rod and Gun Club in the Blue Ridge Mountains, Pa reported: "This morning, at about three bells, I shot and killed two wild turkeys (a fine larger gobbler and a magnificent hen) with *one shot*." He supplied the details later: "My companion was in a prone position behind a thick bush, calling to the wild ones—I, in a more alert posture, was behind an equally thick bush, gun in hand—suddenly two fine turkeys spring into view. So keen were their senses and so swift their reactions that they were practically in full flight before I could get a shot 'from the hip.' The results of this shot are now matters of local pride and history."

He was not bragging. At the moment he aimed at one bird, another flew into his sights. He dropped them both. Father, joking perhaps to overcome envy of Pa's freedom to go wherever his legs could carry him, came up with another memo, "Subject: Charges filed against Colonel E. M. Watson."

> Rather than incur the expenses of a Court Martial it is suggested that General Baruch tie Colonel Watson and Admiral Grayson to convenient trees, distant one hundred paces, that each be armed with a bow and arrow, that each be blindfolded, that each be required to emit turkey calls, and that thereafter firing shall begin. It is believed that this will prove:
> (a) That neither of them ever shot a turkey.
> (b) That they would not recognize a turkey at ten feet.
> (c) That both of them should be released on good behavior. . . .

It would be hard to find two more dissimilar men than Pa Watson and Tom Corcoran, the brash young lawyer in the Reconstruction Finance Corporation, yet "Tommy the Cork" came close after Watson in father's regard until Harry Hopkins, his ambitions soaring, began to shoulder Corcoran aside. Tom's access to Father made his influence in Washington much greater than his official position indicated. Like many another political shooting star, he was not above letting people imagine that he carried more clout than was entirely true.

He was a congenial spirit, who cracked a good joke and sang Irish ballads, so Father encouraged him much of the time. He soon found himself on the short list of those who were invited as friends to Hyde Park, where he would play his accordion or guitar while he improvised jingles and did imitations to enter-tain the company. Unlike the majority of men around Father, Tommy the Cork drew a sharp distinction between times for work and times for play. He would not dream of buttonholing Father to talk politics in the middle of a party, as others did. He was the source of another pleasure for the housebound President. Going the rounds of Washington, Tom picked up the latest tidbits of gossip—who fell down drunk in Georgetown; what secret one Congressman whispered to another in the Capitol cloakroom; which ambassador had found a new mistress. Father liked to be regaled with a *soupçon* of scandal from the social circuit.

Beneath the Irish charm, Corcoran was as tough-minded as the man who employed him, a wheeler-dealer who manipulated politicians and bureaucrats with equal ease. The other "Gold Dust Twin," as the columnists labeled them, was Ben Cohen, the shy, brilliant legal technician on the staff of the Public Works Administration. Ben had a rare talent for devising fresh attacks on any problem the administration encountered. He, too, became one of the Kitchen Cabinet, a backroom theoretician whose part in engineering the New Deal was more important than that of any member of the official Cabinet, with the possible exception of Ma Perkins and "Honest Harold" Ickes. Father had enormous respect for Ben's intellectual attainments, but he was never as close as the other, more dazzling Gold Dust Twin.

Missy's humor was a powerful factor in the relationship. She could be serious enough if the occasion called for it, but never solemn. There would be at least one smiling face responding to Father's when she joined the family for dinner, as she did most evenings. I remember her being put to the test when she was seated toward the end of the table next to Hall, who had enjoyed a few cocktails in advance. He had a penchant for applying a playful squeeze to a person's knee on the nerve just above the joint. I can testify that it could be painful.

In the middle of the first course, a shriek from Missy rose above the conversation of the fourteen other guests, and she leaped up from her chair. We knew that Hall had been up to his tricks again. Father looked down at them with a tolerant smile. Mother's face darkened. "I wish you wouldn't *do* those things," she said, frowning at her brother.

Mother's frequent absences left Missy as the true hostess of the White House much of the time, but the intimacy she had enjoyed with Father for nearly a dozen years underwent a marked change. There were fewer hours to share with her. I believe that he deliberately chose to discipline himself in order to concentrate on the task for which he had been elected. The decision would be easier now that he had entered the sixth decade of life, with his needs less peremptory than before. Missy would not question the new turn in their association. She took it to be her unique obligation to conserve his energies in all respects. As the one he called "my conscience," she could not contest the choice he made. She lost little of her value to him as confidante, companion, and counselor, which was enough for her at the age of thirty-six.

The increase in distance between them restored a little of the freedom she had long since given up for Father's sake. Other men responded to Missy's sparkling blue eyes, her instinctive charm, and her access to the President. She began to go out on dates, not always alert to the fact that she might be invited for subterranean reasons.

Earl Miller, the muscular New York State trooper who was something of a pet of Mother's, was one of Missy's admirers. If he had an ulterior motive it could be that he hoped to ingratiate himself with Father, who had no desire to see Miller around the White House.

Joe Kennedy struck up an affectionate alliance with her and took to dropping her letters, always with some official business matter in mind, signed off with "love and kisses," which Missy answered in the same vein. "My two assistants—F.D.R. and G.G.T.—join me in sending you best wishes," said one flippant note she sent Joe.

Bill Bullitt took her out, eager for any passed-along crumb of the information she was privy to. Bernie Baruch added her to the long roster of White House people, starting with my parents, whom he remembered with gifts. As in Kennedy's case, he made his money by playing the market. Both of them capitalized on any hint they could pick up in advance of Father's intentions in fiscal policy, just as the Kennedy clan continued to probe for early clues when son Jack was President nearly thirty years later.

My often gullible mother used to say, "Every President, I am

sure, leaves the White House poorer than when he went in."
On the contrary, I am confident that in the twentieth century
that has applied only to Father.

Baruch was a polished flatterer, particularly of women. He
set himself up as a sage in Mother's eyes by sending her a check
for $22,000 toward the cost of establishing an experimental
school at Arthurdale, extolling her "rare combination of intelligence and great heart."

Father was wiser to the ways of the veteran speculator who, at
the urging of public relations counsel, made a practice of encouraging reporters to interview him as he sat on a favorite
bench in Lafayette Park, nurturing the impression that he had
that very moment left Father in the White House across Pennsylvania Avenue. The truth was that Father tried to avoid office
appointments with Bernie, whom he found to be a blowhard.
Besides, he had been a leader of the "stop Roosevelt" faction in
the Democratic Party before Chicago. His present generosity
had to be interpreted as an attempt to recoup, though all contributions to future campaign funds as sizable as his must be
gratefully accepted.

So Bernie succeeded in infiltrating the White House, thanks
to Mother, Missy, and, while he lasted, Hugh Johnson, whom
Bernie had introduced into the brain trust *after* the Chicago
convention as a further contribution toward winning Presidential favor. When there was no escaping it, Father would listen
patiently to Baruch's pontificating about how to run America,
but administration policies showed what little weight was attached to the overblown discourses of the self-proclaimed
"adviser to Presidents" by the incumbent and the enthusiastic
young men like Corcoran and Cohen with whom he surrounded himself.

Johnson lasted less than a year as the barnstorming boss of
NRA. In his haste to get things rolling, he clobbered together
an unmanageable, Rube Goldberg contrivance in which the
wheels of industry grated together and the luckless consumers
of the end products had no voice at all. The squeals of protest
could no longer be ignored by the spring of 1934. A review
board appointed by Father reported that the Blue Eagle codes
had given big corporations a golden chance to dominate lesser
ones.

He promptly cut down NRA's power and, to Baruch's dismay, eased Johnson out, to work briefly as administrator of the WPA in New York City. The old cavalryman roared his protests and almost immediately signed on as a newspaper columnist for United Press. His peppery attacks on Father, the administration, and the New Dealers—"the hot-dog group," in his phrase—made lively reading.

Bernie was aghast, though Johnson was advocating in print the appointment of his former boss as Secretary of the Treasury to replace Morgenthau. Baruch tried in vain to reach Father by telephone. He had to content himself with pressing a little unsolicited advice on Margaret Durand, otherwise known as Rabbit, who was Louis' secretary and who took the call. It would be "unwise" for the President or anyone else to be drawn into answering Johnson, said Bernie. There was no indication that Father had the slightest desire to do so.

"You will phone Mr. Baruch today, won't you?" said Rabbit's plaintive memo to Louis. Father would not. He replied to Baruch in twenty-three crisp words: "It is only because I, like you, admired Hugh for his many fine qualities that this kind of thing makes us deeply sad." He let the general down less lightly on a later occasion, when he berated him as "a liar, a coward and a cad," which brought tears to Johnson's squinched-up eyes.

One other group employed Missy as a dependable channel of communication with Father. She proved herself to be a faithful servant of the church whose dictates she did not otherwise take altogether seriously. A cardinal or other Catholic dignitary was seldom refused a White House appointment. Her personally chosen assistant, Grace Tully, was equally amenable to requests from their church.

Mother questioned the propriety of it. She had overcome the anti-Semitism of her younger days. Possibly her partiality for Baruch represented some kind of overcompensation. She was still strong in her disapproval of what she looked on as the tyranny of Catholicism. She had no compunction about bringing in spokesmen for causes she believed in, to sit at the dinner table and attempt to convert Father, whether or not he wanted to listen to them. One of the faults she saw in Missy was her complicity in opening doors for fellow Catholics.

The arrangement suited Father then and later. In his search

for reinforcements in his war on the President, Huey Long found a willing ally in Father Charles E. Coughlin of the Shrine of the Little Flower in Royal Oak, Detroit, a round-faced priest who had built an audience of millions for his weekly radio sermons, which were rabble-rousing political tirades rather than exhortations to righteousness. Eighty thousand letters a week, more mail than arrived for Father, brought in $500,000 a year for the "radio priest."

My parent had to reckon with him as a power in the land, and had been happy to have his early support. "The New Deal is Christ's Deal," proclaimed Coughlin, who in the week he denounced "Hoover prosperity" saw his mail soar to the million mark. The priest, said Father in 1932, "is a friend of mine." As a fellow practitioner of the art of persuasion via the microphone, Father respected the priest's professional prowess in swaying unknown millions of Catholic votes. Nevertheless, he had a quiet probe conducted of Coughlin's finances. It was discovered that his principal backer was a dealer in the foreign exchange market. The priest's cries for inflation and "a living annual wage" were a smokescreen.

Coughlin was quick to respond to the Kingfish's overtures. Soon he was ranting against Father as "the scab President," castigating him along with his other perennial targets: Jews, "Red atheists," "godless capitalists," and "international plutocrats." He created his own Fascist-flavored action group, the National Union for Social Justice, which Louis smelled instantly as a threat to split the Democratic Party against Father.

Somehow Coughlin had to be outflanked. Missy's personal open-door policy for the Catholic hierarchy was used to good effect. Friendly priests and laymen were ushered into the White House office to be enrolled in the undercover mission of curbing Coughlin, while Jim Farley was commissioned to check at the Royal Oak post office to assess the effectiveness of the radio priest's constant fund-raising appeals. Louis had another agent at work in Hall, who kept him supplied with regular reports on the priest's private activities in Detroit. Louis by now was bedridden most of the time. He worked on his knees in the effort to get more breath into his collapsing lungs, but he kept up the flow of daily dictation to Rabbit and telephoned the Boss at all hours of the clock. Coughlin scored a major victory against "the

scab President" after Father concluded that one way to counter
isolationists like the radio priest and the Kingfish, and simultaneously strengthen the crumbling structure of European security, would be to push for a Senate resolution putting the
United States on record as supporting the World Court of the
League of Nations.

The shrill voice from the Shrine of the Little Flower denounced the move as a bankers' plot that would lead to war.
"Keep America safe for Americans and not the hunting ground
of international plutocrats," he raved. On orders from San
Simeon, every newspaper of William Randolph Hearst hammered away on the same theme. Forty thousand hostile telegrams cascaded onto the Senate two days before the vote was
taken.

The World Court resolution required a two-thirds vote for
passage. It went down, 52 for, 36 against. Of the nays, Father
fancied "if they ever get to Heaven they will be doing a great
deal of apologizing for a very long time—that is if God is
against war—and I think he is." In a note to "Dear Harry" Stimson, he nursed the wound.

> You are right that we know the enemy. In normal times, the
> radio and other appeals by them would not have been effec-
> tive. However, these are not normal times; people are jumpy
> and very ready to run after strange gods. This is so in every
> other country as well as our own. I fear common sense dic-
> tates no new method for the time being—but I have an unfor-
> tunately long memory and I am not forgetting either our ene-
> mies or our objectives.

The objectives had moved farther left of center. Father pur-
posely waited until the Seventy-third Congress adjourned in
June before he went on the air for his first fireside chat of 1934.
Two more pieces of legislative mosaic had been cemented into
place. The new Federal Communications Commission had interstate authority and control over transmissions overseas. The
Federal Housing Administration would hold sway in the home-
building industry. Just before the lawmakers departed, he gave
notice that from the next Congress convening in the coming
year he would seek what he privately described as "new

manifestations of the New Deal, even though the orthodox protest and the heathen roar." These manifestations would include, he said, social security insurance, development of natural resources, and a long-range housing program.

A week later, he taunted his enemies over the radio, "Are you better off than you were last year?" he asked the listening millions. In the November elections, the voters answered with a resounding yes by slicing Republican representation in the Senate from 35 to 25 and in the House from 117 to 102, unprecedented figures for an off-year election. In Missouri, a former Kansas City haberdasher rode the tide into the Senate with the backing of that city's notorious political boss, "Big Tom" Pendergast. Unlike some other newcomers, Senator Harry Truman received no admission to Father's inner circle, which was frustrating for "the Senator from Pendergast," as he was called. It proved no easier to get close to Father when Big Tom went to jail for income tax evasion five years later.

The Democrats' sweep at the polls put Father in position to hit hard at the American Liberty League, chartered in August to serve as rallying ground for his archenemies. His pet name for it was the "I Can't Take It Club." Members were easier to identify now that they had emerged into daylight. Al Smith was an organizer, and so was the Wall Street corporation lawyer, John W. Davis. Both were Democrats. Father had begun his political comeback after polio by nominating Al for the Presidency in 1924's seventeen-day convention, but the choice fell on Davis. My parent relished the irony of the present turn of events.

Irénée du Pont was another incorporator of the league, which dedicated itself to combating radicalism, upholding the Constitution, and protecting property rights. William Knudsen, the production genius of General Motors, was a member, along with cranky Sewell Avery, the hard-shelled boss of the Montgomery Ward mail-order house. Pew of Sun Oil signed up, a paladin of free enterprise in an industry whose less successful operatives still pressed for the government to take over the East Texas fields and fix a minimum price of one dollar a barrel for crude.

At a press conference two days after its birth, Father twitted the league as an organization which boiled down the Ten Commandments to only two: love God and forget your neighbor.

There was no mention, he continued, about the government's concern "to try to make it possible for people who are willing to work to find work to do, for people who want to keep themselves from starvation, keep a roof over their heads, have proper educational standards."

He ad-libbed as clear a definition of his goals as he ever put into words: "Another thing that isn't mentoned is the protection of the life and liberty of the individual against elements in the community which seek to enrich or advance themselves at the expense of their fellow citizens. They have just as much right to protection by government as anybody else." He broke off with a broad beam on his face. "I don't believe any further comment is necessary after this—what would you call it? A homily?"

When the Seventy-fourth Congress convened in January, the transforming of America picked up speed again. Identified usually only by the initials of their titles, and often derided as "alphabet soup," new agencies of government proliferated like self-dividing amoebas all over Washington. The key members of their staffs were the bright young attorneys assiduously recruited from Harvard by Vienna-born Felix Frankfurter, who taught law there. His contacts with Father dated back to World War I days. In a scathing *Saturday Evening Post* article, Hugh Johnson termed him the "most influential single individual in the country."

Johnson erred once more. If that tag fitted anyone apart from Father, it belonged to Tom Corcoran. He and Ben Cohen had together drafted the Securities Exchange Act. Now they had a major hand in most items of New Deal legislation, tightening it to match the increasingly leftist mood of Congress, adjusting it under protest to appease conservative old-timers on Capitol Hill. Tommy the Cork was spotlighted as Father's ablest frontline fighter. Only Tom, it seemed, worked harder than his chief, who invariably had to order him at verbal pistol point to take a vacation—and set him a little homework to do while he was away.

Mother did not take to Tom. He was too pungent a personality to suit her. He was also one more Catholic in the President's entourage, and his views were too radical for Mother's taste at that time.

I had my first experience of being used as an entrée to the White House on a mission that was far from radical and, in my opinion, just. William Randolph Hearst deputized me in my capacity as aviation editor to go with his son George from Los Angeles to Washington to lobby for a reversal of Administration policy. I had been writing articles about the need to expand American air power. I had contacts with aircraft manufacturers like Donald W. Douglas and, in the United States Army Air Corps, with the lieutenant colonel in charge of March Field, whose name was "Hap" Arnold.

As an economy measure, Father canceled the government contracts that paid commercial airlines to carry mail. The army's planes would take over that job, he ruled. These aircraft were little changed from the outdated models that existed at the end of the war. The crews sat in open cockpits. Radio communication facilities were primitive. These machines lagged far behind commercial planes in their ability to fly safely with the help of up-to-the-minute weather briefings for their pilots.

Father's cost-cutting backfired. The price of delivering letters was heavy losses in planes and pilots who were not trained for making transcontinental flights in every kind of weather. At all levels of command in the Army Air Corps, the decision was recognized as a mistake. Its effect on the passenger-flying companies was financially crippling. I knew that much from C. R. Smith, promoted now as president of the renamed American Airlines by his chief, E. L. Cord, who wrested control from its principal shareholder, Averell Harriman. Smith had served as best man at my wedding to Ruth.

Not for the first time, I got embroiled in a fierce one-sided argument with Father. "It's probably as great a mistake as you've ever made," I lectured him, "to just outright cancel those contracts. If you weren't satisfied with the commercial carrier's performance, why not put in a federal overseer and allow the airlines to do a job that they're equipped for? Then you'd avoid this needless cost in lives."

He heard me out, but he was not to be budged. As an apprentice lobbyist, I had to judge myself a failure. The immediate net result of the mission was my learning that George Hearst had only limited capacity for handling his liquor. But, as happened so often, Father digested what I had told him, together with less vehement opinions from all sides. Eventually, he produced a program to allocate individual routes to the air carriers and so end cutthroat competition between them. He gave the mail contracts back to them, too.

His relation with Hearst, always uncertain, deteriorated into mutual enmity after the defeat of the World Court resolution. At about the same time that he sent federal investigators into Louisiana to prove the financial shenanigans of Huey Long and company, Father had the Internal Revenue Service conduct a similar scrutiny of every corner and crevice of Hearst's empire, trying to catch the predator of San Simeon off base in his manipulations. Ickes suggested what he thought was a better idea. Why not force the California banks to call in their loans to WRH, who survived only on borrowed money? The Old Curmudgeon neglected to cite precisely what Constitutional powers might give Father that authority, so the proposal got nowhere.

My father may have been the originator of the concept of employing the IRS as a weapon of political retribution. Each of his successors followed his lead. If the situation called for it, he was ready, in his own words, to be "a tough cookie." There was a significant difference between his approach and that of one of his most recent successors. Father ordered no fishing expeditions on the off-chance that they would turn up something damaging to be held over the head of an adversary. He had to be convinced first that a strong likelihood of wrongdoing existed, and he was impartial between his opponents and his friends, like Vincent Astor, who appeared later on a private list of suspected tax evaders. Justice meant a lot to Father.

Tax investigations of Hearst failed to unearth anything actionable, but there was some satisfaction when he suffered considerable financial setbacks in a hasty tidying up of his intricate affairs. Father had better luck in the case of Moe Annenberg, who parlayed his publishing business from a racetrack tipsheet into a highly successful, Roosevelt-hating newspaper, the Philadelphia *Bulletin*. A close look at his tax returns resulted in a prison term.

5

Granny, of course, was against it and so were some of his Cabinet, notably including Henry Wallace, when Father announced seven months after taking office that the United States was to resume diplomatic relations with the Soviet Union. Congress had no formal voice in the matter. The terms of the Constitution gave the President sole authority to accord or withdraw recognition of a foreign power. The decision to reopen an American embassy in Moscow was very much my father's.

His action pleased many Republican businessmen as much as any segment of the country. Ideologies didn't count for much against their soaring hopes of selling more machinery and heavy industrial equipment to help the Russians achieve the latest of their five-year plans. If they had dollars to spend as customers, they could be forgiven for godless Bolshevism. Some objections were heard from the oil industry, which feared Soviet competition.

Suspicions of the deal were stronger on the other side. Father's knowledge of history led him to expect that. Mistrust of foreigners had been instilled in the Russian character by a succession of invading hordes that swept in from the east, starting with Genghis Khan's. The aftermath of the Bolshevik revo-

lution intensified xenophobia in the newborn Union of Soviet
Socialist Republics, when the Allies poured in arms and men to
support the White Russian counterrevolutionaries in warring
against the Reds.

"Volunteers" fought under the command of General Kol-
chak in Siberia and under Denikin in southern Russia. Woodrow Wilson sent in an expeditionary force led by General William Graves. American and British troops on guard duty at the
Allied munition dumps at Murmansk and Archangel were deployed to join the Whites in battle against the Red Army. One
British force occupied the oil center of Baku, another roved the
Afghanistan frontier.

The British Secretary for War, Winston Churchill, denounced "the baboonery of Bolshevism" in 1919 and persuaded the Allies into massive intervention, while he contributed
$500,000,000 worth of tanks and armaments to the cause. At
Omsk, a moment came when it seemed that the effort to stamp
out the revolution might succeed, but the so-called all-Russian
government set up in the town was short-lived. The raggle-tag-
gle Red Army, led by Leon Trotsky, defeated the Whites and
ousted the invaders. It was no surprise to Father that bitter memories died hard.

Yet a persistent respect for the material achievements of
American capitalism colored Soviet planning. In 1921, after
famine swept great sections of the country, the Moscow regime
sought American capital for industrial expansion. United
States engineers were recruited to the task of rebuilding the demoralized land. Twelve years later, the Soviet leaders demonstrated their eagerness to see diplomatic relations restored by
agreeing in advance to cease support of American Communists
in their attempts to foster a homebred revolution.

Bullitt had gained a foothold in the government as a special
assistant to Cordell Hull when Father chose him as the first
American ambassador to the USSR. He had gained previous
experience on a visit to Moscow on behalf of Woodrow Wilson,
when he returned convinced that the Reds would prevail.

He ran into trouble in finding quarters for the new embassy.
The original idea had been to buy a site and build on it, but
ownership of private property was alien to basic Soviet principle. He resolved the difficulty by renting Spaso House, the one

time home of a czarist textile tycoon, which with additional
office space cost an annual $51,750.

He literally flew headfirst into another predicament when the
two-seater American plane carrying him to Leningrad crash-
landed upside down on the airfield. Our breezy ambassador by
then was actively cementing American-Soviet relations according to his own lights. This called for Moscow to be introduced
to baseball and for Red Army cavalrymen to be taught how to
play polo with helmets, mallets, and the rest of the equipment
shipped in from the United States. He was also learning Russian in expectation of being allowed to confer with Stalin without an interpreter. In fact, his one dependable contact in the
Kremlin was Foreign Minister Maxim Litvinov. Any time he
was away from the Soviet capital, hustling Bill Bullitt found
himself stultified.

The thorniest problem was already germinating when he installed himself in Spaso House. Talks about settling debts incurred by czarist governments were timed to coincide with
United States recognition of the USSR. The Bolsheviks saw no
reason in the world why they should pay. Bullitt came to believe
that an understanding had been reached with Litvinov for the
obligation to be honored, but the Russian's interpretation of
what had been agreed to was entirely different. So the pattern
of suspicion began to weave itself again. The debts were never
paid, and Bullitt's rosy enthusiasm for the Soviets was lost soon
after he arrived in Moscow. It was not long before he was hint-
ing to Father that he would appreciate a transfer elsewhere.

Trade with the Soviets was the primary but not the only reason for diplomatic recognition. By the end of March, Adolf
Hitler had grabbed complete dictatorial power, with an announced program of rearming Germany. The Chiefs of Staff in
Washington did not as yet rate him a serious threat to European peace. The Treaty of Versailles, which he rapidly repudiated, had left the Germans stripped of the means of making war.
Japan was the international firebrand that must be prevented
from making further conquests. It would be useful for the
United States, therefore, to have closer ties with the USSR,
which straddled half the globe from the Baltic to the Bering
Sea.

Until now, the prime exponent of Fascism in Europe had

been the meaty former newspaper editor who rallied the middle classes of Italy against native Communists, naming his followers *Fascisti* after the symbol for justice in ancient Rome. A dozen years had passed since Benito Mussolini had marched his legions into Rome to be handed control of the government. Like most Western statesmen, Father hoped that the Italian dictator would stand by the League of Nations and not line up with his German apostle. Breck Long, just appointed ambassador in Rome, where he resided in splendor at the Villa Taverna, had quoted Mussolini's praise for Father. The Depression, in the Italian's opinion, was bound to be defeated by the New Deal, and perhaps the United States could gradually be led into taking on a more responsible role in world affairs.

"I do wish I could have been there with you," Father wrote to Breck. "There seems no question but that he is really interested in what we are doing and I am much interested and deeply impressed by what he has accomplished and by his evidenced honest purpose of restoring Italy and seeking to prevent general European trouble." My parent's view of his "honest purpose" changed abruptly when Mussolini resolved to invade Abyssinia two years afterward.

Where he immediately understood the dangers inherent in Hitler's rise to power, Father was as ambivalent as many of his richer friends toward Mussolini's brand of National Socialism. To them, the corporate state amounted essentially to a face-lift for capitalism to correct the ugliness which the Depression had revealed. He was personally well acquainted with one recent convert to Fascism in the person of Sir Oswald Mosley, who had spent vacations in the 1920's with Father, together with his wife, Cynthia, a delectable woman in my parent's eyes.

Mosley was expelled from the British Labor Party for refusing to recant his belief that England's road to recovery from the Depression lay in public direction of industry, regulation of overseas trading, and government spending to expand the economy—a program not too far removed from Father's. Sir Oswald, a mixture of intellectual and demagogue, founded what he initially called the New Party, renamed the British Union of Fascists, applauded by many a right-wing Briton and idolized by Lord Rothermere's *Daily Mail*. Twenty thousand black-shirted members stood ready to parade through the dismal streets of London's East End, harassing radicals and Jews in a weak imitation of German Brown Shirts as their leader's adulation of Hitler grew.

Der Führer did not lack admirers on either side of the Atlantic. In British newspaper articles, Winston Churchill found kind words for him as well as for Mussolini. Stalwarts of the Tory Party and the American Liberty League alike welcomed Hitler as a bulwark against Communism in Germany. His systematic massacring of Jews alienated some of them, but they saw no danger to themselves in that. They still regarded Communists as the primary menace to a way of life which they very largely controlled. In those early months, Father's attitude was that of most liberals, who trusted that Nazism would soon burn itself out. "My only hope," he said, "is that German sanity of the old type that existed in the Bismarck days when I was a boy at school in Germany will come to the front again." He stood by his appeal to world nations to work together to disarm, with an agreement providing for continuous international inspection to ensure that none of them was breaking the pact. He could go no further than that. Congress would not tolerate American intervention in European affairs.

"I still operate under the laws which an all-wise Congress passes," he always insisted.

How to maintain peace was a problem to which there was no apparent answer. "Collective security" against aggression was the League of Nations formula, but its fifty-two member nations could not agree among themselves on how it might be implemented. Father personally could give only verbal approval as an individual, not as President. The Senate vote against the World Court tied his hands.

The League had no muscle to enforce the peace. In their present state, poverty-ridden nations were unwilling to strain precariously balanced budgets to provide men and arms to remedy that weakness. The only exceptions were the dictatorships, which forced their subjects to forgo butter in favor of guns. For the rest, disarmament had an irresistible appeal. War would be impossible if no country had the means to fight, so the argument ran, and if any nation proved recalcitrant, why then the most frightening weapon of all could be applied—a blockade of its exports and imports would drive it into deeper economic trouble and rapidly bring it to heel. Such was the theory.

The Senate proceeded to tie a second rope around Father's wrists to curb him in formulating foreign policy. The endless debating at the Geneva Disarmament Conference aroused minimum interest among Americans, but the prospect, no matter how dim, of another war in Europe created a public furor. If there was going to be a next time, the United States must stay clear, no matter what. A rising swell of isolationism was Hitler's first victory in the United States.

In April, 1934, the Senate authorized an investigation of the arms industry in the expressed belief that wars were fomented by "merchants of death" who sold munitions indiscriminately to all nations. It was a timely move when masses of the population were assuring one another that no American would ever consent to fight again to pile up profits for armament manufacturers. A flurry of magazine articles appeared to argue that blood-sucking capitalists had been responsible for starting World War I. It had not been the Germans' fault at all. Some of Father's leftist supporters speculated that Germany's new crop of admirers had a hand in spreading that impression.

Because no one else seemed eager for the job, a hard-eyed young Senator from Nebraska, Gerald Nye, was put in charge of the probe. On his first meeting with Father, he assured him, "Mr. President, I've got a hundred percent voting record against you—banking, economy, and beer."

Father, who at first was willing enough to cooperate with the Nye committee and allow access to White House files, assured him, "No, Senator, you were only twenty-five percent against me. There are some things in those bills that neither of us liked."

He did not much care for what followed, when the Nye hearings packed the public galleries for three years on end with dramatic allegations of bribery in high places, tax evasion, and deals in death, while peace societies sprang up on all sides and a steady flow of devoted isolationists were voted into Congress.

At one point, Nye investigators sought to prove that a cabal of Colonel House, Secretary of State Robert Lansing, and Walter Hines, ambassador to Britain, had contrived to maneuver Woodrow Wilson into making loans to the Allies with the effect of driving the United States to join the fighting in 1917 simply to protect its financial stake. Father dictated a letter to House about that:

> You may be interested to know that some of the Congress-
> men and Senators who are suggesting wild-eyed measures to
> keep us out of war are now declaring that you and Lansing
> and Page forced Wilson into the war! I had a talk with them,
> explained that I was in Washington myself the whole of that
> period [as Assistant Navy Secretary], that none of them were
> there and that their historical analysis was wholly inaccurate
> and that history yet to be written would prove my point.
>
> The trouble is that they belong to the very large and per-
> haps increasing school of thought which holds that we can
> and should withdraw wholly within ourselves and cut off all
> but the most perfunctory relationships with the other nations.
> They imagine that if the civilization of Europe is about to de-
> stroy itself through internal strife, it might just as well go
> ahead and do that and that the United States can stand idly
> by.

The letter was sent in September, 1935, six days after Sir Samuel Hoare, Britain's wily Foreign Secretary, announced in Geneva that his country would resist Mussolini's claims to Abyssinia—but only on condition that all other league members would do the same. Any such unanimity was rare in Geneva. Mussolini was not deterred. Less than a month later, the Italian army launched its invasion, pitting tanks, bombers, and poison gas against the spears and muskets of Emperor Haile Selassie's warriors.

It was a world disaster in my parents' view. As early as August of the previous year, Breck Long had reported that Italy intended to wage war on Abyssinia. Father had urged Mussolini to reconsider his plans for building an African empire. It was too late for that, said the reply transmitted from Rome. Italy must have a hold on Abyssinia similar to that of Britain's on Egypt. Empire-building was a game that any number could play.

That spring, Father had been turning over in his mind a variety of methods for throwing United States weight into the scale of peace and stopping Hitler's race to rearm and put half a million Germans into uniform. He saw one way in which he might achieve that when Ramsay MacDonald, Mussolini, and Pierre Laval, Premier of France, met at Stresa, Italy, to decide how they should respond to German belligerence.

Suppose they agreed to blockade the Reich by land and sea, closing off its frontiers with Poland, Czechoslovakia, Austria, Switzerland, France, Belgium, Holland, and Denmark, while the British navy sealed its ports? The United States could not join in actually establishing the blockade without action by Congress. But if such a boycott became an accomplished fact, Father had the Presidential power to recognize it and so align America on the side of peace without reference to Capitol Hill.

It was only a dream, remote from reality. Laval, a renegade Socialist, was one of the battalion of Frenchmen who secretly favored coming to terms with Germany. Mussolini, already far along on his plans to take Abyssinia, had no desire to strengthen League of Nations machinery that might be employed to curb him. The British government was only two months away from closing a private deal with the Germans, allowing Hitler to rebuild a navy up to 35 percent of the British fleet, with U-boats in a category of their own—45 percent or 100 percent to be permitted in the event of danger from the USSR.

Stresa produced nothing more than pious platitudes. That summer Father was confronted with a direct consequence of the Nye hearings in the first of a series of Neutrality Resolutions, passed almost unanimously by both chambers of Congress, prohibiting for six months the shipment of American "arms, ammunition, and implements of war" to any fighting nation. Father and Cordell Hull wanted a distinction made between victim and aggressor, empowering the President to withhold arms only from the invader. Riding high on Capitol Hill, the isolationists would have none of that. Father signed the bill, unwilling to take on Congress in a bout he could not win, trusting that the embargo would hit the mechanized Italian army harder than it would hamper Haile Selassie's barefooted tribesmen.

The Neutrality Act was like a doughnut through whose center unlimited supplies of raw materials could still legally be sold to Italy—scrap steel and copper ingots for conversion into guns, wheat for army rations, cotton for uniforms. Father

could not stretch the act to bar those, much as he was tempted
to try. He had to revert to moral persuasion. "I do not believe,"
he declared, "that the American people wish for abnormally increased profits that temporarily might be secured by greatly extending our trade in such materials; nor would they wish the
struggles on the battlefield to be prolonged because of profits
accruing to a comparatively small number of American citizens."

The "comparatively small number" was not listening. Shipments to Italy of raw materials with war-making potential increased from United States ports.

One item in particular poured through the hole in the
doughnut both before and after the League went through the
motions of imposing sanctions on Italy. The background story
on a proposed oil embargo was as slippery as the stuff itself.
Cutting off oil to Italy would stop Mussolini's tanks in their
tracks and ground his air force. The rest of the League's sanctions, which left oil unlisted to date, had been little more than a
bluff. They had not worked, and his war in Abyssinia continued
unchecked.

The British made a show of concern by approaching Hull to
ask if the United States would follow suit and halt oil shipments
to Italy if the League agreed on that step. It was only a show because the government in London, fearful of shadows, had
scared itself into believing that Mussolini might wage general
war to contest an oil embargo. The British Foreign Office had
no desire to be responsible for toppling Mussolini. He was too
valuable as a potential ally against Hitler. Beyond that, the British were afraid that if they joined in a League embargo, they
would lose the entire Italian market to American oil companies.

Father faced a choice between philosophy and expediency.
Cordell Hull learned that the ten biggest United States oil producers might conceivably go along with a curb on exports, but
Jim Moffett of Standard of New Jersey pointed out the problems involved. They were spelled out in a memorandum to Father:

"Japan is a non-League of Nations member and as such cannot be bound by the League and will deliver oil to Italy in any
volume needed by Italy for military or other purposes. Oil subsidiaries in this country are under contract to deliver oil to Ja-

pan. These contracts legally have to be filled regardless of the ultimate disposition of the oil by Japan. Hence Japan is in a position of obtaining oil from the United States and under no control or restraint for the use of that oil." In a different context, similar arguments on behalf of the supranational oil corporations were to sound strangely familiar in 1973.

Oil sanctions would also be negated, Father was told, by an inflow for Italy from Germany, Rumania, Hungary, Austria, Brazil, and Argentina. Up-and-coming American producers such as Sid Richardson, Clint Murchison, and Charles Roesser would not agree to cut back on oil for Italy in any way. The market there was too tempting. This much I knew, because in the mid-1930's, after I left Los Angeles to return to Texas, I became the tool of the oil lobby in Washington.

I introduced my three oilmen to Father and on one occasion arranged for Roesser and Richardson to spend two days at Warm Springs, conferring with him. I watched, not always on the sidelines, the industry's uninterrupted maneuvering to hold onto the fat oil depletion allowance, passed originally in the 1920's, which enabled them to write off drilling costs and minimize income for federal taxation.

At the Treasury, Henry Morgenthau was equally persistent in trying to slash the allowance in order to boost the yield from income taxes, but he got nowhere. The oil industry succeeded first in ensuring a fixed minimum price of one dollar a barrel, the foundation on which my Texas friends and others built their multimillions. And Father could not be convinced of any need to change the law on oil depletion.

I was in distinguished company in my role with the oil producers. Cactus Jack Garner seldom failed to speak up for his Texas supporters at Cabinet meetings if he was in Washington to attend them. His longtime crony, Sam Rayburn, Speaker of the House, was another who did his best for the folks back home in the Lone Star State.

Oil sanctions were never imposed against Italy. Instead, with no advance notice to Washington, Sir Samuel Hoare crossed from London to Paris in December to hatch a plot with Laval. Italy might call off its war if Mussolini were handed the fertile plains of Abyssinia, while Haile Selassie would be permitted to retain his old domain in the distant mountains. They would present the plan at Geneva.

Jesse Straus, our ambassador to France, who gave up the presidency of R. H. Macy & Company's department stores to take on the job, had no inkling of what was afoot. The State Department and the White House were equally in the dark. Someone tipped off a Paris newspaper, and the storm broke. This cynical betrayal of "collective security" sickened internationalists in America and everywhere else in the Western world. At first, the British government tried to blame Hoare. Lanky Lord Halifax, who had joined the cabinet as Lord Privy Seal, concocted a story that Sir Samuel had been ailing and tired, uncertain of what he was doing, which was transparently untrue. Hoare finally was compelled to resign in tears, and Anthony Eden replaced him.

The Hoare-Laval pact was dead, and so was the League of Nations. In a letter to Jesse Straus two months later, Father spelled out the situation as he saw it:

> The whole European panorama is fundamentally blacker than at any time in your life time or mine. . . . The armaments race means bankruptcy or war—there is no possible out from that statement. . . . Heaven only knows I do not want to spend more money on our Army and Navy. I am initiating nothing new unless and until increases by other nations make increases by us absolutely essential to national defense. I wish England could understand that—and, incidentally, I wish Japan could understand that also.

The panorama grew darker still within three more weeks. On March 7, Hitler sent a token force of the Wehrmacht to occupy the Rhineland. In Paris and London, there was a flurry of talk about applying sanctions against Germany, but when the Council of the moribund League met, only Maxim Litvinov formally proposed that punishment, and he was a Red, so nothing was done about it. Hitler promised that he had "no territorial claims in Europe," and Father foresaw four tough years ahead. "The crisis," he told his Cabinet, "will break in 1941."

On May Day, Haile Selassie fled from Abyssinia into exile in England. Mussolini trumpeted that a new Roman empire was now born. In July, he alerted his triumphant bomber squadrons for battle duty in Spain. There, General Francisco Franco assumed command of an army rebellion against the Popular

Front government in Madrid, just voted into power in the country which five years ago had been converted from a monarchy into a republic. In the middle of the month, the plump little general marched on the Spanish capital, confident of a walkover victory.

Relations between Washington and London were uneasy, as Father's letter to Straus indicated. Over there, a reconstituted National government was led now by pipe-puffing Stanley Baldwin, who despaired of involving Britain in a future war because "the bomber will always get through." Churchill, a pariah to the Conservative Party, voiced a similar line with wildly exaggerated claims about the strength of Hitler's air force, accepting British Intelligence estimates that Germany was spending twice as much on preparations for war than was, in fact, the case. Bluff was one of Der Führer's original secret weapons.

Yet the British were as loath to unbalance their shaky budgets by diverting funds for rearmament as they were to stop selling guns to customers overseas. They resented Father's insistence that, in sea power anyway, the United States must start rebuilding—he quietly earmarked $500,000,000 dollars of NRA money for that. Britain's disenchantment with the man in the White House dated back to a proposal made by Cordell Hull at the Geneva Disarmament Conference, calling for open inspection and control of each nation's manufacturing and trade in arms and munitions. The plan got bogged down in committee, and Father knew precisely where the blame belonged. He told Hull:

> The only practical way of keeping German armaments down to an agreed-to level [is] to inspect German armament supplies. England dashes this hope by declining to be inspected herself . . . the British decline to accept detailed publicity as to armament orders on the ground that it would prejudice their armament trade. At some future time it may be advisable to pull this rabbit out of our hat as proof that the present British Government is not sincere in seeking limitation or reduction of present world armaments or present world trade in warlike weapons. I am much discouraged.

He faulted the British, too, for their failure to stand squarely with the United States against Japanese demands for a fleet as big as ours or Britain's. Two days before the close of FDR's first full year in office, Japan's ambassador, Viscount Makoto Saito, notified the State Department that his country intended to break the twelve-year-old treaty which set the sizes of the United States, British and Japanese fleets at ratios of 5:5:3. "The barrier was down," in Cordell Hull's words, "on the race for naval rearmament."

A glance at a map was enough to show that parity for Japan would make Tokyo the dominant power in the Pacific, a threat to the ocean defense of the Philippines, Hawaii, and Alaska. Father's anger was directed momentarily more at "the Tories" of England than at the belligerents of Japan. He directed Norman Davis in London to make plain to the government there "the simple fact that if Great Britain is even suspected of preferring to play with Japan to playing with us, we shall be compelled, in the interest of American security, to approach public sentiment in Canada, Australia, New Zealand, and South Africa in a definite effort to make these Dominions understand clearly that their future security is linked with us in the United States." The threat was not carried out. In the war which was becoming increasingly inevitable, the Dominions would sense the truth of his words without having it spelled out for them.

Another conference was called in London, this time in hope of settling once and for all the relative sizes of the battle fleets of the United States, Britain, Japan, France, and Italy. It met in December, 1935; the Japanese withdrew the following month. The treaty concluded there was meaningless without them. World peace through disarmament had proved to be another of mankind's illusions. The next challenge to be met by FDR was finding means of convincing the people that America must be armed when the slogan dearest to the hearts of most of them was an unequivocal "Never again."

"Never again" had a different significance in his attitude toward Latin America. Hull promised in the Inter-American Conference held at Montevideo in December, 1933, that no longer would the United States intervene in the internal affairs of its neighbors in the Americas. Father's conscience was affronted by the history of *yanqui* meddling, which smelled to him like colonialism masquerading as what George Orwell later referred to as "Big Brother."

He meant exactly what he said in his Inaugural Address: "I

would dedicate this Nation to the policy of the good neighbor—
the neighbor who resolutely respects himself and, because he
does so, respects the rights of others." The trick now was to
prove as much in acts as well as words.

Mother went off in a state of carefully concealed excitement
on her first overseas mission for him the following year. He
wanted her impressions of Puerto Rico and the Virgin Islands
before he called there in person. She had not yet begun her
fifteen-minute weekly radio talks—at $500 a minute—which
she took on primarily to provide her with money to donate to
Arthurdale. She brought back a report of poverty, squalor, and
sweatshop labor, so that he would know what to look for when
he boarded the USS *Houston* on July 1 with Franklin Jr. and
Johnny for a month-long, 14,000-mile cruise around the Caribbean, then through the Panama Canal to Hawaii before disem-
barking at Portland, Oregon.

As usual, he scheduled a little fishing along the way. The
Houston hove to for nine hours in the Bahamas for Father to be
lowered into a powerboat with my brothers, all of them pulling
in good catches. The next morning brought the first official
stop, at Cap-Haïtien, and a welcome from President Vincent
and the entire Haitian Cabinet. They had an advance idea that
this might be a different kind of *yanqui* after Father's refusal to
commit United States Marines to Cuba during the revolt
against Machado.

He reinforced that impression by venturing into French, the
country's official language, for the start of the speech he made
at Cap-Haïtien, "but when I got to the serious part I shifted to
English," he reported in a jubilant letter to Mother. The speech
was momentous by local standards. Within forty-one days, he
announced, all American troops would be pulled out of the island, an American protectorate for the past eighteen years.
"Many guns and much ceremony all day," said his account of
the festivities.

"Perhaps the Haitians will recognize the vast amount of good
things we have done for them. . . . The *people* do, but the ruling mulatto class doesn't, I fear."

Twenty-four hours later, he was landed at Mayaguez, Puerto
Rico, in torrential rain. "Cheering crowds all along the way—
and really pathetic *faith* in what we are trying to do," he told

Mother in his next letter. "Everywhere they spoke of your visit." He had nothing dramatic to announce on this island, won as a prize in the Spanish-American War, but in San Juan he lectured the American administrative staff on the evils of "too much government" in frustrating native aspirations toward independence.

A rough crossing took him to Cartagena and the greatest challenge of the voyage so far. Colombia had never forgiven the United States for Uncle Ted's crude carving out of territory nearly thirty years ago for building the Panama Canal. Woodrow Wilson had recognized the wrong and urged Congress to offer Colombia a formal apology. Father made a speech in Cartagena and opened up a new chapter in neighborly relations. "The people were most enthusiastic," he noted, "and I am happy over this . . . especially in view of the bitter feeling about the Panama Canal episode."

With the satisfied feeling that he had managed to give the Americas fair evidence of his intentions, my parental "good neighbor" pushed on out into the Pacific for the twelve-day voyage to Hawaii. His schedule would not permit the further 3,400-mile trip from there to the Philippines, but his plans for those islands were advancing, too. By signing the Tydings-McDuffie Act the previous March, he committed the United States to grant the Philippines independence in 1946. The warlords in Tokyo had something new to consider in their timetable.

The radio room of the *Houston* buzzed day and night with messages in and out. In San Francisco, an eight-week-old strike by longshoremen suddenly flared into a general walkout. Hull and Homer Cummings, left by Father to watch the situation, debated whether the National Guard and the Army should be called out to quell it. Radiograms from Washington urged Father to turn back and intervene. Louis convinced him that there was no need for that, so Father authorized Ma Perkins to make whatever statement in his name that she saw fit, while offering arbitration to all employers and unions involved. He did not hesitate to delegate authority, especially when he was otherwise engaged in enjoying himself. Secretary Perkins turned out to be right in thinking that her two Cabinet colleagues were alarmists. The general strike soon fizzled out. The President's testing time in crucial labor relations was postponed, and without interruption he completed "a perfectly heavenly cruise . . . too lovely."

6

The pace of the New Deal was erratic in 1935, running like an engine with water in its fuel lines, faltering, then picking up again. The first quarter of the year brought one ominous set-back—the World Court vote in the Senate—and only one victory, though that was of a scale to cause near hysteria within the Liberty League. The Works Progress Administration, with Hopkins as administrator, was the largest public-works pro-gram of any government anywhere. It placed nearly $5 billion in Father's hands for priming the pump of industry to make jobs and end the business of soul-sapping relief handouts.

Tom Corcoran and Ben Cohen weighed into the struggle to steer the bill through Congress, where the right wing fought to cut the funds down into old-fashioned doles for the unem-ployed. Rex Tugwell thought for a while that this effort on be-half of the enemy would succeed. Big business interests, he told Ickes, had Father stopped.

He was disinclined to plunge into the fray, and the specta-tor's role left him unusually irritable. "This 'rumor factory' called Washington almost gets under my skin," he complained. He was preoccupied with calculating the other side's strategy for next year's Presidential election. Now that the economy was sailing into smoother water, he expected to hear a chorus crying "Don't rock the boat," which was hard on a confirmed boat-rocker who saw a long voyage ahead.

His social security bill spun slowly in the doldrums of committee hearings. The rest of this session of Congress, he thought, "will be more or less of a madhouse—every Senator a law unto himself and everyone seeking the spotlight." Still, he put off participating in the day-to-day turmoil. "Out of it all," he said, "I am inclined to think that there will be such disgust on the part of the average voter that some well-timed, common-sense campaigning on my part this spring or summer will bring people to their senses."

In his upstairs bedroom, Louis was kept alive on oxygen, pestering Mrs. Nesbitt with an invalid's food fancies from mouse-trap cheese to charred steaks. His voice, once as robust as an actor's, was so faint that she could scarcely understand him on the telephone. "I want," he said one evening, "two hot and two cold codfish balls, and after that I want some corned-beef hash, with a poached egg and chowchow."

But he continued to mastermind the study of the odds facing Father in the warm-up for next year's election. The two of them agreed that Gerald Nye was a possible Republican contender now that he had made himself a skyrocket reputation as a knight of isolationism, with sympathetic backing even from like-minded Socialists and Farm-Laborites.

Old guard Republicans had a fancy for Senator Arthur Vandenberg, a former newspaper editor in the present heartland of isolationism, Michigan, and even for Herbert Hoover, both of whom Father felt he could lick with his hands tied.

But it was Huey Long who took up the most time in the deliberations of Father and Louis. They judged that his opening tactic next year would be to try his arm against Father in a series of primaries in states where his "Share-the-Wealth" clubs had the strongest hold. Republican money was already filtering into the clubs in readiness for the trial. Then the Kingfish would pull out to form a third party as Uncle Ted had done in 1912, when the Bull Moosers split the Republican vote and sent Wilson to the White House instead of William Howard Taft.

On the Senate floor, Long ranted by the hour like a man deranged. "I am a dyed-in-the-wool party man. I do not know just

what party I am in right now, but I am for the party," he declared in the middle of one filibuster. "The rich earn more and
the common people less," he reiterated, and administration
leaders on the Hill waited for lulls in his tirades so that they
could hurry bills to a vote.

On the radio, he peddled "share the wealth" with the same
huckster's tricks used earlier in his career to sell books and pat-
ent medicines door to door. "All the people of America," he
cried, "have been invited to a barbecue. God invited us all to
come and eat and drink all we want." His private army, reminis-
cent of Mussolini's Black Shirts, led the applause. In the view of
the White House strategists, the Kingfish was more dangerous
than any Republican. If he achieved his ambition to be President in 1940, he was likely to tranform America into an overt
Fascist state.

In his newspaper columns, Johnson kept up his drumfire
against Father. From the Shrine of the Little Flower, Father
Coughlin seldom let a week go by without a fresh attack on
"plutocratic government." If capitalism stood in the path of social justice, said the priest who was secretly in capitalism's pocket, it ought to be "voted out of existence."

Father justified his inaction on grounds of "public psychology," a subject on which he judged himself an expert. The kind
of moral appeal that only he could make as President had to be
timed with the utmost care. "People tire," he knew, "of seeing
the same name day after day in the important headlines of the
papers, and the same voice night after night over the radio."

Had he tried to maintain the tempo of the past two years,
"the inevitable histrionics of the new actors, Long and Coughlin
and Johnson, would have turned the eyes of the audience away
from the main drama itself," he said. The time was coming
soon for what he called "a new stimulation of united American
action." He proposed doing that "before the year is out." Meanwhile, he could not resist the temptation to get in some more
sunshine and relief for his sinuses by fishing in the Bahamas
aboard Vincent Astor's *Nourmahal.*

He left Washington only after having assurances that Louis
was apparently on the mend, with his wife Grace at his bedside,
on leave from the job with which Father had rewarded her long
patience with her cantankerous husband: She was the postmis-

tress of Fall River, Massachusetts. Mother was left with a commission to perform. Would she give Louis Father's love "and
tell him I expect him to be sitting up in bed when I get back?"

He set sail on the day his public-works bill, keystone of the
entire recovery program, which had already passed the House
and Senate with a variety of amendments, was sent to conference for discrepancies between the two versions to be ironed
out. Conservative Senators seized this eleventh-hour chance to
cut out the heart of the proposed Works Progress Administration.

Radiograms deluged the *Nourmahal,* begging Father to intervene. My brother Jimmy flew from Puerto Rico to join in the
vacation and go on a diet of milk, eggs, and potatoes to soothe
the stomach ulcers which he was developing as an insurance executive. "Bursting with health," as he put it, Father was reluctant to cross swords with his distant opponents, whom he considered "too childish for grown-ups." "It is as well," he concluded, "to let them try to work it out themselves."

He was having fun, as he itemized it in a hasty memo to Marvin McIntyre, an old public-relations hand in the Navy Department when Father was Assistant Secretary, who was now one of
his "assistant secretaries" in charge of White House appointments: "I could write columns about sea & sky and palm trees
and big & little fishes, and bathing beaches and coral and sunburn but no lousy paper would print it even though they (most
of them) specialize in 'colored' news stories!"

The team he had entrusted with the task in Washington did
not let him down. He contributed one pungent cablegram to
their efforts; the bill passed in much the form he wanted; and
the billions of dollars it made available begin to build low-cost
housing, new schools, highway bridges, and tunnels, along with
more "alphabet soup" administrations: National Youth, Resettlement, and Rural Electrification.

The *Nourmahal* cruise ended in April. The following month,
Father was jolted into a do-or-die contest with the Supreme
Court, which threatened to undermine the basic premise and
structure of the New Deal.

He had anticipated trouble with the nine black-robed justices
of the Court—average age, seventy—the previous winter, when
they were called on to assess the legality of one of Father's early

moves to stave off national bankruptcy. Measured against that hallowed metal, gold, the buying power of the dollar had jumped about 60 percent during the Hoover years. On Father's first inauguration day, United States law required that borrowed gold be repaid in the same commodity. Many contracts, including home mortgages, carried a so-called "gold clause" to achieve that end. It meant, in substance, that at going rates a creditor could collect $1.60 for every dollar owed. That had been financial dynamite when bank failures and business bankruptcies were plaguing the economy.

So one of the crucial actions in the First Hundred Days was to set aside the gold clause and make all debts, public or private, repayable in any currency. When the issue reached the Supreme Court in February, 1935, Wall Street was confident that the move would be declared illegal. Father had the same thought. He had a speech ready to meet the emergency, pledging himself to strike back at the Court's anticipated decision "by proclamation and by message to the Congress of the United States."

However, the nine old men backed him in this instance, 5 to 4. He blithely kidded Joe Kennedy as chairman of the year-old Securities and Exchange Commission: "How fortunate it is that his exchanges will never know how close they came to being closed. . . . Likewise, the Nation will never know what a great treat it missed in not hearing the marvelous radio address the 'Pres' had prepared for delivery to the Nation Monday night if the cases had gone the other way."

On May 27, the nine old men, black robes somber against the crimson draperies of their chamber, voted nine to none to declare the National Industrial Recovery Act unconstitutional. The government's interference in interstate business was illegal. Congress, they said, was "running riot" in delegating power to the Executive.

If the New Deal were barred from tackling problems on a national basis and states' rights were paramount, there could be no New Deal. Father spent four days reflecting on his next move while the country waited for an explosion. He set the stage in his oval office. Mother sat beside him knitting a sock when Steve Early, his press secretary, ushered the usual hundred or so reporters in for one of the 998 press conferences Father gave in his White House years. Next to a can of Camels, a stack of telegrams was piled on his desk. He knew most of the men facing him and addressed them by their first names. He lit a cigarette in the inevitable holder and proceeded to talk for eighty minutes.

The hand-to-hand struggle for power between Father and the Supreme Court that was to engage both sides for the next three years began quietly that day. He sounded more disappointed than angered. The issue raised by the "dictum" of the nine justices was not a matter of left- or right-wing politics. What they had done, he said, was to make a nationwide attack on national economic problems impossible. Their narrow interpretation of what was legal in interstate commerce thrust the country back to the "horse-and-buggy era." Yes, the newspapers could quote him on that.

What did he plan to do about it? "We haven't got to that yet," Father replied, squinting to keep cigarette smoke from his eyes. "Better run now," he said, and the conference was over. "Thank you, Mr. President," said by the senior correspondent present, was the traditional response, signaling a hasty but orderly mass exit, then a race down the corridor to the pressroom telephones.

Radio bulletins and the headlines in the afternoon papers gave the impression that Father had declared war on the justices, which was not his intention as yet. His old Republican friend, Henry Stimson, took the "horse-and-buggy" statement to imply that Father was going to seek a Constitutional amendment, a prospect which dismayed him. He approved the Court's decision, he told Father, because Congress was delegating so much power to the New Deal agencies that an irresponsible bureaucracy was springing up in Washington, threatening the rightful authority of the individual states.

Father tried to calm his old counselor. "I can assure you," he said, "that I am trying to look at several angles and that I hope something practical can be worked out." He was no partisan politician, but a pragmatist, hoping to help all groups, anxious to save himself from the strain of argument.

Not for the first or the last time, he had misled the reporters. The New Deal would push on despite the Court's decision. A stack of new bills was ready for action. Speculation filled the newspapers that Congress could only adjourn in face of the stalemate. Father had totally different plans. He circulated a memorandum to his legislative leaders on June 4, listing nine new laws "that I must get this session."

The most far-reaching in its implications was the Social Security Act, which for the first time in history recognized the government's obligation to protect its people from some of the inevitable hazards of life. As his trial of will with the nine old men began, Father sent Corcoran and the rest of his lieutenants out to ginger up the legislators. When they ran into heavy argument, he would pick up the telephone to add his personal persuasions. On August 14, the bill was passed with massive majorities, and laissez-faire in social conscience came to an inglorious end. Now the law provided for old-age retirement payments financed through payroll taxes on employers and employees. It called for unemployment benefits, for aid to the aged, the blind, the needy, for dependent mothers and neglected children. What might the Supreme Court have to say about *that?*

The iron was hot again. Another Hundred Days of Congress saw the enactment of all the "must" measures on his list, along with several more. The Wagner-Connery National Labor Relations Act salvaged those sections of the moribund NRA covering labor's right to organize and bargain for collective employment contracts. The Motor Carrier Act gave the Interstate Commerce Commission direction of bus and truck traffic across state lines. Electric power companies fell under Federal Power Commission authority and the gas industry under Federal Trade Commission rule by the terms of the Wheeler-Rayburn Act. Mineowners felt the bite of the Guffey-Snyder Act, which allowed the government to fix prices, force them to negotiate with miners' unions, and pay a 15 percent tax on coal, largely refundable as a reward to producers who complied with the law.

It took a lot of pushing by telephone on Father's part to ensure passage for one bill that was a particular pet of his. In the whole structure of big business, the feature causing him the greatest concern was the operation of giant holding companies, made up themselves of smaller ones. This pyramiding of financial power meant, as he often said, that "eighty men control the United States." This was an evil which must be overcome. He had been itching to nobble them for half a decade. The current temper of Congress gave him the opportunity. Into the legislative hopper went the Public Utilities Holding Company bill, which emerged as an act limiting the control those companies could exercise over their direct subsidiaries and dissolving the giants whose end product was nothing but paper profits.

The uproar this caused among the Liberty Leaguers and the Chambers of Commerce was mild compared to the tumult stirred by his Wealth Tax package. He sprang it as a surprise to his followers and as a shock to the enemy. In one sweep, he asked for increased taxes on inheritances, gifts, and on personal incomes of $50,000 or more. Corporations would be taxed according to size, and a levy would be imposed on dividends to discourage evasion. What would the electorate think about *that* in November of the following year?

He stayed on in the White House after Congress went home toward the end of August in a state of exhausted confusion over the new, much more radical course Father had set for the New Deal. He could count on nothing but further obstacles being raised by the Court when other laws fundamental to the New Deal came up for judicial review. Could the nine justices thwart his programs indefinitely?

The lull gave him time to assess the men, their backgrounds, and his chances with them. All of them had reached their places on the topmost bench before he entered the White House. It was the most aged Court in United States history. Parchment-skinned Louis Brandeis, appointed by Wilson, was the oldest member at seventy-eight. The archconservative Willis Van Devanter was three years younger. Grouchy James Clark McReynolds, seventy-three, another Wilson appointee, was a consistent spokesman for right-wing opinion. George Sutherland, a well-whiskered seventy-two, owed his place to Harding, and Chief Justice Charles Evans Hughes, who was the same age, to Taft. Harding had put sixty-eight-year-old Pierce Butler on the high bench. Hoover had rewarded snowy-haired Benjamin Cardozo, sixty-four. Sixty-three-year-old Harlan Stone, whose expression matched his name, a Coolidge man; and the Court's junior at fifty-nine, Owen Roberts, another Hoover appointment.

They all seemed content to sit on the bench for as long as life continued. At least four of them—Van Devanter, McReynolds, Sutherland, and Butler—had to be categorized as obstructionists who would drive their "horse-and-buggy" philosophies to the last ditch. By no reckoning could a majority of these men, whose common credo had been formed in the era of unfettered private enterprise, be looked for to approve any realistic program of reform.

The long-term outlook was as black as the old men's robes, but a momentary flash of light brightened the political horizon in September. To avenge the Kingfish's slurring of his family's honor, Dr. Carl Weiss dogged Huey Long in the halls of the graft-riddled State capitol at Baton Rouge and shot him. Long's bodyguards gunned down the young doctor on the spot. As the Senator fought for life, Father's condolences were brief. When he died two days later, his sympathy note to the widow was distinctly formal.

The President and his Cabinet felt not pity but a sense of relief. Jim Farley, always an astute counter of heads, figured that in the forthcoming election, Long would have pulled at least six million votes. A Louisianian minister of the cloth, smooth-tongued Gerald L. K. Smith, took over the mailing lists of the Share the Wealth movement and attempted to drape himself in the Kingfish's shoddy mantle. The Long machine was still in being, but infinitely less effectual without a national leader. Father continued his harassment by keeping IRS agents on watch and withholding patronage from the heirs of the dead demagogue.

He was of the opinion that the rabble-rousers, Old guard Republicans and the Liberty Leaguers would inevitably fight among themselves before the country went to the polls again. The "new stimulation of united American action" with which he intended to .op their squabbling would, in all probability, keep him in the White House for four more years. Not all of the Cabinet shared his confidence. Ickes, for one, imagined that Father was "defeating himself" in fighting the Court. "We are in grave danger of losing the election," Honest Harold told Father whenever the opportunity came up.

Cabinet opinions interested him less than those of freer spirits in the official family. The Cabinet met regularly in the big white-walled room opening on the far side of Missy's office, which stood next to his own. No transcripts were made of what was said as cigarette and cigar smoke tainted the red damask curtains under the gaze of Jefferson and Jackson, whose portraits hung on the west wall, and Wilson, who stared down over the fireplace. Voice-activated tape recorders had not yet, of course, been invented.

Father was careful about what he told the group as a whole. It was hard to discuss anything in the White House without someone leaking word to the newspapers, and he had reason to suspect Cactus Jack as the prime culprit. He had greater respect for New Dealers like Hopkins, Corcoran, and Cohen, Sam Rosenman, and Louis than for most of the political appointees who gathered around the octagonal mahogany table in the Cabinet room with a yellow pad and pencil set at each place.

He was nevertheless punctilious about calling meetings, which he tried to make as informal as possible. Little was ever settled there, but everyone had a turn to speak. Father preferred to deal with people one or two at a time, and some members—Ma Perkins, Ickes, and Morgenthau in particular—were forever anxious to reach him alone.

"Cordell, what's happening abroad?" was a standard opening, which as often as not brought an equally stock reply: "Nothing very encouraging." Then the elder statesman from Tennessee would fuss with his papers and make his report. He could write a scathingly crisp memorandum, but verbally he was almost as long-winded as Baruch.

Morgenthau usually spoke next. "Henry, what have you to tell us?" This would have Henry adjust his pince-nez and limit himself to the fewest possible words, saving his thoughts for a hoped-for private desk-top luncheon later. Wallace was introverted, guarded but amiable. Frances Perkins was worth listening to, even if she seldom knew when to stop. Dern's limitations as War Secretary were all too obvious when he could not see the implications of what Hitler, Mussolini, and the Japanese were up to. Swanson sometimes nodded off to sleep.

The truth of the matter was that, for most practical purposes, Father was his own Secretary of State, of War, of the Navy, and of Commerce, never hesitating to take over in any situation if the Cabinet member concerned was falling short of achieving results. He kept the rest of them on a loose rein, but only Ickes came close to Louis in talking back to him. He welcomed the assertiveness of Honest Harold, even though he threatened to resign with tedious regularity, affronted by the fancied slights he received from Father.

Cabinet meetings were outwardly cordial so long as the "Pres" was on the scene, easing tension among his colleagues with a joke. Frances Perkins remembered the day he left the room to take a confidential telephone call, apologizing for the interruption. As soon as the door, with its Secret Serviceman stationed outside, had closed behind him, she was appalled by the backbiting that suddenly erupted among men who rarely had the courage to criticize him to his face.

The Works Progress Administration had the effect of pitting Ickes and Hopkins directly against each other. Each imagined that he should have control over the billions involved, and the feud erupted into headlines. Harry, according to Harold, was a desperate, self-seeking gambler who could not be trusted with the intelligent spending of his own paycheck.

Father had enough under way with the Supreme Court without having civil war within his team. He ventured a Solomon's judgment by dividing responsibility between the pair: Hopkins would handle projects costing up to $25,000, Ickes would take over after that. "My dear fellow," Father would assure each of them, "you mustn't get the idea that I am working at cross-purposes with you."

So that they might learn to get along better with each other, he took them with him on a fishing trip. On October 3, they boarded the *Houston,* where he settled himself as before in the admiral's quarters—private bath, bedroom, and bookcase-lined sitting room with a dining table at one end. He would introduce them to the soothing joys of rod and line, while they cruised to the Cocos Islands, then back through the Panama Canal to Charleston, South Carolina. Pa Watson would come along, as would Gus Gennerich, the burly ex-New York policeman who had been promoted as Father's personal bodyguard—a dear friend. Congress had done well in its Second Hundred Days, and Father was ready to relax again.

He and Pa reeled in some sizable sailfish, but Harry could not pick up the art. Father reveled in a change from Mrs. Nesbitt's brand of cooking with meals prepared by his favorite Filipino

galley crew. Harold complained about the coffee and the stale
drinking water. Father, who rated himself as a proficient newspaperman after his spell on the Harvard *Crimson* as an undergraduate, contributed a few paragraphs to the ship's paper, *The
Blue Bonnet:*

> The feud between Hopkins and Ickes was given a decent
> burial today. . . . The President officiated at the solemn cere-
> mony which we trust will take these two babies off the front
> page for all time. . . . Hopkins expressed regret at the un-
> kind things Ickes had said about him and Ickes on his part
> promised to make it stronger—only more so—as soon as he
> could get a stenographer who would take it down hot. The
> President gave them a hearty slap on the back—pushing them
> into the sea. "Full steam ahead," the President ordered.

They had been at sea only twenty-four hours, steaming off
the California coast, when a radiogram from Hull brought the
news that Italy had invaded Abyssinia. The before-dinner cocktails that Pa Watson mixed that evening were heavy on the gin.
Father was irked because the State Department proposed delaying publication of a drafted proclamation of United States
neutrality that he had left with Hull; the League should act
first, Hull's aides said.

"They are dropping bombs—and that is war," Father insisted, as he pored over the chartroom maps. "Why wait for Mussolini to say so?" At dinner, he scribbled an instruction for the
proclamation to be issued next morning. During the rest of the
cruise, he waited eagerly for reports on the progress of the
fighting, jubilant if it seemed to swing in favor of Haile Selassie's pathetic forces, gloomy over the Italians' easy successes.

Neutrality could only be tried as a policy because that was
what Congress had ordered, but he disliked having his hands
bound so tightly. He speculated on what might happen if some
European power attempted an invasion in South America. "We
should have to take sides," he reasoned, "and might, without
going to war ourselves, assist the South American nation with
supplies of one kind or another." That fall, he questioned
whether the United States could save civilization, "but at least
by our example we can make people think and give them the

opportunity of saving themselves. The trouble is that the people of Germany, Italy, and Japan are not given the privilege of thinking." He was, of course, equivocating, and he knew it, but it was the best he was allowed to do.

The new year was three days old when the Supreme Court dealt another blow to the New Deal. Mr. Justice Roberts delivered the majority opinion to a packed chamber that waited for the verdict like a prize-ring crowd impatient for a knockout. In the judgment of Roberts, Hughes, Van Devanter, McReynolds, Butler, and Sutherland, the Agricultural Adjustment Act was unconstitutional. Only Stone, Brandeis, and Cardozo disagreed.

The country had been shorn of an operable farm program, the Treasury had been deprived of $500,000,000 in taxes, but Father smiled enigmatically when he learned what the Court had done. The need to challenge the nine old men grew more imperative with every decision they handed down, but he held his fire. "If one is to wage war," he believed, "it is best not to talk until the other fellow gets himself into an untenable position." He was more worried, he said, about events overseas than any domestic problem, including the November election.

For the first time in his political life, he had to plan without Louis. The man who had taught him mastery of politics lay in the Naval Hospital, losing his last personal campaign. Mother took him there, with his secrets and his safe, in a black White House limousine. He still clung to his routine of telephoning Father day and night, though he could barely breathe. He had Rabbit stop by to take a few lines of dictation several times a week. It was only a matter of time, he told her, before he would be on his feet again, with a suite in the Biltmore Hotel, New York, as his base for reelecting Father. He died in his sleep on April 18. His shrunken body was borne into the East Room of the White House to be laid in state, surrounded by flowers, and the flags on the roof flew at half-staff.

Father, who had visited him in the hospital when he could, felt that "for him it must be a blessed release." Of the most querulous of her permanent guests, Mrs. Nesbitt acknowledged, "There was greatness in him."

The Court continued to batter down the New Deal. In a span of two weeks, by 5-to-4 majorities, the old men demolished most of the Bituminous Coal Conservation Act, the Municipal Bankruptcy Act, and New York's minimum wage law, with effect on all the other forty-seven states.

Big business had found its ablest protectors at the same time as it agreed on the candidate to be run against Father in November. His Republican backers hopefully labeled Alfred M. Landon "the Kansas Coolidge." He described himself as "an oilman who never made a million, a lawyer who never had a case," but he had, in fact, made a comfortable fortune from his oil wells before he was elected governor of Kansas in 1933. He was, said Father, "a very good friend of mine for three and a half out of every four years."

The Republican Party chiefs saw in the Kansan's middle-class respectability the ideal qualities for enticing an electorate which they told themselves must be as sick as they were with New Dealing and the histrionics of that man in the White House. At their Cleveland, Ohio, convention, Landon was nominated on the first ballot, and the ballyhooing of the "Topeka Tornado," another optimistic label for him, was launched in the press and on the radio. The usual 85 percent of newspapers united against Father, with many of them printing a daily, front-page warning: ONLY — MORE DAYS TO SAVE THE AMERICAN WAY OF LIFE.

Father Coughlin weighed in with more abuse of "the scab President," the "liar," the "betrayer." On direct orders from "the Chief," every Hearst paper pilloried the "Raw Deal" in editorials and in news columns. As Jim Farley forecast, it promised to be a singularly dirty campaign.

Father blocked out the overall strategy, assigned jobs to be done, vetted other men's speeches, examined budgets, and analyzed the studies from Steve and Mother, whom he made his principal contacts with Democratic headquarters. Without Louis to turn to, Mother was swamped with questions, which she relayed to Father. Who was responsible for studying news reports? For planning a radio campaign? For research? Who would "check on all inconsistencies in Landon's pronouncements?" How was publicity to be unified? Who was to handle newsreels, contact friendly editors, work on speeches? Where were black speakers to be recruited for church meetings and the like?

"More and more," Mother concluded in July, "my reports indicate that this is a close election." The Democratic National Committee thought so, too, heedless of the fact that Father was enjoying considerable financial backing from my friends in Texas, Charley Roesser, Sid Richardson, and Clint Murchison. Among them, they had interested a number of their friends in joining them in large contributions to the campaign. They were sending people out in farm states, cattle-raising areas, and oil-producing areas and were receiving uniformly encouraging reports. They had me pass on these reports to Father. To bolster his courage, each time they told me to pass on the news that their contributions were rolling in from all points of the Middlewest, Southwest, the Rocky Mountain states, and the Far West. Needless to say, these reports from me were looked forward to as an offset to otherwise gloomy predictions. Emil Hurja, the Democrats' statistical seer, detected a heavy drift to Landon and predicted only 376 electoral college votes for FDR. *The Literary Digest* went further than that. In a suicidal gaffe, the magazine that had never before been wrong in spotting a Presidential winner in advance announced that Landon would romp in with thirty-two states' 370 electoral votes, leaving sixteen states and only 161 such votes for Father.

The strangely assorted opposition—Liberty League, the Republican National Committee, Gerald Smith's Share-the-Wealth clubs, Coughlin's National Union for Social Justice, and the anti-New Deal Democrats—did its damnedest to draw Father into declaring open war on the Court, which would have given Landon a glorious opportunity to stigmatize him as a desecrator of the Constitution. My parent was far too cunning to allow himself to be set up like a fairground coconut. The platform which he drafted for the Democrats skirted the issue. If national problems could not be solved "by legislation within the Constitution," then its "letter and spirt" would be maintained by seeking a "clarifying amendment" to allot the government and the states their respective share of responsibility for safeguarding recovery, regulating industry, and protecting the public.

His opponents fell back on the Red menace as the heavy artillery of their attack. Somehow Bolshevism and the New Deal must be equated in the voters' minds. The President must be depicted as a tool of Moscow, working surreptitiously to convert the United States to Communism. Abandoning his own more moderate views, Landon bowed to the will of his masters, and his speeches soared off into fantasy. His running mate, Frank Knox, an ex-Rough Rider under Uncle Ted's command who now published the Chicago *Daily News,* showed less enthusiasm for the dirty work.

The Roosevelt-haters, as expected, fielded a third-party candidate in hope of splitting the Democrats. Representative William Lemke of North Dakota had incurred Father's wrath when the New Deal was no more than a month old by claiming he had Presidential endorsement for a bill requiring the Government to buy up every farm mortgage in the land. Lemke figured the total cost at $3 billion in newly issued money, but White House calculations set the price at more than five times as much—an outrageous proposition.

Now Lemke announced his candidacy on the ticket of the Union Party, an organization begotten by Father Coughlin, Gerald Smith, and a rangy old Californian, Dr. Francis Townsend, who had a simple panacea for the troubles of everyone aged sixty or older: give each of them $200 a month on condition that the money was spent within thirty days. Two or three thousand "Townsend Clubs" flourished across the land, and the founder urged his followers to vote for Landon in states where Lemke could not get on the ballot.

Father regarded the Union Party as a momentary aberration that would have no effect on the outcome. He was confident that he would be reelected as he swung himself behind the podium in Franklin Field stadium, Philadelphia, after he was nominated by acclamation for a second term. Behind the curtains moments earlier, as he reached out to shake a friendly hand, he had lost control of his braced legs, fallen from my brother Jimmy's grasp, and almost toppled to the floor. But, like other crowds that saw him at mass rallies and ball parks, the 100,000 people watching him that Saturday evening never guessed that from the hips down, his muscles were paralyzed.

He had made some overnight revisions of the speech he was to deliver. With his tense face close to the microphones, dazzled by the glare of the spotlights, he laid down his challenge to "the enemy within our gates":

"The royalists of the economic order have conceded that political freedom was the business of the government, but they have maintained that economic slavery is nobody's business. . . . These economic royalists complain that we seek to overthrow the institutions of America. What they really complain of is that we seek to take away their power. Our allegiance to American institutions requires the overthrow of this kind of power. . . . This generation of Americans has a rendezvous with destiny. . . . I am enlisted for the duration."

It seemed as though the cheering would shake the stadium down. Even my ever cautious mother sensed victory in the air that night. "I am quite overcome," she said, "when I think of four years more of the life I have been leading."

The economic royalists listened and stepped up their contributions to the other side. The du Ponts, makers of chemicals and munitions, stood high on the list of Landon's angels. So did Alfred Sloan, chairman of General Motors, and his Detroit associate, John J. Raskob, who as one-time chief of the Democratic National Committee thought that the more conservative Roosevelt of earlier days could be made a showpiece of the American Establishment, "one of those pieces of window dressing that had to be borne with," as Father put it.

The Republicans spent roughly $9,000,000 on the campaign, not counting undercover money that went to their disreputable allies. The Democrats had a little more than half that sum at their disposal—$5,194,741 to be precise. So some $15,000,000 represented the total expenditure on both sides, which was considered a vast amount of cash by party treasurers, who never dreamed that the time would come a generation later when that kind of money would be poured into electing a single Senator.

The Democrats' fighting fund was drawn from a broader spectrum than their opponents'. The unions handed over $770,218. The city of Philadelphia put up $200,000. If General Motors, Walter Chrysler, and union-busting Henry Ford himself were numbered among the enemy, Henry's son Edsel was a renegade among the automobile titans. His closeness to Father originated with the illness of his wife, a polio patient at Warm Springs shortly after Father bought the place. Edsel Ford was important as a donor of funds for the war chest as well as an intelligence agent in the opposite camp.

Joe Kennedy ventured to put his name to a book, *I Am for Roosevelt*, addressed to the business community and designed to defend the New Deal in terms of the profit system which it had preserved. Democracy was endangered, he declared, by "the unreasoning malicious ill-will displayed by the rich and powerful against their common leader."

His fund-raising project for the party was a series of businessmen's dinners, but tickets went begging. "Some of my friends," Joe commented, "in the business and financial world have told me I might as well make up my mind I have had my last job from anyone in the business world. . . ."

The Good Neighbor League, which Father set up, was a kind of testimonial to Louis, whose idea it had been in the first place. It was a front organization, secretly funded by the Democratic National Committee, designed to win votes from independents who would not work within the party machine. A lofty-minded missionary-turned-newspaperman, Stanley High, was brought in to run it, with cooperation from feminists such as Carrie Chapman Catt, who thought so well of Mother that she hung her picture on her library wall, and philanthropists like George Foster Peabody, who introduced Father to Warm Springs in the 1920's and sold him the property in Georgia.

With his nomination over and done with, Father removed himself from the floodlights for the better part of a month. He did not want the people to tire of his voice on the radio and his picture in the papers. Let his opponents wear themselves out if they so chose. He would take a personal "look-see" at a few areas hit by the summer drought when he returned to the White House in August. He planned one or two nonpolitical pronouncements in September. Four or five major speeches in October should take care of his campaigning. Meanwhile, he was going to charter the schooner *Sewanna* for a leisurely sail with Jimmy, Franklin Jr., and Johnny up to Campobello again.

Mother would go on ahead to the summer home on the island. She asked Harry and Barbara Hopkins to join her. Mother was increasingly drawn by Harry's rough-tongued integrity as an embattled New Dealer. He deserved a vacation, but certainly no more than Barbara, who he knew was dying of cancer. The disease had killed his father, and he wondered whether he, too, had some of the symptoms. The three of them would greet

Father when he brought the *Sewanna* into Welchpool harbor, brown from the sun and sporting a temporary set of sideburns.

He had delegated the jobs to be done while he was gone. Under opposition attack as "czar of all he surveys in the relief world," Harry would soon take to the road, carrying a banner for the Works Progress Administration and for FDR. Farley grudgingly agreed to that, though he cut short Hopkins' assignment later. Farley's heart was never in the New Deal, and he viewed Harry as a campaign liability. Every willing or able member of Father's team had a specified task to perform, save one.

Jack Garner, waiting his turn at the Presidency in 1940, preferred to sit out the campaign at home in Uvalde, sipping bourbon, going fishing, and hunting deer. He felt that thirty years of service as a Congressman entitled him to establish his own tradition of making only one speech in any campaign. That year, holding an office "not worth a pitcher of warm piss," he was inclined to avoid even that, when he had just come back from Mexico and the formal opening of a section of the new Inter-American Highway. Aboard the *Sewanna,* Father wrote to Jack, oiling him with flattery, quoting a letter he said he had been sent by Josephus Daniels, his old chief in the Navy Department, now ambassador in Mexico City: "I doubt if any public man has ever visited Mexico who was more warmly received, or who left with more sincere friends, than Vice-President Garner. . . . His frankness and genuineness, which we know and admire so much, won the hearts of the Mexicans."

My parent handled his man with kid gloves even though he seldom trusted him. "I want you, of course, to have a thoroughly good holiday," he assured Garner, "but I am wondering if you cannot make one little trip into a section where the Republicans are making a very definite drive. If you could make one speech in Kansas, one in Nebraska, one in Wyoming, and one in Colorado, I am inclined to think it would be very helpful. . . ."

Jack reluctantly conceded that he would spend a few weeks in New York at the disposal of the national committee.

Much of Father's long-range thinking was done at sea, where he could soak up the sun and pare day-to-day chores to a minimum. On this trip, foreign affairs and the dictators' march to conquest occupied him more than the impending political contest. He turned over in his mind a plan for calling a conference of the seven great powers—the United States, Britain, France, the USSR, Japan, Germany, and Italy—as a step toward preventing the spread of war beyond the frontiers of Spain, where factory workers and peasants armed by the left-wing government amazed the world by fending off the rebels. The Italian air force—and 100,000 Italian troops—remained Franco's most powerful striking force, but German aid was being added to his side, Soviet arms and advisers to the other.

The concept of a peace conference had to be kept a highest-priority secret. Any whisper of the plan would be explosive with the United States blinkered by isolationism and with the election coming up. Father saw the problems of world Fascism and the future of America as indivisible. "The election this year has, in a sense, a German parallel," he wrote as soon as he reached Hyde Park from Campobello, on his way back to Washington. "If the Republicans should win or make enormous gains, it would prove that an 85 percent control of the Press and a very definite campaign of misinformation can be effective here just as it was in the early days of the Hitler rise to power. Democracy is verily on trial."

He instructed Ambassador Dodd in Berlin to carry out a delicate mission: to sound out Der Führer. "What would happen if Hitler were personally and secretly asked by me to outline the limit of German foreign objectives during, let us say a ten year period, and to state whether or not he would have any sympathy with a general limitation of armaments' proposal?"

Dodd did not get to see the dictator personally, but the answer he obtained from Baron von Neurath, head of the German Foreign Office, and Hjalmar Schacht, the Finance Minister, was plain enough. Hitler would sit down at a peace table only if the Soviet Union were first condemned and excluded, and Germany and Italy would want guarantees in advance that colonies lost to them after World War I would be restored. Father's undoubted ambition to issue a call for a great-powers conference soon after he was reelected foundered on that rock.

In Spain, the grinding down of the republic's battalions, which included the volunteers from the United States and elsewhere in the International Brigade, made slow progress. Leon

Blum, Premier of France since June, initially wanted to send arms to the elected Spanish government, but his country was swept by a wave of sit-down strikes and so dangerously divided between a frantic Right and a rebellious Left that he feared aid for Spain would provoke a French civil war. In Britain, Stanley Baldwin's Conservative administration sought to wash its hands of the whole Spanish mess. The official policies of London and Paris called for nonintervention, to which the United States was already committed by the latest Neutrality Act, though legally it did not cover civil war.

Hindsight convinced Father that neutrality was a gigantic error. "Nonintervention" in Spain was a grim farce when Italy, Germany, and then the USSR boasted of their cheating. The hands-off attitude of the great powers resulted in nothing more than appeasement of dictatorships. A blockade of Spain by the French and British fleets, assuming that were possible, would simultaneously end intervention and the war. The only necessary move for the United States to make would be to give approval for such a blockade.

That summer, Father dared not propose anything that the opposition propagandists could distort as a step on the road to war. His sympathies had to be concealed. What he could do was stamp down on efforts to evade the law that made American neutrality work against the Spanish Loyalists. American ships, sailing under sealed orders, were supplying oil to Franco. Ostensibly, these Texas Oil Company tankers were bound for Antwerp. At sea, when their captains opened their orders, they found that their actual destinations were ports held by the Spanish rebels.

Father was incensed when he learned of the trick. Any captain joining in the deception should have his license revoked, he ordered, and their employers could possibly be indicted for conspiracy. The inequity of the situation in Spain bothered him, though not to the same extent as Mother, who openly backed the cause of the government in besieged Madrid. He endeavored to explain that he could not hope for backing from Congress for intervention.

"By trying to convince me that our course was correct," she noted, "he was simply trying to salve his own conscience."

He stuck to his program of avoiding partisan politicking until the month before election day, but his first major speech, on August 14, disclosed the passion of his thinking. War anywhere in the world was a threat to peaceful nations, he said, as he reviewed American efforts to promote peace through the Good Neighbor policy.

"I have seen war," he declaimed, "I have seen war on land and sea. I have seen blood running from the wounded. . . . I hate war." The isolationists were to toss those words in his face five years later, out of context, ignoring the rest of what he said. No law like the Neutrality Act, he pointed out, could cover every eventuality, "for it is impossible to imagine how every future event may shape itself."

The forces behind Landon tried fresh scare tactics to stir up a stampede for their hero. The Works Progress Administration, they claimed, was nothing but a spoils machine, pouring out its billions to buy votes for Father. Social security was a device for bilking workingmen of their wages; they would never get back a cent of the money withheld from their pay packets because Congress was going to grab it. Bribery and corruption were the name of the game that man in the White House was playing, or perhaps, as some of them said, it was "tiddlywinks with the universe."

"Turn the Rascals Out!" thundered the Chicago *Tribune,* and syndicated cartoons depicted my parent as a wild-eyed professor racking America with half-baked theories of revolution. At trade association luncheons, in railroad Pullman cars and in what he called "well-warmed and well-stocked clubs," fantastic stories circulated. They told of shrieks of mad laughter being overheard outside his oval office or alleged that Roosevelt was really *Rosenfeld,* the creature of an international conspiracy of Jews to take over the United States.

A private information sheet distributed that year by the McClure Syndicate to some 270 newspaper editors carried the following item:

> At a recent private dinner in New York an official of American Cyanamid expressed in extreme form the bitterness towards the Administration which is typical of the personal reactions of many right-wing leaders in business and finance. The gentleman in question asserted in so many words that the

"paranoiac in the White House" is destroying the nation, that a couple of well-placed bullets would be the best thing for the country, and that he for one would buy a bottle of champagne as quick as he could get it to celebrate such news.

Father quoted that at one of his press conferences. Wasn't it actionable under law, he was asked. "The President of the United States does not sue for libel," he replied, "and the Department of Justice does not proceed for libel."

Mother came in for more than her share of abuse. Trying to split the Solid South, the smear specialists centered their attentions on her expressed concern for Negro rights and her friendships with blacks. She took it to be her moral duty to invite blacks into the White House, treat them as equals, have her picture taken with them, and argue their causes with Father. He largely shared her concern, but he disagreed with her over the speed at which racial equality could be introduced. Political wisdom convinced him that "hasten slowly" was the best rule to be applied. Unless white bigotry could be overcome by a steady process of education, too much speed would be dangerous.

Landon's operatives paraded the specter of a further four years for Father starting in 1940 to alarm the Constitutionalists. Cousin Alice Longworth, who had seconded the Topeka Tornado's nomination in Cleveland, spread the word in one of her newspaper columns: "The talk is quite general that Mr. Roosevelt now is laying the groundwork for a third term." He had no such ambition at that time. The canard made no more impact than the feather duster to which Alice liked to compare him and his "mollycoddle philosophy." The three separate charges—that Mother was a Negro-lover, Father Jewish and power-hungry—found expression in a jingle popular among some of his more ardent opponents:

> You kiss the niggers,
> I'll kiss the Jews.
> We'll stay in the White House
> As long as we choose.

In spite of the incitements, Father kept security arrangements to a bare minimum. Getting into the grounds was no

problem at all, and at least one stranger entered the mansion itself unchecked. The visiting groups that Mother brought in
were only casually inspected. A signed pass was supposedly necessary to obtain admission to a Presidential press conference,
but one newspaperman came and went for three months with
no such credential. In the matter of death, Father was a fatalist.
What had to be would be. As somebody once said, he could never be categorized as a dictator because he chose to sit with his
back to his office window.

Apart from his first vote, cast for Uncle Ted in 1904, he was a
lifelong Democrat who firmly believed that his party's campaigning was done "on a far higher plane of ethics" than the
Republicans'. As he set out West with Mother in October, he
proposed to keep it that way. He ignored the smears and refused to mention Landon or any other Republican candidate by
name. He ordered his henchmen to accord "the Kansas Coolidge" similar anonymity in their speeches because it was a mistake "to advertise the other fellow." Father would stand or fall
on the carefully spelled out record of the New Deal as he joked
and laughed with the crowds that flocked to hear and see him
for themselves.

Security precautions remained negligible by later Presidential standards. One or two Secret Servicemen made a preliminary check of the routes he would travel in an open car. The
car itself would have an agent on each running board, Gus
Gennerich would be constantly on hand, and that was the extent of it. Father liked to soak up the warmth of contact with
people. One day in Oklahoma City, when a man pushed forward out of the throng and was promptly flung to the ground
in a flying tackle by one of the bodyguards, Father was dismayed by the victim's indignant explanation: "I only wanted to
touch him." Similar incidents were by no means rare.

The campaign train trundled along at a steady 35 miles an
hour so that he could study the landscape for telltale signs of
progress as he had taught Mother to do. For comfort's sake, he
would ride with his braces and his trousers off, having the valet
dress him and restore the ten pounds of steel for his appearance at the next stop. When his legs grew chilled, as they often
did, he would massage them gently or, toward evening, take the
cocktail which the doctors prescribed. One of the dozen or so

standard Pullman cars making up the train was equipped temporarily with radio for direct contact with the White House. There was no special Presidential car until 1940. At night, the locomotive crew put on steam to keep up to schedule for another back-platform chat to a waiting trackside crowd early next morning, or for a more ceremonious rally, when a ramp would be lowered for Father to make his way down on his own two legs, no matter what the effort.

Late in October, he left on his second and last tour, this time of the New England States. The glowing welcome he had found in the Midwest clinched his certainty that he would be the winner. Everything was going magnificently except in Maine and Vermont. Pad and pencil calculations told him that he would collect 360 electoral votes against 171 for the unnamed other fellow.

He covered the nine-day trip in an open car, hemmed in along the highways by cheering masses of admirers, penned in city streets by surging seas of humanity. In private, he was careful not to give way to unwarranted optimism. "I think we have a real possibility in Massachusetts and some chance in Connecticut and Rhode Island" was as far as he would allow himself to go.

He could afford to tease the enemy within its own gates. He chose Wilmington, Delaware, as the ideal place for quoting Abraham Lincoln on liberty—"The world has never had a good definition of liberty, and the American people, just now, are much in want of one." Wilmington happened to be home to the du Ponts, the Liberty League's most devout supporters.

He waited for the climactic speech of the campaign before he opened up on the foe. He had to pause for minutes on end to make himself heard above the clamor of applause that rattled the roof beams of Madison Square Garden after every other sentence. At last, he got to the crux of the matter, and the words rolled from the heart:

"We had to struggle with the old enemies of peace—business and financial monopoly, speculation, reckless banking, class antagonism, sectionalism, war profiteering. *They* had begun to consider the government of the United States as a mere appendage to their own affairs. And we know now that government by organized money is just as dangerous as government by organized mob." The anger, suppressed until now, put an edge on his voice. "Never before in all history have these forces been so united against one candidate as they stand today. They are unanimous in their hate for me—and I *welcome* their hatred."

He paused to give the crowd time to celebrate. He had one more statement to complete the thought, so he must be patient. When the words came, his tone was soft, but it rang louder with every phrase. "I should like to have it said of my first administration that in it the forces of selfishness and of lust for power met their match. I should like to have it said of my second administration that in it these forces met their *master*."

In a betting pool organized at New York party headquarters, on November 1, Jim Farley predicted that Father would carry every state except Maine and Vermont. Yet the Republicans, gulled by the pollsters, still blindly banked on Landon's victory.

The news tickers spelled out the most stunning Republican defeat in Presidential history. Roosevelt, 27,752,869 votes; Landon, 16,674,665; Lemke, 882,479. Of 531 electoral college votes, Father had 528, the biggest ratio in 116 years. Farley had hit it right on the nose. Around midnight, Landon conceded. At some Grand Old Party gatherings early that Wednesday morning, any man who ventured to a toast to the President of the United States was shouted down. At other parties, the orchestra just went on playing.

So far as the rest of the world was concerned, something more important than an American election took place that fall. The Germans and the Japanese coordinated their plans for victory and the Berlin-Tokyo-Rome Axis emerged. From the German capital, William Dodd warned Father, "These dictators mean to dominate Europe, and there is a fair chance of their doing it without war."

7

The best that the enemy could do immediately was to resort
to wishful thinking and pray that his health would fail, so that
his shoes could be filled by Garner, retained as Vice President,
much more malleable and increasingly cool toward Father's
policies. The McClure Syndicate picked up and spread another
unchecked rumor:

> A New York specialist high in the medical field is an au-
> thority for the following, which is given in the strictest confi-
> dence to editors. Towards the end of last month Mr. Roose-
> velt was found in a coma at his desk. Medical examination dis-
> closed the neck rash which is typical of certain disturbing
> symptoms. Immediate treatment of the most skilled kind was
> indicated, with complete privacy and detachment from official
> duties. Hence the trip to southern waters, with no newspaper-
> men on board and a naval convoy which cannot be penetrat-
> ed.

The truth of the matter was that he wanted some time at sea
to seek a solution to the escalating Consitutional crisis created
by decisions of the Supreme Court. "It is a mighty difficult one

to solve," he admitted, "but one way or another I think it must be faced." As yet, he had no clear-cut plan.

He could combine a spell of reflection with something else he had a mind to do. By showing his face in Latin America again, he hoped to foster good relations there and set an example to the Germans and Italians of how to conduct foreign affairs without waving a blackjack. An important diplomatic appearance would be made in Buenos Aires, where an Inter-American Conference was to attempt setting up machinery for handling disputes within the hemisphere and for consultation in the event of war erupting elsewhere in the world. Sumner Welles rated it an epochal gathering. Cordell Hull, who rarely saw eye to eye with his studiously solemn Undersecretary, was not so sure.

As Father cleared his desk for leaving, one letter that was shuffled to the bottom of a wire basket came from Mussolini, congratulating him on his reelection and "hoping that our relations, now reestablished, may not undergo any further interruption." Il Duce had to wait nine months for a reply.

All that was holding up departure was another shipping strike in San Francisco. The rest of the details had been taken care of. Mother would once again stay behind. Pa Watson would come along as a guarantee of shipboard fun, "Doc" McIntire to give sinus treatments. Another member of our family was slated for the trip, too; my brother Jimmy was starting his training as an aide to Father, and he had been commissioned a lieutenant colonel in the Marine Corps Reserve to give him appropriate rank.

The buildup of my brother had just begun. Father's way was to develop closeness with each of us three older children in turn. It was his method of encouraging us when time was too scarce for him to play the parental role in all our lives simultaneously. We took that for granted, the two who were currently more remote as well as the present favorite, whoever that might be. The loss of Louis had left a void in the innermost circle around Father. When he picked on Jimmy to try to fill it, Granny's pleasure at seeing her eldest grandson on the first step to glory could not be restrained.

Before they boarded the cruiser *Indianapolis* at Charleston, North Carolina, on November 18, Father fancied that he would send Jimmy to London next spring for the coronation of Edward VIII, King of England since the death of his father, George V, the past January. The morning newspapers beside Father's breakfast tray were happily reporting the bachelor Edward's courtship of Mrs. Wallis Simpson, a lively American who less than a month previously had obtained a divorce from her second husband. The British press conspired to keep the romance secret.

Easygoing days at a steady 25 knots through smooth seas provided my parent with a rare opportunity to devote a few hours to making up for his neglect of Granny, always playing on her joy over my brother's rising star. "Jimmy will be a great comfort on this trip and it will do him good," said one note to "Dearest Mama." When the ship anchored off Port of Spain, Trinidad, to refuel, Father spent three hours fishing from a whaleboat, catching nothing, but content that he had dispatched my brother to repay a courtesy call by the governor. "Jimmy is in fine form and does his daily work with the Navy and Marine Corps officers," said another chatty letter to Granny.

They entered Rio de Janeiro's magnificent harbor before breakfast on a Thanksgiving Day that crammed in a formal luncheon, a speech to the Brazilian Congress, a reception, and a banquet before the *Indianapolis* upped anchor at ten P.M. to make for Buenos Aires. Mother radioed to say that she was hurrying to Harvard, where Franklin Jr., in his senior year, was laid low with an attack of Rooseveltian sinusitis, which needed surgery.

A souvenir of Rio was carried aboard for her—a tea set of ancient hammered silver, a gift from President Getulio Vargas. "A great rarity and not at all bad looking," Father commented. She had no great liking for such extravagant tributes. Towels, sheets, and pillowcases were the kind of presents she asked for on her birthdays, to his irritation. His own choices would have been a trifle less utilitarian.

Four days of sailing brought them to the mouth of the Rio de la Plata, where the Argentinian fleet steamed out in welcome. Every yard of the four-mile drive from the ship to the United States Embassy, where Cordell Hull waited, was lined with orchid-tossing crowds, yelling *"Viva la democracia!"* With men, women, and children darting out to press closer to the limousine, Gus Gennerich had his hands full. "It was a jumpy sort of day," Father said afterward, the kind that set Gus off dreaming of the farm which he was buying for retirement.

He had a breathing spell at seven o'clock when Father bathed and dressed for a late dinner. Gus was off duty that night, but he had no appetite for dining. He drank only a bottle of beer when he went out to a café with George Fox, the White House pharmacist, and Charlie Claunch, who was slated to be a White House usher. From another table, Pa Watson watched the big, lumbering ex-policeman dance his way through the evening. An hour or so past midnight, Gus went back to this own table, cracked a joke with Claunch, then slumped across the table-cloth. In ninety seconds, his heart stopped beating.

Father was told the news when he woke next morning. He ordered a simple service in the embassy's reception room, where the ship's chaplain read the prayers and marines mounted an honor guard. The coffin was borne up the gangplank for another later ceremony in the same White House room where Louis had lain seven months ago. Mother was alerted by radio to make arrangements.

In every other respect, the trip was a sensational success. From the Uruguayans of Montevideo, Father received the same kind of amazing reception he'd had in Brazil and Argentina, a zenith point in Latin American goodwill for the northern Big Brother. From President Justo of Argentina, he had another present for Mother, which she would think no more of than the silver tea set—a bronze bust of Father himself. "Have seen worse" was his own underwhelmed assessment.

On the opposite scale, affairs in Europe preyed on Father's mind. "There seems to be no step that we can take to improve that situation," he said pessimistically. And shadowing all the achievements of the trip was the fresh gap in the ranks of his true intimates, the loss of Gennerich. "Good old Gus was the kind of a loyal friend who simply cannot be replaced," Father said over and over again. That was one more reason why Jimmy had to become his private secretary.

A radiogram from London on the homeward voyage quashed the plan to send him there for the coronation. On the eve of the public announcement on December 11, Father learned that Edward would abdicate for the sake of "the wom-

an I love," leaving his frail, chain-smoking younger brother
Albert, Duke of York, to take the title of King George VI. "Awful dilemma," said Father, since he would be going ashore the
next day to lunch with the governor of Trinidad. Should he
propose a toast, "the King," on the very day Edward was quit-
ting the throne?

He was fascinated by kings and queens, half-amused, half-
impressed, by the pomp and pageantry that enveloped royalty.
Granny, naturally, found nothing at all amusing in a matter of
such gravity. To her, reigning monarchs were among the few
people in the world ranking in dignity with herself. Hyde Park
became a sort of *petit palais* when royalty visited. She covered
the top of her grand piano with rows of their autographed photographs in gilt frames, arranged like a pictorial *Almanach de
Gotha.*

Characteristically, her son decided to play the problem by ear
in the governor's mansion, not according to protocol as laid
down by the stripe-trousered gentlemen of the State Department. Plain good manners, instilled in him as a child by Granny, would tell him what to do.

Mother's solid commonsense warned her it was a mistake for
Jimmy to resign from the insurance business and go into the
White House, inheriting Rabbit as his secretary. She argued the
point endlessly with Father and my brother, but there was no
changing the verdict. "Franklin did not like opposition too
well—as who does?" she remembered.

She knew that Jimmy's allegiances to his former colleagues
were not completely severed. By her code of morality, it was
perfectly permissible to use influence with Father for a good
cause, relentlessly if she must. Nepotism was a different story.
She feared that Jimmy's daily contact would be turned into a
financial asset by his former associates and that my brother
would open doors for them, as I was guilty of doing for Texas
oilmen.

Father did not see it that way. "Why should I be deprived of
my eldest son's help and of the pleasure of having him with me
just because I am the President?" he asked. Jimmy went on the
payroll. The "Crown Prince," as the newspapers began to call
him, and his wife Betsy seemed to be fixtures of Washington society. The barrage of criticism and the pressures of a job which

was impossible to handle objectively eroded his health. His ulcers bothered him increasingly, to the point where, at a not too distant date, it was suspected that he might have stomach cancer.

This trip to South America and the appointment as secretary to Father marked the era when Jimmy truly became an adult confidant of his father. This period of his life brought home to him, for the first time, the rare warmth and love which our father had to give to his offspring. True it may be that Mother's fears of his susceptibility to outside influence might damage his service to Father. But I am certain in my heart that Jimmy gave much more than loyal service. He labored heroically to be worthy of Father's trust. He permanently damaged his health, but it was a measure of Father's respect for his ability that he entrusted him with such a demanding task. He can always be proud of those years of service, no matter what may have happened in the ensuing years. One other period in the life of son James should be noted before the ink dries on the pages of history. As the son of the Commander in Chief of the armed forces of the United States, when Pearl Harbor came, he was already a volunteer in the Marine Corps. With one-third of a stomach, ineligible for combat service, he still managed to go on active duty and he served throughout the war, much of it in combat with Carlson's Raiders, as a distinguished and fearless leader. His valor and integrity have been vouched for many times by the men who served under him. They have told me so. For these reasons, I would like to record that, no matter what the rest of the chronicle may be, my father loved and was proud of his son James.

No answer to the quandary of what to do about the nine old men had come to mind by the time the *Indianapolis* docked after 12,000 miles of cruising. James Clark McReynolds, Father joked, would still be wearing his judicial robes when he reached his hundred-and-fifth birthday. Yet McReynolds, reaction's clearest voice on the high bench, supplied the key to a solution.

Before he sailed from Charleston, Father left Homer Cummings to study legal history for guidance. One December morning, he came to the Presidential office with something that Father categorized as "the answer to a maiden's prayer." In 1913, when McReynolds was Wilson's Attorney General, he had proposed a scheme for the President to provide substitute federal judges to replace any who were disabled or who clung on past retirement age. This was it. Cummings was ordered to draft a message to Congress in secret. Father would spring it on the Hill as soon as possible after Inauguration Day, which for the first time he had advanced from March to January. The new law he wanted would give the President power to appoint a new man to the Supreme Court, up to a total of six, for every justice who failed to retire on full salary within the six months following his seventieth birthday.

Don Richberg, successor to Hugh Johnson at the National Recovery Administration, was delegated to help Cummings by putting a hard bite into the language. Knowledge of what was afoot was confined to these two, Father, and self-effacing Sam Rosenman. The Gold Dust Twins, who generally would have been let in on the plan from the onset, were kept in the dark. Why? The best guess was that Father envisaged the scheme as a sword that he personally would unsheath to slay dragons. As he saw it, the election had given him a mandate to battle the Roosevelt-haters to the ground. First, he had to eliminate their protective shield, supplied by the Court, which up to now had struck down nine out of eleven basic measures of the New Deal.

The age of the old men was the crux of the plan. If he could get this new law through Congress, five of the nine—Brandeis, Van Devanter, McReynolds, Sutherland, and Hughes—would be off the bench almost immediately, replaced by appointees of Father's who would give him a virtually automatic majority.

The November landslide had resulted in a Senate made up of seventy-five Democrats and only twenty-one Republicans. In the House, the victors were represented by 334 members against the opposition's meager eighty-nine. With those overwhelming majorities, Father hoped during this second term to destroy the ability of the handful of financial and industrial tycoons to control the business of America.

Meantime, the most loyal of his lieutenants should be rewarded. In the afterglow of the Latin American triumph, he wanted a special tribute for Cordell Hull to recognize the work he had put in at Montevideo. Cordell deserved next year's Nobel Peace Prize, he thought, but he wondered whether the recommendation could properly come from himself as President.

Endless correspondence on this theme started before the year was out. In 1937, Father himself was nominated, though the honor went elsewhere. He kept plugging away for Hull, however, and finally Cordell received the prize. By then, my parent had been dead for nine months.

He celebrated New Year's Eve, 1936, in the style he liked best—with Mother and others of the family in his oval study, comfortable in his big chair, listening to the radio tell how the rest of the country was seeing in another twelve months that should put the United States well along the road to restored prosperity. The eggnog that night was laced with some of "those most excellent examples of Dominican manufacture"—rum sent from Moscow by our new ambassador there, Joseph E. Davies, a tycoon who sided with Father.

Bill Bullitt's wish had been granted, and he had been posted from the USSR to France to succeed Jesse Straus, who had died a few weeks after resigning. A vehement anti-Communist by now, Bullitt decided before he left that he would put on a show to stir the natives. He proceeded to stage a party in Spaso House which he reckoned was the brightest Moscow had been privileged to see since the days of the czars. Davies went one better than that. With the fortune of his wife, Marjorie Post, a breakfast cereal heiress, behind him, there were no luxuries known to man that Joe could not afford. He anchored at Leningrad in their 250-foot yacht, *Silver Cloud,* air-conditioned, square-rigged with diesel auxiliaries, its lockers crammed with frozen food. If the proletariat was not impressed, Father certainly was. He had a predeliction for this rare species of super-rich Democrat.

January was hectic. A budget message had to be prepared, an Inaugural speech written, and all the official dinners for the Cabinet, legislators, the judiciary, and diplomats crowded into the calendar, together with the receptions that delighted social Washington and bored him beyond belief. Behind the scenes, the strategy for assault on the Supreme Court was taking shape.

Cummings protested that he felt like a conspirator, but he and Richberg, jealous of outside legal advice, kept Corcoran and Cohen at arm's length. When Tom got a hint of what was going on from Rosenman, he tried to caution Father against the stratagem for circumventing obstruction from the nine old men. Father did not want to hear him, any more than he was prepared to give advance notice to the newspapers or even to his party leaders on Capitol Hill. He had to strike fast and with maximum surprise. He dismissed the idea of overcoming the Court problem by way of Constitutional amendment. There was no time for that, and besides, he could never count on its winning approval from the requisite thirty-six states when their legislatures were perennially subject to local pressure from business lobbyists.

"Give me ten million dollars," Father would say, "and I can prevent any amendment to the Constitution from being ratified by the necessary number of states."

The team of speech writers, headed by Rosenman, assembled drafts of his words for Inauguration Day. He would start by inventorying the gains of his first four years, then look ahead to fresh priorities. "Shall we pause," he would ask, "and turn our back upon the road that lies ahead?" The answer was obvious, yet the country had to be roused from a recent mood of complacency that he detected, a feeling that the Depression was just about over and little more need be done about it.

Washington, to his way of thinking, had looked like an emergency hospital in 1932, "and now most of the patients seem to be doing very nicely; some of them are even well enough to throw their crutches at the doctor." That was too flip a comment for an inaugural. As he went over the drafts for the speech, committing the words to memory so that they became his own, he leaned back in his swivel chair and studied the ceiling. Then the phrase came that would dominate the headlines. He scribbled in, "I see one-third of a nation ill-housed, ill-clad, ill-nourished." There was no better way to pinpoint the situation the New Deal had yet to remedy.

Rain drenched Washington on January 20 when he stood bareheaded in the downpour to take the oath once again on the massive old Dutch Bible brought down from Hyde Park. In the speech he delivered, one sentence might have given Chief Justice Charles Evans Hughes a clue to what was in store for the Court: "The Constitution of 1787 did not make our democracy impotent."

Throughout the afternoon of February 4, Louise Hackmeister, who ran the White House switchboard, was worked to a frazzle, placing calls. Father summoned the Cabinet and leaders of Congress to meet him in the morning. Stenographers were ordered to report in at six thirty A.M. to get the documents ready. The plan for forcibly retiring aged Court justices was about to unfold.

The meeting was held one hour before the Presidential message went to Capitol Hill. The group in the white-walled Cabinet Room listened in silence while Father read excerpts to them. He asked for nobody's opinions. He was in too great a hurry for that. Reporters were due to gather in his office at any minute, brought in by Steve Early, who had only just learned that this was the day for attack. Cactus Jack said not a word before Father was wheeled off to the press conference. Later, in the Senate lobby, Garner applied a thumb and forefinger to his nose. His disenchantment with his President was close to being complete.

Corcoran persuaded Missy to squeeze him onto Father's schedule for a few minutes that morning. Tom had two serious reservations in mind. By failing to take the Senate leaders into his confidence earlier than this, Father was bungling his chances of gaining Senatorial approval for his scheme. By withholding any clue to what he intended from the aged but more liberal-inclined justices like Brandeis, Father was deliberately affronting them.

He saw some validity in what Tom said and sent him off immediately to the Supreme Court building. Corcoran invaded the sanctuary of the justices' robing room to find and tell Brandeis, then stood beside him in the hall while his eight colleagues filed by on their way to take their places on the immense mahogany bench. The eighty-year-old judge was grateful for the courtesy, but he told Tom that he was "unalterably opposed" to Father's action.

All nine were seated and the first hearing of the day begun when a messenger emerged from behind the backdrop of crimson curtains and presented a sheet of paper to each of them. Proceedings were halted for a moment while they digested the bulletin. Father intended to change not the Constitution but the makeup of the Court.

"Court packing" was the label Herbert Hoover attached to it

in the commotion that embroiled the country as soon as the news was out. "What a grand fight it is going to be!" Father said with a chuckle, supremely confident of another victory.

The affray brought on some strange switching from one side to the other. Hugh Johnson somersaulted to the microphones to praise my parent for doing "what he was elected to do." Hoover and Landon itched to get on the air to blast Father, but the Republican high command dissuaded them. The Democrats in Congress were in such turmoil that the Republicans had best sit back and enjoy the squabble.

Even among New Dealers, there was strong feeling that Father had been devious. "Too damned clever" was a standard comment. The Liberty League issued no public protest, but it was no coincidence that hostile full-page newspaper advertisements, purportedly placed by outraged local groups, erupted across the land. Tens of thousands of letters descended on Capitol Hill, and a return flood of printed copies of Congressmen's speeches, pro and con, deluged the voters. Father continued to convince himself, "The people are with me."

Possibly they were, but his majorities in both Houses of Congress grew shakier and shakier. The Gold Dust Twins led the corps of proselytes ordered out to hold the line. To Corcoran, it was one more cause to be pushed, even if this time his heart was only half in it. On the whole, he considered, "the President's messengers were incompetent and perhaps disloyal."

Tom believed some compromise could be negotiated—perhaps to reduce the maximum number of new appointees to the Court to three and so avoid the appearance of steamrollering. Cummings and Richberg, insulated from the hurly-burly, advised Father against that. In the middle of the struggle, Cummings took a vacation, which rankled with Tom. Cactus Jack sat on his hands, counting the days until he could make off for Uvalde.

The court-packing issue snapped the threads of some of Father's oldest friendships. One morning's mail brought from Jerome Green, Harvard treasurer and valued friend, a copy of a letter he had just written to the New York *Times*. "For one who knows the President," it said, "it is impossible to believe that he is aiming at a future dictatorship; but it is also impossi-

ble not to recognize the packing of the Supreme Court as exactly what a dictator would adopt as his first step. The President
may not know where he is going, but he is on his way."

Father thrived on criticism from distant "enemies within the
gate," but he was peculiarly sensitive to thrusts from those he
felt should know him better. From Warm Springs, where he
had gone in the vain hope of a few days of sunshine, he
whipped off a cutting reply: "I think you will have a right to
send similar letters to any paper twenty-five years from now
just as you do today. There are some of us who believe, however, that unless this nation continues to act as a nation—with
three branches of government pulling together to keep it going—you might find yourself unable to write to the papers a
quarter of a century hence."

He was still in Georgia when the Judiciary Committee
opened hearings on the bill in the Senate caucus room. There,
Burt Wheeler turned on him with savagery of his own and a
bludgeon in the form of a letter from Charles Evans Hughes.
The hot-tempered Senator from Montana had been among the
first to boost Father for the Presidency in 1930, when Burt led
Progressive opposition to Hoover. In the past election, he had
campaigned for Father in Kansas, Iowa, and Wyoming, as well
as in his own state. Now, here he was floor leader of the counterattack against the Court plan. What had happened to him?

In the first place, he hated Cummings. In the second, he felt
slighted because the seven years he had put in for Father had
brought him few rewards. It was time to vent his animosity, and
the most damage he could do was to draw the Chief Justice
himself into the fight. The immaculately bearded old lawyer
had not forgotten the cut-and-thrust crafts of a politician, acquired when he challenged Wilson for the Presidency in 1916
and lost by a margin so narrow that he went to bed imagining
he had been elected. The letter he wrote for the Judiciary Committee at Wheeler's prompting presumed to speak for all nine
Justices. They opposed enlargement of the Court, it said, because that would reduce its efficiency, on which they set great
store.

Father was reluctant to accept the fact that from now on
Wheeler was to be a commander in the opposing army. "I am
sorry about Burt," he noted regretfully. "His last attack on me

seemed to me to be a little 'below the belt.'" Naked bitterness between them developed later.

He continued to listen to the pro-Administration voices that told him the fight was being won, that the well-marshaled forces of reaction were on the defensive. The one danger was a possible filibuster, the soothing counselors said, and even then they would lack, according to present count, only 6 of the needed 64 votes to cut off debate by enforcing cloture.

"We'll smoke 'em out," said Father gleefully. "If delay helps them, we must press for an early vote." There would be no compromise.

Hughes defended his Court by cutting more ground out from under the Presidential feet. On their previous records, a majority of the nine old men was expected to turn down the Wagner Act, under which John L. Lewis' new Congress for Industrial Organization was recruiting millions of steel, auto, and other assembly-line workers into union ranks, blocking out the more conservative American Federation of Labor. Certainly, the autocratic Chief Justice, on past performance, promised to be an automatic nay.

Nobody in White House circles could overestimate the consequences if the Wagner Act were declared illegal. The generation of union militants hit industry after industry with demands for more money and easier conditions. Sit-down strikes inside the factories on the French pattern were the latest weapon, added to the armory of instant walkouts, mammoth parades, and violent picketing, which sparked ever more violent counteraction, like the bloody encounters between goon squads and demonstrators at Henry Ford's River Rouge plant.

But Hughes did not aim to join in a Court ruling that would have had the irresistible effect of driving the forces of organized labor onto Father's side. The Chief Justice outsmarted him by casting his vote with those of Brandeis, Cardoza, Roberts, and Stone to find that the Wagner Act was unassailable within the framework of the Constitution.

Father had anticipated a veto to sharpen the edge of the conflict, but he behaved as though everything were going according to plan, joking with Pa Watson, clearing up his affairs as the mood for a spring vacation with some guaranteed sunshine crept up on him.

Pa had gone off to the racetrack the previous weekend with a lighthearted instruction to put a few dollars for Father on any horse "whose name smacked of the sea." Naval Cadet, running in the fifth race, met that requirement. Pa reported the result: "I placed the bet as follows: $2 to win, $2.00 place, $2.00 show. The horse ran third, paying $6.70. It gives me great pleasure to enclose 70 cents."

Twenty-four hours after Hughes' counterstroke, Father dictated this memorandum to Pa:

1. You are hereby appointed Chief Bookmaker to the Dictator.
2. The next time you go to the track change the lay by picking a horse with an Army name.
3. If the horse has an artillery name, double the bet.
4. Don't let the horse see you.

As usual, he had paid up his income tax on the dot, none too pleased with the financial situation in which that left him. Like millions of others, he was being pinched by higher taxes. He worked out his own returns and filled them in himself in his neat handwriting. Not even Missy was allowed to type them. In 1936, his net income had fallen to $62,939.74, on which he paid tax of $12,963.70, leaving him with slightly less than $50,000. Out of that, he had college fees to pay for the education of Franklin Jr. and Johnny, as well as their allowances, which he kept up after they graduated. He had cut Jimmy off the allowance list when his schooling was finished, and my allowance ceased even earlier, which was good for our self-respect, but, in Mother's excuse-finding for our behavior, another factor making us susceptible to the wrong kind of employment offers.

She filed separate tax returns. She had achieved a long-felt ambition of her own by making herself financially independent. The few hundred thousand dollars of inherited capital worth which she brought into her marriage were ineptly managed by trustees, and the income shrank to roughly $5,000 a year. Nowadays, she earned twenty times as much from her rounds on the lecture circuit and from her ingenuous column, *My Day*, which appeared in some sixty newspapers. There was more money in the offing for her. That year, *Ladies' Home*

Journal paid $75,000 for serial rights to her memoirs, *This Is My Story*. Along with the rest of her income, she gave most of it away to charity or to the hopeless task of turning Val-Kill Industries into a paying concern.

She no longer expected to be asked to share a vacation with Father. In any event, the load of commitments she undertook in leading her separate life made it virtually impossible to coincide their schedules. Going fishing was an exclusively male business for him now. The days when Missy joined in the fun aboard the plodding old houseboat *Larooco* in and around the Florida keys were long since past.

He again prescribed fishing as a temporary cure for the tension between Ickes and Hopkins, whose feud had flared as fiercely as ever. In the middle of his own preparations for another spell at sea, Father packed them both off for Florida waters in the *Houston*. He would not sail with them this time, since he had different plans.

A telegram from Harry indicated that, for a few days at least, he and Harold could enjoy a joke together, especially at each other's expense: PLEASE TELL YOUR SO-CALLED MILITARY AIDES THAT I GOT MY ALLIGATOR YESTERDAY AND WHEN I RODE HIM BACK TO THE SHIP HE TOLD ME HE WAS A CLASSMATE OF PA'S . . . WHEN HAROLD GOT A STRIKE THE OTHER DAY . . . FIRST THE ROD AND REEL AND THEN HAROLD WENT OVERBOARD AND WE HOPED FOR A BRIEF MOMENT THAT WE HAD LOST THE BEST FISHERMAN IN THE CABINET. . . .

Father's response went to Ickes because the Old Curmudgeon was touchy when he felt left out of anything. GREATLY DISTURBED ABOUT ALLIGATORS. AS SENIOR OFFICER PRESENT PLEASE INSIST HOPKINS DELIVER TO YOU COLONEL WATSON'S BOTTLE OF BAIT . . . NATIONAL BUDGET ALMOST IN BALANCE. IF YOU BOTH STAY AWAY ANOTHER WEEK DEBTOR NATIONS WILL PAY WAR DEBTS AND WE CAN ALL HEAD FOR SAMOA.

The crisis over court-packing had occupied him for weeks. He felt unusually remote from the world overseas, where the future of peace looked darker by the day. "Every week changes the picture," he observed, "and the basis for it all lies, I *think*, not in Communism or the fear of Communism but in Germany and the fear of what the present German leaders are meeting for or being drawn toward."

The reports coming in from our ambassadors were uniformly discouraging. Bill Phillips in Rome found Mussolini obsessed with the idea that Communism and Fascism were locked in a fight to the finish. The flood of Italian arms and men into Spain was lapping around Madrid, prompting Ambassador Claude Bowers to move his center of operations out of the Spanish capital to safety across the French border. He was neither the first nor the last of his rank to feel queasy under fire.

Bullitt in Paris learned that the French had warned Austria they could not defend that country, already undermined by Nazi agents, against a German invasion. Dodd in Berlin saw a search for food supplies as the driving force behind a hungry Germany's aggressions. John Cudahy in Warsaw prophesied that Hitler was on the verge of another coup to bolster his prestige, and Father, in a startling act of prevision, promptly commissioned his ambassador to assess the ability of Poland and Czechoslovakia to defend themselves against the Wehrmacht.

He had a "not wholly crazy" fancy about a Big Five conference of King George VI, Stalin, Mussolini, Hitler, French President Lebrun—and perhaps himself. "If five or six heads of the important governments could meet together for a week," he wrote Dodd, "with complete inaccessibility to press or cables or radio, a definite, useful agreement might result or else one or two of them would be murdered by the others!"

For the present, since a Gallup Poll disclosed that 94 percent of Americans favored staying out of foreign wars, all he could do was rocket the Navy Department, because the building of new warships was falling behind schedule, and seek to ensure that the revised Neutrality Act gave him discretion to allow a belligerent nation to buy American supplies on a cash-and-carry basis.

He looked for any scrap of amusement to keep his spirits at their optimum level in the gloom that prevailed at home and abroad. He must have chuckled when he handed Missy for his private files a "list of historical, contemporary, and literary personages to whom the President has from time to time been compared by friends and critics," compiled by an unidentified jester. Along with "Kerensky" on the debit side stood the names of Machiavelli, Iago, Stalin, Hitler, Mussolini, Napoleon, Nero, Lochiel, Mr. Chadband, Mr. Pecksniff, Augustus Caesar, Theodore Roosevelt, Joab, Pontius Pilate, Judas, and Santa Claus.

On April 28, he took the train from Washington to New Orleans for a fishing trip on which I joined him. "I haven't a care in the world," he declared just before leaving, "which is some going for a President who is said by the newspapers to be a remorseless dictator driving his government into hopeless bankruptcy."

II

THE PRICE OF POWER

8

I n all his years of deep-sea fishing, before and after polio, Father had never caught a tarpon. He had put out in whaleboats, sailing dinghies, and power skiffs. He had cast his line over the side of the *Larooco*, from chartered cruisers' after-decks, and from the fantails of rich friends' yachts. He had reeled in marlin, swordfish, jewfish, groupers, and sharks beyond number. He was proud of landing near-record rainbow runners and blue cavalla, but never a tarpon, and we both agreed it was time he did.

From the ranch outside Fort Worth where Ruth and I lived, I urged him to come down to try in the waters off Port Aransas, Texas. His arms needed no twisting from me. This was a fish that had eluded him too long. Besides, cruising would give him the opportunity he needed to take a long-range look at Washington and the world.

"I don't give a Continental damn whether I catch a fish or not," he told one press conference, but that was not entirely true. He had his heart set on a tarpon.

The arrangement was for me to meet him at the Roosevelt Hotel, New Orleans, to which he would be driven from the train. The customary combination of pleasure and politicking was scheduled. Our hosts that evening were all eminent members of the still mighty Huey Long machine, the subject of the continuing probe by agents of the Internal Revenue Service.

It made for a certain piquancy to sit at dinner in Antoine's under the glazed stare of the dead Kingfish, whose photographs hung on the walls. Father enjoyed his first taste of oysters Rockefeller, but the pleasure did not compare with twitting such notables as the governor of Louisiana, the mayor of New Orleans, and Seymour Weiss, owner of the hotel, on the hazards implicit in undiluted political power. A bill to trap the tax dodgers was due to go to Congress in little more than a month. Weiss and the governor were among those many disciples of Long subsequently indicted for income-tax evasion and sentenced to prison.

Soon after dawn the next morning, we boarded what the newspapers invariably described as "the Presidential yacht," which had come down from Washington to await us. The *Potomac* was, in fact, an old Coast Guard patrol boat, the former *Electra*, which had been refitted at no great expense for Father's use. He slept below decks in a stateroom that few admirals would have looked at twice. On the main deck, there was a combination saloon-dining room, with direct access to the galley. The cushioned fantail provided a spot where visiting dignitaries could be entertained.

"I'm surprised she survived the trip down," Father said with a smile. The *Potomac* was geared for sedate voyaging at a maximum 16 knots up and down the river for which she was named. It was a standing joke that in any kind of sea "the Presidential yacht" was likely to turn turtle.

We went down the Mississippi, through the delta into the Gulf of Mexico, then along the Louisiana and Texas coasts. The sun was warm enough for him to sit out under his ancient panama, freed from the weight of steel. The first day was spent unwinding, "to get sufficiently far away from the forest," in his words, "to look at it as a whole without being lost among the individual trees."

We anchored in Port Aransas harbor the following day. Rented sportfishing boats came out as scheduled to take us trolling. Father's hopes were high as he sat in a swivel chair, big freckled hands firm on his rod. The tarpon were striking. In the channel leading out of the harbor, he got his first bite. The charter-boat captain took us out slowly to the channel mouth, past the piers, to give him space to play the leaping silver fish, shaking water as it arced in the air.

It gave him a good fight. For better than half an hour, he sat with his withered legs outstretched and his great arms tensed while he reeled in his catch. The smile on his sweat-drenched face was as broad as a house as Pa Watson and I congratulated him.

"This one has to be yours, Bunny," he said. It weighed in at sixty-five pounds, and he had it mounted for me.

The pattern of the days was much the same. We fished from Port Aransas and from Port Isabel, near the mouth of the Rio Grande and the Mexican border. Every morning, the little charter boats arrived to take us out into the gulf. Father hooked more tarpon, including one that he had mounted for himself, and other game fish that were running. In the early evening, the visitors would come aboard the *Potomac* for drinks on the fantail—the governor of Texas and an assortment of politicos, looking for patronage jobs and federal aid for local projects, to be quizzed by Father about the pace of recovery in their districts.

Ruth drove down to stay with friends at one of the cottages used for fishing and hunting just outside Port Aransas. She came aboard for drinks and dinner, bringing some of the natives we knew—oilmen whose business was prospering again, cattlemen in a similar happy state now that the New Deal had restored healthier prices in agrobusiness. Father went to his stateroom early and slept as usual, without a worry on his mind, bothered by nothing except a touch of spring fever.

Washington could have been on a different planet. A week went by without so much as a mail plane arriving. "There is no news outside of an occasional tarpon!" said a note he sent Granny. The gravest bulletin came in a later letter from her. Feebler now at eighty-two, and using a crutch sometimes, she had fallen and chipped an anklebone. He joshed her about that. "As you have so often said to me, 'It will give you a rest in spite of yourself'!"

The otherwise frustrated family man surfaced as usual on this trip, when he had time to catch up with his children's progress—or lack of it in some cases. Mother had flown out to Seattle while we were away to visit Anna and her new husband, John Boettiger, in their new house in the city where he had been rapidly promoted to publisher of Hearst's *Post-Intelligencer.*

Father hoped to see the Boettigers along with Sistie and Buzz at Hyde Park the coming summer. "I think we could pay for their trip—don't you?" he wrote Mother. "It will be a pity if they don't manage to come home once a year."

His spring fishing season ended when he took the train from Port Aransas to San Antonio for talks with more Texas bigwigs and a brief speech or two, then on to Austin for the same purposes. In San Antonio, a beanpole-thin young man whom I had met once or twice before approached me to ask a favor of Father. Lyndon Baines Johnson was fresh out of teachers' college and a Houston high school job when he originally worked in Washington as secretary to Texas Congressman Richard Kleberg of the King Ranch Klebergs, elected in 1931. Two years later, with a $2.50 ring from Sears Roebuck, he married Lady Bird Taylor. Now he had just completed eighteen months as state director of the National Youth Administration, which lent money for building schools and libraries for some hundred thousand students—a promising political-power base for a cocky go-getter like Lyndon.

When a special election had to be called to fill the Congressional seat in the Tenth District left vacant by Representative Buchanan's death, Lyndon's hat went straight into the ring. He was twenty-eight years old, hungry and already under the wing of Representative Sam Rayburn of Texas, House Majority Leader and an old friend of his father's. Contest for the seat ran hot. Lyndon's tactic was to place himself to the left of his more conservative rivals and convince his audiences that a vote for himself was a vote for Franklin D. Roosevelt.

He won handily, and now he wanted to have it appear that he had Father's blessing. What he sought from me was clearance to ride the Presidential train with him from San Antonio to Austin. "I'd really appreciate it," he said, "if we could slow down where there's people living close along the track, and maybe the President could stand on the rear platform with me beside him, giving a wave of his hand."

I was not sure about that. "Well, in that case," he said, "I could stand there by myself, waving as we went by, to show I was riding with the President."

Father could not resist such brass. Asking him to move to and fro between his private compartment and the swaying platform time and again was too much. But Lyndon was welcome to come aboard. The train could be slowed as requested. "I *will* keep my shade up and wave through the window," Father promised.

Lyndon spent the journey scurrying out onto the platform and back in again, overjoyed that, though Father did not explicitly endorse him, everyone in the Tenth District would know about the ride. He swiftly received another mark of my parent's esteem, a place on the House Naval Affairs Committee. He had other qualities besides energy that made him useful to Father. Lyndon would serve as a go-between in dealing with "Mister Sam," the Majority Leader. And Lyndon was a stalwart New Dealer in a state where conservative Democrats like Garner and Jesse Jones swung a lot of weight. The day was approaching when FDR would involve himself in yet another battle, this time inside his own party.

Father broke his journey home to spend a night at our Benbrook ranch. At an afternoon barbecue that we gave for him there, he met, as scheduled, the kingpins of the beef industry from Texas and the rest of the country, who converged on this gathering to convince the President that he should bar Argentine meat from the United States. Here was another instance of how a member of his family was employed to gain access to the President and corner him into listening to the persuasions of a pressure group. He took it all in good part; he was used to special-interest spokesmen homing in on him. My contribution was no more effective than my lobbying for the airlines' mail contracts had been. Father was as affable toward his fellow guests as ever, but the flow of canned beef from the Argentine continued into the United States without interruption.

He returned to the White House resigned to the fact that victory over the Court would take longer than anticipated. "Even if we have to part with some more of ultraconservative friends, we have the overwhelming majority of Democratic voters with us and a substantial majority of all the voters," he said.

The fight over the Court virtually monopolized Congress. Almost without exception, every other major piece of New Deal legislation was stalled in committee hearings. The business of government was bogged down in no-man's-land between Executive and Judiciary authority. The split among the Democrats deepened.

One week after the fishing trip ended, the opposition let off two more shots. At Burt Wheeler's prompting, Justice Van Devanter, aged seventy-eight, gave Father two weeks' notice of his retirement from the bench. Minutes later, the Senate Judiciary Committee voted 10 to 8 against the court-packing plan. Among the nays were six Democrats.

If Van Devanter's strategically timed resignation was a prelude to others, what was the need for Father's bill? If his own party could not agree on it, what were his chances of success? He could abide no longer by the counsel of Cummings and Richberg to stand pat. Compromise would have to be tried next. Perhaps he could pull together the divided Senators by nominating the majority leader, Joe Robinson of Arkansas, to the vacancy on the Court and saddle him meanwhile with the job of rounding up support for a watered-down version of the court-packing proposal, empowering the President to substitute no more than one justice a year and raising the age of compulsory retirement from the bench to seventy-five. Joe was willing. A place on the Supreme Court would be some kind of compensation for having lost the Vice Presidency, which he tried for in 1928 as Al Smith's running mate against Hoover and Charlie Curtis.

The intimidating coalition of minority Republicans and conservative Democrats gave other evidence of hostility, if not of pure spite. When Harry Hopkins lodged a request for a new Works Progress Administration appropriation, the House of Representatives cut his salary from twelve to ten thousand dollars a year. "It was a pleasant sight to see someone slap the smartalecky Harry Hopkins down," crowed one Washington *Post* columnist.

Slapping Harry was one way of getting at Father, who had pulled him so closely into the inner circle that many Washingtonians believed Hopkins was being groomed as the next President. At that time, Father had no thought whatsoever of a third term, though he was determined to live up to his promise to master "the forces of selfishness and of lust for power" by 1940. There lay the nub of his mounting problems with members of his party whose loyalties were divided between him and the enemy.

"Some of our Democratic 'friends' do not at all like the idea," he said, "that I may keep on making speeches and radio talks for the next three and a half years. They think that a second-term President should be duly grateful and retire into innocuous desuetude."

Harry's mixture of idealism and back-alley ruthlessness made him a first-class adjutant. He might be a political liability to Father, but he believed wholeheartedly in the New Deal. He, too, had been drawn in tight to help fill the emptiness created by the death of Louis, but there was an immeasurable difference between Harry and his predecessor. Louis' ambitions were only for Father. As early as the spring of 1937, Harry dreamed of winning his own way to the White House, and Father did nothing to discourage him.

So the counteragents of both parties singled out Hopkins for attack. Democrats tried to eradicate him as potential candidate in the interests of their own candidacies. Wallace undoubtedly envisaged himself as a future choice. So did Jesse Jones. Cordell Hull was not immune to hopes of the Presidency. Neither was Jim Farley, though he saw the Vice Presidency as his first step. Garner would have the priority claim to the party's supreme nomination next time around. He was sixty-seven years old, and 1944 would be too late.

At Uvalde, where he had gone to ground, the poker-faced old man began staking out the territory on which to challenge Father. The vacation in itself, taken when the Senate dispute was reaching a climax, was a clear sign that he disagreed with Father's plan. Jack lacked all enthusiasm for the New Deal as such. Except for their belief that big-money interests controlled the country, the two men had little in common. Garner nourished deep distrust of Eastern bankers—notably Andrew Mellon, who, by Jack's account, made himself an extra $1,000,000 while he was Hoover's Secretary of the Treasury—but the new breed of Texas bankers were not to be put in the same dark category.

Cactus Jack and Father were poles apart on the question of executive power. It must grow, in Father's opinion; it had grown too much already, according to Garner. He was against the outpouring of federal funds, against the new unionism and the epidemic of sit-down strikes. He was in favor of balanced budgets and a return to less spectacular ways of running the government. In many respects, apart from his party label, Jack was a good Republican.

Father needed all the help he could drum up. He tried to coax Jack into cutting short his vacation. "Frankly," he wrote him, "I honestly think you ought to be coming back pretty soon, timing it so that it would not be said that you were rushing back to save the amended Court Bill by trying to call off a filibuster. . . . I really think it would be fine if you would come back before the Bill reaches that stage, *i.e.* in a week or ten days. . . . I want to tell you again how I miss you because of you, yourself, and also because of the great help that you have given and continue to give to the working out *peacefully* of a mass of problems greater than the Nation has ever had before. So do come back very soon and make me and a whole lot of others very happy."

Jack remained in Uvalde. It took a funeral to bring him out of seclusion. In the sixth month of the struggle over the Court, Joe Robinson died of an overtaxed heart as he got out of bed one morning. Garner joined the mourners at Little Rock, Arkansas, and took the opportunity to sound out Senate colleagues on the Bill's prospects. When he reached Washington, he laid it on the line to Father: "You are beat. You haven't got the votes."

It fell to Jack to work out a last-ditch compromise. There was no evidence that he tried to rescue much from the wreckage. The shredded bill that Father reluctantly signed represented defeat for court-packing. And yet. . . .

A majority of the nine old men did approve the Social Security Act when it came up for survey. Father did get his first New Dealer onto the high bench when, as Van Devanter's successor, he appointed a dynamic Alabama lawyer, Senator Hugo Black; he was in such a hurry that he neglected to find out in advance that the new Justice had briefly belonged to the Ku Klux Klan.

By 1940, Father could claim, "I lost the battle, but I won the war." The Court had been made over on the pattern he desired. Five more of the original nine were gone—Brandeis,

Cardozo, Sutherland, Butler, and McReynolds. In their places sat Stanley Reed, Felix Frankfurter, William O. Douglas, Robert H. Jackson, and Frank Murphy, who once gave Hall Roosevelt a job in Detroit.

The mournful finale of the fight over the Court bill overlapped a program for striking out the "economic royalists" from a different angle. The shrinking of his own net income under the impact of higher taxes was a powerful factor in Father's shying away from a third term. The family budget was no closer to being balanced than the nation's, and Granny was digging deeper and deeper into her capital. He knew for a fact that he could earn more money in retirement than as President.

Flagrant tax evasion by the rich infuriated him. He had the evidence on his desk, and he yearned to publish a list of the biggest names, which included Vincent Astor along with Colonel Robert McCormick, owner of the rabidly hostile Chicago *Tribune*, and some of the du Ponts. These last names caused him some mischievous delight. Franklin Jr. was engaged to marry Miss Ethel du Pont of Wilmington, Delaware, as soon as he graduated from Harvard. To shield him from any suspicion that he was marrying only for money, Father would continue to support him while he went through the University of Virginia law school.

On the first day of June, my hard-pressed parent recommended to Congress a new law designed to combat tax-dodging. In the accompanying message, he had a dig at the wealthy who incorporated their yachts as a method of frustrating the Internal Revenue Service, and we wondered exactly whom he had in mind.

One week later, the Croesus of Wall Street himself, John Pierpont Morgan, was interviewed by shipboard reporters on his return from England. "Congress," he rumbled, "should know how to levy taxes, and if it doesn't know how to collect them, then a man is a fool to pay the taxes. . . . You only do what you are compelled to do by the law, for it is never any pleasure for anyone to pay taxes."

Father's wrath rose by degrees. "What do you think of JPM's exposition of Christianity when he landed the other day?" he asked one distinguished attorney, Charles Burlingham. "How many Englishmen occupying a similar position in London would publicly express the same ethical viewpoint? And, incidentally, what British courts have ever handed down opinions on tax avoidance or tax evasion similar to the opinions of some of our courts with which you are doubtless familiar? Finally, ask yourself what Christ would say about the American bench and bar were he to return today."

I fancied that there was a quizzical glint in his eyes when he presented himself along with Mother in Wilmington for Franklin Jr.'s wedding. If ever there was a lions' den, it was the mansion of the parents of the bride. The du Ponts undoubtedly wished that her choice could have fallen on someone more to their taste than a son of that man in the White House. The bridegroom comported himself very well, though they could scarcely help feeling that Ethel was marrying into the most horrendous family in the land.

In top hat and morning coat, Father carried it off in great style. He greeted every du Pont within range like an old friend, even though he did allow that the press of duty would oblige him to leave the reception somewhat early. To one and all, he said in as many words: "Come on down to the White House at any time. I'll be glad to sit down with you so that we can take a look at your problems."

The sins of the tax evaders continued to stir his scorn. A Harvard classmate of his, Alexander Forbes, now a professor of physiology at the medical school there, ventured to speak up for Morgan in a letter to the Boston *Herald* and then send Father a clipping. Since one of Forbes' aunts had married into Uncle Ted's family, the professor's sentiments might be taken as those of the Oyster Bay branch as a whole.

"Look," he wrote, "at the sorry spectacle presented by long rows of beneficiaries of the 'boondoggle,' leaning on their shovels by the hour, at futile projects, and contrast it with the great universities, museums and research laboratories which have come from the wise and generous giving of such as Morgan, and then consider which is the major constructive force in building a stable civilization."

Father took aim and replied. "Your argument is perfectly clear to me," he told Forbes, "and put in very simple English it is this:

It is true that under a representative form of government the Congress of duly elected Senators and Representatives has passed certain tax laws. I do not agree with this method of taxation. It is true that the same Congress has made appropriations for many purposes. I consider many of these appropriations are for futile projects. Therefore, because I do not agree with laws passed by a majority, I have a perfect right to evade or avoid any of the taxes just so long as I can get away with it!

My dear cousin and old classmate—that being your belief, I do not hesitate to brand you as one of the worst anarchists in the United States. And, incidentally, I use "anarchist" in its pure Greek sense. You are saying in your letter to the Boston Herald—"let every man who does not agree with the law violate the law at his discretion."

Other men's tax returns continued to fascinate Father in the thirties. He was convinced that Al Smith, for example, who kept up his sniping on the Liberty League's behalf, was in the pay of the "big fellows." He made no effort to take a private peek at Al's income picture, but he was more than interested in the returns of some Senators who talked with no other voice but that of big business. His curiosity was piqued by no more than a handful of them. That was one difference between him and one of his successors, who between 1969 and 1973 prompted ninety-nine Internal Revenue Service investigations of "ideological, militant, subversive and radical organizations," which included the Urban League, the National Council of Churches, and the John Birch Society.

In one case, at least, Father's curiosity took a further turn. Boake Carter was one of the currently popular strains of radio commentators who jumbled news and editorializing together to the point where it became impossible for a listener to distinguish between them. The craft had produced a dozen or so national celebrities such as Walter Winchell, Drew Pearson, and H. V. Kaltenborn, all classifiable as "liberal," Carter and Fulton Lewis Jr., who were rightists. I had some familiarity with the business, since I preceded Lewis as a commentator on the Mutual Broadcasting System network.

Carter's speciality was the Far East, where, he alleged, administration "meddling" was risking United States involvement in war with Japan. Father classed Carter with Father Coughlin as a liar and menace to the democratic process. He ordered an undercover investigation of the commentator's record, not forgetting his tax returns, and he mentioned to Frances Perkins that he would be happy if she could discover that Carter, an alien, had no right to be in America. Either the results of the checks were disappointing, or Father decided to stay his hand. Carter went on harassing him, unrestrained.

The Japanese extended the frontiers of war that summer. A clash with Chinese guards at the Marco Polo Bridge near Peking provided Tokyo with the pretext for a major incursion into China. The inglorious response of American isolationists was to demand the complete withdrawal of United States troops and businessmen, too, from Chinese territory. Clamor for peace at any price in the Orient produced a problem which was to become exceedingly familiar in the years ahead—an attempt by America's armed forces to make their own policies.

Admiral Harry Yarnell, commander of the United States Asiatic Fleet, informed his officers that no ships under his command would be withdrawn; they would stand by to protect and help Americans in China. The Navy Department compounded this usurping of Presidential prerogative by relaying his statement to reporters here. The first Father knew of the affair came from his breakfasttime newspapers.

In a rare ill humor, he snapped at Cordell Hull, "Will you let me know confidentially just what happened and whether the announcement was made with your approval or not?"

The answer was Not. No one in the State Department had any knowledge of Yarnell's outburst until the statement was released in China. Now, said Hull, State had concluded that it should not intervene. The problem was a matter for Navy and Yarnell on one hand, and Navy and Commander in Chief Franklin D. Roosevelt on the other.

True to a solid tradition in the armed forces, the admirals and the generals who ran both the Army and its Air Corps were scheming again to find ways of eliminating civilian control. At about this time, the armchair brass in the Navy Department were buttonholing Congressmen about the possibilities of setting up a General Staff to undermine sickly old Claude Swanson.

It was a kite that had been flown every few years since the time Father was Assistant Navy Secretary. Swanson was equipped neither by health nor practical experience to haul it in. Father would take over in "watching the situation out of the corner of my eye," he said. Claude received a gentle hint about what to do: "I think it would be a good idea to pass the word down the line through Operations and Navigation that any-body caught lobbying for a General Staff will be sent to Guam!"

The Navy had more substantial business to attend to. Japan's thrusts into Manchuria and now China were proof of the brutal effectiveness of her armies in their undeclared war. Her rapidly evolving sea power was untried as yet, but the day seemed bound to come when Japanese battleships and aircraft carriers would test their strength somewhere in the Pacific. Suddenly, the atolls and specks of land stippling that vast ocean acquired new importance for the major powers. They would make bases for warplanes.

Canton Island, in the Phoenix group, lying roughly halfway between Honolulu and Fiji, was a case in point. Sea birds had been its only inhabitants for more than a century, apart from a twenty-year stretch beginning in 1860 when Americans occu-pied the place to collect, sack, and export guano. This June, Canton Island looked so enticing to both American and British high commands that the two countries claimed it simultaneous-ly.

An expedition of United States astronomers had landed there, finding it an ideal spot for telescopic probes of the night skies. When New Zealanders arrived with a war sloop to back them in ordering the sky-watchers off the island, Father's dan-der was aroused again. On his orders, researchers combed the old records of American whalers that put out from Nantucket, Gloucester, and New Bedford between 1791 and 1828. Sure enough, Canton Island had been discovered by some of them in those years.

As something of an old salt himself and a lawyer, too, Father knew that this was not a decisive factor. He delivered a pocket lecture at one Cabinet meeting to make the point clear to Hull, whose perceptions were sometimes sluggish. "Discovery," said Father, "does not constitute national possession for the country to which the discovery should belong unless discovery is fol-lowed within a reasonable period of time by permanent occupa-tion." Two decades of guano trading were insignificant. "A purely temporary occupation . . . does not give sovereignty to the country to which the guano company belongs."

What he recommended was to call Britain's bluff. Canton Island had been unoccupied for years. "It is open to occupancy to us today," he declared in a subsequent memo to the Secretary of State. "I suggest immediate action from Honolulu." In blunter words, have the United States fleet claim the island.

Father's opinions of the British were at a low ebb and still descending. Stanley Baldwin had survived as Prime Minister until the coronation in May of George VI, who reigned only because Baldwin had demanded his elder brother's abdication as the price for marrying Mrs. Simpson. The Westminster Abbey ceremony involved our ambassador, Bob Bingham, in a dilemma which Father facetiously referred to as "the famous case of Trousers vs. Breeches." Bob had elected to wear striped trousers, until the Lord Chamberlain stipulated that knee breeches were *de rigueur* for the London diplomatic corps, including the current Soviet envoy, Max Litvinov.

Bob received a consoling note from the White House. "My ruling is," wrote my parent, an authority on almost everything, "that Ambassadors should wear trousers unless the Sovereign of the State to which he is accredited makes a personal demand for knee-breeches. I am fortified in this ruling by the pictures I have seen of Comrade Litvinov in the aforesaid short pants. If Soviet Russia can stand it I guess we can too."

Baldwin's replacement, beak-nosed Neville Chamberlain, was largely unknown except by name to Father. He thought it would be useful to see the new British leader at close quarters, so he extended him an invitation to come to Washington in the interests of the United States and Britain cooperating to promote peace and stability among nations.

Chamberlain turned down the idea, cloaking his rejection with the polite excuse that more time was essential to lay the groundwork for such a meeting, which, held too hurriedly, could only raise false hopes in Europe. It was the Prime Minister, in fact, who was motivated by false hope—and groundless fears.

British service chiefs, along with the rest of the world's, grossly overcalculated German air strength. They accepted Hitler's word about the destructive might of the Luftwaffe. They estimated that German bombing could be kept up for sixty days nonstop, to kill 600,000 Britons and injure twice that many. In the previous year, if Winston Churchill were to be believed, Germany spent 12,000,000 Reichsmarks to rearm. Hitler bragged that his arms budget ran to 90,000,000 marks. The real figure, revealed subsequently, was 40,000,000, spread over the six years preceding March, 1939.

Chamberlain took it to be his mission to make a deal with Hitler so as to stave off British disaster. He dared not risk antagonizing him in advance by first talking with another world leader on the far side of the Atlantic who by no stretch of imagination could be considered friendly toward the Nazis.

Churchill's influence on British affairs fell to zero. He had been a leader of "the King's men," who resisted Edward VIII's abdication and hoped, instead, to topple Baldwin. Churchill now was totally discredited, a man spurned by every political party, his career apparently over. In the wilderness, he preached that Hitler was bent on war and Britain must prepare to defend herself, but the Prime Minister and the vast majority of his government were set on appeasement. In private, Father allowed that he hoped for a "a little more unselfish spine" in the British Foreign Office.

He also had hopes that Mussolini might yet be kept out of Hitler's pocket. When at last he answered the Italian's nine-month-old letter, he felt "confident, my dear Duce, that you share with me the fear that the trend of the present international situation is ominous to peace." He dangled the notion of a face-to-face meeting between the two of them without actually offering an invitation. "We both realize the great difficulties that stand in the way," but "some day you and I must and shall meet in person." As early as 1937, Father never questioned his gifts for winning over anyone to his point of view once they sat down together.

The air force chiefs of the Western powers escalated their demands for money to spend every time they revised their estimates of the Luftwaffe's striking power. They took it as a truism that bombers would always get through, as Baldwin had said, and that the only defense was retaliation. Building bombers must have priority over the battleships, submarines, tanks and all other traditional weapons of war.

In this respect, the United States was badly handicapped. It had no independent air command. The Air Corps, such as it was, belonged to the Army. The new generation of Army Air Corps officers, like Hap Arnold, Carl Spaatz and Ira Eaker, all felt that the regular Army was stifling them, blind to the vital importance of long-range bombers. In the view of the older generation entrenched at the top, aircraft had a purely tactical mission to perform, in support of men on the ground.

Father took counsel from the young mavericks and came up with a characteristic compromise. It was rare for him to interfere in Army policymaking. The Navy was something else, since the Commander in Chief knew the ins and outs of that department. He sensed the inevitability of war in Europe. He would do his best within the strict limits set by Congress to employ whatever moral force the United States could exercise to stave off the conflict. In the meantime, the country should be made ready for any eventuality. Since bombers were called for by men whose word he accepted, bombers would be built as a third arm.

He gave the junior generals autonomy to develop a strategic air force against the day when it might be needed. Aircraft factories began tooling up to produce the planes, giants of the era, which later became the legendary B-17's, B-24's, and B-29's of future war.

One more omen of trouble ahead with Japan appeared before the summer was over. A flotilla of Japanese vessels showed up in the Bering Sea. They were crab fishing, according to Tokyo, and instructing students aboard in the pursuit of salmon. One of the academic craft was accompanied by eleven other trawlers, the other by eight or nine support ships. Father was sufficiently intrigued to call for action from Admiral Bill Leahy, his purse-lipped Chief of Naval Operations, due to retire in two more years. He had spent nearly half a century in the Navy, with service in the Spanish-American War, in putting down the Philippine rebellion of 1899, and in China during the Boxer Rebellion.

"It seems to me," Father told him, "that we have almost enough to go on to have a counter-study made to see what this particular area could be used for by the Japanese in the event of war, and what should be done by us in our plans to counteract it."

9

An omen of a different kind could be sighted on Wall Street. For no obvious reason, stock prices started to slide. There was nothing at first to cause Cabinet alarm, and Father clung to his ambition of balancing the federal budget for the coming year, since tax receipts were running ahead of estimates and $400,000,000 were being cut in government spending.

The decline accelerated. Waves of selling forced down stocks close to Depression levels. Father began saying that "if" not "when" the budget could be balanced, he would try to have a museum wing added to the east of the White House. But Ma Perkins assured him that Labor Department projections indicated that the worst would soon be over. Father concluded that he might conveniently take another "look-see" at the country to scent the mood of the people and keep his contacts with local party men warm.

During the next two weeks, the Presidential Special trundled across the continent to the Northwest Pacific states and back. He drew crowds every bit as big and enthusiastic as if he had been in the thick of an election campaign. So far as he could tell, his defeat in the Court battle had cost him nothing in popular support. He wished that the newspapermen aboard would concentrate more on the simple speeches he made in meeting halls and from the train's rear platform instead of feeding their readers columns about "whether I shake hands with Mr. X with my left hand, or looked away when Mr. Y greeted me, or spent forty seconds longer talking with Mr. Z than with his colleague," but he was reconciled to that kind of reporting.

"It would be a lot cheaper," he told Steve Early, "if all your newspapers would hire Walter Winchell and save railroad fares." Walter was in Father's camp as a Sunday-evening radio gossip and in his daily column.

My parent saved his fireworks for Chicago, stronghold of isolationism and the last stop on the trip. He had sweated out the speech he was to deliver there with Sam Rosenman, Tommy the Cork, and Don Richberg, boiling down and polishing the words, because he expected to cause a sensation. Harold Ickes contributed the key thought: "quarantine."

The occasion was the dedication of a new Public Works Administration bridge, the subject was war and peace. Ten percent of the world's people were threatening the peace, freedom, and security of the remaining 90 percent, Father declared. "The peace-loving nations must make a concerted effort in opposition to those violations of treaties and those ignorings of humane instincts which today are creating a state of international anarchy and instability from which there is no escape through mere isolationism or neutrality."

Then came the crucial words that leaped from the next editions' headlines: "When an epidemic of physical disease starts to spread, the community approves and joins in a *quarantine* of the patients in order to protect the health of the community against the spread of the disease." The administration was seeking "to minimize our risk of involvement, but we cannot have complete protection in a world of disorder in which confidence and security have broken down." The crowd cheered so loudly it was hard to believe that the significance of what they had just heard had sunk in.

He had taken a first cautious step toward educating the country about the realities of the danger facing America. The response was pretty much what he anticipated. Germany and Japan took violent exception to his words. Britain, France, and the Soviet Union applauded. At home, six prominent pacifist groups, including the No-Foreign-War Crusade, which Mother served as a keynote speaker, complained that he was marching the United States down the same road that led to war in 1917. A Philadelphia *Inquirer* poll of Congress registered two-to-one opposition to America's taking common action with the League of Nations in the new Far East crisis. Some Congressmen, breathing fire, talked about impeaching Father. On most of the population, the speech apparently made no impact whatever.

"I am fighting against a public psychology of long standing," he recognized privately, "A philosophy which comes very close to saying 'Peace at any price'." He thought there might have been more criticism, which would be preferable to apathy. "It's a terrible thing," he said to Sam, "to look over your shoulder when you are trying to lead—and to find no one there."

More, much more, must be done to instill something of his own thinking and his own confidence into the people of the United States. He could do that. "I verily believe," he wrote, "that as time goes on we can slowly but surely make people realize that war will be a greater danger to us if we close all the doors and windows than if we go out in the street and use our influence to curb the riot."

There was no letup in the cascade of stock market prices. At the first Cabinet meeting after the Western trip, he reported to his colleagues on what he had seen. Conditions, he had found, were "good." Some of those around the octagonal table still prattled about "a corrective dip." His recommendation was to "sit tight and keep quiet," but not for anyone to make Pollyanna statements along Herbert Hoover lines, promising that recovery was just around the corner.

Down, down went the market until averages had fallen from a high of 120 to a low of 81 by the year's end. New Deal recovery programs had pushed up national income from $46 billion under Hoover to a present $68 billion. Farm income stood at $8.5 billion, almost exactly double the 1932 figure. Wages and salaries had soared from $31 to $42 billion. Corporate profits had experienced a swing of more than $10 billion, from $4 billion in deficits to $6.5 billion in black ink. Was all this to be lost?

Henry Morgenthau's nerves, never strong, began to crack. He showed signs of sharing the panic which was taking over in the financial community. "We are headed right into another

Depression," he advised Father and added the usual question: "What are we going to do about it?"

Father tolerated almost anything from Henry. He liked to tease him with such admonitions as, "Be sure not to get the plus and minus signs mixed up." He tried to calm his anxiety with a frivolous memorandum: "When you were getting all that money out of me Monday morning while I was in bed, I forgot to tell that Jim Townley would be very grateful to get some money from you. . . ." Roosevelt of Hyde Park and Morgenthau of Fishkill both pledged an annual $750 to the Dutchess County Democratic organization: chairman, Jim Townley.

The "Pres" could not yet get very excited about what he called "the Stock Exchange debacle." One reason was his system of conducting private spot-checks of conditions as they affected ordinary citizens, which had produced an encouraging report. In a sample community in upstate New York, 108 families out of a total 150 had been pummeled by the 1929 crash because they bought stocks on margin. Last week's poll showed only six of them in that predicament.

"The present decline," said Father, "has directly hit only a comparatively small number of people who insist on continuing to speculate with margin accounts."

He was mistaken. Stock prices went on sliding. The business of America was going rapidly downhill again. Production was down, and unemployment was mounting toward the ten million mark.

When he came to analyze the position, he found the cause but not the immediate solution. He saw what he described as "an unconscious conspiracy" on the part of the economic royalists to force his hand. The big investors were pulling out of the market and drying up the supply of risk capital. They had found an infinitely more effective weapon than rumors about insanity to smite him with. What they triumphantly berated as the "Roosevelt recession" was a counterattack on everything the New Deal had accomplished in controlling big business and the banks. They had turned on the man who had proved to be their salvation in 1933. They were out to blackmail him, compelling him to roll back taxes, slash relief spending, call off the policing operations of the Securities and Exchange Commission, put down the strikers, and curb the unions.

Their determination to do battle was sparked by two circumstances. One was the crackdown on corporate and individual tax evasion, not yet six months old. The other was a brand-new poll, addressed to editors and leaders of industry, business, and labor, asking whom they foresaw as the Democratic candidate in 1940. The overwhelming opinion was that Father would be the nominee and the first third-term President. Missy was delighted to pass along that piece of news.

The Roosevelt-abominators could not stomach the thought. They wanted the lost days of privilege and power restored to them, and they stood ready to reduce the country to chaos again to achieve their desire. With Father discredited as Hoover had been, they could make sure that the next man in the White House, Democrat or Republican, was a manipulable puppet, a Mussolini for preference, a Hitler if need be. It was a pity that the Kingfish was dead, because he would have been perfect for the purpose. Coughlin and Gerald L. K. Smith were pale imitations, but Detroit money and railroad money kept them in full voice as part of the strategy.

On Wall Street, one corporation lawyer started a fund-raising drive, with full attendant publicity, to put together a $1,000,000 purse for dangling in front of Father as an inducement to resign. He should presumably be grateful for such consideration, so much more humanitarian than other men's talk about seeing him assassinated.

He could smell the cause of the manufactured pandemonium, but how to cure it remained uncertain. Priming the pump with billions of federal dollars had been the treatment prescribed four years ago, to make jobs, stimulate spending, and reopen padlocked factories. This time, "reflation" was perhaps the wrong medicine, as Morgenthau said. Driving prices up again would hit hardest at that third of the nation to whom Father had pledged his help—the ill-housed, ill-clad, ill-nourished. The best means of protecting them and the rest of the country in the present storm was to balance the budget, even if he had to crack the whip over spendthrifts on Capitol Hill to get that done.

"If the Congress exceeds my budget estimates, which will provide a balanced budget, the Congress can stay in session or come back once a week in special session throughout the full year until they give me additional taxes to make up the loss," he said.

When he summoned the lawmakers into special session in mid-November, he did not play with words to hide the truth. "Since your adjournment in August," he told them, "there has been a marked *recession*. . . ." He had nothing revolutionary to propose as a palliative: a national farm act; a wages-and-hours bill; a regional planning program; a plan for streamlining the government, whose enactment would call for vigorous pushing from Senator James F. Byrnes of South Carolina, chairman of the Committee on Reorganization. That push was not supplied. When Congress went home for Christmas, not one of the four bills had come up to a vote.

Toward the end of November, Father resolved on a private meeting with representatives of those interests that were tightening the screws on the market. He invited a number of big businessmen to Hyde Park. So far as I can discover, no record was kept of what either side told the other. His patience was thinner than normal as the result of a jaw infection. A subtle hardening of his overall personality was discernible to those of us who knew him best. Father was showing battle scars. Nothing indicated that a truce was even considered. In the matter of his health, he felt, he said, "rather like a boiled owl."

His jaw still bothered him when he left for the Florida keys and another brief fishing bout in the wallowing *Potomac*. Ross McIntire went along to apply surgical dressings morning and night. Jimmy and Pat Watson were in the party, as well as Assistant Attorney General Robert Jackson, destined for the Supreme Court one day. Ickes and Hopkins completed the group, but their feud was suspended for the present.

Harry had lost his wife, Barbara, a few weeks earlier. He had known there was no cure for her cancer, and he was not sure whether there might be for his own suspected case. Harold, a widower himself for two years, had him to stay at his Maryland farm while he pondered and mourned. When the *Potomac* sailed home again, Harry would go to the Mayo Clinic in Rochester, Minnesota, to have half his stomach cut away. Meantime, five-year-old Diana Hopkins found a new godmother. She must live at the White House, my mother said, and feel that she was one of our family, to be treated just like another grandchild.

It was singularly joyless cruise. The infection left Father so listless that he could scarcely bother to cast a line. The last vestige of joy disappeared when they reached the little harbor of old Fort Jefferson, where Dr. Samuel Mudd spent four years imprisoned for doctoring John Wilkes Booth's broken leg after he killed Lincoln. A radiogram from Cordell Hull intimated that Japan would probably declare open war on China within the next few days. Demands by Tokyo for the withdrawal of all United States land and sea forces from China would almost certainly follow. Congress would call for another proclamation of American neutrality, "which," said Father despondently, "will actually favor the Japs." There seemed to be no stopping the advance of the Axis powers, east or west.

He cut short the cruise to head straight for Washington to have his jaw X-rayed and lanced. At the Mayo Clinic, Harry survived surgery, though the operation left him literally prone to starvation through malnutrition, and then went to Joe Kennedy's Florida house to recuperate. One clue to my parent's financial straits and Granny's role as Santa Claus came in a note he scribbled to her: "Ever so many thanks for the check. It is far too much—so I will straighten it out when I get back." Another clue showed itself in the gift he had bought Mother on her past birthday—a fur lining for a cloth coat. "I hope it keeps you warm," he said, "but it ain't much of a present."

The expected declaration of war on China did not come, but Japan tried the first serious test of American resolve. On December 12, Japanese bombers flew over the United States gunboat *Panay* twenty miles up the Yangtze from Nanking. To identify herself as a neutral in a battle zone, the ship had two large Stars and Stripes painted on her upper deck. She was sunk by Japanese bombs, along with three Standard Oil tankers on a delivery run.

Father had Hull into his office the next morning to instruct him what to tell the Japanese ambassador at a scheduled one o'clock meeting. The line must be firm enough but reasonable. It was "hoped" that Tokyo would "be considering definitely . . . full expressions of regret," full compensation, and guarantees that similar attacks would not occur in future.

When the Japanese claimed the sinkings had been an unfortunate mistake, the State Department submitted the findings of

an official United States Navy inquiry that pinned the blame
where it lay. Two days before Christmas, Japan complied with
each of Father's wishes, still protesting that the bombings were
to be taken as pilot's error in identification.

In the middle of this confrontation by diplomacy, a titillating
new rumor about the man in the White House floated around
the clubs and fashionable cocktail lounges: Father had died
aboard the *Potomac*, and his body lay hidden in the sand of Dry
Tortugas in the Florida keys.

Not every Republican joined in the chorus of hate. A notable
exception was Henry Stimson, Secretary of War under William
Howard Taft, Secretary of State under Hoover, and a pillar of
integrity in Father's eyes. As President-elect, he had arranged
through Felix Frankfurter, with Hoover's approval, to have
Stimson up to Hyde Park for an extended briefing session, covering disarmament, war debts and, most important, the Far
East. The old statesman's attitude toward Japan had hardened
as far back as September, 1931, when Japanese troops grabbed
Mukden as a prelude to overrunning all Manchuria. Stimson
proposed to respond with force and an economic blockade in
cooperation with the League of Nations, but Hoover's isolationism would not countenance any such thing.

At the present juncture, Henry and Father were in total
agreement that China's cause was also ours and a neutrality act
for the Far East would only help the Japanese invaders. Stimson urged that the United States go it alone in aiding the Chinese. That was something Congress would never condone, but
Henry was a man of conviction, to be kept in mind for some future day.

Not every business Goliath took part in the conspiracy on the
stock market. One or two of the more enlightened were willing
to help look for ways out of the current dilemma. There might
be more imaginative solutions than Morgenthau's dream of a
balanced budget. Father was persuaded of that after Henry the
Morgue was hooted down for advocating his pet theory in a
speech at the Academy of Political Science in New York.

Father welcomed a proposal made by two senior New Dealers, Rex Tugwell and Adolf Berle. They would invite a handful
of the top men in industry, finance, and labor to work out a
different means of halting the slide into a second Depression.

Acceptances came from Owen Young of General Electric; Tom Lamont, Harvard, 1892, and a J. P. Morgan partner; Charles Taussig, president of the American Molasses Company; Philip Murray and John L. Lewis of the Congress for Industrial Organization.

Lewis' participation had been uncertain. He felt that he had been cheated out of the nearly $500,000 he donated to the 1936 campaign. Where was the expected payoff from Father? Lewis' letters to Ma Perkins went unanswered. He had not even been extended the courtesy of being allowed to nominate an Assistant Secretary of Labor. In their sit-down strikes against management, Father had declined to say a word in support of the unions. Only an ingrate would exclaim, like Father, "A plague on both your houses," which stung all the more because it was a quotation from Shakespeare, whose lines the Ohio Welshman loved to spout.

The previous Labor Day, Lewis had poured on the rhetoric: "It ill behooves one who has supped in labor's house to curse with equal fervor and fine impartiality both labor and its adversaries when they become locked in deadly embrace."

There was an additional, more personal reason for his discontent. As the result of an oversight by one of Missy's assistants, Lewis was omitted from a White House luncheon for labor leaders and invited only to a reception that followed. "He who tooteth not his own horn, the same shall not be tooted" was an aphorism he set great store by, and he blew a blast of anger.

By way of appeasing him, he was asked to bring his wife to tea with my parents. Some urgent family business took Mother off out of town just before the Lewises arrived. Missy poured tea that day, which John L. interpreted as a second deliberate slight. Forever after, he was lost as an ally of the President, whom he derided as a tricky weakling, to Cousin Alice's joy.

But he sat in at the meetings that Tugwell and Berle arranged and did not argue with the general conclusion that, Wall Street debacle or not, "No one must starve." Balancing the budget must be a secondary consideration. Father did not entirely trust this little council of advisers. Perhaps they, too, should hear the crack of a whip over their heads. He had a couple of suggestions for Rex Tugwell:

"One thing that might be brought out: the control of business through the holding company method. I think it is probably true that the electric utilities have thirteen billions of securities outstanding but are controlled by the owners of six hundred millions of securities. If that is true in the case of a utility, it is probably equally true in most other large industrial groups.

"Also, if you want to throw a bit more of a scare you can point out that there is growing sentiment on the Hill for the government to own the Federal Reserve banks and have these banks make direct loans when the private banks appear to be shutting down on credit. We are, of course, against it but it is a growing sentiment in the small towns and more remote sections."

Christmas in the White House was subdued. "We all had great fun with Diana," said a note to Harry Hopkins in Florida. "She is a lovely youngster and stole the show." There was a tree, of course, and a turkey, which Father carefully carved into paper-thin slices as a matter of pride in the skill, and economical besides. It was a day for an extra drink in celebration. "How about another little sippy?" he would say as he stirred the martinis or his own special formula for rum punch. "Love thy neighbor and thine enemy, too" was the gist of his message to the nation.

The New Year brought another attempt on his part to stiffen Neville Chamberlain's approach to Hitler. Father still felt that an international conference, possibly under United States auspices, where every country's grievances could be ventilated, was a workable idea. He took Hull's advice and offered that thought to the Prime Minister. Chamberlain turned him down flat again. He had already sent Halifax to Berlin to assure Der Führer that German claims to Danzig, Austria, and Czechoslovakia could be resolved in his favor so long as "far-reaching disturbances" were avoided.

As before, Chamberlain used the excuse of needing more time to give his "measure of appeasement" of Germany and Italy a chance to bear fruit. Privately, he allowed, "It is always best and safest to count on nothing from the Americans but words." His reply went off while his Foreign Secretary, Anthony Eden, was vacationing in the south of France. One month later, Eden resigned, in protest, and Halifax succeeded him.

Eden hankered after a personal meeting with Father in the belief that it would have what he termed "a steadying effect upon the dictators," but there was no chance of that. Churchill, looking back a decade later, termed Chamberlain's action "the loss of the last frail chance to save the world from tyranny otherwise than by war," but that was Churchillian exaggeration. British government leaders lacked the will to stand up to the German bogeyman for fear that the Luftwaffe could bomb England into ruins, and the American President lacked authority to support such a stand. And even if he had Congressional approval, what could actually be done? Rearmed Germany was a land power, the mightiest in Europe, but the Reich lay more than 3,000 miles from America's Atlantic seaboard, far beyond the range of United States striking forces, which were uniformly feeble. Economic sanctions were a possible countermeasure, but too many businessmen in Britain, the United States, France, and elsewhere in the Western world were trading with the Germans to make an embargo a serious consideration.

What else was left? Nothing but the intangible influence of moral indignation if by some miracle it could be aroused on a worldwide basis. His own indignation about the evils of dictatorships made that seem worth a try to Father. Through Missy's "Catholic mafia," he contacted George Cardinal Mundelein, the liberal-minded priest who headed the diocese of Chicago. He was asked to sound out the Vatican about a special envoy of the President being assigned to Rome as the first step toward enlisting Pope Pius XI in an organized outcry against international aggression. Likelihood of success was as dim as the catacombs. The Church openly backed Franco, whose ultimate victory as the savior of Spain from the Reds seemed ever more certain.

Chamberlain's flabby response marked a turn in my parent's thinking about the closeness of war. Perhaps peace could not survive the coming summer. The pace of American preparedness was perilously slow. He must push harder to have men and machines in better shape for the sure day when Europe would catch fire again. There were new ambassadors to appoint for Berlin and London; Hugh Wilson, who had been our minister in Switzerland, to succeed Dodd in Germany, Joe Kennedy, rich and socially ambitious, to replace Bingham at the Court of St. James's.

As soon as Joe had established himself in the London embassy, Father joshed him: "When you find that British accent creeping up on you and your trousers riding up to the knee, take the first steamer home for a couple of weeks' holiday."

He conferred with "Black Jack" Pershing, the only officer since Washington to hold the title of General of the Armies, about bringing the ground forces closer to par. He virtually took over running the Navy from his White House desk, delving into the fine details of building ships of war and recruiting their crews. One order called for buying up civilian powered-yachts for use as patrol boats, just as they had been utilized in the last war, when Father sold his auxiliary schooner, *Half Moon*, at a knockdown price.

On January 28, a message to Congress requested $800,000,000 for more ships, and the isolationists had another field day. A Navy of the size he contemplated was meant for action overseas, not for defending the shores of America, they proclaimed. Church groups and pacifist organizations joined in deluging the White House with protests against his "hysterical" rearmament policy and his "counsel of despair."

On Capitol Hill, a move was under way to forge another shackle to limit Presidential ability to conduct foreign policy. In the past eleven months, support had grown for amending the Constitution so that, even after a declaration of war by Congress, only the approval of a majority of voters in a national referendum could make it legal, the exception being actual invasion of the United States. An Indiana Democrat, Louis Ludlow, introduced the resolution. When it came before the House, it was defeated by a narrow 209 to 188, but Ludlow and his followers refused to let the matter die there.

Father passed some thoughts on the subject along to Jimmy. "National defense is a current, day-to-day problem of administration in the hands of the President under our Constitution, and it has been on the whole wisely administered. The safeguard is that war shall not be entered into except by Congressional sanction. National defense represents too serious a danger, especially in these modern times when distance has been annihilated, to permit delay. . . ." Vietnam did not exist in 1938; French Indochina was simply a faraway slice of France's colonial empire.

On the Chinese mainland, Nanking fell to the Japanese. The

invading troops celebrated with a rampage of looting and arson that wrecked the property of Americans all over occupied China. Father promptly urged on Hull the idea of making Japan accountable in dollars for her soldiers' crimes by holding Japanese-owned real estate within the United States in escrow until the damage had been paid for.

The momentum of Axis victories quickened, helped by the kind of mutual aid so flagrantly evident in Spain. Rumors reached the White House that Mussolini was sending planes and pilots to Japan. On February 4, Hitler in a bloodless purge rid his Foreign Office of its few surviving old-time diplomats and his army of those generals who spoke up against war. A month later, as Commander in Chief, he sent his tanks rolling unimpeded into Austria.

Father said nothing in public. It fell to Mother to drum home the lesson she read in the dictators' easy picking off one country after another. "Nobody can save his own skin alone," she preached in lecture after lecture. "We must all hang together." But she knew the message went unheeded.

Behind the scenes, he continued to fit together a preparedness program in bits and pieces, like somebody starting on a jigsaw. The actions of the State, Navy, and War should be synchronized, so Hull set up a liaison committee, under strict orders to minimize its importance to the outside world and keep its discussions secret lest the isolationists accuse the White House of taking a further step toward war. Father had State open discussions with the British to make air bases on Canton Island and neighboring Enderbury available to both countries as refueling stops between Hawaii and the South Pacific, while he simultaneously laid claim to any other unoccupied Pacific island "we decide we want to use."

He still kept his silence over the seizure of Austria. The "Roosevelt recession" was the primary reason for that. For him to speak his mind about Hitler might set the market diving more precipitously. "I hear disturbing reports that some people with politics as a foremost consideration really don't want much in the way of recovery until next winter," he told Walter Teagle, board chairman of Standard Oil of New Jersey.

The problems of Nazi aggression and domestic recession dovetailed, in Father's analysis. The forces behind the business slump and the forces that would strike a deal with Hitler were one and the same. "They would really like me to be a Neville Chamberlain," he decided, "and if I would promise that, the market would go up and they would work positively and actively for the resumption of prosperity. But if that were done, we would only be breeding far more serious trouble four or eight years from now."

He mulled over the question of who would lead the dual struggle for peace abroad and recovery at home when he stepped down three years hence. His intention to retire had not changed. Mother was as adamant as ever on the subject of a third term. "You know I do *not* believe in it," she used to tell him. The candidate he hoped would fill his shoes was Harry Hopkins. It was a personal decision in which Mother was not consulted.

"I saw no one actually being prepared to take Franklin's place," she said long afterward. Her own choice was Cordell Hull, but Father considered him too antique. He ruled out Ickes as too pugnacious, along with Henry Wallace, too indecisive, and Farley, "clearly the most dangerous." Garner did not merit discussion. Father had taken to making him the butt of his edgier jokes at Cabinet meetings. In return, as Ickes confided to his diary, Cactus Jack "sticks a knife in the President's back."

When Harry's convalescence in Florida was over and he reported back for work, Father had him stay in the White House for ten days, to satisfy himself about Hopkins' health and unfold his plans for 1940. In his opinion, Harry's tragically brief marriage to Barbara made his earlier divorce insignificant. The essential course for his protégé to follow was to get himself fit and keep his hat out of the ring for the time being, so that his enemies within the party could not gang up on him.

According to the scribbled notes which Hopkins kept of their meeting, Father repeated to him something that he had previously, I believe, confided only to the family: that if he had been able to continue treatment at Warm Springs after 1928, use of his left leg would have been restored. When he yielded to Al Smith's urging to run for governor of New York, Father sacrificed the opportunity of ever walking alone again.

He would be both physician-consultant and back-door cam-

paign manager for Harry. For a start, Hopkins should be
brought into Cabinet meetings. The reshuffling of the Cabinet
that Father contemplated would make an opening for him.
Harry Woodring, former Democratic governor of Kansas, was
not shaping up as Secretary of War, the job he had held since
George Dern's death in 1936. There was a strong streak of the
isolationist in Woodring. Dan Roper, "funny as a crutch,"
would need replacing as Commerce Secretary. That would be
the better of the two appointments for Hopkins, Father concluded, though Baruch, dipping his oar in again, advised Harry
otherwise.

A *My Day* column of Mother's showed that, while she was not
consulted about the plans for him, she completely approved of
Harry's impending stardom. "It was good to see Mr. Harry
Hopkins yesterday," she wrote, "and to have him spend the
night with us. . . . He seems to work because he has an inner
conviction that his job needs to be done and that he must do it.
I think he would be that way about any job he undertook."

The coalition of Republicans and conservative Democrats in
Congress followed up its humbling of Father in the Supreme
Court controversy by tossing out his recommendations for improving working efficiency in the Executive Branch more than
a year after he had first proposed them. His aim, simple
enough, was to put the operations of the White House, the
management agencies, and Cabinet agencies on a businesslike
basis, as outside experts had been urging since the Taft era. At
the same time, he wanted to eliminate the overlapping of responsibilities between Cabinet members and staffs. One accusation leveled against him as an administrator was that he liked to
commission two people to do a particular job for him at the
same time. True enough, but there was no established chain of
command, nothing remotely resembling the organizational
charts so beloved by the business schools.

The President's so-called household included all the aides
who worked for him. Instead of the cohorts of chieftains, depu-
ties, assistants, and secretaries that were added to insulate
subsequent Chief Executives from contact with reality or reason, Father had nobody standing between himself and his Cabinet. The lines of authority ran straight to himself. Department
heads reported directly to him because the Constitution gave

him no right to interject a substitute. Conflicts between departments had to be resolved by Father for the same reason. The whole thing was a mishmash that he hoped to disentangle.

His staff, located in the fancy-sounding executive wing, which was more accurately described as "an old, rickety shanty or lean-to," could do with half a dozen more assistants, "young men," as he put it, "with a passion for anonymity." Congress at one point seemed willing to afford him these, but nothing more.

"I would hardly know what to do with six executive assistants if I do not have any authority to put the government as a whole on a businesslike basis," Father remarked plaintively. "It is a little like giving the President the envelope of the letter without any letter in it!"

When the blueprint for reorganization came before the Senate in February, his opponents in and out of Congress pulled out all the stops on the propaganda organ once more. "A dictator bill," snapped the men who had already attempted to pin him with the blame for the "Roosevelt recession." He was "plunging a dagger into the very heart of democracy." Mysteriously financed committees for "Constitutional government" jumped in with mass mailings and advertisement campaigns. A hundred horsemen in Paul Revere outfits trotted past the White House bearing banners demanding NO ONE-MAN RULE.

He had not counted on such pandemonium. He had little cause to. There was nothing radical about the plan, which had been drawn up by independent consultants in the first place.

He recognized the instigators of the outburst and named them in a hastily prepared announcement. "I have no inclination to be a dictator," it said. "I have none of the qualifications which would make me a successful dictator. I have too much historical background and too much knowledge of existing dictatorships to make me desire any form of dictatorship for the United States of America." Who had conjured up the "silly nightmares"? "Those who would restore the government to those who owned it between 1921 and 1933" or "those who for one reason or another seek deliberately to wreck the present administration."

It did no good. A little more than a month after it became a Congressional target, the reorganization bill was laid to rest for another year. Father made a note of those Democrats who had thwarted him for the second time. He thought he saw a way to have some scores settled before the year was over.

Six days later, he had another message to submit to the Seventy-fifth Congress, which was so clearly in uncheckable rebellion against him, desperate to find any pretext for reasserting itself against expanding Executive authority. The cure for the recession, he said, performing a 180-degree turnaround, lay in the resumption of federal spending, $300 billion worth, to put a figure on it.

Veteran New Dealers like Cocoran and Cohen, who had been saying as much for half a year, celebrated his conversion. Leon Henderson, an economist who worked for Hopkins and had the rare distinction later of calling Father "you son of a bitch" in an argument over a fishing catch, could growl, "I told them so." Leon had predicted the slump six months before it started, which won him a place in Father's attention. Hopkins could take a healthy share of glory, too. It was Harry who acted as principal spokesman for the advocates of pump-priming in talking with Father. The $300 billion appropriation was approved.

Morgenthau was left out in the cold. When he heard from Mr. President in person that budget-balancing was jettisoned for the present, Henry wailed that he might feel compelled to resign. If he did, my parent warned him, history would judge him as a coward who quit under fire. Henry pulled himself together, and no resignation was tendered.

Father let two weeks go by and then got off a further request to the Hill. He had complained long enough about the perilous concentration of financial and industrial power in the hands of a few rich men. The private enterprise system left one-third of the nation short of jobs, income, and opportunities for an improved life. It was time to take a hard look at the workings of the profit system. Congress proved willing on this count, too. The outcome was the Monopoly Inquiry Act of June 16, which created the Temporary National Economic Committee to study the makeup of trusts, check on pricing, profits, investment, savings, and on down the line in the most exhaustive examination of American economic life ever undertaken. The New Dealers chalked up a second much-needed success, and Leon Henderson had additional cause to celebrate: He was appointed director of the committee.

The anti-Roosevelt partnership on the Hill evened the score in that year's Revenue Act, which repealed the steep taxes on undistributed corporation profits and cut the tax bite on capital gains. When Father declined to sign a bill so diametrically opposed to his convictions, it was voted into law nonetheless. The economic royalists were resourceful enemies. In this encounter, they had found an ally in Baruch. Testifying before a Senate committee, he attributed the drying up of risk capital to the taxes on profits and capital gains. In headline words, New Deal policies were deepening the recession. Mother could not understand why Father thought Bernie a slippery customer in spite of his repeated protests that the newspapers had misrepresented him.

One more clash in Congress between Rooseveltians and reactionaries ended in a draw, disappointing to both sides. The bill to control wages and working hours on a national basis had been hanging fire for a year. The original draft had been chewed between the labor bloc, which sought to gain advantages above those envisaged by the text, and Southern Democrats, who wanted to exempt any number of industries below the Mason-Dixon line from meeting minimum wage and maximum hours provisions.

Without some kind of nationwide standards, the fundamental concept of the New Deal was insecure. Some of his lieutenants were so pessimistic about the bill's chances that they thought it should be withdrawn. Father was so certain of its need that he was ready to compromise up to a point and agree to two separate wage scales, one North, the other South. The Southerners were still not satisfied, in particular Martin Dies of Texas, who looked for concessions in behalf of a local sacred cow.

It was, Father exploded, "the weakest, most dangerous proposition" he had ever heard. "If we start to legislate for the oil industry, we'll be aiding and abetting those people who want to exempt the canners, the cheese factories, and the lumber mills, and that is completely unsound."

In any event, a heavily rewritten, watered-down version of the bill was locked up in the House Rules Committee, under the sway of Southern Democrats, when Father gave way to the desire to "clear away my personal cobwebs" and spend a week in the Caribbean aboard the cruiser *Philadelphia* on her shakedown trip. One stop took the ship into Samaná Bay on the northeast coast of the Dominican Republic. A United States destroyer was also there. He had ordered it sent in as a reminder of American naval power when he heard that a German warship would be cruising in the vicinity.

He was at sea when the news came that he had hoped for. Senator Claude Pepper, an "FDR rubber stamp" by his opponents' description, had been renominated in Florida's May 3 primary. During convalescence from surgery, Hopkins had helped plan Pepper's strategy, and funds had been diverted for the campaign. The only real issues were the President, the New Deal, and the languishing wage-hours bill. The Senator's clear majority would give the hostiles in Congress something to think about. "The voters' hearts (and heads!) seem still to be in the right place," Father crowed.

There were other grounds for quiet satisfaction on that voyage—and more evidence of his intention to retire when his term expired. For months, he had been chewing over the notion of achieving a certain immortality for the New Deal and inferentially for himself by gathering in one spot all the documents, personal correspondence, and other source materials of the Roosevelt era. He could scarcely be charged with undue egotism, since he would be out of office by the time the myriad pieces of paper had been gathered together.

He had raised the topic with Charles Eliot, grandson of the Harvard president, and now Father was in the throes of conferring with more scholars and historians about setting up the first Presidential library in the United States. According to a tradition beginning with John Adams, a President's papers were his personal property, and they went with him on retirement. The records of both John and John Quincy Adams were shut up in a Boston vault, accessible only to their descendants. Mary Todd Lincoln gave away her husband's documents as souvenirs. Other Presidents' memorabilia were lost, eaten by rats, deliberately destroyed, or auctioned off piecemeal. With a personal regard for history, Father was bent on setting an altogether different precedent.

Just as he planned to the last detail the homely Warm Springs cottage known in journalistic hyperbole as the "Little White House" and the equally unpretentious Hyde Park retreat called "Hilltop Cottage," so he took a few minutes that spring to pick up a pen and sketch the single-story, fieldstone building in Hudson River Dutch style which he envisaged as a repository for the collection, to be erected on a site close by Granny's house. Henry Toombs, the New York architect who supervised both the other construction jobs, worked over the scratchy drawing, made on a sheet of ruled yellow paper. He came up with a provisional estimate of $290,000,including $75,000 for air conditioning and his own $20,000 fee.

Father admitted to being a "a bit appalled" by the size of the library, as Toombs contemplated it, "but you know more about the total volume of the papers than I do," he told the architect. Nobody had more than a vague idea when my parent, a compulsive hoarder, tended to save every scrap that fell into his hands, not excluding menus and match covers.

Very soon, the library became another hobby like his stamp collection to take his mind off the losing struggle with Congress. It was a matter, he confessed, "which lies very close to my heart," though he had no wish to have the project named for him, any more than a bridge or a highway should be. "Crum Elbow Library" to commemorate Granny's estate, or perhaps "Hyde Park Library" for the village itself, struck him as suitable choices.

How to pay for it all when he would not dream of asking for federal funds? Once it was up, title to the building and everything in it would be vested in the government, which would pay for running the place, but it must be a gift to, not from, the country. He made a start by earmarking the net, after-tax proceeds from publication and serial sale of *The Public Papers and Addresses of Franklin D. Roosevelt,* five volumes edited by Sam Rosenman and published by Random House. The rest of the cost was raised by private subscription from some 28,000 citizens. Granny donated sixteen acres of the Hyde Park estate.

His enthusiasm mounted as he pondered what should go into the collection. Hoover had been the first President to preserve all his papers and correspondence. His mail amounted to some 400 letters a day; Father's was ten times more. (Hoover, incidentally, took the cue from my parent and rapidly organized his own Presidential collection after the Hyde Park Library was opened.) New Deal correspondence files alone would overflow a house. Stored up in Albany were sixty packing cases full of his New York governorship papers. A similar cache in Washington occupied more than 5,000 feet of shelf space.

He decided to add to the trove his own collection of United States naval history, assessed by experts as the finest in existence outside of museum walls. The 400 prints and pictures, the twenty-seven ship models, the log books and manuscripts dated back in some instances to 1775. He owned approximately 15,000 books and pamphlets, many of them rare autographed copies from their authors. "Far more than my children could possibly use," he concluded, so he donated most of these, too.

By the time he had finished, the Hyde Park Library held about 50,000,000 items in all categories, from the diaries of Rebecca Howland Roosevelt, his father's first wife, to Granny's account books; from his baby shoes and cradle to one of the bullets fired at him by Giuseppe Zangara; from Louis Howe's old bank statements to a humidor for cigars, a gift from Fulgencio Batista.

For the items he donated to the library, he claimed somewhat less than the $500,000 valuation which one of his successors attempted to set on his Presidential papers in a 1972 tax return. For all his papers and all the physical property, including the priceless naval collection, Father claimed $9,900 as a tax deduction.

The glow produced by Claude Pepper's Florida victory lasted long enough to see Father back at his desk and the watery wage-and-hours bill safely through Congress. It fell so far short of his original intention that Father signed it sighing, as he sometimes did. "Well, that's water over the dam. Now we'll go on to chapter two." But this time there was no chapter two. The Fair Labor Standards Act, as it was labeled, was the last important achievement of the New Deal.

The hostiles on the Hill bounced back into action as the result of another primary race, where Father's candidate lost the Democratic nomination for governor of Pennsylvania. Tom Kennedy, secretary-treasurer of the United Mine Workers, was beaten by his rival, Claude Jones, who had the support of the state's party machine. The New Deal had apparently lost its magic not only in Congress but now with some voters, too.

10

His reasoning as well as his temper told Father that he must avenge himself. The desire to slay dragons was irresistible. The party must be purged of as many as came within reach. The sword to be used was his personal standing with the vast majority of voters, which he believed to be high as ever. Before they went to the polls in November, Father would single out the Congressional evildoers one by one to block their being returned to either House.

He had not intervened in local elections since he entered the White House. "In spite of fool stories in fool newspapers," as he phrased it, his policy toward these contests had been strictly hands off. He had refused to say anything for publication about his preferences between candidates. Not even the use of his name was condoned explicitly.

He liked to relate the tale of what happened during a municipal primary campaign in Cleveland when Hugh Johnson, heading the National Recovery Administration at the time, went there to make a speech about his organization.

"When he arrived," Father would tell, "he was met, wined, dined, and introduced by the leader of one faction. The next morning, the newspapers and campaign committees of that faction proclaimed loudly that the administration and the President were supporting them. Like an idiot—who, however, will know better next time—I sent word that this claim was wholly unauthorized and wholly untrue.

"Thereupon, the opposing faction got out large headlines and made extravagant claims that of course I was not supporting the first faction—that I had made public denial of it and that therefore I was supporting their faction."

The idea of taking the fight against conservative Democrats to the voters did not originate with Father. In their enthusiasm for this, Hopkins and Ickes had found something else to unite them. Sam Rosenman was another who accepted the logic of disciplining the rebels who had dragged the New Deal to a halt. Without them, there would have been no conceivable way for the twenty-one Republican Senators and eighty-nine Representatives to defeat FDR in the Supreme Court encounter, to knock down his reorganization plan, to reverse his tax policy, and to bleed the Fair Labor Standards Act into a ghost of the original.

Yet Father had no relish for political civil war. He had spent too many years cultivating many of the Congressmen who deserved now to be ousted. He hated to break up any friendship, but he saw no alternative. The party as a whole had to be taught that crossing up the President did not pay. The maximum possible number of Democrats elected to the next Congress must be men prepared to go down the line for him.

He cherished a long-term vision beyond that. The past five years had seen the beginnings of a realignment in both major parties. There were liberal Republicans whose views were far more progressive than the conservative Democrats. Traditional political allegiances were becoming outmoded. For the country to be kept on course and headed away from the rocky coastline of reactionism, the votes of enlightened Republicans as well as Democrats would be required. Cracking the right-wing opposition in his party would be a step in that direction.

On June 24, in a fireside chat, he made his first plea for liberals to be nominated in the forthcoming party primaries, men who realized that new conditions demanded new remedies, impelled by an "inward desire to get practical needs attended to in a practical way." The headline writers seized on a key sentence:

"As President of the United States, I am not asking the voters of the country to vote for Democrats next November as opposed to Republicans or members of any other party."

As usual in these roundups of problems and their solutions that he reeled off in front of the microphones, he touched on some other topics, one being the present state of the recession. Capital and labor, he urged, should unite against cutting wages, since that would only bring on more trouble by reducing spending power.

"Today," he added, "a great steel company announced a reduction in prices with a view to stimulating business recovery" without wage cuts. "Every encouragement should be given to industry which accepts a large volume of high-wage policy."

In the big black type of the next morning's headlines— ROOSEVELT DECLARES WAR ON PARTY REBELS—a disclaimer from one of his corporate antagonists was lost. "No official of the U.S. Steel Corporation has given any assurances that wage reductions will not follow steel price reductions," the statement said. The "war" on dissident Democrats was only one battle in the to-and-fro struggle with forces that were trying everything possible to put a different man in the White House.

In a matter of days, he was aboard the train, heading West like a genial avenging angel. He had Anna and John Boettiger along for company. Jimmy had gone with Mother to Minnesota to put himself into the Mayo Clinic, with symptoms not unlike those of Harry Hopkins. When he was discharged, he would spend some time at Campobello before returning to the job that was obviously getting the better of him. The strain showed in the gastric ulcers that wrecked his health and in the developing tension in his marriage to Betsy. Father was one of the few people left in Washington who thought that Jimmy should continue to work for him.

He let the circumstances of the local scene and the records of the men involved decide his choice of weapon. Some of his targets received the silent treatment, others were roundly denounced, but a parade of sham courtesies was standard on both sides. Every candidate, for or against the New Deal, maneuvered to be seen with FDR as the train wound a path through Ohio, Kentucky, and Oklahoma. Senator Robert Buckley of Ohio was given only a lukewarm recommendation. In Kentucky, grizzled Alben Barkley, the Senate leader, received an accolade from Father. In Nevada, foxy Pat McCarran was frozen out.

In Texas, my parent had some kind words for Lyndon and Maury Maverick, who was so passionately pro-Roosevelt that he had signed the text of the court-packing bill the minute it reached Capitol Hill and tossed it into the House hopper without reading it. Cactus Jack stayed out of sight. Neither he nor Farley could condone what Father was doing. They wanted the Democratic Party to remain what it had turned into since 1933, a hybrid creature, part labor, part black, part liberal, part reactionary, but probably attractive enough to the electorate to put Jack and Jim into office as the next President and Vice President.

In California, Father recommended that Democrats give their votes to Senator McAdoo, whose dreams of the Presidency had withered in old age, not to Sheridan Downey and the "thirty-dollars-every-Thursday" pension plan that was the main plank of his platform. The cheers there for FDR matched the reception the crowds gave him throughout this journey. He felt assured that he had accomplished what he set out to do when he was hoisted to the deck of the *Houston* in mid-July for a three-week cruise, taking him south across the equator again, to go collecting specimens of flora and fauna from the Galápagos.

"We don't care who wins," he reported back blithely to Marvin McIntire as the ship reached Cocos Island. One cruise was almost indistinguishable from another in the easygoing life at sea. Among his reading this time was a new book Uncle Fred gave him—Winston Churchill's angry survey of world affairs between 1932 and 1938, which he entitled *While England Slept*.

Father maintained his flow of banter. "Pa got a sailfish today—the only one & he is asking to succeed Pershing as General of the Armies" . . . "I caught a 230 lb. shark yesterday—1 hr. and 35 minutes—so I win the pool for Biggest Fish!" . . . "Pa hooked a fish—brought it to within ten feet of the boat, looked at it and screamed, 'A huge shark! Sergeant, Sergeant, shoot the blank of a blank!' The marine shot said fish through the head, whereupon Pa brought him in and he turned out to be an innocent little, two foot mackerel." He promised Ickes, who was off in Alaska with his new wife, the former Jane Dahlman, aged twenty-five, "When you get back, I will tell you how Pa lost $30 and I won—another shark episode."

After the *Houston* docked in Pensacola, Florida, he broke his homeward train journey twice to lambaste two men who stood close to the top of his blacklist. In the little crossroads town of Barnesville, Georgia, Senator Walter George reposed in dignity on the platform behind Father. The Senator was being challenged in the primary by young United States Attorney Lawrence Camp, whom the administration had put up for the task.

George did not stir when he heard Father say, "My old friend, the senior Senator from this state, cannot possibly in my judgment be classified as belonging to the liberal school of thought. . . . If I were able to vote in the September primaries . . . I most assuredly should cast my ballot for Lawrence Camp." Camp, also on the platform, sat frozen-faced.

When he had finished, Father swung himself around to shake George's hand. "Mr. President," said the Senator, "I want you to know that I accept the challenge."

"Let's always be friends," came the reply. "God bless you, Walter."

In South Carolina, "Cotton Ed" Smith, a white supremacist, faced a rival in Governor Olin Johnston, who entered the contest after a heart-to-heart talk with Father. Employing his technique of not advertising an adversary by mentioning his name, my parent proceeded to flay Cotton Ed in a speech at Greenville. "I stepped on the gas," he chuckled afterward.

He waited until he was back in the White House to lay into Senator Millard Tydings of Maryland, whom he castigated for seeking reelection "with the Roosevelt prestige and the money of his conservative Republican friends both on his side." Father wanted his man, Representative David Lewis, to win so badly that he took two days off from the White House to stump the state for him.

There was a further name on the roster of intended victims. Even though Representative John O'Connor was Basil's brother, he must be disposed of. As chairman of the House Rules Committee, he had been a particularly painful thorn in the Presidential flesh. Hopkins and Tom Corcoran were assigned to boost the chances of Jim Fay against O'Connor in Manhattan.

In the first half of September, Father had to drop all other business and hurry out to Minnesota, where Jimmy had been readmitted to the Mayo Clinic, with Mother again at his side. Six weeks of medication and diet had done nothing for the ulcers. His condition was critical. Surgery was the one hope left, and there was a serious element of risk in that. The doctors were prepared to wait only until Father reached Rochester in the Presidential Special. Harry Hopkins went with him.

Mother's account of Jimmy's operation in her newspaper column was a study in self-restraint. She could not allow that she or Father or the rest of us had feared for my brother's life. She had a sympathetic word for the surgeon, who "looked as though he had been through quite an ordeal"—it was a characteristic device to ascribe her own concealed suffering to somebody else. And she pretended she discovered that "one real advantage for which a President could be grateful" lay in having a doctor keeping him posted on how the hours-long procedure in the operating room was progressing.

On September 12, Father sat in his private railroad car in the Rochester yards with Hopkins, listening to the radio. He knew more than enough German to understand exactly every poisonous word that Hitler was shouting above the chants of *"Sieg Heil!"* from the ranks of his uniformed Storm Troopers, massed at the Nazi Party Congress in Nuremberg. "Oppression" by the Czech government of Germans living in the Sudeten area of the country must end, screamed Der Führer, or the Fatherland would be compelled to rescue them.

Father's response was to order Harry to fly to California to make a secret survey of the production capability of aircraft manufacturers there. Soon after, from the White House, he proclaimed that the United States needed 8,000 planes. Generals and admirals joined most of the newspapers in the land in jeering at him for ludicrous daydreaming. "The President," said Hopkins' notes, "was sure then that we were going to get into war and he believed that air power would win it."

The failure of Father's missions of vengeance was overshadowed by the sudden quickening of the European race toward destruction. A less urbane man would have judged from the results of the primaries that Democratic voters had all but repudiated him. The tally was depressing. Maryland? Tydings swept in. South Carolina? Another win for Cotton Ed. Georgia? Walter George an easy victor. Nevada? Pat McCarran took the nomination. Manhattan provided a crumb of consolation. Jim Fay did manage to squeeze out the detestable O'Connor. But in general the only lesson to be learned was that people resented what they saw as Presidential interference in purely local politics.

The Axis buildup of a coordinated war-making machine had gone into higher gear with the German takeover of Austria. Hitler spent a week in Rome that spring with an entourage of 120 men, reviewing mammoth parades of Italian troops performing an imitation goose-step, rechristened the *passo Romano,* and exchanging blood oaths with Mussolini during a banquet at the Palazzo Venezia.

"What a show it must have been!" Father commented at the time. "It must have cost a lot but I suppose it could be justified on the plea that it is just like FDR's policy in spending money for public works!"

Mussolini copied more than the German goose-step. Two months later, anti-Semitism was made part of Italy's legal code, barring all Jews from schools and universities, expelling those who had settled in the country after 1919. Another multitude of refugees was driven to look for shelter, joining the legions who had fled Germany starting in 1933. These German Jews counted themselves among the blessed of God as Nazi pogroms reached new depths of barbarity.

The task of finding homes and raising funds for the persecuted was largely left to private philanthropy by the governments of the West. It was a matter of policy for them to encourage it, and when they met in the Evian Conference, they began searching for places on the map for Jews to colonize. In England, Baldwin's only radio speech after retirement was a fundraising appeal. The first hint of dissatisfaction with Joe Kennedy's performance as ambassador came in a report that he had to be prodded into taking an active part in working on the refugee problem. Sumner Welles confirmed to Father that, from all he could gather, this was unquestionably true. It was possible, it seemed, that Joe was being infected by the attitudes of those upper-class Englishmen who kept Jews out of their clubs and out of some of the more celebrated public schools, hoping at the same time that Hitler's attentions could somehow be diverted from the West toward the Russians.

Joe had already received one rebuke from Father on a completely unrelated subject—for granting an exclusive interview to a London correspondent of Hearst's Boston *American,* which appeared as a "special message of advice" to its readers. That drew a sharp radiogram from Hull, then Father added his own slap: "We were all greatly disturbed. . . ."

In the course of September, when torrential rains doused the United States, Europe reached the edge of the precipice.

Monday, the fifth. France suspended all army leave and recalled all reservists to the supposedly impregnable steel-and-concrete fortresses of the Maginot Line defending her frontiers.

Wednesday, the seventh. Speaking for Chamberlain, the *Times* of London urged President Eduard Benes of Czechoslovakia to cede all Sudetenland to the Germans.

Tuesday, the thirteenth. The day after Hitler's Nuremberg threats, Sudeten Germans attempted a revolt, which the Prague government put down without difficulty.

Wednesday, the fourteenth. Mussolini announced that he backed Hitler, and the French government panicked. France would no longer singlehandedly guarantee the security of Czechoslovakia. "Entry of German troops . . . must at all costs be prevented," said the message sent to Chamberlain by Premier Édouard Daladier.

Thursday, the fifteenth. Chamberlain flew to Munich and saw Hitler at Berchtesgaden, to offer him the Sudetenland after a pretense at negotiations. Hitler accepted the proxy surrender.

That day, Father wrote to Bill Phillips in Rome. "Chamberlain's visit to Hitler today may bring things to a head or may result in a temporary postponement of what looks to me like an inevitable conflict within the next five years. Perhaps when it comes the United States will be in a position to pick up the pieces of European civilization and help them to save what remains of the wreck—not a cheerful prospect. . . .

"If we get the idea that the future of our own form of government is threatened by a coalition of European dictators, we might wade in with everything we have to give. If a war starts now . . . I think ninety percent of our people are definitely anti-German and anti-Italian in sentiment—and incidentally, I would not propose to ask them to be neutral in thought. . . ."

The following morning, he called a Cabinet meeting. Chamberlain, he told the group around the table, "is for peace at any price." He judged that in a showdown Britain and France would abandon the Czechs, he said, and "wash the blood from their Judas Iscariot hands."

Sunday, the eighteenth. Daladier went to London to argue with Chamberlain that Hitler intended to conquer Europe. Would Britain join France in guaranteeing what remained of Czechoslovakia after the Sudetenland had been amputated? Chamberlain agreed to that.

Wednesday, the twenty-first. Benes was driven to accept the proposed surgery by an Anglo-French threat to desert him.

Thursday, the twenty-second. Chamberlain flew for another meeting with Hitler at Berchtesgaden, deluding himself that appeasement had succeeded. Hitler promptly escalated his demands: he must occupy Sudentenland *immediately*, not after more time-wasting talk. He finally consented to wait until October 1. "It's up to the Czechs now," said Chamberlain forlornly as he went home.

The Poles and Hungarians had sessions with Der Führer, then added their own claims to slices of Czechoslovakia when dismemberment began. Britain prepared for sudden war by issuing 38,000,000 gas masks. Experimental air raid warnings wailed over the radio. In London, workmen dug zigzag trenches across the parks as emergency shelter from German bombs, and four parents out of five signed up their children to be evacuated from the city.

Monday, the twenty-sixth. The hand of Winston Churchill showed in a warning he persuaded the British Foreign Office to issue: "If German attack is made upon Czechoslovakia . . . France will be bound to come to her assistance, and Great Britain and Russia will certainly stand by France." Lord Halifax, the foreign secretary, authorized it without his signature, so Georges Bonnet, the French Foreign Minister, denounced it as a forgery. Chamberlain disowned it. Britain, he said, stood ready to concur with Hitler's demands.

Father appealed to London, Paris, Rome, and Berlin, urging all four countries to keep negotiating.

Tuesday, the twenty-seventh. Hitler replied to Father: War or peace was for the Czechs to decide. Reports reaching the White House gave Father, as he said, "a definite feeling that Hitler would not wait until Saturday, October first, but would move his troops before that." At two o'clock the following afternoon, to be exact. Starting at midday on the twenty-seventh, Hull and FDR began to pile on the pressure. A second cable flashed to Berlin: PRESENT NEGOTIATIONS STILL STAND OPEN. THEY CAN BE CONTINUED IF YOU GIVE THE WORD. Another went to Bill Phillips in Rome, instructing him to ask Mussolini to intervene and perhaps persuade Hitler to reopen negotiations.

Radio signal towers pulsed throughout the day with a two-way flow of messages between Washington and the major capitals of the world as the effort to stave off war grew more frantic. Hitler remained as silent as a cat hunting mice. The Western leaders pursued their separate inspirations. Benes wanted Father to rally Anglo-French support for the Czechs. Chamberlain wanted permission to address the American people by radio. Father urged all the nonaggressors to hasten their appeals for talks to be resumed.

In London, Chamberlain mobilized the British fleet and sent his chief foreign affairs adviser, Sir Horace Wilson, flying off to beg Hitler not to start his tanks rolling yet. The Prime Minister, too, had the British ambassador to Italy, Lord Perth, appeal to Mussolini to calm down the German dictator.

Wednesday, the twenty-eighth. At nine forty five A.M., Mussolini was told of Father's message, though Phillips did not get an appointment until four P.M. Shortly before eleven A.M. Il Duce saw Lord Perth. In Westminster, the House of Commons met in special session to listen in fear to Chamberlain's recital of the crisis to date. He was still on his feet when Mussolini's response was passed to him hand-to-hand along the government benches. Hitler had agreed to meet in Munich with the British, the French, and the Italians. There were sobs of relief mixed in with the cheers from the benches and in the visitors' gallery. Only Willie Gallagher, the solitary Communist in Parliament, openly scorned the moment of apparent salvation.

On September 29, Chamberlain again flew to Munich. The agreement to give Hitler the Sudetenland was signed there before midnight, while Czech government representatives waited outside in the lobby. The following morning, the Prime Minister came up with a statement which he wished Hitler would also put his signature to. "We regard the agreement signed last

night . . . as symbolic of the desire of our two peoples never
to go to war with one another again," it said. Der Führer was
willing to oblige. When Chamberlain spoke from his window at
10 Downing Street that night, his gravelly voice rose above the
cheers.

"This is the second time," he said, "that there has come back
from Germany to Downing Street peace with honor. I believe it
is peace for our time."

Father could neither bring himself to share in that illusion
nor see any workable means of telling Americans his own dark
beliefs about the future. Only disgruntled Leftists and a few
fireaters called the Munich pact peace through fear. One of the
fireaters was Churchill, whose point of view Father had
warmed to after reading *While England Slept*. But Sumner
Welles echoed the opinions of many in the administration three
days after Munich, when he declared that the way was now
open for building a new world order based upon "justice and
law."

Father's sinuses had been acting up all summer, and many of
his messages during these past days had been dictated from his
bed. "I have had a pretty strenuous two weeks," he allowed,
"but the cruise made it possible for me to come through except
for a stupid and continuing runny nose. A few days ago I wanted to kill Hitler and amputate the nose. Today, I have really
friendly feelings for the latter and no longer wish to assassinate
Hitler."

His feelings about the likely outcome of Chamberlain-style
appeasement colored the final words in a kidding letter he dictated to Missy for Marvin McIntyre, whom he had ordered to
take a prolonged rest cure for symptoms of tuberculosis. "I am
often touched, but seldom have I been so touched as by your
letter to Miss LeHand," he said. "It was one of a very small
number of letters which occasionally she shows to me. Both of
us were dissolved in tears. . . . You are such a fine citizen that
if we have to go to war with Hitler I am sure you will be the first
to enlist." The date was October 6, 1938.

The task of arming the country and simultaneously educating an insular people about the need to do so required a
specialized blend of deviousness and audacity. When Hopkins
came back from California, he had a visitor in the person of the

new deputy chief of staff, Brigadier General George C. Marshall, whose promotion had been recommended by Pershing. Between them, they worked out another of Father's magician's tricks for shuffling money, taking it from where it was most readily available for spending where it was most needed. Millions of Works Progress Administration dollars were surreptitiously diverted to make machine tools for producing small-arms ammunition, some of which, with equal secrecy, he allowed France and Britain to buy.

He was anxious to get an altogether different slant on affairs in Britain than that available from Joe Kennedy, who followed an increasingly pro-Chamberlain line, or from the Prime Minister himself. He pushed ahead with a plan to invite King George and Queen Elizabeth to the United States, counting on their "essential democracy" to make a good impression on Americans.

"I need not tell you how happy I am," said his letter to Buckingham Palace, "that Great Britain and the United States have been able to cooperate so effectively in the prevention of war even though we cannot say that we are 'out of the woods' yet." That was a not-too-delicate hint that he did not share Chamberlain's rosy expectancy of "peace for our time."

As the November, 1938, election day drew nearer, the Democrats' prospects looked increasingly bleak. This midterm year had produced no clear-cut campaign issue between themselves and the Republicans. Every electoral district seemed to have picked its own subject to argue—the abortive purge, the "dictator" in the White House, the sit-down strikes, the rights and wrongs of white supremacy.

At the last minute, Father attempted to have the voters believe that what was at stake was the New Deal itself. In a broadcast to the nation, he gave warning that "if American democracy ceases to move forward . . . then Fascism and Communism, aided, unconsciously perhaps, by old-line Tory Republicanism, will grow in strength in our land."

For all the effect it had, he wasted his breath. On a visit with him to Hyde Park, Hopkins paraded his political callowness by predicting only minor Democratic losses. Father knew better, but the outcome was worse than pencil-and-paper calculations led him to expect. The unprecedented majorities of his disrupted party fell catastrophically in the House from 244 to 93 and in the Senate from 58 to 46. The Republicans held onto every seat they had and captured thirteen governorships. Prow-jawed Martin Dies limbered up to start a probe by the House Un-American Activities Committee of Hopkins' Works Progress Administration to discover just how its funds were being spent. The government, he said, must be cleansed of such "Communists and fellow travelers" as Harry, Ickes, and Ma Perkins.

Father preferred as a matter of habit to look on the bright side. He considered the election results as being "on the whole helpful" in that "we have eliminated certain individuals and certain intraparty fights which were doing positive harm." He blamed the Democrats' losses on the fact that "our officeholders and our candidates had not measured up," brushing aside the unpalatable truth that the alliance of Republicans and conservative Democrats was in a stronger position than ever to block any FDR program they objected to.

Events overseas and their impact at home had first place in his priorities. "Our British friends," he thought, "must begin to fish or cut bait. The dictator threat from Europe is a good deal closer to the United States and the American continent than it was before."

He could summarize his objectives in a single sentence: "I am working at the present time on two very important things—first, national defense, especially mass production of planes; and, second, the establishment of a better system of constant publicity with the idea not only of making clear our objectives and methods, but also nailing the deliberate misstatements of fact as fast as they are made."

He persuaded himself that the new Congress would "meet us two-thirds of the way," but he would need Garner's help to achieve that. After pleading first that he had a cold and then that he figured on going deer hunting, Cactus Jack came up from Uvalde two weeks before Christmas. Their White House meeting turned out to be seasonably chilly. Farley had already attempted to read the moral of the election to Father. Garner repeated much the same conclusion. The administration, they both said, must swing rightward. The future of the New Deal should be surrendered to appease the conservatives in the party. They had as much chance of winning over Father as they had of converting him to isolationism. The breakup of two more political friendships was very near.

Post-Munich euphoria faded fast. The dictators' smooth victory over Chamberlain was a signal for them to step up their aid to Franco and crush the final resistance of the Spanish Loyalists. In his frustrated desire to do something more positive than stand by and watch the death of a cause he believed in, Father looked again for some frangible link in the chain of restrictions placed on him by the neutrality resolutions of Congress, which embargoed arms for Spain on grounds that shipping them while the war there was at a peak would threaten the peace of the United States. But he might be permitted to revoke the embargo if he judged that the conflict was nearly over and so danger to America had passed. Would Homer Cummings let him have a legal opinion on this fine point—but not in writing, please?

Once again, Stimson had proved his caliber by arguing that Father could permit shipments to the Loyalists simply by Presidential proclamation, without reference to Capitol Hill. Nothing was finalized either way. Ickes privately placed responsibility for inaction on the State Department, where some of Herbert Hoover's adherents lingered on in key positions. With no information on that score, American liberals accused Father of callous indifference to the fate of Spanish democracy.

My parents asked Hopkins to spend Christmas Eve together with Diana in the White House, where the rituals of the holidays followed their unbroken pattern. Wreaths in the windows; Granny in dignified attendance; piles of packages more spectacular in their wrappings than in their contents; an enormous East Room tree, where Father would read and act out his abridged version of *A Christmas Carol.*

Harry had received his major gift forty-eight hours early. He was sworn in as Secretary of Commerce by Justice Stanley Reed, a newcomer to the Supreme Court, on Christmas Eve. Washingtonians remembered that Hoover had made the job his stepping-stone to the Presidency. To most of the country, Harry was identifiable now as the heir apparent. To Senator Tydings and some others who had escaped Father's purge, Hopkins was known as the "White House termite."

11

The turkeys, plum puddings, and all the trimmings were served in the State Dining Room, where Father cocked an eye at the fieldstone fireplace, picturing its lintel carved with the quotation from John Adams which he'd had unearthed: "I pray Heaven to bestow his best of blessings on this house and all that shall hereafter inhabit it. May none but honest and wise men rule under this roof."

Much of the time, he was preoccupied with the matter of what he would tell the country when the Seventy-sixth Congress convened two weeks ahead. He had the conclusion of his message clear in his mind, another quotation he remembered, words of Abraham Lincoln. "This generation will nobly save or meanly lose the last best hope of earth. . . . The way is plain, peaceful, generous, just—a way which if followed the world will forever applaud and God must forever bless." He jotted down some other thoughts in the privacy of his study.

Mother sought out Harry. As a new entrant into the family, he should be taken under her wing. If his health held up and his career developed as it might, what would become of Diana? If his health failed, the question would be that much more urgent. He outlined his financial situation and gave her details of his life insurance. She must have felt that something more was needed because she promised to see that, no matter what, his daughter would be well educated and have money in reserve when her schooling was over.

"I was, naturally, quite overcome by her suggestion," Harry told Diana years later. At Mother's urging, he had a new will drawn, naming her guardian of the six-year-old child, who stayed in her care for the next three years.

The place closest to Father which Louis once occupied was empty again, and Harry moved in to fill it. The experiment of training Jimmy as Presidential right-hand man had been called off. The surgeons found no trace of cancer when they took away two-thirds of his stomach, and he was out of the clinic in ten days. The stay was long enough to start his domestic life on a fresh turn. The friction that had developed between Betsy and himself made him susceptible to other attentions. He fell in love with one of his nurses, Romelle Schneider.

Father had looked forward to the day of my brother's return to work after some weeks of convalescence, fully prepared to ignore constant criticism that Jimmy's inside track at the White House was turned to good advantage by his friends and former associates. Our parent believed that his oldest son would conform to the plans he had made for him.

When Jimmy broke the news of his attachment to Romelle, Father was outraged. A divorce from Betsy had no place in the schedule. His reaction revealed the more dominating streak which the family had recently detected in him. My brother was not to be let off lightly. When he offered his resignation, pleading poor health, Father accepted it without hesitation and arranged to have Basil O'Connor, one of the toughest attorneys in New York, represent Betsy in the forthcoming divorce action in order to make things difficult for my brother.

As an unexpected outcast from our parent's favor, Jimmy made off for California. Through connections he established there, he landed a $25,000-a-year job as Sam Goldwyn's assistant in the motion-picture business. Mother accepted an appointment to the board of Roosevelt & Sargent to look after his interests in his absence, while he waited to marry Romelle.

My brother had no invitation to the White House that Christmas. The hue and cry about nepotism had been raised again, with references to John Boettiger and myself added for good measure, and not without justification. Would Hearst have hired me as head of his radio chain if a Roosevelt had not been President? one editorialist asked. Would Hearst have promoted Boettiger as a publisher "almost the moment he married the President's daughter if it were not for his admittance into the Roosevelt family?" Would Jimmy have been employed by Goldwyn "if papa hadn't been sitting on the throne?"

Jimmy remained in Father's bad books for disposing of Betsy, but our parent was incapable of staying angry with anyone in the family for very long. Jimmy was soon forgiven. Mother saw the breakup more objectively. She was relieved that the job she had opposed before he started in it was over for my brother. Her views on divorce, which she had once sought herself at the height of Father's romance with her Catholic secretary, Lucy Mercer, in 1918, were possibly flavored by that memory.

In a questions-and-answers column which she wrote regularly for *Ladies' Home Journal,* she once stated her opinion. The matter-of-fact words held clues to her personal history when they were read by those of us who were beginning to understand her nature at last:

> Divorce is something which should never be taken lightly, but I think the real emphasis should be laid upon the seriousness with which we undertake marriage in the first place. Sometimes even when a marriage begins with every apparent prospect of success, people develop differently and find themselves, over a period of years, unable to live together in harmony. When that happens it seems to me that there is nothing to do but resort to divorce. . . . Certain religions do not recognize divorce, and of course I am not talking about people who belong to those religions. . . ."

To the best of her knowledge, Lucy, now the gentle and statuesque Mrs. Winthrop Rutherfurd of Tranquillity, New Jersey, and Aiken, South Carolina, had been erased from Father's life. She had no idea in the world that Mrs. Rutherfurd had been provided with a White House limousine to watch both his Inaugurals to date, or that the onset of disaster in Europe would stir him like an Ernest Hemingway hero to look again for more of Lucy's company.

The hostility of the Seventy-sixth Congress that assembled on January 4 did not deter Father. In his opening message, he gave fair notice of his line of thinking. "There comes a time in the affairs of men when they must prepare to defend not their homes alone but the tenets of faith and humanity on which their churches, their governments, and their very civilization are founded."

He repeated the words he had spoken in Chicago in accepting the 1936 nomination. "'This generation has a rendezvous with destiny.' That prophecy come true. To us much is given; more is expected. *This generation will nobly save or meanly lose the last best hope of earth.*"

World war, he told the lawmakers, may have been averted at Munich, but "all about us rage undeclared wars—military and economic." The democracies could not "forever let pass" acts of aggression "which automatically undermine all of us." The least the United States could do was reexamine its neutrality laws to make certain that they did not continue to aid the aggressors. Dreams of a balanced budget were brushed aside. Government spending would have to be cut by one-third unless Congress agreed to deficit financing, and Congress would have to tell him where such cuts were to be made.

Horrified by the prospect of pump-priming for no matter what reason, the conservatives and isolationists squealed on cue. "I think our antediluvian friends have got themselves in a bit of a jam," Father considered. "I have told them some simple home truths and intimated that they had every legal right to go their own way but that if they did, they would bear the full responsibility." He thought the session would "settle down and be comparatively quiet"—if peace could be preserved in Europe.

His budget message provided the hostiles with a bigger shock. For the fiscal year starting July 1, 1940, he called for spending $8,996,000,000, a little more than double the deficit inherited from Herbert Hoover. Of the total, $1,319,558,000 was allocated for arms, an increase of $309,351,000, but only a puny $170,000,000 for aircraft as such. Father was so far from being satisfied that he promptly belabored the legislators with a supplementary request earmarked for buying planes—$500,000,000 worth of them.

To keep war away from the United States called for more

than weapons and men in uniform. The aggressors must be forestalled from infiltrating, or perhaps invading, America's neighbors north and south. Cordell Hull could be relied on to nurse the benign relationships that had been established in Latin America. Father preferred to retain in his own hands all dealings with Canada and Prime Minister William Mackenzie King, with whom he had developed a friendship when, as Governor Roosevelt, he delighted in boarding a launch and inspecting New York State waterways as far as Lake Ontario and the Thousand Islands.

President and Prime Minister together had produced some tangible testimony to their cordiality. In Father's first term, they tweaked the noses of British Tories, who preferred an "Empire first" policy for Canada, by signing a trade agreement to ease the movement of goods to and fro across the border. The previous summer, the two of them had joined in dedicating the new international bridge that spanned the Thousand Islands.

It was Father's hope that the day would come when he and Mackenzie could "drop in and visit" with each other as casually as members of the same family. When Hitler was drawing his plans for the Czech takeover, Father added a few lines of his own to a speech prepared by the State Department for him to make in Ontario. The commitment exceeded the authority granted him by Congress, but for once there were no complaints when he promised, "The people of the United States will not stand idly by if domination of Canadian soil is threatened by any other Empire."

He was still pursuing a dream of binding the United States and Canada together by the use of shared hydroelectric power from the cascading St. Lawrence River. That, too, dated back to his governorship years. A treaty drafted to accomplish the power project was turned down in 1934, by the Senate, where approval required a two-thirds majority. Now, five years later, prospects seemed brighter, as Father hastened to tell "Dear Mackenzie" in a letter devoted principally to the impending visit of King George and his queen in the early summer, when the Prime Minister would bring them down to the White House and on to Hyde Park.

"If it is terrifically hot," Father joked, "can't you discard that very good looking gray morning coat and design for yourself a white Naval uniform, with gold maple leaves to denote Prime Minister rank? I might even try my hand at designing the same sort of thing for the Commander in Chief of the United States Army and Navy. It has never been done but I fear that is one precedent I do not dare to break." In those distant days, male White House staff members had been spared the wearing of Graustarkian shakos and tunics on dress occasions.

He was sadly off in his guess about prospects for a St. Lawrence treaty. The Senate was no more enthusiastic than before. Two more years were to pass before Canada and the United States devised an agreement, instead of a treaty, to develop power and navigation in the river's basin. A simple majority in Congress was needed for approval, but the votes were not there.

At the end of January, he invited a group of Senators in for a cram course in foreign affairs, hoping that his sense of urgency would rub off on some of them. Those idols of isolationism, Gerald Nye and Champ Clark of Missouri, were included. Father went down a list of more than a dozen European nations "whose continued independent political and economic existence is of actual moment to the ultimate defense of the United States."

If the Baltic states fell to Hitler, he said, America's position would be weakened. The same held true for Scandinavia, Holland, Belgium, Portugal, Greece, Egypt, Turkey, Romania, Bulgaria, and Yugoslavia. Czechoslovakia had once been a link in United States defense against future German and Italian aggression, but that link lay broken now. He excluded Britain, France, and the Soviet Union from his list that day. The service chiefs of most of the major powers imagined that the British and the French has been saved from war by Munich. If Hitler struck again, it would be to the east, against the USSR.

Father's pocket lecture gave the isolationists too good an opportunity to miss. "A few silly Senators," he related afterward, "reported the conversation in a wholly untruthful way." They spread word to the newspapers that he had said America's frontiers reached to the Rhine. Columnists and commentators picked up the phrase so fast that most Americans accepted the invention as a fact of history. The opposition vilified him as a warmonger, but the outcome was not altogether unsatisfactory. Europeans also accepted the "frontiers on the Rhine" fabrication, with the result that the democracies took heart and the dictatorships turned their fury on Father.

His talk to the Senators, which left them notably unmoved, was part of a concerted effort from our embassies and consulates around the world. Our envoys were under instruction to stress at every opportunity that fresh aggression would bring serious repercussions in the United States. The effect was minimal. Knowledgeable diplomats discerned that Father's efforts to repeal the arms embargo were getting nowhere, which explained the absence of another country's name from his list, much as he regretted it.

The Loyalists had lost all Spain but for Madrid, where the outnumbered, outgunned defenders were putting up last-ditch resistance. Chamberlain still reckoned on Mussolini's services in calming down Hitler. After a visit to Rome, the umbrella-brandishing Prime Minister bestowed on Il Duce a token of his regard by recognizing Franco as the lawful ruler of Spain on February 27. Madrid held out for one month longer. Five days after its capture, the United States followed Britain's lead in acquiescing in a dictator's victory and recognized the Franco regime.

When the State Department asked for assurances that Loyalist captives would be safe from reprisals, Father sent ambiguous replies. Within our family, Mother took the fall of Spain more to heart than anyone. Leon Henderson heard her rebuke Father for what she could only interpret as his sins of omission. "You and I, Mr. Henderson," she said, "will some day learn a lesson from this tragic error over Spain. We were morally right, but too weak. We should have pushed *him* harder," she added, as though her husband were not in the room.

He lacked the power to send arms overseas, but he could have the Navy put on a show. For the first time in five years, the United States fleet was concentrated in the Atlantic. Father boarded the *Houston* to join in maneuvers in the Caribbean—and get in a few hours of fishing. The isolationists made hay while he was gone with a concerted attack on him for embroiling America in war. They came forward with a novel explanation for what was evolving in Europe. War was coming there, they said, because the democracies were provoking Hitler.

Not surprisingly, Stalin held a diametrically opposite opinion. On March 10, he denounced the free nations of Europe for their failure to check the Axis and accused them of egging on the Nazis against the Soviets. There was reason for the undertones of fear in what he said. Red Army capabilities were at an ebb. The USSR was suffering the debilitating effects of a three-year purge of diplomats, old-line Bolsheviks and, more significantly, its top military leaders, many of whom had faced the firing squads. The chiefs of staff of the Western nations dismissed the Russians as an effective fighting force. They were not to be reckoned with as a deterrent against Nazi belligerence. What pressure could they possibly exert when the routes to Germany stretched across hundreds of miles of Polish plains in the north and were blocked in the south by the Carpathians? Besides, the governments of those East European buffer states were not far away from outright Fascism themselves.

The next few days brought into crystal-sharp focus the prospect of an all-Fascist Europe, secure for use by the Germans as a springboard into Latin America, where Fifth Column sympathizers were already preparing the way. The combination of fomented unrest, military threats, and coercion by economic pressure had worked faultlessly so far. The Nazis were preparing to start the squeeze on Portugal, to thrust that country into Franco's orbit and open the path into Brazil, where Vargas ruled as President only with the sanction of a military junta.

On March 14, Wehrmacht tanks and troop carriers rolled out from Sudeten territory into Prague, with contingents of black-clad Gestapo in their wake, primed to impose a rule of terror by extermination of Leftists and Jews. Hitler spent the following night in the Czech capital, prancing with delight. Chamberlain's "peace for our time" had lasted half a year.

Still the British Prime Minister would not concede that the Munich agreement lay in the wastebasket. Nobody, he claimed, "could possibly have saved Czechoslovakia." The spirit of appeasement was not dead yet. War with Germany was unthinkable. Britain would be devastated, and if the Reich were destroyed, Eastern Europe would be left as a Soviet prize. In the past six months, the British rearmament picture had greatly improved. He felt that he could be firmer and safely present a braver face to the Germans. He must try to make them see the possible consequences if they refused to call off further conquests. Joe Kennedy's reports from London gave every sign that he sympathized with Chamberlain.

The Englishman wanted France, Poland, and the USSR to join in a declaration of resistance as a warning to Hitler that he would risk encirclement if he went to war. The French were willing and the Russians, too, provided that the French and the Poles signed ahead of them. But the Poles balked, rejecting any form of alliance with Communists. Chamberlain decided that Britain could go it alone. Poland had seized on the bone extended by Hitler and taken Tesin from the Czechs at the time of Munich. The Poles must be kept from slipping farther under German influence. Without consulting Paris, he promised Poland full Anglo-French support in the event of attack.

Father found his understudy, Harry Hopkins, in need of some Rooseveltian instruction in foreign affairs. The new Commerce Secretary, his appointment confirmed after some testy cross-examination by the Senate, was undergoing intensive grooming, with a more businesslike veneer applied over the previously overt radicalism. His department carried its own Business Advisory Council, some of whose members were eager to take a hand in Harry's transformation. The council's spokesman, Averell Harriman of the Union Pacific Railroad, Wall Street, and Groton, was one of these "tame millionaires." Another was square-jawed Edward R. Stettinius, rich by inheritance and by virtue of being board chairman of United States Steel. Jesse Jones found it expedient to devote some time to reeducating Hopkins and so, of course, did Bernie Baruch.

They discovered the one-time social worker to be an apt pupil. Harry reveled in the company of the rich. He was scrupulous in handling government funds, he had no desire whatever to amass a personal fortune, but he loved to share in the pleasures of the wealthy. He enjoyed being a guest at their estates on Long Island and in their splendid mansions south of Washington. The racetrack fascinated him, though his gambling was concentrated on politics, not the parimutuel windows. Fresh fields and greener pastures claimed him as their own, and his old stamping grounds saw him no more.

Harry's progress in making himself more acceptable to the business community delighted Father, but his protégé's overview of the outside world was still immature. Harry could be trusted to carry forward the banners of the New Deal, but he

Father's first official photograph, in color, after becoming President in 1933.

(above) Queen Elizabeth of England and Mother drive to t
White House in 1939, on the occasion of the visit of
the King and Queen to the United States, markin
the first visit of a British Monarch to this count
since the War of Independence. (below) Father takes
General Pershing for a drive, accompanied by Secret
of the Navy Swanson, to attend a Memorial Day
celebration during his first term in the White Hou
General Pershing had been confined by illness fo
some time at Walter Reed Hospital.

(above) Mother and Father pose in the oval study on the second floor of the White House for the Christmas card photo—Christmas, 1933. (below) General Eisenhower greeting President Roosevelt and welcoming him to La Marsa, Tunisia, at the headquarters of my command, the 90th Allied Reconnaissance Wing.

(above) Father's first tarpon that he had ever caught. He made this catch off Port Aransas, Texas, in 1937. (bottom left) Mother teaching Elliott, Jr. (Tony) to swim at the Val-Kill cottage swimming pool, summer of 1940. (bottom right) Father at the wheel of his Ford at Hyde Park, inspecting the progress of construction of his Top cottage where he hoped to spend many hours writing and relaxing when he retired. The cottage was nearing completion in 1939.

Mother arriving Burbank, California, airport to be greeted by me, summer of 1933. I was operating Gilpin Airline, owned by Isabella Greenway, which operated from this airport.

Jim Farley, Mother, Father and Franklin as they left the New York house, 47-49 East 65th Street, to go to Washington for the Inauguration in March, 1933. (Below) Father with General George Patton, reviewing the invasion troops at Rabat, Morocco, in November, 1942.

A birthday dinner for Major David Brooks at the Headquarters mess of the 90th Reconnaissance Wing. General Bedell Smith is talking while Gen. Spaetz, Father, General Eisenhower, Gen. Curtis and Gen. Spaetz's B-4 pay careful attention. Colonel Roosevelt, 90th Wing Commander, Lt. Col. Polifka, deputy wing commander, Lt. Col. Grey and Major Brooks with backs to camera.

This is a picture of Mother inspecting the facilities of the 3rd Photo Reconnaissance Group which I commanded, in England at Steeple Morden just prior to our departure for the invasion of North Africa. The picture was taken in October, 1942, on the occasion of her visit to England.

Mother poses for her picture in the Inaugural Ball gown, which she wore in March, 1933.

(above) Father and I conferring just before the arrival of General Charles de Gaulle at the Casablanca Conference, November, 1942. (below) Father's funeral cortege proceeds down Pennsylvania Ave. to the White House after his body had been brought by train from Warm Springs, Georgia, where he died on April 12, 1945.

was some distance away from sharing Presidential perspectives on the approach of war and the demands that placed on Americans, whether or not they wished to get involved. The pacifist in Hopkins, which had been an early bond between himself and Mother, still persisted in his makeup, whereas she now saw as clearly as anyone the menace of Fascism on a global scale.

The opportunity to improve Harry's understanding of affairs overseas came at the end of March. He had delivered just one major speech as Commerce Secretary on a nationwide radio hookup when he fell sick again with what he dismissed as "a touch of the flu." Jim Farley's sensitive ears detected the carefully modulated "something for everyone" appeals in the text and promptly labeled it "Hopkins' acceptance speech."

The "flu" got no better, so Hopkins gladly accepted an invitation from Baruch to rest for a while at Hobcaw Barony. Bernie took the occasion to relay to Harry a forecast that the old intriguer's good friend Winston Churchill had made to him: "War is coming very soon. We will be in it and you will be in it." Harry's attention was hard to hold. The question of cancer occupied his thoughts again, but Baruch was not to be put off.

He was riding high at this time with Father, who had conceived a grandiose scheme for resettling Jewish and other political refugees in a "United States of Africa" and sketched out a map for Bernie to explain the possibilities. State Department emissaries had broached the subject with Hitler. Bernie's enthusiasm soared to the point where he spoke of raising $500,000,000 in seed money and having Herbert Hoover brought in to make a preliminary engineering study—if Hitler did not slam the door on the idea.

Further clinical tests allayed Harry's cancer fears, but, as nurse and mentor, Father had Harry go down with himself and Missy to Warm Springs. Diana stayed with Mother. Harry liked Missy, and Father was "the grandest of companions." Hopkins' lessons began most mornings after breakfast, by which time my parent would have read the newspapers and a chapter or two of a current detective novel, if time allowed. With his pale, shaky-kneed trainee beside him, he would take the daily telephone reports from our embassies in Europe and from Hull and Welles, interspersing them with explanations to Harry of what every move signified.

Harry's notes pictured a quiet week in the plain little cottage, which lacked even a refrigerator. After an hour spent on international matters, the secretarial staff would come in to tackle the mail and the appointments calendar, while Father remained in pajamas and his old robe. An eleven o'clock swim and massage at the indoor pool—a gift of Edsel Ford—then a scoot around the grounds in the open Ford touring car specially equipped with manual controls, which Father loved to drive.

Harry and Missy usually made up the only luncheon guests. The food was invariably "medium to downright bad," and the service no better, but the conversation more than compensated for these deficiencies, in Hopkins' judgment, since the host discussed everything under the sun "with the utmost frankness." After a brief nap, he took the two of them driving up and over the Georgia hills, returned at four thirty to take care of the mail, then prepared the ceremonial cocktails which they would sip until seven o'clock dinnertime. Gin was a staple of most of his drinks—in the shape of two, occasionally three, smooth martinis, or mixed with ginger ale or grapefruit juice. In spite of his nutritional troubles, Harry liked to have a glass in hand, and he was hypercritical of Father's "low and uncultivated taste."

Dinner was punctuated by Father's reminiscences. A good anecdote was worth endless retelling. His recall of what had happened to him throughout life was as impressive as his habit of collecting every kind of souvenir along the way, but he never bothered to remember how many times he had told a story before. Missy's appreciative smile gave him no clue. After coffee, he would leave his two guests to play Chinese checkers while he read magazines and more newspapers or turned to his stamp albums before a rubber on the foundation staff arrived to give his legs a final soothing massage before his ten o'clock bedtime.

Father, Missy, and Harry left Warm Springs together in the Presidential Special, but Hopkins was too ill to return to his cavernous, wood-paneled office in the Commerce Building. During the next crucial eighteen months, he was never fit enough to spend more than a few days at a time working. Both he and "Dr. Roosevelt" accepted the inevitable, unpalatable truth that Harry must give up his ambition to be President. His "acceptance speech" was the last of its kind that he made. Early that summer, he launched his personal campaign to keep Father in the job.

"How is President Roosevelt going to get around the third-term bugaboo?" he was asked at a news conference.

"You have got the answer when you say 'President Roosevelt,'" he told the reporter.

But my parent's mind was not yet made up. Mother had no clue to his intentions, which he rarely discussed with anyone. She would dearly love to be out of the White House and completely freed of First Lady responsibilities so that she could pursue the life, parallel to but seldom touching Father's, which she had fashioned for herself. She thought that he had made his contribution to history by now and was getting bored with his job. She sat with Hopkins and her knitting for three hours in the White House gardens one day, confiding in him. The essential thing for Father to do, she said, was to choose another successor, then see to it that his choice was nominated in 1940, but she had doubts that he would do any such thing.

Without Father's cooperation, nothing could be done. "He, without intending to do so, dominated the people around him," said Mother, who secretly pretended that she was among the "dominated."

He had been back from Warm Springs less than a week when, late one Friday night, he had two long, identical cablegrams put into the State Department pipeline for delivery the following morning, one addressed to Hitler, the other to Mussolini, who on Good Friday had snatched another laurel for the Axis by seizing Albania.

"You realize I am sure," the messages said, "that throughout the world hundreds of millions of human beings are living today in constant fear of a new war." He refused to believe, nevertheless, that the world was necessarily "a prisoner of destiny," when its leaders "have it in their power to liberate their people from the disaster that impends."

What he asked of the two dictators was a pledge of ten years of peace, and he enumerated one by one the thirty-one nations to be spared attack in Europe and the Middle East. In return, he promised to bring about a world conference to resolve the twin problems of how to disarm the nations and assure them of supplies of raw materials and products essential to prosperity. "It is still clear to me," he declared, "that international problems can be solved at the council table."

The choosing up of sides for war had gone too far. The British and the French welcomed his idea. Soviet President Mikhail Kalinin talked of the Roosevelt initiative finding "the warmest echo in Russian hearts." The Germans sneered that the message had been delivered to the wrong addresses. The Japanese dismissed it as "a mere diplomatic circular." In Rome, where Hitler's rotund deputy, Luftwaffe chief Hermann Goering, was visiting Mussolini, Father's cable was stigmatized as "the most incredible document in the whole history of diplomacy." Goering interpreted it as a symptom of mental derangement on the same day that the tiny Italian monarch, Victor Emmanuel, was allowed to add "King of Albania" to his string of meaningless titles.

Generally in Europe, the impetus of the messages was brief. It was overshadowed by a fresh alarm, a rumor that the Germans were about to march into Danzig, established as a Free City in 1919, to provide Hitler with a suitable fiftieth birthday present. Father was too great a realist to feel any great disappointment.

"I am none too hopeful but my conscience is clear," he told Mackenzie King. "If we are turned down the issue becomes clearer and public opinion in your country and mine will be helped."

No reply to "the most incredible document" came from Mussolini. His Axis partner waited two weeks, then in a two-hour speech to the Reichstag, went through Father's message line by line, ripping it apart, storming that if any of the countries on the list believed themselves to be menaced by Germany, they should approach him, Der Führer, in person. America's home-bred isolationists chuckled that Hitler had Father stymied. "He asked for it," said Gerald Nye.

Repeal of the arms embargo became the primary task my parent set himself. He had House of Representatives leaders in for a briefing, followed by senior Senators. There was no convincing either set of them. Senator William Borah of Idaho, slouching in a chair in the White House study, put isolationism's credo in a single sentence: "All this hysteria is manufactured and artificial." War was out of the question this year, said Big Bill, because "Germany isn't ready for it." He knew that, he added, because he had "more reliable" sources of information than the State Department's in Europe. Cousin Alice liked Bill.

Cactus Jack, also present, took pleasure in counting heads as he had at Joe Robinson's funeral. He had the same satisfaction as before in telling Father, "You haven't got the votes, and that's all there is to it." When Congress adjourned that summer, the embargo remained intact.

12

As a practitioner of the arts of persuasion, Father wanted the welcome he planned for the King and Queen of England to act as a symbol of American affinity for a country whose present political leadership he did not trust. Britain sooner or later, he felt, would be compelled to confront Hitler. Poland might be the flash point, now that the Nazi dictator had answered Chamberlain's dithering alliance with the Poles by repudiating the nonaggression pact Germany had signed with that country in 1934. To date, however, not a single sterling pound's worth of credit or a single British rifle had gone to Poland, and the alliance itself remained unconfirmed by the British Parliament.

Britain's service chiefs convinced the Prime Minister of the altogether obvious truth that giving military aid to Poland was an impossibility unless the Soviets were brought in, too, capable in theory of rushing troops across their western frontier. But Chamberlain shied away from an Anglo-Soviet alliance. "I must confess," he confided in private, "to the most profound distrust of Russia. . . . I distrust her motives, which seem to me to have little connection with our ideas of liberty, and to be concerned only with getting everyone else by the ears."

Necessity, as ever, was the mother of compromise. Negotiations with the USSR were opened in April with sounds of approval from Churchill, whom the Prime Minister continued to keep standing in the wings. As the date of King George's arrival in Washington approached, the talks had reached deadlock, only to be started up again. The British wanted a one-way promise of Soviet assistance if it were called for. Molotov, the new Commissar for Foreign Affairs, was angling for equal partnership in a fully fledged military pact with Britain and France.

Father did not place total reliance on the reports he was receiving from several of his departments, War, State, or Treasury. Too many of them took an openly sympathetic line toward the Germans, who were provocatively dumping exports at cut prices on the United States, much to Morgenthau's dismay. "Germany must have markets for her goods or die," said one apologetic message from the United States Embassy in Berlin. In London, our ambassador had grown so enamored of the Prime Minister's policies that Ickes wisecracked, "Chamberlain has decided to increase his Cabinet so that he can give Joe Kennedy a place in it."

No detail of the preparations for the King and Queen was too minute for Father's personal attention. With Congress resisting almost everything he asked, from repeal of the Neutrality Act to sanction for a $1,850,000,000 domestic loans program, masterminding the royal visit was a rare form of escape, more enjoyable even than browsing over a stamp collection. He manifested some of the signs of a nervous host. "I devoutly hope everything will go through without any upsets," he said on the eve of their arrival in the White House.

He drew up the guest lists and specified the seating arrangements for every formal meal with due regard for the most delicate points of protocol. He ordered the bindings for the presentation copies of his *Public Papers and Addresses* for the King, and Mother's memoirs, *This Is My Story,* for the Queen. For the visitors' weekend at Hyde Park, he solicited the neighbors and relatives like Aunt Betty, his half-brother's Cockney widow, who lived next door, to provide their spare bedrooms for members of the British contingent. He enlisted Bishop Henry St. George Tucker, presiding divine of the Protestant Episcopal Church, to preach the Sunday-morning sermon in the little stone church of St. James's, down the road from Granny's house, and he allocated the pews for the service.

Edith Helm, Mother's social secretary, was halfway drowned

in his memos. Why had Lady Nunburnholme been omitted from the list for tea? How about Franklin Jr. for one of the Hyde Park dinners? The roster for what became a celebrated picnic, replete with hot dogs and strawberry shortcake, to be served on the lawn behind his new cottage on the far side of the highway at Hyde Park, was okay, except that Secretary and Mrs. Morgenthau rated to be put one rung above Bishop Tucker.

Mother kept a wary distance between herself and most of the hoopla. Her homespun notions of hospitality extended to the scrambled eggs she prepared for all seasons and square dancing in the East Room of the White House after a simple supper. Her sense of the ridiculous was tickled by a pages-long memo volunteered by Bill Bullitt, stipulating in terms worthy of Lord Chesterfield exactly how a President should cater for a king and queen down to the placement of furniture, quantities of bed coverings, and the number of hot-water bottles deemed necessary in midsummer.

She could not escape Father's memos, some of them businesslike to the extreme. For instance:

> Please let me have complete list of (a) All British visitors at Hyde Park or in Poughkeepsie or on Royal train. (b) All American officials attached to them at that time. (c) All houses of our neighbors where the British will stay Saturday night, June 10th. I can think only of Mrs. J. R. Roosevelt [Aunt Betty], Mr. and Mrs. Gerald Morgen, Mr. and Mrs. Lydig Hoyt and Mr. and Mrs. Vincent Astor. (d) List of all the family who will be in Hyde Park for the picnic on Sunday. (e) List of all Americans attached to you and to me—aides, secretaries, etc. All of this is for the seating arrangements in the church. I figure that the above list will take about sixty people and the church will hold only 150. The Rector will distribute to the regular congregation these extra seats by ticket so that no outsiders will be able to get in. Could you let me have this information tomorrow?—F.D.R.

As the mistress of Hyde Park, Granny was in a greater tizzy than Father. The house was scoured from attics to cellar, glassware and her best china borrowed from Aunt Betty, the ser-

vants advised that, much as she disapproved, White House domestic staff, and blacks at that, were to be brought in for the
momentous weekend. Her butler was so taken aback that he resigned.

Her determination to queen it a little herself may have been
influenced by some recent days spent in Texas with Ruth and
myself. Granny's eyes "just naturally turned" to the West and
not the East for the first time at the age of eighty-four. She arrived by train in Fort Worth with one large suitcase. On the
drive from the railroad station through the city, her eyes were
bright.

"How very *large* the buildings are!" she exclaimed, and I
knew that she had expected to find a frontier town surrounded
by a wooden stockade to fend off Indian raids. When we arrived at our ranch, her wonderment increased.

"What a handsome house you have, and *such* a beautiful
countryside!" she said glowingly, amazed that we weren't living
in a log cabin with cow ponies hitched to the fence. When she
learned that we planned to take her to a garden party toward
the end of the afternoon, her eyebrows lifted.

"But, my dear, I have brought only one formal dress with
me—" That would be fine, we said. The shot-silk purple tea
gown that she dressed herself in turned out to be twenty-five
years old, a relic of Wilson's Presidency and the most venerable
garment in her wardrobe.

Our host had made his millions in oil. The house was as elab-
orate as anything in Texas, surrounded by landscaped gardens
with expanses of flowers and manicured boxwood hedges like a
French château. After Granny had been introduced, she murmured, "My dear, I'm a little tired from the journey. I should
like to sit down. You can have the people come by, and I shall
be happy to meet them."

She was escorted into the garden and seated in a comfortable
lawn chair in the arbor, where she greeted her fellow guests
with the style of an empress. "When I saw all those other beautiful clothes," she told us afterward, "I was so ashamed of what I
was wearing that I thought it best not to make myself obtrusive
by standing up."

There was a sequel to that incident. Ruth, who measured not
much more than five feet tall, was exceedingly pregnant. Gran-

ny, who topped her by almost ten inches, had a present for her before she returned to Hyde Park. "I want you to have this dress," she said. "You can have it cut down as a maternity gown."

Preparations for the royal visit were close to complete when the deceptively smooth surface of Anglo-American relations began to grow choppy. Chamberlain's policy of appeasement had shown up in another guise in Palestine, and Father felt "a good deal of dismay." Axis anti-Semitism had brought a flood of immigrants into the land, setting off a chain reaction of Arab violence. Two years earlier, a British commission had recommended partitioning Palestine into separate Jewish and Arab states, with British control retained over Jerusalem and Bethlehem. Zionist dissatisfaction soared so high that another commission was set up twelve months later, only to conclude that Jewish and Arab communities were so interwoven that partition was out of the question. The pattern of violence continued.

Less than three weeks before King George descended on Washington, the British government surrendered to Arab pressure in the hope of securing the Middle East against Axis subversion in the event of war. Whitehall ruled that, after a further 75,000 Jews had been admitted during the next five years, immigration must come to an end. The Balfour declaration of 1917, promising "a national home for the Jewish people," was abandoned. Arabs would outnumber Jews two to one in Palestine.

"It is something that we cannot give approval to by the United States," Father told Hull. At the end of May, Cordell relayed the same view to Congress.

Five hundred thousand people packed Washington's steamy avenues on the June morning when the King and Queen came in, from Canada, with Mackenzie King in attendance. Cutaway coats were *de rigueur* for Father and his Cabinet, rented in one or two instances for the day. That evening we dined in splendor, though Mrs. Nesbitt's kitchen lived down to its reputation. Father followed the dictates of protocol by seating Queen Elizabeth, glittering with diamonds, on his right, Mrs. Garner on his left. Mother was flanked by King George and Cactus Jack. At the far end of the horseshoe table, I had Pa Watson and Ethel Du Pont Roosevelt for company.

Father had lacked either time or inclination to prepare a formal speech. When he rose with an aide's help to toast the King, all he had in his pocket were a few scribbled notes: "Life of nation. . . . Give thanks—bonds friendship. Greatest contrib. civiliz. example conduct relations. Because each lack fear—unfortif. neither agress. no race episode. . . . May understanding grow closer—friendship closer—Drink to health." That was good for five minutes.

"May this kind of understanding between our countries grow ever closer," he concluded without a glance at his scribbles, "and may our friendship prosper. Ladies and gentlemen, we drink to the health of His Majesty, King George VI."

Mother had arranged for the children of Cabinet members to catch a glimpse of the "royals" in the White House, but Diana Hopkins somehow missed the opportunity. Mother mentioned the omission to the dimpled little Queen, who fancied that the solemn little girl might like to see her in her jewels and tiara. So the following evening, Mother took Diana to stand in the hall outside the visitors' suite to goggle, lost for words, as she curtsied to Her Majesty. Mother thought the Queen was "a little self-consciously regal," but she kept that opinion out of her column.

At Hyde Park, she pointed up the difference between the two of them by darting about in a brown gingham dress, supervising luncheon, while King George wandered around, taking home movies. In the matter of regality, Granny more than held her own with the Queen, with some new clothes to bolster her dignity. The two visitors, who looked little bigger than midgets next to the lofty Roosevelts, had a spin in Father's Ford. Dinner on Saturday night was interrupted by the clatter of falling dishes behind the serving screen. The look on Granny's marble face said that no such disaster would have occurred if she and her staff had been in charge. When the party boarded the train at Hyde Park station after Sunday church service, the waiting crowed broke into "Auld Lang Syne."

Father, who had sat up until one thirty that morning talking with the King, jotted down his impressions of his guests. "They are very delightful and understanding people, and, incidentally, know a great deal not only about foreign affairs in general but also about social legislation."

Since he was writing to an Oyster Bay Roosevelt—Nicholas, once editor of the New York *Times*—he felt compelled to add a punchline concerning *The Red Network,* a volume described by its compiler, Elizabeth Dilling, as a "Handbook of Radicalism for Patriots." On the basis of guilt by association, it named Mother as a revolutionary, along with such assorted figures as Mahatma Gandhi and Albert Einstein. There were Americans who accepted every word of it as gospel truth.

King George and Queen Elizabeth, Father wrote, "would qualify for inclusion in that famous book, which is constantly quoted by some of *your friends—not mine*—to the effect that Eleanor and I are Communists!"

Not long afterward, a similar tally of the "guilty" reached Father's desk in the shape of a confidential report prepared by the Federal Bureau of Investigation for Martin Dies' investigating committee. It listed organizations considered to be subversive, un-American or Communist-inspired, along with their members or financial contributors who, *ipso facto,* were suspects. Among the contributors stood the names of Henry Stimson, Frank Knox—and Granny, a latter-day Tory if there ever was one.

John Edgar Hoover's appointment as director of the FBI dated back to Coolidge's first term. He had extended his web of influence throughout Congress to secure himself bipartisan support for his job. Father dealt with the bullet-headed boss at arm's length. He recognized his efficiency by reappointing him, though he suspected that in many matters Hoover was not a member of the administration team. But his competence was unquestionable, so Father made it a practice never to interfere, this in spite of the fact that he knew there were many rumors of Hoover's homosexuality. These were not grounds for removing him, as Father saw it, so long as his abilities were not impaired.

The confidential FBI report enraged Mother when she was shown it. She felt strongly that Hoover had overreached himself and should be taken to task. She had been active herself in raising money for some of the organizations on the list. Most of them, she insisted, were in no sense Communist fronts. She was probably mistaken in that. A great many were supported in part by Communist funds and included Communists in their ranks, holding positions of responsibility.

The concept of the Popular Front to unite opposition to Fascism attracted enormous mass support. It had started in France, where a coalition of political parties, with little in common except hatred of the Axis dictators, seemed to be the only means of forestalling the right-wing Establishment from striking a bargain with Hitler and turning the country over to native Fascists. In the United States, similar conditions prevailed. Anyone with the conviction that the Nazis were bent on world conquest was likely to find himself donating money, time, or both to some organization dedicated to the same belief. Communist Party policy was to have its members join those organizations, where by dint of hard work they usually rose to levels of leadership. Since the USSR was the only other major power apart from the United States which consistently followed an anti-Axis line, a certain regard for that aspect of Soviet foreign policy was almost universal within the Popular Front, with or without prompting from the Communist faithful.

Mother shared this viewpoint. Father was more skeptical. He had no fear of Communism as such. So far as he was concerned, the New Deal had erased any danger of a Communist takeover in the United States. He could cite the party's barrage of criticism of himself and his acts as proof of success. The blindness to this fact that existed among America's upper classes was a constant irritant. "I am a bit fed up by very rich people," he said, "who say that they have to pay 75 or 80 percent of their income in personal income taxes." He was "reasonably sure that in the great majority of cases these people have very large 'spendable income' on which they pay no income taxes."

But American tycoons, for all their grumbling, had not succumbed to the same inferiority complex as their British counterparts. "The rich there," said Father, "fear Communism, which is no threat, and throw themselves in the arms of Nazism."

He discounted the FBI report. People like Stimson and Granny were no closer to being Communist sympathizers than Hoover himself. They responded with donations when they were approached by friends who had become interested in these anti-Fascist groups. He knew exactly how it came about because of Mother's own fund-raising for some of these causes. A number of names on the confidential list were there as a result of her direct overtures. She had no hesitancy in asking for contributions or in asserting her point of view. The shyness which had frustrated most of her previous years was shed within a few months of her entering the White House, when she accepted the fact that she was indeed First Lady in the land. By 1939, she had turned into something very close to an evangelist.

The talks between the British and the Soviets ground on, getting nowhere. Agreement on a military alliance would be reached only if Poland consented to aid from the Red Army in the event of attack, and this the Poles refused to accept. Trying to break the new deadlock, Molotov invited Halifax to Moscow. The invitation was rejected. When Eden volunteered to go, Chamberlain said no. On the Soviets' Eastern frontiers, Japanese tanks, planes, and artillery began hammering at Russian troops. Each side claimed to have shot down 150 planes with few losses, but Father was glad to learn that the Japanese had actually taken the worst of it.

In the final hours of June, the House of Representatives by a vote of 159 to 157 declined once again to lift the arms embargo. The telephone calls from our European embassies that Father took the following day confirmed his fears. "The vote last night," he said, "was a stimulus to war."

Two more steps remained to be taken before Hitler struck. On August 21, twenty-four hours before Father got back from a cruise to Nova Scotia to escape Washington's sweltering summer, the British and Russian diplomats met for the last time, having achieved precisely nothing. That night, Joachim von Ribbentrop, former champagne salesman, now German Foreign Minister, flew to Moscow. It took only two days for him and Molotov to sign the Nazi-Soviet pact, pledging the USSR to neutrality if Germany went to war.

At Chamberlain's urging, Father cabled Warsaw. The Poles would accept his effort to conciliate. From London, Joe Kennedy reported to Hull: "After all, they [the British] cannot save the Poles." Father cabled Hitler. He received no reply. For reasons of his own—elation, perhaps, over closing his deal with Stalin—Der Führer postponed the invasion of Poland, originally set for August 25. Halifax urged the Poles to negotiate with Germany. They would not.

The order to attack came on Thursday, August 31. At four forty-five the next morning, the Wehrmacht began to move across the Polish frontier. Seventy-five minutes later, the first Luftwaffe bombs fell on Warsaw. The clocks in the White House stood at one A.M. Father was asleep when his bedside telephone rang at ten minutes of three. Bill Bullitt was on the line from Paris, where, as a young man, he had watched from his aunt's balcony as German shells bombarded the French capital.

Anthony Biddle, our ambassador to Poland, had just got through to him with the news. Wehrmacht armor was already deep into Polish territory. "It's come at last," said Father. "God help us all." Within minutes, he called Hull, Woodring, and Acting Navy Secretary Charles Edison. Windows in the State, War, and Navy Departments soon blazed with light.

Edison made notes of what Father told the Cabinet meeting that afternoon about his reactions:

> I was almost startled by a strange feeling of familiarity—a feeling that I had been through it all before. But after all, it was not strange. During the long years of the World War the telephone at my bedside with a direct line to the Navy Department had time and again brought me other tragic messages in the night—the same rush messages were sent around—the same lights snapped on in the nerve centers of government. I had *in fact* been through it all before. It was *not* strange to me but more like picking up again an interrupted routine.

At five A.M. he got around to calling Mother in Hyde Park. "Turn on the radio," he told her. "Hitler is about to talk to the Reichstag."

Sometime before dawn, my parent willed himself back to sleep for a while to charge his strength for the day ahead. Before breakfast, Kennedy telephoned from London. Reportedly, he declared that Britain would fight. If he said that, he was premature. An appeal from the Poles met with a guarded response from Chamberlain. The British Cabinet clung to the fancy that war could be averted if the Germans would halt their advance and consent to pull back across the border. A message to that effect reached Hitler in the course of the day.

Bullitt was apparently equally misinformed. A second call from him reported that he had Daladier's personal word that France, too, would fight. In point of fact, the French general staff wanted to defer any declaration of hostilities until every last reservist had been recalled to the colors. The Paris government still dreamed that Mussolini would be willing to mediate.

Saturday, September 2, came and went while German armor blasted through Polish defenses and the issue of general war or a patched-up peace remained undecided. In the Oval Room, Father played a few hands of poker with his cronies, interrupted by a steady inflow of dispatches. Nobody was ever encouraged to curry favor by letting him win. He was down $35 when the cards were put away. "War," he said, "will be declared by noon tomorrow."

The belated British ultimatum, delivered to Hitler in his Berlin Chancellery at nine o'clock London time on Sunday morning, declared in essence, "Withdraw or we fight." It expired, unanswered, at eleven, and almost immediately, Chamberlain's rasping voice was heard around the world, announcing the outcome. The wail of air-raid sirens—it was a false alarm—provided an epilogue.

That evening, Father went on the air to talk about the consequences for the United States. "When peace has been broken anywhere, the peace of all countries everywhere is in danger. . . . This nation will remain a neutral nation, but I cannot ask that every American remain neutral in thought as well. Even a neutral has a right to take account of facts. Even a neutral cannot be asked to close his mind or his conscience. . . . As long as it remains within my power to prevent, there will be no blackout of peace in the United States."

He waited for two days before he issued the requisite proclamation of neutrality, giving the British and French that much more time to pick up American munitions. But this was a pitiful palliative. The vital task was to lift the arms embargo. All other business with Congress must be put aside for that when the lawmakers were summoned into special session on September 21. By then, the German blitzkrieg had shattered Polish resistance. To keep his newfound allies as far as possible from the Soviet border, Stalin sent the Red Army to overrun eastern Poland in October. "Hitler's path to the east is closed" was Churchill's satisfied comment.

Father's speech to the special session, ad-libbed from a few notes on a sheet of paper, laid the subject squarely on the line. He regretted ever signing the 1935 Neutrality Act, he said, whose very title was a misnomer, since its effect was to put America on the side of the aggressors in every case. It must be repealed.

"I am almost literally walking on eggs," he said in private afterward. "I am at the moment saying nothing, seeing nothing, and hearing nothing." A triumvirate of Senators—Jim Byrnes, Alben Barkley, and Sherman Minton—was responsible for steering repeal through the Upper House. At last, the prospects looked good for them.

With Poland knocked out, its President Moscicki hiding in Rumania and a government-in-exile set up in France, fighting in Europe came to a sudden standstill. There were no battles, no air raids, no alarms. The French army sheltered behind the Maginot fortresses. A British Expeditionary Force, only four divisions strong, improvised fresh defense works along the Franco-Belgian border. The Allies lacked all desire to provoke Hitler by attacking Germany. Hitler hoped that they would bow to the inevitable and call off hostilities now that the Polish campaign was ended.

Father took it into his own hands to move ahead with his preparations while he waited for a decision from Congress. For more than a month, the top secret War Resources Board of military men, business leaders, economists, and key government officials had been coming to grips with problems of stepping up production of munitions and mobilizing manpower. Half a dozen of them reported verbally to FDR; virtually nothing was committed in writing. If the isolationists got wind of it, they were bound to raise the cry of warmongering again.

He plotted an end run around the laws that prohibited incurring any deficit in the budget as a result of spending funds which Congress had not authorized. Capitol Hill approval was obtained for calling up an extra 100,000 soldiers, sailors, and marines, but there was no money for housing them. He ordered the War and Navy Departments to go ahead, anyway. One hundred thousand men in uniform, he reckoned, represented a *fait accompli*. The lawmakers could not refuse to come up with a further appropriation to provide barracks, beds, and medical care.

He made the White House the setting for an international conference on refugees and rattled his audience with a forecast that before the war was over there would be perhaps 20,000,000 of them, Jews and Gentiles. The time to start planning a future for them was now, he declared.

He guessed that millions of Catholics would be included among the homeless, which was a subject that ought to be discussed as soon as possible with the Vatican. Before the year was over, he sent a special ambassador to Pope Pius XII in the person of a carefully chosen "tame millionaire," Myron C. Taylor, a director of United States Steel, American Telephone & Telegraph, the First National City Bank of New York, the New York Central Railroad, and a Protestant, too.

In Berlin, Hitler's propaganda chief, the cripple Josef Goebbels, embarked on a peace offensive, designed to give Hitler the armistice he was after, along with his half of Poland. Newspapers everywhere swallowed the bait, made up of planted rumors, broad hints, and statements from "authoritative sources." Father was the selected focus of Der Führer's attentions. TRUCE PROPOSAL FROM ROOSEVELT WOULD BE ACCEPTED, BERLIN HEARS, said a New York *Times* headline.

Father was not to be drawn. The role of international peacemaker had enormous appeal, but he refused to make any move that would only give Hitler time to consolidate his capture before he went on to new conquests. "Not a day passes without my trying to see if a favorable opportunity exists," he wrote to Joe Davies, shuffled around now as ambassador to Belgium. But any American initiative must wait until "it has become abundantly clear that the path towards which we may point does in fact lie in the direction of peace."

Two of the men close to him had an informal peace plan of their own. Pa Watson and Steve Early let it be known that they would pay $1,000,000 to anyone who would "get Hitler." "Where they will get the money from I do not know," said Father, tongue in cheek.

He was as sure as he knew his own name that the "phony" war in Europe was only a prelude to further blitzkrieg. He drafted two cablegrams, one to King Leopold of the Belgians, the other to Queen Wilhelmina of the Netherlands. In the event of invasion of their countries, Mother and he hoped they would send their children to safety in the United States, where they would be cared for "as members of our own family."

Josef Goebbels was not the only source of hints that Father should make a move toward "peace" for the Nazis. Joe Kennedy joined in, following a line of appeasement that even the Chamberlain government had abandoned. The British told themselves that time was on their side, that Germany could not afford to continue the war, that at some unspecified future date the Allies would gain a virtually effortless victory, leaving both sides only moderately damaged and the Reich preserved under new leadership as a bulwark against Communism. Joe was less nonchalant and more scared. Like Bullitt in Paris, he fancied that Hitler might emerge as the victor in a drawn-out conflict, and even that might be preferable to seeing Germany defeated and Central Europe swept by Communism. He urged that Father should take the initiative in trying for an armistice. There was not a chance of that. Instead, at one point, Kennedy received a hint or two designed for his own edification.

"I do not think people in England should worry about Germany going Communist in the Russian manner," Father told him. "Also, while the World War did not bring forth strong leadership in Great Britian, this war may do so. . . ."

Throughout these months, Hopkins lived in expectation of death. He had checked in again at the Mayo Clinic for seemingly endless testing to discover what had reduced him to a near skeleton. The diagnosis was "severe malnutrition," so severe that his doctors gave him only four weeks to live before he starved to death. Father would not accept that prognosis. He had Ross McIntire call Navy experts in on the case. They promptly had Harry brought back to Washington for a series of experiments, looking for some means of nourishing him. Father would not dream of accepting his resignation.

"Why you'll be back in your office in a couple of weeks and going great guns!" he said, but Harry's recovery took the best part of a year.

With Hopkins out of the running completely, Henry Wallace came forward with his own recommendation about whom the Democrats should nominate next year. Speaking in Cincinnati, he declared that the war made a third term for FDR a matter of necessity. Hank's stock in the White House sank like the Dow-

Jones index. The struggle on the Hill to lift the arms embargo was reaching its climax. Led by Big Bill Borah in his shabby suits and shiny shoes, the isolationists got in some telling shots. The man in the White House, they thundered, was playing the same crooked game as Wilson in 1914. Unless he were checked, a similar price would soon be paid in American dead on the fields of France.

It was inexcusable for Wallace to talk about a third term at this juncture, interjecting Presidential politics in the middle of the grappling in Congress, stirring up a deeply rooted public sentiment that eight years in office were enough for any President. White House pressure, pleas, and promises had evoked some amazing support for repeal of the embargo—from Al Smith; from influential Catholics like Bishop Sheil of Chicago; from Frank Knox, Landon's running mate in 1936; even from Landon in person. Wallace, with his own eyes fixed on the Presidency, saw his best hope in being Vice President to Father after 1940. But he had spoken out of turn and deserved to be slapped down, which Steve Early proceeded to do with my parent's blessing.

"It would have been kind," Steve told reporters the next morning, "and polite of the speaker to have consulted the victim before he spoke." Most Senators enjoyed hearing Wallace being chastised. A memo from Pa reported the result: "Jimmy Byrnes phones that everything is all right and they think they can get the vote by tomorrow night. He says that the statement at the White House regarding Wallace's announcement was regarded on the Hill as being 100% and wiped out all the damage Wallace had done. "

Sixty-three Senators voted to raise the embargo, thirty were against it. The House followed their lead. The new law was riddled with compromises. The most serious was its cash-and-carry stipulation. The Allies could shop for arms and ammunition as they liked in the United States, but American ships were forbidden to deliver the supplies that were bought. In the nine months of "phony" war, the British lost 800,000 tons of merchant vessels to the U-boat packs that patrolled the seas to the alarm of Churchill, whom Chamberlain had finally brought into his government as First Lord of the Admiralty. The British treasury came in for a shock, too, when it found that the British, not the Germans, were running short of cash, compelling them to hold down spending in America to $600,000,000 a year.

In that same month of October, a meeting took place in Father's office that was to have infinitely greater consequences for mankind than anything Congress did. The caller was Alexander Sachs, Wall Street economist, a director of the Lehman Corporation, and an amateur student of science. The subject he wished to discuss was nuclear fission. Early in August, Father had received some preliminary briefing from one of Elizabeth Dilling's alleged Communists, Albert Einstein, a refugee from Berlin. Disturbed by German progress in atomic research, he wrote to Father. "This new phenomenon would also lead to the construction of bombs," said his letter. "A single bomb of this type . . . might very well destroy . . . some of the surrounding territory."

Dr. Sachs came armed with another letter from Einstein, a memorandum from another refugee from Fascism, Dr. Leo Szilard, who was carrying out his own experiments in atom-splitting, and a paper by Szilard that had appeared in the April issue of the *Physical Review* with the opaque title, "Instantaneous Emission of Fast Neutrons in the Interaction of Slow Neutrons with Uranium."

Sachs found Father preoccupied with the progress of the embargo debate, which was still in progress in the Capitol. The visitor refused to be fobbed off. He began to read aloud the pages he had brought with him. Once Father's attention had been caught, the irresistible doctor read on through to the end.

"Alex," said Father then, "what you are after is to see that the Nazis don't blow us up."

"Precisely."

My parent took the first percipient step toward spending $2 billion of totally unauthorized money on building the atom bomb by ringing for Pa Watson. He filled him in briefly, then left him to contact the Bureau of Standards. "Don't let Alex go without seeing me again," he said. Dr. Sachs came back to the White House that night.

The whole idea that, by instantly converting rare metals into exploding energy, a city could be destroyed was preposterous to most of the old-line military, who still found it hard to fath-

om the successes of Wehrmacht blitzkrieg. Pa had a stock answer for them: "The Boss wants it, boys. Get to work." An
"advisory committee on uranium" was assembled, composed of
scientists and armed forces officers. The most fateful secret in
the country's history was in the making.

Stalin acted again that fall to keep war away from the Soviet
Union, first by occupying Latvia, Lithuania, and Estonia, then
on November 30 by invading Finland after the Helsinki government had refused Red Army control. The League of Nations, united at last in outrage, promptly expelled the USSR,
the only country to be censured in that fashion. An Anglo-
French expeditionary force of 100,000 troops made ready to
land to help the hard-fighting Finns.

Father shared the League's feelings. "The whole of the United States is not only horrified but thoroughly angry," he informed Ambassador Joseph Grew in Tokyo. "People are asking
why one should have anything to do with the present Soviet
leaders because their ideas of civilization and human happiness
are so totally different from ours. We have not got that feeling
about Japan but things might develop into such a feeling if the
Japanese government were to fail to speak as civilized twentieth
century human beings."

Father's partiality for the Finns was genuine, not influenced
by the fact that Finland was the one country that had not repudiated its World War I debts to the United States. But sentiment was one thing and business another. When Herbert Bayard Swope came forward with the suggestion that the embattled government in Helsinki be allowed to waive payment of the
next debt installment, he got nowhere.

"I may be a benevolent dictator and all-powerful Santa
Claus," Father replied, "and though the spirit has moved me at
times, I still operate under the laws which the all-wise Congress
passes."

Since communication between Washington and Moscow was
close to nonexistent, he did not know what to make of present
relations between Hitler and Stalin. Nothing coming in from
any embassy left him any the wiser. Some advisers held the view
that the Germans were as much concerned as anybody about
the Soviet occupation of eastern Poland and the Finnish invasion. They foresaw further Red Army moves against Norway,
Sweden, Rumania, and Bulgaria.

Other Washington seers argued that Hitler and Stalin as a team intended to divide Europe between themselves, then press ahead into Asia Minor, Iran, Africa, and the colonial empires of the Allies. Father was inclined to this latter view. He suffered during that dark, bewildering winter from a nightmare vision of a Hitler-Stalin victory, with America's world trade subject to their mercy "unless we were willing to go to war . . . against a German-Russian dominated Europe."

Mother's disillusionment with some of her cherished Leftist causes was clinched, as was the case with millions of other Americans, by what Father described as "the rape of Finland." Up until the signing of the Nazi-Soviet Pact, she had thought of a Nazi as being automatically more evil than any Communist. "I have always felt that, in theory, Communism was closer to Democracy than Nazism," she allowed to Anna Louise Strong, a professional American Communist whom Mother introduced into the White House.

Her innocence about the regimented workings of the party was ended by the political flipflop executed by the nimble Miss Strong and her colleagues when they averred that, by signing with Stalin, Hitler was transformed automatically from the devil incarnate into a victim of imperialism, but Mother's naïveté about some Popular Front groups remained intact. She was too ingenuous to realize that she was being used, much as her children were, because of her unchallengeable access to the President of the United States. Her ego made her susceptible, and her evangelism made her willing.

One organization that enjoyed her devoted support was the American Youth Congress, in which overt Communists and fellow travelers held positions of power. Mother felt especially deep affinities for any collection of young people whose aim was to build a different world along lines that she approved of. I am convinced that she was motivated by a profound psychological hunger. None of us children in our growing-up years had turned to her for comfort, guidance, or protection. We saw her principally as an austere, rather distant woman who seldom could communicate with us. The warmth in our lives came from Father and Granny.

As Mother matured, she did her utmost to make amends. It was always she who came hurrying if one of us fell into trouble. She would fly to Seattle to see Anna, to Los Angeles to keep in touch with Jimmy, to Fort Worth to visit me. But we were too old to be mothered, and the damage had been done. So she was unconsciously impelled to find substitute children to care for as her own, like every other sentient creature deprived of its young. That gave her the chance to expend on them her enormous energy and her largely untapped emotion, rewarding her with the feeling that she was taking a constructive part in molding their lives. As she awakened, she yearned to give affection and have others show affection for her.

She mothered a wide variety of people. Earl Miller was one. Another was Mayris Chaney, nicknamed "Tiny," a professional dancer introduced to her by Miller. Tiny, together with other surrogate sons and daughters, had the run of Mother's little New York apartment on East Eleventh Street in Greenwich Village, which she shared with her secretary, Malvina ("Tommy") Thompson.

A young man and woman who later became husband and wife had a double hold on Mother's heart. Joseph P. Lash and Trude Pratt were the next-best thing to being a son and a daughter, and they were Popular Front activists. Joe, short in stature and towered over by Mother, was the formal head of the Student Union, whose viewpoints were pronouncedly left-wing. He also served in the American Youth Congress when Martin Dies' Red-baiting committee fixed its sights on that assemblage of fledglings.

Trude was a social worker, whose marriage to Elliott Pratt, son of a wealthy New York family, ended in divorce. She came to Mother's notice first, and it was she who introduced Joe into the maternal circle, as I remember. My mother, who was not averse to matchmaking, encouraged the romance. Joe and Trude became such frequent overnight guests of hers in the White House that they were there more often than any of her children. In return for sharing their confidences, she felt obliged to help them out by any means within her power. This included lending them her little cottage with its rabbit warren of rooms at Val-Kill, to which Father's principal contribution was a check toward dredging the reedy pool for purposes of swimming.

One ability of his, missing in Mother, was to know instantly when he was being led down anybody's garden path. He had none of the impulses that drew her to Joe. He was irritated by her throwing herself so wholeheartedly into youth-group causes, though she received no clear-cut instruction to stay away from them. He maintained his hands-off approach, while he gave her to understand that neither personally nor as President could he condone all she did. He also kept a finger on the internal affairs and policy switches of the Popular Front organizations by way of the FBI reports on them. J. Edgar Hoover was asked to do nothing beyond the limits of the law, and his own respect for legal process was such that he would have refused any commission which he regarded as improper. It fell to Father's immediate successor in the Presidency to set up the Central Intelligence Agency—and the fourth President after that to subvert the CIA into something close to a domestic Gestapo illegally involved with most segments of life in the United States from business to labor, from the churches and universities to the news media, from government to burglary.

On the occasions when two or three of us children met, we liked to speculate about the people who swarmed around our parents. As insiders close to the scene, we found a certain pleasure, for instance, in watching the infighting going on in preparation for the 1940 convention; in wondering how far Bill Bullitt would progress in his evident ambition to be a future Secretary of State; in trying to analyze the regard that Joe Lash and Mother had for each other. Our sympathies could be described as mixed. Though the four oldest of us were Democrats, we fell far short of being left-wingers, and Johnny was a secret Republican. He had embraced the opposition as a prelude to his recent marriage to Anne Sturgis Clark, who came from a family of staunch GOP voters, but he left his conversion unannounced until after Father died.

Joe stayed in the White House at the time that he and other officials of the Youth Congress were called before the Dies committee, which was busy extending the "Red network" line of guilt by association in an effort to prove that the administration was riddled with Communists. One Cabinet member, Ma Perkins, had been malhandled for failing to deport Australian-born Harry Bridges, a West Coast labor leader who would strike his longshoremen at the drop of a cargo hook. Jim Farley was another who wanted Bridges shipped out of the country to end embarrassment to the Democratic Party. Father ruled otherwise. Unless there were solid ground for expelling Bridges, he must be allowed his legal rights without any surreptitious trial by a Star Chamber.

The Dies committee's hearings had been under way for an hour or so on the December morning when Mother appeared in the House caucus room to lend moral support to Joe and his associates. "The committee was on the defensive," Lash wrote gratefully in his subsequent account, while the temporary chairman, Representative Joe Starnes of Alabama, was "at his courtliest" in his interrogation.

Mother took Joe and a handful of other witnesses to lunch and then to dinner in the White House. Lash reported later that Father's "appreciative laughter" interrupted the relating of the day's encounter. It should be noted that Father was given to letting a laugh cover a multitude of feelings.

Neither of my parents had much to smile about one rain-sodden weekend two months afterward when the White House gates were opened to let in more than 4,000 Youth Congress marchers on a pilgrimage to Washington. Mother put on her rain cloak to mix with them for a while before Father went out on the south portico to deliver a piece of his mind. They listened in silence while he quickly checked off the accomplishments of the New Deal to date and warned them that utopias could not be built overnight. Then he turned to affairs in Europe.

"More than twenty years ago, while most of you were very young children, I had the utmost sympathy for the Russian people. In the early days of Communism, I recognized that many leaders in Russia were bringing education and better health and, above all, better opportunity to milions who had been kept in ignorance and serfdom under the imperial regime." The murmurs of approval among the crowd died with his next words. "I disliked the regimentation under Communism. I abhorred the indiscriminate killings of thousands of innocent victims. I heartily deprecated the banishment of religion. . . ."

He had once hoped that Russia would eventually become a peace-loving nation with free elections, but that hope was today "either shattered or put away in storage. The Soviet Union, as everybody who has the courage to face the fact knows, is run by a dictatorship as absolute as any other dictatorship in the world."

His eyes took in the damp and mostly sullen faces of the crowd below. "It has been said that some of you are Communists. That is a very unpopular term these days. As Americans you have a legal and Constitutional right to call yourselves Communists, those of you who do . . . but as Americans you have not only a right but a sacred duty to confine your advocacy of changes in law to the methods prescribed by the Constitution of the United States—and you have no American right, by act or deed of any kind, to subvert the government and Constitution of this nation."

A storm of booing broke out among the pilgrims as they brandished their battered placards at him. Mother's face darkened as she followed him inside. She felt that, much as she deplored the abuse, he should have avoided lecturing his bedraggled audience in such strong terms.

That afternoon, she went over to the Labor Department auditorium for an indoor session of the pilgrimage, to hear a sulky John L. Lewis lash out at Father and invite the Youth Congress to join in a campaign to slash arms spending and keep America out of war.

At Lash's prompting, Mother had invited a band of the pilgrims to Sunday tea. "I do wish you would come over, Franklin," she said, "to meet these young people and at least say how-do-you-do." She was confused in her own mind about what deserved priority for the United States. Perhaps it was a mistake to divert so many federal millions into armaments. The Finns were worthy of financial aid as victims of aggression, but she could not rid herself of the suspicion that these youthful objectors might be partially correct in their views about the imperialistic nature of the war. Father should hear them out at least, she said.

With no great enthusiasm but out of consideration for her, he agreed to attend the tea party. The jeering of the previous day bothered him only momentarily, and not at all as a politician. Open opposition from Communists of whatever age was invaluable for solidifying public opinion in his favor.

Mother's guests had assembled in the East Room when he

was pushed in to greet them from his wheelchair. They proceeded almost immediately to gather around and harangue him face-to-face. They could find nothing right with his policies at home or overseas, and their angry voices told him so. He was responsible for mass unemployment running into the millions and he was dragging the country into war. When he tried to speak to them, they shouted him down.

Mother stood up in righteous indignation, and the booing was finally hushed. Her cheeks were flushed, and her words fluttered. "How dare you be so rude to the *President* of the United States?" she stormed at the entire group. "Even if you *disagree* with him, you should show more respect. The President of the United States should not be insulted in such a *disgraceful* fashion." This did not sit well with her visitors. For her pains, she got booed, too.

She was as shocked as she had ever been in her political career. It was traumatic to her to discover that young men and women for whom she felt such affection in her heart could turn and insult her. Father was wheeled away in anger, but there were no recriminations. "I rather think it was a mistake for me to have gone," he said. The demonstration was no more than he might have expected from Communists and party sympathizers when the Youth Congress was torn by dissension over the rights and wrongs of the Nazi-Soviet Pact.

He might have handled the situation more adroitly if he had not been bothered by his sinusitis acting up in the damp weather. He was looking forward to a few days aboard the *Tuscaloosa,* combining a little fishing with an inspection of defenses in the area of Panama. Before he embarked, he would send Sumner Welles off to London, Paris, Rome, and Berlin for a final cast-around to see if there was a remote possibility of concluding a just and durable peace. To Father, the odds seemed to be a thousand to one against, but it was worth a try. Moscow was omitted from Welles' itinerary. Father could see no useful purpose being served by talks with Stalin, whose troops were making slow headway against the Finns. Along with most Western statesmen, my parent still fancied that a chance existed of keeping Italy neutral, so a handwritten introduction for Welles went to Mussolini ("I still hope to meet you some day soon!") as well as to Chamberlain and Daladier. Hitler did not merit any such personal touch.

Mother held Joe guiltless for his part in the tea-party debacle. She did not blame him for the behavior of the others who had come with him. The fondness she felt for Joe was undented. For a few more months, she continued to help raise funds for the Youth Congress, while she allied herself with those members who strove to keep its Communists in check. Before the spring was over, Father consented to talk once again with some of the tamer representatives of the organization whom Mother brought in for a three-hour session of questions and answers. He had his own scrupulously concealed opinion of many of the college youngsters, male and female. In his book, they were simply "shrimps."

I had an encounter of my own with a few of them, including Joe, at Hyde Park that summer. I had not expected to find them there when I stopped in to discuss a decision I had reached with my parents. Hitler was rampaging over Europe by then, and only Britain stood against him, but the line of argument purveyed by Mother's guests took nothing of that into account. According to them, America had no more business than before in getting involved in an imperialistic war. I disagreed rather forcefully, since I had come to the conclusion that it was time for me to volunteer for the United States Army Air Force. I hopefully applied for service somewhere in the sunshine—the Philippines, Hawaii, Panama, Bermuda. There was no trace of nepotism in the posting I ultimately received—as an air intelligence officer assigned to the Twenty-first Reconnaissance Squadron in the woebegone wastes of Newfoundland.

13

In the spring of 1940, Father's effectiveness as a leader was at its nadir, his influence over Congress close to zero. The two-term tradition—which was an accident of history, since the Constitution said nothing on the subject—left him only eight more months before another man was elected to replace him. With Hopkins out of the picture, Father had neglected to find another political heir. In the firm belief that next year would see him in retirement, a flock of publishers were tempting him with offers—$75,000 for a series of articles for *Collier's* magazine, a United Features Syndicate contract for one or two newspaper columns a week, propositions for his memoirs, a history of the New Deal, or any other work he chose to write.

None of us in the family had a clue to what he intended. He spoke so often of all the books he was going to write, the good times at Hyde Park he was looking forward to, the travels he would undertake with Mother, that we concluded that he had made his choice.

In the weekly radio commentaries I made over the Texas network which Charley Roesser, Sid Richardson, and I had put together, I reiterated my guess that FDR would not be a candidate. In consideration of the local banks and entrepreneurs who backed the network, I joined in promoting the man they wanted to see in the White House. "If the President does not run," I proclaimed without shame, "Jack Garner is the ideal candidate for the Democratic Party." That was enough to damn me forever with Harold Ickes, who viewed the leather-tough old Texas as the administration's archtraitor.

It also provoked John Boettiger to publish a vitriolic front-page editorial in the *Post-Intelligencer,* which was rapidly bandied about in other newspapers to the joy of the Roosevelt-haters, who smelled a family squabble. He took the hide off me and insisted that the Democrats' only possible nominee was FDR. It seemed as though the son were disloyal, the son-in-law tried and true. All I could do to allay my own hurting was to tell interviewers, "If Father does decide to run, naturally I shall be for his candidacy, but I have felt all along that he will not be a candidate."

Garner was by no means the only Cabinet member with his eyes on the Presidency, though his enmity toward Father was profound enough to make his overriding aim the barring of a third term for my parent. Cactus Jack made it evident that he detested everything the New Deal stood for, which provided Lyndon Johnson with a chance to confirm his position in Father's good books. When Garner's supporters drew up a curious document testifying that Jack's reputation as a hard-drinking man was based on nothing but rumor, Lyndon declined to sign it on the grounds that it was a transparent lie.

Jim Farley had already made his own ambitions plain by having his name filed in the Massachusetts primary. Father's judgment of Jim was that he deserved to be Postmaster General, nothing more. In domestic politics, his single standard was expediency; in foreign relations, he was an ignoramus. But, plotting together, the seventy-one-year-old Texan and the fifty-one-year-old New Yorker might turn out to be an unstoppable combination.

Cordell Hull had too much cautious dignity to go angling for the nomination, but he was certainly Mother's choice, and Father did not discourage him. At sixty-eight, Cordell would have liked to see his venerable political life suitably rewarded. Like Barkis in *David Copperfield,* he was willing, but he would have to be asked, and nobody went so far as to do the asking.

Henry Wallace dreamed of some future day when the lightning would strike. Harold Ickes was not totally lacking in similar ambition. Robert Jackson, Attorney General since the previous January, felt stirrings toward greater renown. Outside the Cabinet, there were other men enamored of the thought that they, too, might be in the running when the party convened in Chicago the following July. Millard Tydings, the suave Senator from Maryland; Alben Barkley; Herbert Lehman, governor of New York; Paul McNutt, recently appointed head of the Federal Security Agency, all figured on the speculative list.

Father made a practice of dropping a few words of good cheer to most of them in turn as part of his strategy in keeping everyone guessing. One exception was Garner, whom he now disdained to the point of hoping he would stay away from Cabinet meetings. If Father let it be known that he would not run again, he would lose what little hold he had on Capitol Hill, and his Presidential ability to conduct foreign policy would be gravely impaired. If he announced that he was willing to be drafted, he would precipitate an uproar over a third term when public opinion polls showed an impressive majority of people opposed to it. To crown everything, he had an attack of flu that he could not shake. So he kept his intentions a mystery and stomped down on attempts to make him the party's standard-bearer for the third time.

At the end of March, he spelled out his credo. "We are fighting for the ideals of government and not merely for the individual man. Under our political system it would be a great pity if the continuance of liberal government were dependent on one person in the Presidency. . . . Especially do I deprecate the attitude of some of our friends that unless I run, no other Democrat can be elected. That is sheer defeatism."

In London, the approach of spring produced an itch for action on the part of the redoubtable First Lord of the Admiralty. When Churchill delivered his tirades, the War Cabinet, of which he was now a member, listened politely enough, but persisted in the fancy that the British fleet's blockade would ultimately force the Germans to capitulate. One of his endless schemes, however, did meet with his colleagues' approval. The Anglo-French expeditionary force assembled to fight in Finland would need to traverse Norway and Sweden before it could be put into battle against the Soviets. En route, it would take the Norwegian port of Narvik, 200 miles deep within the Arctic Circle and a major source of iron ore for Germany, on which the Allied blockade was having next to no effect.

The Daladier government, which was soon to fall, welcomed the plan. It fitted snugly with the current French fantasy of preserving themselves from battle scars by transmuting war against Hitler into war against Stalin. But on March 12 the whole cockalorum scheme was knocked out of kilter: The Finns made peace with the Soviets. Hitler, who had been watching for the Allies to close in on Scandinavia, grabbed his opportunity. At dawn on April 9, the phony war came to an end with the clatter of Wehrmacht tanks rolling unopposed into Denmark. Starting with Narvik, the Germans seized every Norwegian port of strategic significance on the craggy coastline around as far as Oslo, an impossiblity, according to British Admiralty thinking, when the entire operation was conducted within range of the guns of the British Home Fleet. But the warships dared not challenge the Luftwaffe, poised to strike from captured Norwegian airfields.

The half-trained force originally destined to fight for the Finns was thrust into battle, then hastily withdrawn, incapable of holding on within range of German dive-bombing. The Allied commanders had been provided with another lesson in the power of blitzkrieg, and the Chamberlain government began to totter.

"I pray God," said Father, "the Germans will not attack in the West, but judging by the Scandinavian action they are complete experts at hiding their moves." The influx of cablegrams on his desk and daily spate of telephone calls made prayer seem futile. Welles had found no glimmer of hope for peace, but he brought back a reassuring assessment of the British will to fight, as they apparently would shortly be compelled to do, since all the signs pointed to the Low Countries as the next German target.

I am confident that May 10, 1940, could be marked as the day that he resolved to offer himself for four more years in the White House. On that day, German parachutists floated like thistledown onto the airfields of Belgium and the Netherlands, while tanks and troop carriers hurtled across their borders, and Stuka dive bombers screamed down from the clouds.

Father was proud of the Belgian blood inherited from Gran-

ny and even more so of his Dutch lineage on Grandfather
Roosevelt's side. The Netherlands to him was "the country of
my ancestors." He took the dual invasion almost as personally
as if Storm Troopers had goose-stepped up Hyde Park's gravel
drive. That was the day he accepted it as his clear duty to God
to prepare and lead the United States to fend off the encroach-
ments of Nazism, hell-bent on conquering the civilized world.
As his right-hand man, he chose Harry Hopkins, though he
had barely recovered from near-fatal illness. Harry dined with
him that night and was installed as a permanent resident of the
White House during the course of that same twenty-four
hours.

May 10 also marked the stepping down of Neville Chamberlain and the call to Buckingham Palace of Winston Churchill by
King George, whose personal preference for Prime Minister
was Lord Halifax. The series of disasters at German hands had
brought the British public to boiling point. The heaviest attacks
on Chamberlain came from his own Conservatives, one of
whom, Leo Amery, cried out to him in the House of Commons,
"In the name of God, go!" Without a change of Premier, the
government would be swept away.

The British historian A. J. P. Taylor has spelled out the circumstances of the final choice. A majority of Conservatives and
opposition Socialists would have accepted Halifax, "prince of
appeasers." When Chamberlain asked Churchill in a private
meeting whether he would agree to serve under the intended
replacement, Churchill would not answer. He knew that in this
crisis he had the backing of most of his countrymen. If he resigned the Cabinet, the government must fall. The power
would be delivered into his hands if he held out long enough.

The confrontation took place *the day before* Hitler's invasion
of the Low Countries. Churchill's own account of the meeting
in *The Second World War* placed the date as May 10, to make it
appear, to quote Taylor, "that Hitler, not his own implicit
threat, brought him to power." Seventy-two hours later, the
Conservatives still cheered for Chamberlain. The only applause
for Churchill came from the opposition benches when he rose
to his feet to warn his country, "I have nothing to offer but
blood, toil, tears and sweat." What was his policy to be? "It is to
wage war, by sea, land, and air, with all our might. . . ." What

was his aim? "Victory at all costs." The appeasers were afraid he
might say exactly that.

On the next day, the Dutch army surrendered. Father's
thought was for *his* Queen, stolid little Wilhelmina, who had already fled with her household to London. "I need not tell you
that I am proud of the splendid resistance put up by your
armed forces against impossible odds," said his message to her.
However, he foresaw "inhuman bombing of England" as the
next German move. In that event, if she wished to bring herself
and the family to the United States, "I can send a cruiser or
merchant ship with convoy to Irish port but naturally at least a
week advance notice is necessary."

Whenever he reached a turning-point decision, he exuded a
special air of unshakable self-confidence. It surrounded him
during these following days when German fire and armor
turned west into the Ardennes to strike across the haunted battlefields of northern France, leaving hundreds of thousands of
Allied troops floundering in the wake. Two days after Churchill's dark promise, Wehrmacht panzer columns had attained
the Channel coast at Abbeville, Boulogne, and Calais, to stand
within sight of England. Would these last few miles of shallow
water block Hitler from maintaining the momentum of his assault and catapult his armies onto British beaches?

The first portentous cable from Prime Minister Churchill to
Father was dated May 15 and signed, possibly to play on my
parent's well-known fascination with affairs of the sea, "Former
Naval Person." It dwelled on the prospect of paratroop landings and a Luftwaffe blitz as a prelude to a German victory over
all of Europe. It asked Father for the lease of forty or fifty destroyers to hold off a cross-Channel invasion, for military aircraft, antiaircraft artillery, and steel for munitions making. It
promised that, if all else failed, Britain would fight alone.

"We shall go on spending dollars for as long as we can," said
Churchill, "but I should like to feel reasonably sure that when
we can pay no more you will give us the stuff all the same."

The day after this message arrived, Father drove to the Hill
to ask an elated Congress for close to $1 billion for guns, tanks,
and equipment to mechanize the United States army, and for
the production of "at least fifty thousand planes a year." He
must get America into shape to meet attack as the first priority.

He was uncertain as yet whether Britain could hold out. Sending the British navy destroyers, as he cabled Churchill, was a matter for Congress to decide. The same held true for France, whose new Premier, Paul Reynaud, was making similar overtures.

In some partisan judgments, which I shared, Father was "the only one who really understood the meaning of the term *total war*," the one man who saw "the awful mission of the United States in a world running berserk." The isolationists clung to their blinkers. Father Coughlin sounded off about "thieves" attempting "to steal our liberty, our peace, and our automony." Diehards in Congress, with a zealous new spokesman in Senator Robert A. Taft of Ohio, complained that the administration was taking sides in the war by flooding the country with anti-German propaganda. They found a new hero in the legendary Colonel Charles Lindbergh, a folk figure since he had earned a $25,000 prize and international fame by flying alone from Long Island to Le Bourget airfield, Paris, in 1927. He dismissed the alarms that Father was sounding as "hysterical chatter" and spread the word that German strength and Allied frailty guaranteed an early Nazi walkover unless a bargain was struck with Hitler.

White House plans for mobilization were developing fast. "I am hitting on all cylinders about seventeen hours a day," said Father. With Hopkins' help, he established the National Defense Advisory Commission, first of all the wartime agencies devised to gear up the factories, canalize manpower, fix priorities, control prices, and ration food. One of his sternest Republican critics, bluff Bill Knudsen, president of General Motors and formerly of the Liberty League, entered the fold to oversee industrial production, a bellwether for a growing host of the former enemy who enlisted in the cause of national unity, satisfied that New Dealing now had to be left in abeyance.

Not many months passed before Father could josh Knudsen about a list of businessmen eager to serve in Washington. "Bill," he said, "couldn't you find a Democrat to go on this dollar-a-year list anywhere in the country?"

"There's no Democrat rich enough," the Detroit tycoon said, grinning.

My parent debated the advisability of drafting young men into the armed forces, never done before unless the United

States itself was physically at war, but put that aside for the time being. He sent one appeal after another to Mussolini, urging him to stay on the sidelines.

Another crucial cable from Churchill arrived five days after the first. It vowed that he and his colleagues would go down fighting if Britain fell. There were no plans for setting up a government-in-exile in Canada, Australia, or anywhere else. Then Hitler would be free to choose the next rulers of the country. That helped to clinch it, so far as Father was concerned. The British must receive all possible aid short of American entry into war. But in their plight, they appeared to imagine that miracles of production could be achieved overnight. The truth was that it would take time, months running into years, before there would be supplies to spare.

Panzer divisions scythed through France, and the defenders toppled like wheat, abandoning tanks, ammunition stores, guns, and rifles to the enemy. "Evacuate the maximum force possible," said the order from London. The only Channel port left open for that was Dunkirk. The night before the salvage operation began, Father spoke into the bank of microphones set up in his study. "We defend and we build a way of life," he said tensely, "not for America alone, but for all mankind."

On May 28, forty-eight hours later, the Belgians surrendered. During the next week, the British navy, along with flotillas of fishing boats, river steamers, luxury yachts, and leaky sailboats ferried the battered Allied forces from the beaches of Dunkirk—199,129 Britons, 139,097 French. The British army had been stripped bare of most of its weapons. The country's survival depended on the United States.

Father scratched around for whatever was readily available for the British shopping list and nudged Morgenthau, his liaison with the purchasing commission, into coming up with legal justification, no matter how flimsy, for what he was doing. Soon 500,000 World War I rifles were on the way for Britain's civilian Home Guard, who up until then had been equipped with little more than pitchforks and kitchen-knife "spears" as they patrolled the countryside, watching for German paratroops. Eighty thousand machine guns and ammunition for them, some aerial bombs, 900 75-millimeter cannon and shells to fit—it was a drop in the bucket, but it was a beginning. Deliveries of aircraft intended for the USAAF were diverted, too, to bolster defenses against the Luftwaffe. The Royal Air Force had already lost nearly 500 planes.

To Lew Douglas, returning to the administration fold to become War Shipping Administrator after six years of chosen absence, Father explained another stratagem: "We are turning in old Army and Navy material to the manufacturers who have been given orders for new and up-to-date material. I have a sneaking suspicion that the old material . . . will be on its way to France in a few days. . . . The more effective immediately usable material we can get to the other side will mean the destruction of an equivalent amount of German material—thereby aiding American defense in the long run."

Intense objections to "frittering away" war supplies on the Allies were heard from Harry Woodring. Devoid of sympathy for Father's policy, the isolationist Secretary of War clashed day after day with Assistant Secretary Louis Johnson, a devoted Rooseveltian. The morning was not far off when Woodring received a long overdue letter from my parent: "I am asking that you let me have your resignation. . . ."

The campaign in France was as good as over. The crumbling figurehead, Marshal Henri Pétain, who had just joined the government, and General Maxime Weygand, the latest Commander in Chief of the French, were already talking about an armistice. When Bullitt lunched with him on June 4, Pétain swore that the British were preparing to fight to the last drop of French blood before they patched up peace with Hitler, possibly after installing a Fascist as their Prime Minister. Ambassador Bill relayed that thought in one of the stream of cablegrams he directed at the White House, frantically beseeching more help for the country he claimed to love only second to his own, though since last fall he had been looking for a new assignment.

Not all of his appeals were rational, and virtually none could be met. With their fleet intact and without the Channel to defend them, the French competed with the British in asking for American destroyers. Could they buy them or have them built in the United States? Father had Sumner Welles set Bullitt straight on that. Construction would take two and a half years, and Congress would never permit the sale of ships in commission, no matter how antiquated.

On June 10, Mussolini declared war on France. Father had an appointment to keep in Charlottesville with Mother, to see

Franklin Jr. graduate from the University of Virginia Law School. To the dismay of the neutralists in the State Department, my parent stuck some last-minute words of his own into the speech he delivered there that night. "The hand that held the dagger," he declared, "has plunged it into the back of its neighbor." He also gave the first public notice of his long-term plans for Congressional attention. "We will extend to the opponents of force the material resources of this nation. . . . We will harness and speed up the use of those resources in order that we ourselves in the Americas may have equipment and training equal to the task of any emergency and every defense."

The following morning, Churchill and his future Foreign Secretary, Anthony Eden, flew to confer with the French. His army, said Weygand, could scarcely fight any longer. In the detailed account of the meeting that Churchill cabled Father he omitted to note that, on hearing this, he had broken into tears, then clenched his fists and vowed that he would be content if Hitler struck immediately at Britain, giving Weygand time to stabilize his demoralized divisions on the Somme.

Paris was no longer tenable, so the seat of government was moved to Bordeaux. Bullitt, with a change of heart, sought to stay on in Paris, with visions perhaps of repaying a historic debt to Lafayette. Father left the choice up to him "in the best interests of the United States and humanity." Bullitt elected to remain "in a great American tradition," aiming to use his influence to prevent Nazi atrocities after they marched into the city. Both Hull and Welles believed he made the wrong decision. If he had gone along with Reynaud, they thought he might have been able to keep France in the war.

Bill Bullitt tried later to settle an old score with Welles and, at one stroke, take a prime contender out of the running for the job he felt should be his—Secretary of State. On a visit home, he instigated the setting up of Welles for public disgrace, knowing of the sexual duality of this fellow member of the Eastern Establishment. Welles had booked a sleeping compartment on an overnight trip to a Midwestern city, where he had an appointment. At the first stop the next morning, the police were waiting for him, alerted by the Pullman porter, who complained that the Undersecretary had enticed him into the compartment to make homosexual advances.

Father believed Welles' version of the incident—that it was

the porter, bribed on Bullitt's behalf, who had made the overtures. The outcome, no matter what, was that in September,
1943, Welles resigned, and Father, with the war at its peak, lost
the services of the man he regarded as the ablest in the State
Department. But Cordell Hull was still in office, and the overweening ambition of William Christian Bullitt, with his baby-
pink skin and bright blue eyes, never was realized.

To stir the country into realization of crisis, Father activated
a plan that he had been germinating for the past six months,
well before his decision to run again. The moment had arrived,
he concluded, "to put aside strictly old-fashioned party government." The most dramatic demonstration he could make would
be to install two respected Republicans as heads of the armed
forces. He found a new Secretary of the Navy in Frank Knox, a
new Secretary of War in Henry Stimson. Always eager to hit as
many birds as possible with a single stone, he chose June 20, the
eve of the Republican convention in Philadelphia, to announce
the appointments and wait to see how the opposition would respond to that.

He took Hopkins to Hyde Park with him that day, for three
nights' rest from the Washington steam-kettle. Reynaud had
quit that week, replaced by Pétain, who straightway began negotiating for an armistice. The German attack on Britain was
due to start any second now, warned Churchill. He was, in fact,
one month off in his reckoning. Hitler actually ordered preparations for invasion on July 16.

The Republicans reacted just as hysterically as my parent had
expected to his naming of Knox and Stimson. Cries of "double
cross" and demands that his two appointees be drummed out of
their party filled the Philadelphia air. Farley contributed his
own denunciation of the "betrayal" of Democratic purity. The
remonstrating was still going strong when the news reached
Hyde Park that Pétain had bought peace for France by ceding
the northern half of his country plus the entire coastline to German occupation. Bullitt laid the blame for French capitulation
on the British. It never would have happened, he reasoned, if
Churchill had acceded to Reynaud's frantic eleventh-hour appeals for more Royal Air Force squadrons.

In Philadelphia, the Republican rank and file were in open
rebellion against the party managers. "We Want Willkie," said

the buttons and the demonstrators, but Wendell Willkie was the last man that the bosses had in mind as a candidate. For one thing, he was a renegade Democrat who had been a delegate to the 1924 convention where Father nominated Al Smith for the Presidency. For another, he was an internationalist who had no quarrel with administration policies overseas, though as president of the Commonwealth and Southern Corporation he had kicked hard against the Tennessee Valley Authority. The Grand Old Party's kingmakers, isolationists to a man, envisaged one of their own kind, like Robert Taft, as the best match against Father.

But Willkie, "a good, sturdy, plain able Hoosier" in the words of one idolizer, won the nomination, "just a simple barefoot Wall Street lawyer," as Harold Ickes cracked. Father was more than pleased. The Republicans had lit on the hardest man to beat, but Willkie's world view matched his own. If Britain collapsed before Election Day, which seemed more than likely, and my parent's aid-for-the-Allies program thereby fell into disrepute, Willkie might well be the next President, but there was little chance that he would strike any bargains with the Nazis.

The preliminary pounding by the Luftwaffe of British ports and shipping had been going on for the better part of a week when we Democrats gathered in an odor of popcorn and hot dogs at the Chicago Stadium on Monday, July 15. Hopkins had set up headquarters in a suite in the Blackstone Hotel, with a private telephone line to the White House installed in the bathroom. He had made some preliminary trips to the city, but had never attended a convention before. He had to try somehow to fill Louis Howe's shoes. Farley had his own quarters across the street in the Hotel Stevens, where he would cling to the reins as long as possible to get himself in and keep Father out of a third term in office.

My efforts on behalf of Garner had been jettisoned on the word that FDR would run again. As a loyal member of the Texas delegation, led by Sam Rayburn, I had a speech prepared in favor of another local son, Jesse Jones, for the Vice Presidency. As to Father's desires, I had no more information than anybody else. All I knew from him was that he intended to sit it out in the White House, waiting to be drafted. The convention must provide emphatic proof that it wanted *him,* not that he wanted to impose himself on the delegates. To that end, he had given Harry a penciled note, to be read over the microphones. The key words said, "I have not today and have never had any wish or purpose to remain in the office of the President, or indeed anywhere in public office after next January."

Alben Barkley made the message the climax of his Tuesday night speech. The delegates, free to vote for any candidate they chose, squirmed to whisper to each other in their chairs. Then the infamous "voice from the sewers" bellowed from every loudspeaker. Mayor Ed Kelly, consulted in advance by Hopkins, had planted his superintendent of sewage in a basement room equipped with a microphone hooked into the sound system. "W-e w-a-n-t R-o-o-s-e-v-e-l-t!" thundered through the auditorium, obliterating even the ability to judge what was happening, until 50,000 people packed the floor, picking up the chant in a parade that lasted close to an hour.

Father was not nominated by acclamation, which is what he wished for most, but Wednesday's voting came close to that mark. On the first roll call, it was FDR 946½, Farley 72½, Garner 61, Tydings 9, Hull 5. My parent was a long way from satisfied. Sitting in the Oval Room, playing solitaire and realpolitik simultaneously, he must have a running mate of his choice or he would refuse the nomination. He scribbled a speech for delivery saying exactly that. The difficulty was that he had waited to hear his own fate before he named the man he had selected for the number-two place on the ticket.

There were seventeen contenders in Chicago, wheeling and dealing to harness support. Ickes, Jimmy Byrnes, House Speaker William Bankhead, Assistant Secretary of War Louis Johnson—if all the names were put up and seconded, we should never get home. The convention was divided every which way when Mother flew in from Hyde Park in a private plane provided on schedule by C. R. Smith. She had counted on spending the week at Val-Kill, enjoying the simple life there, along with Malvina Thompson, having a few friends like Earl Miller and his newest beloved drop in from time to time. A call from Frances Perkins in Chicago set her wondering whether it wasn't her duty to attend the disrupted convention after all. When she checked with Father, he did not think the trip was necessary, but she went nonetheless.

I had a foot on the steps leading up to the platform, all set to second the nomination of Jesse, whose name Jim Farley had offered to the convention. Mother, met by Farley at the airport, pressed through the crowd to catch my attention. "Father has picked Wallace," she said intently. "Don't you get up there and speak for Jones." I turned around and carried the bulletin to Rayburn.

Why had the choice fallen on Wallace, who ranked none too high in Father's esteem? "He cannot make up his mind on anything" was one of his criticisms of his Agriculture Secretary. Why had Farley shown so eager to see Mother? Why had she hurried here contrary to Father's advice? The answer to the first question was not hard to discover. Hull refused the job when Father approached him, and he had gone to Hull only after concluding that, in spite of the need to hold the party together, Garner was an impossibility. Farley, I suspected, was playing his last card. If the convention, which jeered every mention of Wallace's name, balked at nominating him and drove Father to reject his own candidacy, the anti-Roosevelt factions could name their own man—perhaps even Farley.

Anyway I looked at it, Mother's role remained a mystery. She genuinely admired the liberality of Wallace's thinking and made little of his guruism that antagonized so many, including Father. Whether her desire to get out of the White House drove her to join in a Farley plot was a riddle I could not solve.

In Washington, Father listened grim-faced to the radio commentators' descriptions of turbulence in Chicago. The revolt against Wallace looked like succeeding. My parent had the finishing touches added to his rejection speech. Missy, beside him in the study, tried in vain to hide her pleasure. For the sake of his well-being, she wished with all her heart to see him retire. When the balloting began, Bankhead of Alabama took the lead and stayed there to the end.

Without so much as a fan whirring to cool the room, Father was wet with sweat, his shirt stained dark under the armpits. The recent increase in perspiration was a sign, like the grayness showing in his complexion, of fatigue under the crushing pressure of those days. On the final tally of the first ballot, a handful of states that had asked to pass on the roll call cast their votes to Wallace, for a total 627 out of 1,100. One more fight was narrowly won. Father changed his shirt and, with Missy moist-eyed in the little group around him, delivered his acceptance speech: "I will, with God's help, continue to serve with the best of my ability and with the fullness of my strength. . . ."

Wallace proposed to make a speech of his own in the convention hall, but Hopkins brutally recommended that he should not so much as show his face, to prevent more cacophony. Father predicted that the stupidity of the attacks on his new running mate by what he called "the Hater's Club," with Burt Wheeler, Pat McCarran, and Millard Tydings among its leaders, would cost the ticket dear in November. Nevertheless, he calculated on winning by 340 electoral college votes. Following his usual practice of nonintervention, he turned down a plea from Truman for help in the upcoming Missouri primary and asked Steve Early relay the decision to St. Louis.

Two mammoth problems were incubating on his White House desk. Where to find manpower for the armed forces, which were far below par in spite of soaring voluntary enlistments? How to provide Britain with destroyers, for which Churchill constantly pleaded, to stand off the anticipated invasion fleet? Until solutions were reached, he would stay out of political campaigning and ignore Willkie. Under no circumstances, Father ruled, could he be more than twelve hours by train away from Washington; flying played havoc with his sinuses.

Stimson, the new broom in the War Department, saw the solution to the first puzzle as compulsory military service, relabeled *selective* service for public relations effect in the bill which he helped draw up for introduction in the Senate at the unlikely hands of Edward Burke of Nebraska, isolationist and New Deal foe. When Father put his weight behind it, one of the kingpins of the Hater's Club, Burt Wheeler, declared that its enactment would give Hitler his "greatest and cheapest victory." Battalions of Gold Star Mothers paraded in protest on Capitol Hill.

Of course, my parent appreciated that the draft might lose him decisive November votes. "But if you were in my place," he said, "you would realize that in the light of world conditions it is, for the sake of national safety, necessary for us to prepare against attack just as fast and just as sensibly as we can. . . ." He dismissed the danger of militarism. "There is, however, . . . a real danger of this country being thrown into some form of Fascism."

The other new man in the Cabinet, Frank Knox, urged the release of the warships that Churchill was begging for, but Father had reservations. If he asked Congress for permission, a coalition of the Hater's Club and the Republicans would certainly refuse him. If the destroyers were sent only to fall into German hands after a British defeat, he would willy-nilly be strengthening the forces of the enemy.

The essential preliminary, he informed Churchill, was a British pledge that if their fleet were driven from home waters, every warship would sail to ports of the Commonwealth countries to continue in battle. Former Naval Person would not assent to that. Such a promise would smack of defeatism, which he could not tolerate. Some other approach had to be found.

Negotiations were already under way for the United States to lease seven naval bases and airfields in Bermuda, Newfoundland, and around the Caribbean. Father judged that he could tie one deal in with the other, trade the destroyers for the bases, and have Admiral Harold Stark, Chief of Naval Operations, certify that the end result was a defense bargain for America—$250,000 worth of World War I warships, as my parent appraised their value, exchanged for real estate worth millions. A generation later, a single warplane, the 400,000-pound B-1, cost $76,000,000.

Initially, Churchill scorned this "sordid deal." For the sake of his prestige with Parliament and people, he aimed to keep the two transactions separate and portray each of them as an example of friends helping one another out in a time of need. Picturing Father as a bosom companion as well as a benevolent ally was essential to his home-front strategy. The cables from him came addressed to POTUS, ostensibly the initial letters of "President of the United States," yet subtly flattering to anyone who could decline the Latin verb *posse* and knew the derivation of "potent."

The horse-trading continued through the offices of Lord Lothian, British ambassador in Washington. Joe Kennedy in London was querulous because he was not kept posted on progress. The Nazis were bound to overrun Britain, in his estimation. Father grew tired of hearing Joe's opinion that the British, in anticipation of disaster, should guarantee to order their fleet to Canada.

A memorandum for Kennedy's attention reflected some irritation with Churchill, too: "There is no thought of embarrassing you and only a practical necessity for personal conversations makes it easier to handle details here. I should be glad to have you explain to Former Naval Person that I am totally precluded from giving away any Government vessels or equipment."

The Prime Minister grudgingly accepted a final American compromise. Newfoundland and Bermuda were to be "donated by free will and accord"; the other five bases would be swapped for the destroyers. Willkie, in accepting the Republican nomination, had spoken up in favor of selective service. Tipped off in advance about the destroyers deal, he promised not to make it a campaign issue. His single objection was that it did not go far enough in rendering aid to Britain.

He soon changed his mind when Father, fortified with a legal opinion from Ben Cohen, bypassed Congress and, on the basis of Stark's certifying that the ships were useless for our own defense, handed them over by Presidential decree. This, roared Willkie, was "the most dictatorial and arbitrary act of any President in the history of the United States."

Had he known about it, he could have accused Father of committing a much more "arbitrary act" three months previously, the day after Paris fell. That was when he put Dr. Vannevar Bush, president of Washington's Carnegie Institute, in overall charge of what his terms of reference described as studies "into the possible relationship to national defense of recent discoveries in the field of atomistics, notably the fission of uranium." Bush, Father promised, would have "my continuing interest in your undertakings." The $2 billion Manhattan Project, surreptitiously funded, progressed one stage farther. The appointment was directly traceable to Lindbergh's parlor preachments of German invincibility. When Bush heard him speak at a private meeting, he felt impelled, as spokesman for a group of concerned American scientists, to approach Hopkins and unveil plans for a National Defense Research Council. Hopkins introduced him to Father—and helped Bush compose his own letter of appointment.

The draft bill was still stalled on the Hill when the destroyers-for-bases agreement was announced on September 3. On that day, the German high command finalized its schedule for invading Britain. Four days afterward, the Luftwaffe blitz on London began. From then on, bombs rained on that city every night until November 2. Reports from our embassy there added to Father's concern over Kennedy's morale. When the sirens wailed, Joe was usually the first to head for the air-raid shelter.

Willkie started off confident that he could win without bothering to campaign. On the third-term issue alone, he guessed that he could splinter the Democrats. The lapel buttons sported by the Republican faithful concentrated on that rosy hope. "No Crown for Franklin," said the mildest of them, "No Man Is Good Three Times," sneered the most salacious. "Bring on the Champ!" Willkie shouted in what proved to be a classical error of judgment, but for the present Father could not be enticed. He was saying nothing.

One theory popular with the "America First" Committee, the brand-new, richly financed propaganda spearhead of the isolationists, held that Roosevelt, the British, and the Jews were conspiring to drag the world into war. Chamberlain in his day had blamed the Jews, too. Leaflets spread another rumor that all of us Roosevelts had made millions since 1933. A legend circulated by word of mouth had it that, if elected, FDR in his Kerensky guise would swiftly resign to put Wallace into the White House. Each of these fancies was as wild as the others. After some letters, possibly forgeries, turned up in Republican hands, implying that Wallace was intimately involved with crack-brained mystics, Father briefly wanted his running mate out of the race entirely. The Constitutional experts advised him that there was no provision for a Vice Presidential candidate to withdraw.

He joked with Ickes over the Wallace-for-Roosevelt switch. "I am not of a suspicious nature, but I have a sneaking feeling that these people would like to see me beaten. Isn't that horrid of them? I suppose there should be a categorical denial—as many as necessary. Perfectly simple to make. Perfectly true. Have no thought of resigning but a bomb or a machine gun or a fatal disease might put me out of the way though I do not anticipate any of the three."

As soon as I was commissioned, I became something of a campaign issue myself. I wangled my way into his White House office to show Father my papers. For a moment, he was too moved to speak. At Hyde Park that weekend, where we celebrated Granny's eighty-sixth birthday, which fell on September 21, and my thirtieth two days later, he proposed a dinner-talk toast: "To Elliott. He's the first of the family to think seriously enough, and soberly enough, about the threat to America to join his country's armed forces. We're all very proud of him. I'm the proudest." I felt that my greatest closeness to him dated from that time.

The news that the prodigal son was now an officer in the procurement division of the USAAF was seized on by the Roosevelt-haters as proof that he was using his influence to keep me out of combat with a desk job. In the following weeks, I was inundated with some 35,000 poison-pen letters and postcards, very few of them signed, to be sure. A fresh crop of buttons bloomed across the land with the slogan "Poppa, I Wanta Be a Captain, Too."

Willkie's high-mindedness evaporated when he realized that his chances were fading. The blitz on London and a Japanese thrust into French Indochina, a base from which to invade Malaya, combined to make voters feel that a change in the Presidency in times as perilous as these might be a mistake after all. And the "Roosevelt recession" was over at last, thanks to the pump-in of money for armaments, which had factories crying out for more and more men.

Republican strategists pressured their man to shift tactics. Instead of harping on unemployment and Father's niggardliness in aid for the Allies, the warmonger label must be pinned on him. Like every faltering candidate, Willkie was willing enough to turn ugly. If he were elected, *he* would never lead the country into war, he declared, and in big-city financial districts, he was welcomed with confetti and ticker tape. He repeated the formula until his voice wore down to a gravelly whisper: "If *his* promise to keep our boys out of foreign wars is not better than his promise to balance the budget, they're already almost on the transports."

Passage of the Selective Service Act—limited to one year in uniform with a sixty-day delay built in to see whether a stepped-up recruiting scheme would work better—played into Willkie's hands. The first drawing in the lottery for the draft was due one week before Election Day. The numbers that Father ceremoniously started pulling out of the revolving drum would decide the probable future of 800,000 young men. Couldn't the date be postponed? He said positively not.

Field reports and the incredible volume of hysterical mail reaching the White House might be omens of a tidal wave of panic that would wash Willkie to victory. The hour had come for Father to serve the party. He agreed to make five speeches in the last two weeks of the campaign. The Presidential Special was rolled out of its shed.

Philadelphia was plastered with billboards: SAVE YOUR CHURCH! DICTATORS HATE RELIGION! VOTE STRAIGHT REPUBLICAN TICKET! Father let Willkie know that his wish to meet "the Champ" was about to be fulfilled. "I consider it a public duty," he told the crowd in Convention Hall, "to answer falsification with facts. I will not pretend that I find this an unpleasant duty. I am an old campaigner, and I love a good fight."

Mussolini invaded Greece the night before Father went to New York City, to spend fourteen hours in an automobile driving through the city streets, with interruptions to telephone the State Department. He made no public reference to the assault, apart from expressing his "sorrow for the Italian people and the Greek people." His eloquence was saved in Madison Square Garden that night for skinning isolationists in and out of Congress, in particular *Martin* (Joe), *Barton* (Bruce) *and Fish* (Hamilton) in a derisive chant that his audiences were to repeat everywhere along his route.

On the train to Boston, he worked on the address scheduled for there, along with Missy, Grace Tully, Sam Rosenman, Hopkins, and playwright Robert Sherwood, who had been recruited as a star of the speech-writing task force. The political advisability of refraining from spelling out how close war was approaching the country frustrated Father. He agreed reluctantly to placate the party bosses and include in his text an unexceptional sentence. "I have said this before, but I shall say it again and again: Your boys are not going to be sent into any foreign wars."

To Rosenman's suggestion that the words "except in case of

attack" should be tacked on, Father snapped, "If somebody attacks us, then it isn't a foreign war, is it? Or do they want me to
guarantee that our troops will be sent into battle only in the
event of another Civil War?"

In the Italian section of Brooklyn, his "stab in the back" denunciation of Mussolini had stirred up so much preliminary antagonism that doorbell-ringers for the Democrats could go on
their rounds only under police protection. Two nights before
Father's appearance, John L. Lewis had threatened to lead a
walkout from the Congress of Industrial Organizations if FDR
was returned to the White House. Father saw a chance to ham-
mer away at the ominous alliance between extreme Left and extreme Right.

"Something evil is happening in this country when a full-
page advertisement against this administration, paid for by Republican supporters, appears—where, of all places?—in the
Daily Worker, the newspaper of the Communist Party. . . .
These forces hate democracy and Christianity as two phases of
the same civilization. They oppose democracy because it is
Christian. They oppose Christianity because it preaches democracy."

A swing through the Midwest left him with a few hours one
day to inspect Wright Field, Ohio, in the company of Hap Arnold, a major general now and commander of the Army Air
Forces. I saw Father alone for five or ten minutes on his train to
talk about "Poppa, I Wanta Be a Captain, Too" and the damage
it might bring on election day.

"I'd like to resign," I said.

"You talking to me now as Commander in Chief?" This with
a twinkle in his eyes.

Yes, I was. He had General Arnold come into the lounge car.
"I'm going to leave this one up to you, Hap," he said, turning to
look out the window.

"What do you want to do?" my commanding officer said.
"Reenlist as a private?"

If I couldn't do that, I replied, I was thinking about the Royal
Canadian Air Force.

"Put your request for resignation through official channels.
Give all your reasons. It'll be acted on." In went my application
as prescribed. A week later, down through the echelons of com-

mand, I had my answer. Request rejected. That was when I started the systematic nagging of superior officers that finally got me posted to Newfoundland.

In the closing days of the campaign, Willkie systematically anesthetized his conscience. "In moments of oratory . . . we all expand a little bit," he said lightly afterward. His gambit now was to challenge Father's credibility. "On the basis of his past performance with pledges to the people," he rasped before his voice failed, "you may expect war by April, 1941, if he is elected."

The Champ declined to mention Willkie by name. Not until his windup speech to 40,000 Clevelanders on November 2 did he make any reference to the third-term controversy. Then, while the crowd roared its head off, he put the issue in a nut-shell.

"There is a great storm raging now, a storm that makes things harder for the world. And that storm, which did not start in this land of ours, is the true reason that I would like to stick by those people of ours—yes, stick by until we reach the clear, sure footing ahead. And we will make it—we will make it before the next term is over. . . . When that term is over there will be another President, and many more Presidents in the years to come. . . . Our future belongs to us Americans. It is for us to design it; for us to build it."

On the evening of the day that 50,000,000 people went to vote in the biggest turnout in history to date, he secluded himself with his tally sheets and pencils at the dining-room table in Granny's house. Mother circled endlessly through the house, making sure that the family and members of Father's staff had everything they needed. Granny sat in her own dim little snuggery at the top of the stairs leading down to the library, sewing and gossiping with her circle of other beldames, only half heeding her console radio.

He had figured on winning 340 electoral college votes; he received 449 from thirty-eight states. Along with the ten states that went his way, Willkie gathered 300,000 more popular votes than any other Republican who ran for the Presidency. But against the 22,304,755 ballots cast for his opponent, Father had 27,751,597.

"It was a narrow escape," he told Rosenman. "There were

altogether too many people in high places in the Republican campaign who thought in terms of appeasement of Hitler." He was living, he said to Sam, "in constant dread that the national security might, under remote circumstances, call for quick and drastic action."

Early in December, a call for drastic action came from Churchill. Britain's single-handed struggle against an ever more powerful Germany was running into disaster. Disproportionate losses—1,733 planes against 915 for the Royal Air Force—had driven the Luftwaffe to taper off the blitz of London. The bombers' purpose now was to break down morale by the systematic destruction of target cities, beginning with Coventry, where upwards of 1,000 people suffered wounds or death in a night of terror.

Attrition, not invasion, was the present danger. With uncurbed supplies to draw on from conquered territory, from the neutrals and from Stalin, who was buying time in expectation of a Nazi attack the coming year, Hitler was immune to blockade by sea. On the contrary, with the French ports in their possession, the U-boat packs could strike at incoming British convoys clear across the Atlantic. Thousands of tons of shipping were going down every month. Of the fifty old destroyers assigned by the United States, only nine were in British service by the end of 1940.

Churchill's primary problem, as he repeatedly cabled Father, was neither bombing nor U-boats, but money. Britain's prewar balance of $4.5 billion was all but exhausted. Yet the law as enacted by Congress demanded cash immediately after carriage. Bankruptcy could pull Britain down just as effectively as blitzkrieg. The question that Former Naval Person could not let up on was, what did POTUS plan to do about that?

It was posed again in a five-page, nineteen-point, 4,000-word letter delivered by Navy seaplane landing in the water off Antigua when Father was off on a routine Caribbean fishing cruise aboard the *Tuscaloosa* in the carefree company of Pa Watson. The only guest was Harry Hopkins, out of office as Commerce Secretary and serving instead as Presidential troubleshooter. Their catch so far had been skimpy. Harry hooked a twenty-pound grouper, but he was too weak to haul it in. In this latest missive, the most forceful to date, Churchill reviewed his country's plight in its entirety. He concluded with a ringing affirmation of faith in American support, but scrupulously omitted any thought on how the massive aid he needed could possibly be arranged.

Father had been at sea for a week. The exhaustion of campaigning, which had left him drained and haggard, was forgotten under a healthy tan. With the batteries charged again, he started thinking to himself about the letter, talking to nobody about what was germinating in his head. Before the *Tuscaloosa* reached home port, he had invented what he first called "Lend-Spend." "One evening," Hopkins said afterward, "he suddenly came out with it—the whole program." Its creator did not know exactly how to make it legal, but he would find a way somehow.

"What I am trying to do," said my parent, "is eliminate the dollar sign." He used a press conference on December 17 to put his brain wave into terms every American could understand and possibly agree with: "Suppose my neighbor's home catches fire, and I have a length of garden hose. . . . If he can take my garden hose and connect it up with his hydrant, I may help him to put out his fire. . . ."

Four days after Christmas, spent in the White House, he returned to lining up opinion for what he proposed to do. "We must be the arsenal of democracy," he said in his fireside chat that night. Hopkins supplied the phrase, picked up from an unidentified newspaper somewhere, but it was Father's own addition that said: "I believe that the Axis powers are not going to win this war." He based that "on the latest and best information." That was pure invention. He knew little more than he read in the newspapers.

Less than a week previously, he had told Frank Knox, only half-jokingly, that by July 1 next year, "all of us may be dead."

III

THE SPOILS OF VICTORY

14

I was two months ahead of Father in getting a first look at the indomitable Prime Minister, a roly-poly figure in a dark-blue siren suit that looked like a child's one-piece bedtime outfit. On Saturday morning, I presented myself by invitation at Chequers, his official rural retreat in Buckinghamshire, close by RAF Bomber Command headquarters and the tunneled cliff where Sir Francis Dashwood, the eighteenth-century Satanist, staged the underground orgies of the Hellfire Club. Winston's most superior butler met me at the door of the red-brick mansion, his face a study in incredulity when he asked after my luggage, and all I had to submit for inspection was a toothbrush and a comb.

I flew to England at the tail end of the blitz in the early summer of 1941, when some 30,000 Britons had died in the bombing—more than on the battlefields to date—and the Luftwaffe was regrouping to strike at the USSR. My job was to examine, with the British, the findings of a survey I had been engaged in, locating likely sites on the northern rim of the Atlantic for development as staging points for ferrying United States fighter planes to the United Kingdom.

Former Naval Person's welcome was somewhat preoccupied

but cordial enough for me to be lent a handsome set of his Indian silk pajamas, rather too snug for my frame, which I found split from stem to stern when I awoke on Sunday morning for an early cup of tea and a view of the beautiful formal gardens. Any American who could catch the ear of POTUS was sure to be afforded Winston's personal hospitality. If it was declined, he was sorely offended, as General Marshall, Army Chief of Staff, and Admiral Ernie King, Chief of Naval Operations, discovered one year later, when they arrived in England under Father's orders to confer in secret with General Dwight D. Eisenhower before they talked with anybody else.

Winston telephoned Claridge's Hotel, around the corner from our embassy in Grosvenor Square, where they were installed in the sixteen-room suite which Hopkins maintained on the fourth floor. He was spluttering with anger at their "rudeness." The best way to apologize, Hopkins found, was for himself to depart for a weekend of Chequers cheer.

Harry was the first of us to be wooed—and, in his case, won—by Winston. Father had sent him over for what was meant to be a two- or three-week visit the day after delivering his annual message to Congress at the start of his third term. Hopkins' instruction was to "talk to Churchill like an Iowa farmer" and start arrangements for POTUS and Former Naval Person to meet that spring. Food was scarce for Englishmen, and the railroads had been battered by bombing, but Winston laid on a train with the fanciest Pullman cars, white-gloved conductors, and a first-class meal with accompanying wine to take Harry to London from Poole, the south-coast harbor where the Pan-American Clipper had touched down from Lisbon on the last leg of the flight. The Prime Minister had been fully briefed on his visitor's single-minded devotion to Father and possibly on Harry's taste for some of life's elixirs. I'd catered a different kind of diversion when Harry interrupted his flight over at the new Gander airfield and I took him off on a day's dry-fly fishing for rainbow trout.

My parent felt compelled to reciprocate the Prime Minister's compliments when Lord Halifax came to the United States shortly afterward as the successor to the late Lord Lothian. In an unprecedented gesture of solidarity with the British—and to catch a glimpse of their navy's latest vessel of war—Father made the journey to Annapolis to extend a personal greeting to the aristocratic eminence of Chamberlain's foreign policies as he stepped ashore from the new 35,000-ton battleship *King George V.* Perhaps Halifax's perception as a diplomat could be advanced in Washington. Our next ambassador to the Court of St. James's, Abraham Lincoln's lookalike, John G. Winant, stood waiting in the wings as a replacement for Kennedy, who had been summoned home in bad odor the previous December.

The Lend-Lease bill, HR 1776, had just been introduced in Congress "to promote the defense of the United States," as the text stated. It permitted the President to "sell, transfer title to, exchange, lease, lend or otherwise dispose of" ships, tanks, planes, guns, ammunition, or any war supplies to any country whose protection he considered vital to the United States on any terms he deemed satisfactory. Amendments tacked on later stipulated that Congress would control the cash, doling it out by installments, and not a dollar was to be transferred to any government overseas.

A raging debate immediately engulfed the country. America-Firsters, masterminded by Herbert Hoover, clamored that the country was being sucked into war again. Burt Wheeler bellowed that enactment would mean "plowing under every fourth American boy." Big-business isolationists protested that Britain was looking to Uncle Sap for handouts, while she equipped herself to expand her postwar export markets at United States taxpayers' expense. There were liberals who denounced Father as a tyrant intent on sentencing his country to suicide. Red-baiters screamed that he was asking for a free hand to extend aid to Red Russia if he so decided, which is exactly what he had in mind, as reports began filtering in from the embassies about Hitler's next thunderbolt.

Churchill, who would undoubtedly have preferred his every request to be met by Presidential decree, was alarmed that the hullabaloo on Capitol Hill would drag on past the point where the last British dollars would be gone. How could his Treasury pay for existing orders, and where was the money to come from for subsequent commitments?

Hull's idea was that the British could help their own cause with Congress by providing hard evidence that they had scraped the bottom of their financial barrel bare. Let them settle for their purchases up to date by selling whatever assets remained in the United States, then put up some of their colonial possessions as security for their next round of buying.

Father liked the suggestion in principle, but he thought that, even with Jesse Jones' muscle behind them, they could not raise more than $1 billion cash in the coming weeks. The total lend-lease bill, never rendered as such, was to amount to six times that figure. As for the real estate that might be acquired, he was skeptical of its value. Why should we buy bases around the world at the cost of "two million headaches, consisting of that number of human beings who would be a definite economic drag on this country?"

Willkie volunteered to help swing votes on the Hill, where Jimmy Byrnes was in charge of obtaining safe passage for HR 1776, but first he wanted to take a look at England for himself. He stopped by at the White House to say au revoir before he left, twelve days behind Hopkins. When Father heard that he was waiting in Pa Watson's office, he asked for some papers for camouflage purposes, any papers. "Just give me a handful to strew around on my desk so that I will look very busy when Willkie comes in."

The man he had trounced in November spent two weeks in England. Willkie was impressed not so much with Churchill as with the fighting spirit of the British people, currently being led to expect invasion no later than by May 15. Straight off the plane on his return on February 15, he made a disheveled but decisive champion for lend-lease. As he spoke in the old Senate caucus room, Cousin Alice Longworth sat in the audience, rooting for the opposition. Legions of the bill's enemies, with Elizabeth Dilling in full voice, swarmed throughout the city.

Willkie's glowing testimony more than offset the objections of the first witness who had been heard. Joe Kennedy could discern no hope of British victory. He also suspected Churchill of hiding deep-rooted anti-American prejudices. If this were so, he could scarcely have thrust so hard for the bill now under debate. The conditions attached to it stipulated that British exports must be curbed to prevent unfair competition with American trade overseas. Supplies not covered by lend-lease must still be paid for in dollars. Once her war was over, Britain must promise to allow her tariff barriers to drop.

Hopkins had reached London persuaded that Churchill considered himself to be "the greatest man in the world," but he rapidly fell under the spell of the tempestuous old war-horse. They got along so famously that he cabled for permission, readily granted, to stay on in England until the middle of February, six weeks in all. Most evenings, after a glass or two of sherry, they dined together in a little basement room under Number 10 Downing Street, while Churchill poured out his hopes and schemes along with the wine and the vintage port. He introduced Harry to King George, who had him to lunch in Buckingham Palace. He led him into conferences with every Cabinet Minister and the British Chiefs of Staff. He equipped his guest with a gas mask and tin hat and took him up to Scotland to see Halifax embark at Scapa Flow. He conducted Harry on a cross-country tour to show him bomb damage, defense works—and the respect that the British had for their picturesque Prime Minister.

He had him to Chequers for one weekend after another, where Harry wore his overcoat indoors from morning until night to fend off the winter chill. He plied him simultaneously with war secrets and the astounding assortment of alcohol—scotch, brandy, and champagne—that kept Winston going through the day. To the alarm of the FBI men detailed to keep tabs on him, Harry would leave some of those confidential documents scattered around his hotel bedroom until he came to learn better.

He was won over completely, as the incoming flow of his letters and cablegrams to Father demonstrated, each more fervently pro-British than the last, extolling Churchill and forwarding his shopping lists for weaons and war supplies. "Your decisive action now can mean the difference between defeat and victory for this country," said a key sentence in Harry's concluding cable. Winston himself could not have stated his case more vigorously.

From the time of that visit, Harry fought in Churchill's corner, concerning himself more with presenting the Prime Minister's policies to Father than with putting over FDR's viewpoint to Winston. That was a flaw in the otherwise unblemished record of valor and unbroken loyalty. Churchill came to use Hopkins as a sounding board before he personally tried out his desires with POTUS. The contacts he nursed with Harry came second only to his private and personal exchanges with Father, which before the war was over produced something in the region of 1,700 letters, cablegrams, and other messages. It was left to a British historian to remark that by excluding his communications from normal diplomatic channels, Winston assured himself of a mine of exclusive documents to draw on when he came to write his version of history.

Father was not waiting for passage of lend-lease—the Senate voted 60 to 31 in favor on March 8—to push almost all pending requisitions through to the British or to weave together the strands of Anglo-American cooperation. London teemed with Americans in and out of uniform. British brains were being enlisted to work on the exploration of atomic energy. Staff talks with the British in Washington, under way since the end of January, were at the point of producing the first plans for combined strategy on the assumption that both countries would ultimately be involved in fighting both Germany and Japan. Military intelligence was being pooled. RAF bomber crews were undergoing secret instruction at United States airfields. G-men and their transatlantic counterparts were jointly checking on spying and sabotage by Nazi agents here and overseas. Admiral King had the fleet on intensified battle training.

In April, Father made a deal with the Danish Minister in Washington to keep the Nazis out of Greenland by building transit bases there, and the exiled government of Denmark sacked their envoy in protest. In May, the President ordered the construction, at the rate of 500 a month, of a fleet of strategic bombers, staggeringly big by contemporary standards, that would blitz Germany by daylight in due course. That same month, he created the Office of Civilian Defense; started American warships protecting the Atlantic sea lanes for convoys to Britain; and added China to the lend-lease list to bolster Generalissimo Chiang Kai-shek's vacillating struggle against the Japanese.

But no date was set for the meeting with Churchill. The most peremptory reason was Father's health. He came down with intestinal flu, and a checkup disclosed the cause of the grayness that so often showed in his face. His heart was as sound as a bell, but he was suffering from iron deficiency anemia. The loss of blood resulted from an affliction to which human beings have succumbed at times of excessive tension throughout history, including Julius Caesar and Napoleon Bonaparte. Father had a severe attack of hemorrhoids. The treatment prescribed was ferrous sulfate, not surgery, but July was over before he was fit again.

By that time, Missy was more gravely ill than he. It was surely no coincidence that she was stricken with a condition also produced by stress when she made Father's life her own. The stroke she suffered as a consequence of hypertension left her partially paralyzed and with her speech impaired. Father would assure himself that she was "a bit better now," but for her there was no recovery. She was never again well enough to pick up her burden of responsibilities. Evenings in his study grew increasingly lonely.

The hemorrhaging he suffered could explain the odd reference to dying he had made to Frank Knox. The alarming perception of mortality prompted his interest to flare in Lucy Mercer Rutherfurd. His thoughts dwelt on the days when he was prepared to divorce Mother and give up the Navy Department to enlist in World War I as a step toward making Lucy his bride. Lucy's letters to him in Europe when he was visiting the battlegrounds as Assistant Secretary were found in his luggage by Mother after he arrived home on a stretcher. In the showdown that came while he was still bedridden, Granny's threat to cut him off financially broke up the romance with Lucy, or so Mother believed.

Yet on January 6 Mrs. Rutherfurd had sat in a closed limousine on the fringe of the shivering crowd on Capitol Plaza, listening to the Inaugural speech he had dictated on New Year's Day, with Sherwood, Hopkins, and Rosenman working alongside him. "We look forward," he told Congress and the nation, "to a world founded upon four essential human freedoms: The first is freedom of speech and expression—everywhere in the world. The second is freedom of every person to worship God in his own way—everywhere in the world. The third is freedom from want—which, translated into world terms, means economic understandings which will secure to every nation a healthy peacetime life for its inhabitants—everywhere in the world. The fourth is freedom from fear—which, translated into world terms, means a worldwide reduction of armaments to such a point and such a thorough fashion that no nation will be in a position to commit an act of physical aggression against any neighbor—anywhere in the world. That is no vision of a distant millennium. It is a definite basis for a kind of world attainable in our own time and generation."

He had not changed his thinking up to the moment of his death. I find no cause to question its validity today.

A few weeks later, he relived his memories of the circumstances surrounding the first, scarifying break with Lucy. One of his oldest and dearest friends, Josephus Daniels, his chief at the Navy Department at the time, would remember enough of the details as he had been told them twenty-three years ago to read between the lines of Father's letter to him, recapturing the days when he was only thirty-five:

> When I had nearly finished the inspection work on the other side in September, 1918, I think I wrote or cabled you that after I had come home and reported to you, I wanted to go back to Europe with an assignment, in uniform, to the Naval Railway Battery. Good old Admiral Plunkett had talked with me about it at St. Nazaire in France where the guns were being assembled and were nearly ready. . . . He said that he would take me on, if I came back, in his outfit with the rank of Lieutenant Commander.
>
> A little later, as you remember, I came back on the Leviathan with "flu" and a touch of pneumonia and was laid up in New York and Hyde Park for about three weeks. I got back to the Department, as I remember it, about the twentieth of October, told you of my desire, and you said that you could not conscientiously ask me to stay in Washington any longer. Then I went to see the President and the President told me that in his judgment I was too late—that he had received the first suggestion of an armistice from Prince Max of Baden, and that he hoped the war would be over very soon. That ended the effort on my part because within a few days it was clear that some form of armistice would be worked out.

Seeing Lucy more often, when a rare hour or so could be manipulated into his schedule, became integral to his life. He had no more qualms about keeping this hidden from Mother than in telling her the white lie that covered his departure for Argentia Harbor, Newfoundland, and the long delayed meeting with Former Naval Person.

"I'm going to take a little trip up through the Cape Cod Canal to do some fishing," he announced one Sunday morning in August as he left by train with Captain John Beardall, his new naval aide, and Pa Watson for New London, Connecticut, where the docile old *Potomac* lay waiting. He did, in fact, drop a line in Buzzards Bay the next day, along with some guests who had been picked up for a few hours afloat. One of them was the lively, laughing Crown Princess Marthe of Norway, a refugee living with her two daughters in Bethesda, Maryland, for the past year. She was a great favorite of Father's and a useful source of information about the intriguing that went on among exile governments in London. The *Potomac* did, in truth, traverse the Cape Cod Canal, but the seemingly familiar figure sitting on deck under a panama hat was not Father. For the one occasion in his life that I know of, he resorted to a double.

Late the night before, he had been put aboard the cruiser *Augusta,* with Ernie King in personal command, to steam north escorted by half a dozen other warships toward Argentia, to await a rendezvous. The British battleship *Prince of Wales,* was heading across the Atlantic with Winston and his team, plus a seagoing companion for backgammon in Harry Hopkins, who had wound up a second trip to London. The Prime Minister would have preferred a more spectacular and perhaps sunnier setting than this remote bay hemmed in by bush and stunted pines, but he bowed to Father's wishes.

The most momentous item to be discussed was of recent origin. Hitler's onslaught against Soviet Russia was only forty-five days old, which was twice as long as his generals had expected the despised Red Army to hold out against the lightning thrusts of the Panzers, the screaming dive-bombers, and the pounding of mobile artillery. Much the same assessment of Soviet capacity prevailed among the British and American army chieftains, but that did not deter either Churchill or Father from announcing immediate aid for the USSR. My parent was eager to get shipments delivered before winter ice clogged every Arctic Ocean port east of Murmansk, despite the protests from the military that they would fall into German hands.

The risk was worth taking, in his estimation. The first four days of blitzkrieg had brought no sign of Red Army regrouping when he summed up his thinking about what he termed "this Russian diversion" in a letter to Bill Leahy, whom he had sent as ambassador to Pétain's government in Vichy France. If it amounted to more than that, he wrote, "it will mean the liberation of Europe from Nazi domination—and at the same time I do not think we need worry about any possibility of Russian domination." It was unlikely that Leahy concurred, but he was never a man to argue with a President.

Father wanted the best firsthand information obtainable about Stalin and his people. Hopkins was already in London making final preparations for Argentia. He proposed that he interrupt talks with the British to fly to Moscow. My parent enthusiastically agreed. His authorizing cablegram instructed Harry to ask the Soviet leader in Father's name "how we can most expeditiously and effectively make available the assistance which the United States can render to your country in its magnificent resistance to the treacherous aggression by Hitlerite Germany."

Harry spent most of his waking hours during his two days in Moscow closeted in the Kremlin. There was not a moment to spare for socializing, but the terse-mannered dictator in the baggy tunic and gleaming boots opened up to Hopkins in much the same way as Churchill had, assessing his armies' prospects and their needs like "a perfectly coordinated machine," in Harry's phrase. A lend-lease Catalina flying boat, bucketing through headwinds, carried him back to Scapa Flow on the eve of the *Prince of Wales'* sailing. He was so desperately ill by then that there were fears he would not survive the crossing.

On the basis of preliminary reports from Harry, aid for the Soviets had leaped close to the top of Father's priorities. At the final Cabinet meeting before he left for Argentia, he applied the goad. "Nearly six weeks have elapsed since the Russian War began, and we have done practically nothing to get any of the materials they asked for on their actual way to delivery in Siberia. Frankly, if I were a Russian I would feel that I had been given the runaround in the United States."

The goad was left in charge of his liaison officer with the Office of Emergency Management, Wayne Coy, in his absence. "Please, with my full authority," Father told him, "use a heavy

hand—act as a burr under the saddle and get things moving!"
Two hundred bombers should be sent from stock to the USSR.
If the Germans could be held until October 1, "Russia is safe
until the spring. Step on it!"

At my base, Gander Lake, I received strange secret orders to
pick up the British Minister of War Production, bustling Lord
Beaverbrook, from an incoming British plane, then take him by
train to a transfer point and fly him to Argentia Harbor. I was
in the copilot seat of our little OA-10 Grumman when we
cleared the mountain spur overlooking the bay. None of us
aboard could figure out how the bay had come to be filled with
American warships. The puzzle was solved a few minutes later,
after we had tied to a mooring post and I had been whisked in a
tender to the *Augusta*. Along with Lieutenant (jg) Franklin Jr.,
who was equally surprised to find himself on the scene, I got to
see Father shortly before lunch, which my brother and I shared
with him.

This was to be the first of five world summit meetings that I
was to be privileged to attend with Father. Later, I was to attend
the Casablanca Conference, the two Cairo conferences, and the
one at Teheran. Franklin Jr. joined me for the Argentia meeting and later also attended part of the Casablanca Conference.
I missed Bretton Woods and the Yalta Conference, which my
sister, Anna, was privileged to attend. I must say that these rare
moments of close communion with Father stand out in my
mind as the most satisfying of my life. I gained a special insight
into the mind and heart of FDR. I felt the strong love and pride
he had for all of us children. Above all, I learned what a unique
mind he had and how formidable was his grasp of the course of
human events. All my life I feel irresistible pride that this man
was my father. What a glorious accident of fate, with its not un-
mixed blessings! I may never live up to the heritage of my parents, but I glory in being of their flesh and blood.

Lazing around that afternoon in his quarters—routinely the
captain's—we got to talking about lend-lease schedules for the
British, whose Prime Minister was due in tomorrow. "They'll be
worried about how much of our production we're going to divert to the Russians," Father said. He snapped his fingers, zilch,
as he added, "I know already how much faith the PM has in
Russia's ability to stay in the war."

He had a shrewd idea of what would happen when he and

Churchill got down to cases. "Watch and see if the PM doesn't start off by demanding that we immediately declare war against the Nazis." A courier interrupted us briefly with a satchelful of documents. Then Father went back to rehearsing himself for the next day's conversations.

"The British Empire is at stake here." He cocked an eyebrow. "If in the past, German and British economic interests have operated to exclude us from world trade, kept our merchant shipping down, closed us out of this or that market, and now Germany and Britain are at war, what should we do?"

Though our hearts and our natural interests lay with the British, he said, "we've got to make clear from the very outset that we don't intend to be simply a good-time Charlie who can be used to help the British Empire out of a tight spot and then be forgotten forever. . . . America won't help England in this war simply so that she will be able to continue to ride rough-shod over colonial peoples." There were signs that a little fur was destined to fly when Winston came aboard in the morning.

He arrived in pomp and splendor shortly after the *Prince of Wales* anchored close by in the gray drizzle. I held Father's arm while the two of them met, to gossip about their health, their worries, and their jobs, and to go immediately on to a "Franklin" and "Winston" basis for their private talks.

The PM had brought along platoons of top brass, advisers, aides, secretaries, and a Ministry of Information crew armed with notebooks and cameras. That was surprise number one in the matter of public relations and self-promotion for Father, who had reached agreement in advance with Churchill that no reporters or photographers would cover this conference.

"We'd damn well better get some cameramen and some film aboard in a hurry," Hap Arnold whispered when he saw the size of the turnout, so back to Gander Lake went the Grumman to pick up a couple of men. Arnold had brought along no assistant for what Father had foreseen as a get-together where he and the PM could broaden their personal relationship beyond the limitations of correspondence and telephone calls, while they roughed out what the declared war aims of their countries might be. On the American side, preparations had been so secretive and hasty that not so much as an agenda was ready. When Hap noticed his counterpart, Air Marshal Sir Wilfred

Freeman, flanked three-deep with aides, I was rapidly pressed into service as a notetaker.

The British enjoyed a further advantage in the presence of Averell Harriman, whose London job as expediter of lend-lease shipments brought him into Winston's orbit, to be courted, dined, and entertained for weekends at Chequers. Harriman supposedly was to coordinate all his activities with Gil Winant, but the less obtrusive ambassador was soon pushed into the background. Half the time, to his embarrassment, Gil had no clue to what Harriman was up to. His protests to Father had little effect. Fond as he was of Winant, he regarded Harriman as a go-getter who could produce results in double-time. That judgment was fortified by Hopkins, no friend of Winant, who consistently sang the praises of his one-time mentor in the mysteries of big business when Harry entered the Commerce Department. Harriman could be relied on to push a Churchillian point of view.

He and the much more selective Sumner Welles were included among the guests at the formal dinner Father gave in the captain's saloon of the *Augusta* on Saturday night. On his right, of course, sat Winston, his shoulders hunched forward like a bull's. Around the table were his top team—Sir Alexander Cadogan, Permanent Under Secretary of State for Foreign Affairs; his Chiefs of Staff, Admiral Sir Dudley Pound and General Sir John Dill; Sir Wilfred Freeman; and Churchill's inseparable Lord Cherwell, who as Frederick Lindemann had headed the group of British scientists that invented radar. They all looked so resplendent as to put us Americans—Stark, Marshall, King, Arnold, Hopkins, and the rest—in the shade.

After vegetable soup, broiled chicken, and chocolate ice cream, Churchill launched into a review of the war situation that dazzled every one of us with its brilliance. With an eight-inch Corona slewing around between his teeth, he told of battles lost, "but Britain always wins the wars." His country had been on the brink of defeat, "but Hitler and his generals were too stupid. They never knew. Or else they never dared."

Tonight, Father, who dominated every previous gathering I had attended with him, was content to listen, fiddling with his pince-nez, doodling on the tablecloth with a burnt match, rubbing his eyes when the smoke from a Camel irritated them, throwing in an occasional question.

"The Russians?"

The cigar tilted upward. "Of course, they're much stronger than we ever dared to hope. But no one can tell how much longer. . . . When Moscow falls. . . . As soon as the Germans are beyond the Caucasus. . . . When Russian resistance finally ceases. . . ."

Winston was dicing for heavy stakes. The lion's share of lend-lease should go to the British. Any aid to the Soviets would eventually be wasted. "The Americans *must* come in at our side," he concluded, rearing back in his chair. "You must come in if you are to survive!"

On Sunday morning shortly after eleven, we were piped aboard the *Prince of Wales* to sing "Onward Christian Soldiers" at a joint service on the quarterdeck under the shadow of the sixteen-inch guns. Tears came to Winston's eyes before that hymn was over. As we prayed in unison, an irreverent thought crossed my mind: "Here are a couple of men who are important only as they stand at the head of two mighty nations, united if only for this moment. . . ."

Unity dissolved in the afternoon sessions when the brass on each side got down to business. With much politeness, the British made it plain that they could not go along with the arguments of Marshall, Arnold, and King that tanks and planes and artillery for the Soviets meant more dead Nazis, whereas Britain for the time being could only stockpile much of her lend-lease supplies. The humiliation of Narvik had been followed by further defeats in Greece and Crete. The only land fighting the British were engaged in now was in North Africa, where General Erwin Rommel, a German prodigy, had taken over command from the fumbling Italians and constantly threatened the Suez Canal, British lifeline to the Indian Ocean.

Dinner in the *Augusta* that evening was more informal—Father, Winston, their immediate aides, Franklin Jr., and myself. The brandy disappeared steadily and many a cigar burned to ashes before the session broke up at two o'clock. Tonight, the sizing-up was over. The two giants were ready to challenge each other. Churchill listened with eyebrows knitted to my parent's opening gambit:

"Of course, after the war one of the preconditions of any lasting peace will have to be the greatest possible freedom of trade.

No artificial barriers. . . . Markets open for healthy competition."

Churchill shifted in his chair. "The British Empire trade agreements are—"

"—a case in point. It's because of them that the people of India and Africa, of all the colonial Near East and Far East, are still as backward as they are."

His listener's neck flushed. "Mr. President, England does not propose for a moment to lose its favored position among the British Dominions. The trade that has made England great shall continue, and under conditions prescribed by England's ministers."

Father answered slowly. "It is along in here somewhere that there is likely to be some disagreement between you, Winston, and me. . . . If we are to arrive at a stable peace, it must involve the development of backward countries, backward people. How can this be done? It can't be done obviously by eighteenth-century methods. . . . *Twentieth*-century methods involve bringing industry to these colonies. *Twentieth*-century methods include increasing the wealth of a people by increasing their standard of living, by educating them, by bringing them sanitation—by making sure that they get a return for the raw wealth of their countries."

The Prime Minister was turning red. "You mentioned India?"

"Yes. I can't believe that we can fight a war against Fascist slavery and at the same time not work to free people all over the world from backward colonial policy. . . . The peace cannot include any continued despotism. The structure of the peace demands will get equality of peoples. Equality of peoples involves the utmost freedom of competitive trade. . . ."

It was an argument that could have no resolution. Whenever the two men sat down together, Father would keep prodding Churchill over India, Burma, the colonies, probing his conscience, needling, not out of mischief but from conviction, which was what worried Winston most.

When the British finally said goodnight, I helped Father to his cabin to join in a last cigarette. "A real old Tory, isn't he?" He grunted. "Oh, I'll be able to work with him. Don't worry about that. We'll get along famously." He puffed smoke from his holder. "Winnie has one supreme mission in life, but only one. He's a perfect wartime Prime Minister. His one big job is to see that Britain survives this war. . . . But Winston Churchill lead England after the war? It would never work."

More than any other factor, it was Hopkins' reports on the Russians that persuaded the reluctant British that the Soviet Union should receive its share of lend-lease supplies. Other than that, the Anglo-American brass rarely saw eye to eye on any subject that was introduced. Marshall recommended a British withdrawal from the Middle East to end what the Americans saw as a pointless drain on resources. Arnold could not believe that bombing alone would defeat Germany, but Winston, always remembering the holocaust of World War I, nurtured the fancy that the war would never see great armies locked in battle again. Marshall had different ideas about that.

Much of the talk centered on Japan. The exodus of Red Army troops from Manchuria to meet the German attack in the West had eased Tokyo's fears of Soviet countermoves in that quarter and thereby increased the danger of fresh Japanese incursion elsewhere. With their occupation of Indochina completed, the next probable targets would be Malaya and the Dutch East Indies. The rundown British base at Singapore remained the only obstacle in their path, and the British were short of planes and ships for its protection. Could Father warn the Japanese against further aggression in the southwestern Pacific—and against the USSR, too, to help calm Stalin's nightmares of war on both his frontiers? Father promised that as soon as he returned to Washington he would summon Ambassador Kichisaburo Nomura to tell him that if Indochina were freed, the United States would attempt to come to terms with Japan over supplying essential oil and raw materials to the ravenous homeland.

On Monday, I was in and out of Father's cabin most of the morning as he huddled with Churchill over a document which Cadogan had carried over in his briefcase. What the British wanted, mainly as a publicity handout, was a ringing declaration of principle between two great nations engaged in a common cause. They sought "no aggrandizement," said Cadogan's draft; and "no territorial changes" contrary to a population's wishes. They would work toward sharing essential produce and "effective international organization" to afford security for all nations. The Atlantic Charter was in its birth throes.

After being rowed ashore in a whaleboat, wearing a one-piece jumper with truncated sleeves and shorts cut above the knees, Winston interrupted an afternoon stroll to bombard his companions with a handful of rocks. He returned to dine with us and to wind up his argument. Late that night, he stood over Father, waving a stubby forefinger under his nose. "Mr. President," he cried, "I believe you are trying to do away with the British Empire. But in spite of that, in spite of that we know that you constitute our only hope. And," he whispered, " *you* know that *we* know it. *You* know that *we* know that without America the Empire won't stand."

The background to his outburst lay in some additions to Cadogan's paragraphs that Father had pressed for. A new pledge had been written in: "That they will endeavor, with due respect for their existing obligations, to further the enjoyment of all States, great or small, victor or vanquished, of access, on equal terms, to the trade and to the raw materials of the world which are needed for their economic prosperity." Churchill was acknowledging in his words to Father that the peace could be won only according to precepts laid down by America. British colonial policy would be a dead duck.

My parent took the finished charter much more seriously than the British, to whom it represented little more than a declaration of intent. It was his inspiration to tack on its final paragraph:

> That they believe that all of the nations of the world, for realistic as well as spiritual reasons, must come to the abandonment of the use of force. Since no future peace can be maintained if land, sea or air armaments continue to be employed by nations which threaten, or may threaten, aggression outside of their frontiers, they believe, pending the establishment of a wider and permanent system of general security, that the disarmament of such nations is essential. They will likewise aid and encourage all other practicable measures which will lighten for peace-loving peoples the crushing burden of armaments.

(Of United States spending for 1975–76, the burden of armaments accounted for $100 billion, and the budget carried a $30 billion deficit.)

The Atlantic Charter never existed as a signed and sealed page of parchment. That might have made it look suspiciously like a treaty, to be submitted for ratification by a Senate which blew hot and cold about war and the peace to follow. "There isn't a copy . . . so far as I know," Father cagily told reporters later. "I haven't one. The British haven't got one. The nearest thing you will get is from the radio operators on the *Augusta* and *Prince of Wales.*" But the charter was none the less real for the world's colonial peoples—Indians, Burmese, Malays, and the rest—who soon began to ask if its words truly meant what they said.

A cablegram to the Kremlin summarized the results of the conference for the information of Stalin. The wheels were set in motion for Americans and British to work out details of aid for the Russians at a Moscow meeting in the fall. Harriman was chosen to head the United States team.

With Father's arm on mine, we watched the British battleship slip out of the bay just before five o'clock on Tuesday afternoon. The *Augusta* gave her passing honors, and the band played "Auld Lang Syne." Four months later, the *Prince of Wales* and her crew, a few of whom we had come to know briefly, went down in the waters off Malaya, riddled by Japanese torpedoes.

On the day she sailed from Argentia harbor, Congress delivered a reminder to Father that he was walking on eggs in everything he said or did relating to the war. If it came to a showdown, his preparedness programs could be nullified overnight by a hostile vote. With its ears cocked to the sentiments of families begging to have their sons back home after twelve months spent in training, the House of Representatives was not at all sure that the country needed a conscript army. Tuned in on the debate on the Hill, draftees started chalking O.H.I.O. on latrine walls—Over the Hill in October. Without extension by the lawmakers of the one-year term of service, many a GI was ready to desert. The United States would be left without an effectual fighting force.

Though America-Firsters arranged for a million "keep out"

postcards to be mailed under Burt Wheeler's frank, the Senate recognized the necessity at a time of peril of extending the draft. In the House, passage came by one solitary vote—203 to 202. Senator Wheeler correctly read the moral: "This vote clearly indicated that the administration could not get a resolution through the Congress for a declaration of war. . . . It is also noticed that the Congress does not take seriously the cry of the administration that the so-called emergency is greater now than it was a year ago."

On September 6, when Father was at Hyde Park for the weekend, Granny died in her bedroom over the library in the new wing of her house, the plans for which she and her son had drawn, allocating modest quarters for Mother between Sara Delano Roosevelt and her only child. Father was too deeply involved in his mission to carry the cause of good against evil to victory to spare time for exhibitions of grief.

In a letter to Joe Lash, with whom she kept in close contact, Mother confided her own response. "It is dreadful to have lived so close to someone for 36 years and feel no deep affection or sense of loss. It is hard on Franklin however." She would have liked to make over the house in keeping with her own ideas of what a home should be. Father would not permit that. When it came to sorting out Granny's estate and her hoard of mementos in cellars and attics, he wept to find that she had saved the cradle she rocked him in as a baby and the satin slippers and lace-trimmed robe in which he had been christened in St. James Episcopal Church fifty-nine years previously.

Mother's turn to mourn came a few days after Granny's death. She spent ten of them at the bedside of her brother Hall in Walter Reed Hospital before cirrhosis killed him. "My idea of hell, if I believed in it," she wrote, "would be to sit or stand & watch someone breathing hard, struggling for words when a gleam of consciousness returns and thinking 'this was once the little boy I played with and scolded, he could have been so much & this is what he is.' It is a bitter thing. . . ."

Granny left her son virtually everything she had, including the sum of $920,115. The inheritance came at a particularly critical time in family finances. Father's net income that year amounted to $79,725.28, on which he paid $36,738.64 to the Internal Revenue Service. The payroll at Hyde Park ran to about $3,000 a month. The sole expense to the government there was the cost of maintaining a guard at the entrance gate when Father was in residence.

Inflation was starting to bite as a consequence of the pouring out of money to war production, with wages and prices soaring together. Raw materials, notably rubber, were in short supply; rationing would have to come soon. Leon Henderson had already rocked Washington by proposing that the manufacture of automobiles, refrigerators, washing machines, and other household appliances be cut in half. Father had recommended that $3.5 billion should be raised in additional taxes—the following spring, that figure leaped to $11.6 billion.

When he toted up his income and outgo for 1941, Father got off a letter to the IRS, asking whether on his tax return he could deduct a portion of the expense of White House entertaining, which pushed the food bill to $2,000 a month, over and above his $25,000 a year allowance. With his letter, he carefully enclosed a check for $10,000, one month after it was due, explaining that he did not want to incur any additional interest charges. The IRS turned him down, and these days there was no Missy around to cool his wrath by joking as she had in the past, "Take it out on Morgenthau."

When he died, he left a net estate of $1,974,316.45 and $562,142 worth of life insurance, which went to the Warm Springs Foundation. Claims and debts, including a $44.86 telephone bill and $46.20 owed to Mother for expenses at Campobello, amounted to $36,397.15. His portfolio of stocks and bonds was a mix, ranging from 800 shares of General Electric to one in Safeway Stores. Funeral and administrative expenses—$493,524.17—were the biggest charges, which in all cut the assets on hand for the trust fund to $1,439,171.17. The bulk of this was bequeathed to Mother, passing to the five children after her death.

As the close of the year 1941 drew nearer, the Germans thrust across the Russian uplands to within thirty miles of Moscow, where the regrouped Red Army miraculously turned the attack. Harry Truman was one who espoused the view that the Nazis and the Soviets should be left to "kill as many as possible" of one another. His continued presence in the Senate was not of Father's choosing. He had preferred Lloyd Stark, governor of Missouri, in the 1940 primary, but Truman beat Stark by a hair and went on to win his second term on the Hill.

Truman proceeded to make an unheralded tour of a dozen Southern states, checking out Army bases and munitions plants for waste and inefficiency. On the Senate floor, he spoke tirelessly about the dawdling and shoddiness he had seen, his eloquence possibly warmed by the rebuffs he had encountered in trying to steer defense contracts to Missouri's small-business men.

At fifty-seven, Truman, in one historian's phrase, seemed "little more than a parochial politician with a mediocre record of achievement." But the White House passed the word through Jimmy Byrnes that the Senator from Missouri could be allowed to run a Special Committee to Investigate the National Defense Program. The headlines it made accused the administration of missing schedules, failing to stir an all-out national effort, frittering money away. One noteworthy endeavor deliberately kept concealed from Truman's probing was the Manhattan Project, as it was called on its formal launching the following year. Father was surreptitiously channeling the first millions into the search for the atom bomb, with a new division of the Army Corps of Engineers involved in building secret plants and secret cities. He continued to doubt whether he could ever succeed in obtaining a declaration of war from Congress. His appeal to the Japanese had failed. They had no mind to withdraw from Indochina or from China itself, which would have to be part of a peace package for the Far East. They put out feelers for a meeting to be held somewhere in the Pacific between Father and their Prime Minister, Prince Fumimaro Konoye, but that would be futile without some common ground being established in advance. My parent had no illusions about their relentless ambitions. Every message passing between their Washington embassy and Tokyo was deciphered, thanks to the cracking of their cable code by the process known as "Magic."

On October 17, Konoye resigned, and the militarists took over the government with General Hideki Tojo as the leader. Two weeks later, they formulated the timetable for war. Unless the United States agreed by midnight November 30 to help Japan obtain essential resources in the Pacific, supply a million tons of oil a year, and leave China to its invaders, America would feel the weight of Japanese power.

Reinforcements of diplomats arrived in Washington to back up Nomura, whose Buddhalike figure waddled in and out of the White House and the State Department. One of them was the special envoy, Saburo Kurusu, who looked uncommonly like Gilbert and Sullivan's "Nankipoo." He had romantic memories of one member of the Delano family, which Father, reaching out for anything as he stalled for time, briefly rekindled.

Kurusu let it be known that he would be honored to meet Laura Delano, otherwise our sprightly unmarried Aunt Polly, Granny's youngest sister. Years before, her father had taken Polly to visit Japan, where she fell in love with young Saburo, the scion of rich industrialists. Wanting none of it, Warren Delano hustled her home to the United States. She had not seen or communicated with Kurusu during the intervening decades, but she was happy to accept Father's invitation to greet him again in the White House.

On November 24, Father filled in Churchill about the latest fruitless exchanges with Emperor Hirohito's men, adding a footnote: "I am not very hopeful and we must all be prepared for real trouble, possibly soon." Two days before, after a rendezvous at the Kiril Islands, which stretch like a broken string of pearls between Hokkaido and Kanchatka, the strike force of six Japanese carriers with close to 200 planes aboard, two battleships, two cruisers, and nine destroyers received further orders to make for Hawaii, subject to recall. Magic intercepted no messages to indicate that the mannerly negotiators in Washington were aware of what Tojo planned on doing when their time ran out.

15

On Sunday morning, December 7, I slept late at the ranch in Benbrook, where I was out on a weekend pass. Barely two weeks after Argentia, my unit had been ordered back Stateside; an application of mine to go to navigation school had been accepted; and now I was stationed at Kelly Field, San Antonio, with only a few more days left before graduating as a navigation officer. After a morning's horseback riding, I was back home when one of the children turned on the radio, and I heard a broadcast ordering all officers and men to report back to their stations immediately.

From Kelly Field, I put through a call to Father, which took two hours to go through. "What's the dope, Pop?" I hollered, uptight from delay.

"Well, it looks like we're really in for it. What's new with you?"

"There's a story that we're all going to be shipped out tomorrow, all squadrons to be ordered out to the Philippines. . . . Then we heard that there was a Jap landing force in Mexico. And that there'd be an attack on the Texas air bases any time now. . . . Also there was a story going around that the Japs were getting ready a task force of ground troops to come

303

up from Mexico across the border and attack Texas or California. . . ."

I heard a noncommittal "hmm." "Well, if you hear anything else," he said, "you'll be sure to let me know, won't you? Good luck to you, Bunny." His telephone clicked.

In a threadbare sweater, he had been sitting in the Oval Room that windy, wintry afternoon, chatting with Harry Hopkins after luncheon for two served on his desk top, when Frank Knox telephoned at one forty. "Mr. President, it looks as if the Japanese have attacked Pearl Harbor."

"*No!*" said Father, but it was the target, not the attack, that amazed him. At nine thirty the night before, Captain Beardall's assistant, Commander L. Z. Schultz, had brought my parent a Magic intercept, a multipart cable from Tokyo to Nomura. "This means war," said Father as he read it. A new Japanese attack was imminent, but where? Ten hours afterward, the bombs and torpedoes that decimated the Pacific fleet gave the answer. Seven capital ships lay sunk or foundering.

One of the earlier calls that Father took on his clamoring telephones came from Churchill. He had heard the news on the portable radio given him by Hopkins, which sat on the dining-room table at Chequers, where Harry and Harriman were spending another weekend. The Japanese, the Prime Minister reported, were simultaneously on the rampage in the Malay Straits. Might he make full speed to the United States with his Chiefs of Staff to coordinate battle plans? Yes, as fast as he could, was the reply. In point of fact, because of the five-hour difference in time between London and Washington, Britain declared war on Japan ahead of the United States.

Long into the night, over beer and sandwiches, Father worked on the message to be delivered to a joint session of Congress the next day. He did not like Sumner Welles' draft, and Hull's was too long-winded. Father would choose his own words to describe this "date which will live in infamy." When he stood in the House of Representatives' chamber the next morning, freckled hands clutching the edge of the rostrum, only one prosy sentence was not his in the brief speech he made. It was Harry who had suggested: "With confidence in our armed forces—with the unbounding determination of our people—we will gain the inevitable triumph—so help us God." With just one dissenting vote, Congress declared war. Before it was over, 16,353,659 Americans would serve, and 405,399 of them would die.

One week later, when the havoc done at Pearl Harbor had been tallied, he jotted down his summation of the attack:

> Essential fact is that Jap purpose was to knock U.S. out of the war before it began. Made apparent by deceptions practiced, by the preparations going on for many weeks before the attacks, which were made simultaneously throughout the Pacific. Jap purpose failed. The U.S. services were not on the alert against the surprise air attack on Hawaii. This calls for a formal investigation, which will be initiated immediately by the President. . . .

By then, Hitler's (and Mussolini's) formal entry into battle against the United States was three days old. Father's reply in kind had been voted by Congress, this time without a solitary nay. Der Führer asked for nothing from Japan in return for his show of loyalty. The Germans would tackle the Russians without any help from Tokyo. He had rendered the Allies the greatest possible service within his power, believing that the United States could do no more harm to Germany than was already being done. American soldiers, he thought, "can't stick in a crisis." Winston entertained not entirely dissimilar opinions. In Robert Sherwood's judgment, "he was profoundly skeptical of the ability of American troops to compete with the Germans in ground warfare on a massive scale."

The Churchillian touch showed up in the code name for the next round of Anglo-American conferences. The dictionary definition of "arcadia" is "a place of rural peace and simplicity." His arrival three days before Christmas created further chaos in a White House already disrupted by emergency change. The stepped-up security precautions initiated immediately after Pearl Harbor day annoyed both my parents. Mother, in particular, thought that the installation of antiaircraft guns on the roof passed into the realm of fantasy. Morgenthau, who was in control of the Secret Service, was balked by Father when he sought to circle the grounds with troops and put tanks on guard duty at the gates. Inside the house, the sole military staff on duty might be a solitary junior officer. Henry had an air-raid shelter dug under the Treasury Building up the street, but Father gave him fair warning that he would use it only if Morgenthau would put his Fort Knox gold up as a pot for poker.

Seventeen people sat down for dinner the first night that Winston spent in the White House, installed in the big second-floor bedroom across the hall from the southeast corner suite that was Hopkins' home. Mrs. Nesbitt fancied that the PM "looked poor-colored and hungry" and vowed to fatten him up, even if she was trying to buy close without shopping for "extras." Her budget succumbed to the strain, however, the day sixty-eight guests lingered on for lunch in the Cabinet Room.

Winston's life patterns called for flexibility on everyone's part, from the host to the ushers, who were put on duty around the clock. He took a scalding hot bath twice a day, reveling in the sudsy soap that was unknown in Britain's austerity program. His valet picked up fifty dollars' worth from Mrs. Nesbitt's stock before they left, but she was repaid for that.

The PM was never perturbed to find a visitor in his bedroom as he emerged glowing pink from the tub. I had personal experience on a second visit to Chequers the following September when I was summoned to say good-bye and found him clad only with a cigar. He liked to prowl his room that way, dictating to a male secretary. Father once discovered him in the same state of nature and began a strategic retreat in his wheelchair. Winston stayed him. "The Prime Minister of Britain," he chuckled, "has nothing to conceal from the President of the United States." Churchill subsequently denied the story, insisting that he was wearing a bath towel.

His habit of napping in the afternoon, then working and chatting about the world and its history until two or three in the morning exasperated Mother, a firm believer in the virtues of "early to bed, early to rise." Since Father allowed himself no siesta after lunch yet matched his bedtime hours to his guest's, she complained that "it always took him several days to catch up on his sleep after Mr. Churchill left." Winston liked to down a few brandies as the night wore on, so Father would have himself an extra cocktail or two to keep him company, which was another reason for Mother's objections.

She had no cause for concern now about Father's health. In

fact, there was so much public comment about his air of confidence under stress that he had Grace Tully write a memo about it for Steve Early's background information. It was a document almost as strange as his own reminiscences of World War I sent to Josephus Daniels. Again it harked back to those weeks spent in Europe, when Lucy haunted his mind.

"A good many comments have been made that the President seems to be taking the situation of extreme urgency in his stride," Grace wrote, "that he is looking well and that he does not seem to have any nerves. People sometimes forget that this kind of crisis is not wholly new to him; the only difference is that today he is Commander-in-Chief. . . ." She listed in detail his 1918 travels as Assistant Navy Secretary, not forgetting Dunkirk, "which was under constant shell fire from the Germans," and concluded with a telling sentence: "At the end of September he returned to the United States on the Leviathan with a case of double pneumonia."

I suspect that both my parents were glad to have a houseful of hungry, demanding Englishmen bustling about on the second floor that Christmas. The place would have seemed empty without them, when the only child around was Diana Hopkins. All the grandchildren were absent. Anna was in Seattle, and all four of us sons in uniform, now that Johnny had followed Franklin Jr. into the Navy. Mother had Mayris Chaney to stay as an overnight visitor, Father had Fala by his side for company, the crotchety Scots terrier given to him the previous year by his cousin and special confidante, Daisy Suckley. Murray the Outlaw of Fala Hill, to accord him his full title, was Father's first and only White House pet, a solace in hours of loneliness, a nibbler of tidbits from the breakfast tray, deserving the stocking which was hung for him over the fireplace. Mother, who then had no love for dogs, barred him from the dining room.

POTUS and Former Naval Person went to Christmas morning service at the Foundry Methodist Church, then devoted the rest of the day to business. Bulletins from the battlefronts were singularly lacking in seasonal cheer. Rommel was running riot in the Libyan desert. With Hong Kong, Guam, and Wake in their hands, the Japanese were moving on Manila, leaving General Douglas MacArthur and his men trapped on the Bataan Peninsula and rocky Corregidor. Rumors flew like chaff in the

wind: Warships had bombarded Los Angeles; paratroops had
landed; saboteurs had been put ashore from submarines off the
California coast. Judging by the screaming headlines, the only
war worth considering was in and around the Pacific.

Churchill and his entourage were fearful that American anxiety over Japan's conquests might compel Father to leave the
British alone again to battle the Germans. The initial task was to
reassure them, as Marshall and Stark did, that "notwithstand-
ing the entry of Japan into the War, our view remains that Germany is still the prime enemy and her defeat is the key to victory." On the United States side, that priority had not been seriously questioned.

The second job, again principally for Marshall, was to put
into perspective the cut-and-dried plan, brought in the visitors'
leather dispatch cases, for Anglo-American forces to invade
North Africa before the Germans did. Winston was prepared
to launch Gymnast, as the scheme was coded, within three
weeks. Marshall objected to assigning great numbers of United
States soldiers to what was essentially a peripheral operation,
not the vital attack on Hitler's European fortress. Gymnast, renamed Torch, was finally scheduled for March, with only three
American divisions committed and on condition that an invitation for the North African landings could be wheedled from
the French authorities in Algiers.

What to do about the French was a perennially thorny problem that found Father at odds with Winston. The PM had written off the men of Vichy as tools of Hitler. For their part, they
nursed bitter memories of the British sinking of two French
battleships and a battle cruiser at Oran, Algeria, in July, 1940,
to keep them out of German hands when they might just as well
have sailed for the United States. So Churchill pinned his faith
on starch-stiff Charles de Gaulle, leader of Free France in London. My parent, at Hull's prompting, took a more lenient view
of feeble old Pétain and his corrupt government. By maintaining contact through Bill Leahy, he calculated that the remains
of French fighting potential would not fall completely under
Nazi control, notably their bases in North Africa. Dealing with
Vichy was a policy that won him no medals from liberals at
home, but to him it was a matter of plain necessity.

The third, and possibly most peremptory, undertaking

which George Marshall had to perform was to insist on the principle of unified command, a single, supreme chief of all American and British fighting forces—air, ground, and sea for the Pacific and later for the European theater of operations. Churchill's feet went down firmly on that one. Not until Hopkins as mediator led him into a tête-à-tête session with Marshall could the Prime Minister be won around.

Father stuck to his policy of leaving the conduct of the war to his top hands—the austere Marshall, who had been promoted over thirty-four more senior officers; Arnold; and salt-bitten Ernie King, who, on replacing Stark, joined the exclusive band of shellbacks willing to shout it out with the Commander in Chief whenever tempers rose. Winston, to the contrary, preferred to have a hand in everything his Chiefs of Staff did or contemplated doing. Even his War Cabinet held few formal meetings during the final two years of battles.

"I think," Father said when Arcadia was over, "we must avoid too much personal leadership—my good friend Winston Churchill has suffered a little from this."

There was no reading of Scrooge, Bob Cratchit, and Tiny Tim around the tree in 1941. Starting in the afternoon, he and his guest worked on another declaration, the most engrossing item of business on the agenda, in Father's estimation. After dinner for sixty to an accompaniment of carol singing, the two of them labored on past midnight, putting together sentences to crystallize the ideals which made the war worth fighting. How to describe all the countries, great and small, conquered or free, engaged in hitting back at the Axis? "Allied," said Churchill. "Associated," Father thought.

An early text of their combined effort was cabled to Moscow. On December 27, a familiar face appeared at the White House luncheon table—Maxim Litvinov, deposed when the Nazi-Soviet Pact was signed and now restored to grace as the Soviet envoy in Washington. The bargaining between him, Father, and Churchill was sharp but brief. He would obtain approval from the nonbelievers in the Kremlin for including the words "religious freedom" in the document. He could not agree to Winston's formula for leaving the way open for the French to subscribe as signatories. That was the cue for the Prime Minister to observe acidly that Litvinov "wasn't much of an ambassador."

The Soviets asked for no more than minor changes in the draft they had seen, all designed to make it plain that *they* were not at war with Japan; an assault on his Eastern frontier was the last thing Stalin wanted to provoke. There was still no generic term to cover all the governments who were to sign the document.

It came to Father at breakfast forty-eight hours later, on the day Winston was to interrupt his stay for a quick trip to Canada and risk offending the *Québecois* with a speech denouncing Vichy France. He rolled into Churchill's room at a lively clip while Former Naval Person was splashing in the bath. "I've got it!" Father announced with pride. "*United* Nations." Winston promptly added his blessing. It was essentially a child of FDR's imagination from the start.

The seeds of United Nations contention had already been planted simultaneously in Moscow and London on that day. In the Soviet capital, Stalin demanded that Britain recognize his country's right to the Baltic States and a Western frontier based on the old Curzon Line, restoring half of Poland to the USSR. This, he maintained, was essential to future defense. In London, General Wladislaw Sikorski's Polish government-in-exile would tolerate no such bartering of its lost homeland. Postwar Poland must stretch as far as its 1919 borders.

For the present, neither Churchill nor Father was inclined to bother much about the Poles. "I think Sikorski should be definitely discouraged on this proposition," my parent was soon to instruct Sumner Welles. "This is no time to talk about the postwar position of small nations, and it would cause serious trouble with Russia." Just how much trouble he could not even dimly envisage.

On the evening of New Year's Day, a consort of statesmen and diplomats of twenty-six nations, Poland included, crowded into the White House study, "being convinced," as the declaration avowed, "that complete victory over their enemies is essential to defend life, liberty, independence, and religious freedom, and to preserve human rights and justice in their own lands as well as in other lands, and that they are now engaged in a common struggle against savage and brutal forces seeking to subjugate the world."

Mother, with Lash beside her, watched, close to the door. Father signed first, followed in sequence by Winston, Litvinov, and T. V. Soong, the new Chinese ambassador, brother-in-law of Chiang Kai-shek. The so-called Big Four nations had found something in common for the first time. Then, in alphabetical order from Australia to Yugoslavia, four-fifths of the human race was pledged to cooperate in "victory over Hitlerism."

At the dinner table that night, Churchill reminisced about the days when, at his command, the British expeditionary force had fought for the Russian Whites in 1919. Today, he forgave the Bolsheviks "in proportion to the numbers of Huns they kill," he said.

"Do they forgive you?" Hopkins interjected.

"In proportion to the number of tanks I send," said Winston. Father thought that memories might last longer.

That exchange, and many more like it, might have colored his thinking when he spoke with Mother afterward about the postwar world. "It will be hard for Winston," he said, "and I am sure that in some ways it will be easier to make Mr. Stalin understand certain things."

At the end of the month, I had an after-breakfast chat with him while he made another pot of coffee for himself in his bedroom—he consistently claimed that the White House kitchen did not know how to brew a cup fit for drinking. I was due off to North Africa, one of two navigators assigned to the photographic mapping of the terrain as part of something identified as Project Rusty. I couldn't see the point of taking pictures of desert sand until he spelled out the implications of Torch. It was essential, he explained, to keep hold of the Mediterranean and the Suez Canal to get aid to China by airlift from India and to ship lend-lease arms to the Soviets across Iran.

"What we know is this," he said. "The Chinese are killing Japanese, and the Russians are killing Germans. We've got to keep them doing just that until our armies and navies are ready to help. . . . Look at Africa from another angle. The Nazis aren't in the Sahara just to get a sunburn. Why do they want Egypt? Why do they want central Africa? It's not a long hop from there to Brazil. Pennsylvania Avenue can have its name changed to the Adolf Hitler-Strasse, and don't think it can't!"

Steve Early poked his head around the door to remind him of his next appointment. "Two minutes, Steve," said Father. He had a final thought to pass along. "First place, in spite of the handful of vocal defeatists in this country, the American people as a whole have the guts and the stamina to carry through the job. In the second place, God didn't intend this world to be governed by the few." I went on my way, satisfied with the fit of my humdrum chore into the overall pattern for victory.

The "vocal defeatists" amounted to considerably more than a handful. Nothing on earth, it seemed, could tempt an isolationist to change his spots or convert those people who worked to drag down FDR. He smiled every time he repeated a remark made by Elmer Davis in a Columbia Broadcasting System commentary: "There are some patriotic citizens who sincerely hope that America will win the war—but they also hope that Russia will lose it; and there are some who hope that America will win the war, but that England will lose it; and there are some who hope that America will win the war, but that Roosevelt will lose it!"

The "enemy within the gate" of former days had a new strategic approach for attaining Fascism in America. Some of them advocated the "ostrichlike" policy (Father's description) of pulling back the armed forces to our own shores. Others, with an admiral or two among them, sought to concentrate United States strength in the Pacific theater, leaving the Germans and the Soviets to cut each others' throats. Unanimously, they scented an opportunity to turn back the clock and erase the gains that the New Deal had given to the unions. There was no shortage of Congressmen out to abolish the right to strike and outlaw the forty-hour week "in the interests of war production" as the cost of war edged up to $100,000,000 a day, sending the price of everything skyrocketing.

Measured by the standards he set himself in 1933, Father took his time in coping with inflation. On April 27, a Message to Congress specified the remedies: increased taxes, price ceilings, fixed rents, frozen wages, a "buy bonds" drive, rationing of all commodities in short supply, a clampdown on credit and installment purchasing. Congress took four more months to act, but even so it showed better speed on the track than the thirty-eighth President of the United States in 1974.

The hate mail continued to arrive every weekday morning at the White House. He saved the most noteworthy envelopes for his private collection: "F. D. Russianvelt, President of the

U.S.A., C.I.O." "Benedict Arnold 2nd, Washington, D.C."
"Rattlesnake Roosevelt." "Dishonorable Franklin Deficit Roosevelt."

There was no letup in rumormongering, either. Losses at
Pearl Harbor were far greater than had been reported, said the
whisperers, and the United States coastline was virtually defenseless. A hard-nosed, forty-year-old attorney named Thomas E. Dewey, who looked a certainty to win the governorship of
New York for the Republicans for the first time in twenty years
the forthcoming November, drew a parallel with Chamberlain's
clique of appeasers. He claimed that "there is already an American Cliveden set in Washington and other cities" scheming for
a negotiated peace, seeking to use his party to achieve this "cowardly end." The tittle-tattle of enemy propaganda was recirculated with glee, including one Rome broadcast reporting that
an air raid on the White House drove Father to the cellar, to
find Steve Early "lying drunk with a bottle of whiskey beside
him."

From time to time, my parent let off steam by way of response. As a reward for consistently plugging the isolationists'
America-first line in the Chicago *Tribune,* its publisher, Colonel
Robert McCormick, should be given "the next higher rank than
Field Marshal," Father snapped. At one press conference, he
personally handed Drew Pearson a German iron cross to shame
him for printing confidential and potentially damaging information in his *Washington Merry-Go-Round* column.

Father would often dictate a fiery letter to Grace Tully to get
an opinion off his chest, then destroy it before it was mailed.
Sometimes it escaped destruction, like one ironic shot that landed on a New York banker's desk:

> I have your letter of March second. Let me tell you something terrible. The Japanese never would have attacked the
> United States had it not been for the common cold.
> You wax positively gruesome when you declare solemnly
> that had it not been for the thirty million man-days lost by
> strikes since the defense program began, the Philippines, the
> Dutch Indies and Singapore would all have been saved. You
> sound like Alice in Wonderland.
> So let me tell you something more fantastic than that. If,

since the defense program started, we in the United States had not lost sixty million man-days through that scourge of Satan, called the common cold, we could undoubedly have had enough planes and guns and tanks to overrun Europe, Africa and the whole of Asia . . . P.S. Where is that saving of $100,000,000,000 you were going to make out of unnecessary government expenditures? Perhaps I am wrong and you said only $10,000,000,000.

He had grown impatient with criticism. He was losing his resilience, and his jokes carried a sharper edge as the pressure of his responsibilities mounted. There was no time left to look for proselytes among his enemies, and he was increasingly brusque in the family circle. He complained to the Navy Band that they put too many "frills" into their version of "The Star-Spangled Banner." He grumbled to Mother that Mrs. Nesbitt had served him chicken and then sweetbreads with such monotony that "my stomach rebels and this does not help my relations with foreign powers. I bit two of them today."

He was irritable over having to forgo cruising in the *Potomac*—he was advised the boat made too easy a target for aerial raiders—and often to pass up his evening swim. He flatly refused Mother's suggestion that he follow an example set by some country-house owners and turn over rooms at Hyde Park as a convalescents' home. When fresh income tax increases cut him down to $30,000 net a year, he whipped off an explosive memorandum to her. "SOMETHING HAS TO BE DONE!" Mrs. Nesbitt must manage on a reduced budget, $1,500 a month. The number of servants must be pared. Mother must stop asking so many guests to dinner. She should see to it that he was served only one egg, not two, for his desk-top lunches and arrange to ban second helpings at all meals for everyone.

As early as March 9, he was cabling Churchill that he was "becoming more and more interested" in making the first great Allied offensive an invasion of northern France that summer. The War Plans Division, which was directed by Dwight David Eisenhower, newly jumped from colonel to brigadier general (temporary), had prepared the plan. The logic was unassailable. "We cannot concentrate against Japan," said a memorandum from Marshall. "Successful attack in this area will afford the maximum of support to the Russian front."

But the sheer logistics of assembling enough men and supplies to mount a massive cross-Channel assault from Britain ruled out the hoped-for date. Roundup, as the plan was originally named, would have to wait until the spring of 1943, no matter what Stalin wanted, and he had been entreating the British to open a second front in Europe from the day the Germans swung to attack the USSR. If the Soviet situation became desperate in the meantime, the planners calculated that a limited invasion of Hitler's Fortress Europe, code name Sledgehammer, could be staged by mid-September in the present year.

Father sent Hopkins and Marshall to London to clear Roundup with Churchill. They found him preoccupied with trouble in India, where support for war against Japan was nonexistent in spite of British dread that this once-bright jewel of the Empire might come next on Tokyo's conquest list. The Congress in New Delhi set immediate self-government as its price for fighting the Japanese. That was out of the question in Winston's evaluation. Before many more months had passed, Jawaharlal Nehru, the Nationalist hero, and 20,000 other political figures were back in jail for the duration of the war.

India was one subject on which POTUS and the PM never did agree, and so, for the time being, was Roundup. Winston had no desire to commit British troops in unlimited numbers against a well-fortified enemy. North Africa, he insisted, was the place for an Anglo-American landing. "Our major strategy must be the defeat of Germany this summer in her Russian effort," Father had claimed, perhaps forlornly, but his two emissaries returned from London without any British undertaking to join such an effort.

The failure was obscured by a succession of headlines. Taking off from the carrier *Hornet,* a flight of B-25's commanded by Colonel Jimmy Doolittle, USAAF, scattered bombs on Tokyo. In the southwest Pacific's Coral Sea, Admiral Chester Nimitz's fleet tangled in battle with the Imperial Navy, compelling troop transports under its escort to pull back from an intended landing on Port Moresby, New Guinea, a likely springboard to Australia.

One month afterward, halfway between Los Angeles and Yokohama, the two fleets clashed again. The Battle of Midway, in Ernie King's assessment, was "the first decisive defeat suffered by the Japanese Navy in 350 years." The catastrophic losses we had taken to date at Pearl and elsewhere in this ocean—five battleships, a flattop, two cruisers, seven destroyers, merchantmen by the score—were avenged and the limits of enemy expansion reached at last.

By now, it was obvious that Churchill and Father would have to put their heads together again if differences about the timing and the advisability of opening a second front in Europe were to be resolved. In every diplomatic exchange, Stalin stressed his aim to have the Allies attack before the end of the year to dilute the strength of the Wehrmacht, which was smashing at the Crimean port of Sevastopol to climax eight months of siege.

Winston was haunted by the nightmare of the Channel being turned into "a river of blood." He pinned his hopes on the RAF's ability to bomb Germany into submission now that 1,000 planes had been put in the air for a night raid on Cologne. First as an overnight guest at Hyde Park, then in the White House, he stalled over implementing plans for Roundup which had already been settled. How could Father's staff chiefs guarantee that a premature effort would not end in disaster? Far better try Gymnast, renamed Torch, which had been postponed so far.

Events determined Father's choice, which went contrary to the counsel of Stimson and Marshall, who minimized the impact any North African venture could have on the outcome of the war. The Germans had taken over from the inept Italians in Libya. Rommel's Panzers had come close to destroying the British tank forces there. Winston had been in the United States only two days when Father handed him a telegram with the crushing news that Tobruk, the desert bastion, had surrendered to Rommel, with 25,000 Britons captured.

Father had told me at our last meeting what that might portend. "What's wrong with a giant pincer movement by the Japanese and the Nazis, meeting somewhere in the Near East, cutting the Russians off completely, slicing off Egypt, slashing all communications lines through the Mediterranean?" With that prospect in mind, he sanctioned Torch. Hopkins, Marshall, and King would fly to London to iron out the final details. Harriman would go with Churchill to Moscow with the delicate task of telling Stalin that there would be no Roundup that year because Winston and his staff chiefs had ruled against it.

A later cable from Father had some thoughts for Winston on

how to handle a tricky job: IT IS ESSENTIAL FOR US TO BEAR IN MIND OUR ALLY'S PERSONALITY AND THE VERY DIFFICULT AND DANGEROUS SITUATION THAT HE CONFRONTS. I THINK WE SHOULD ATTEMPT TO PUT OURSELVES IN HIS PLACE, FOR NO ONE WHOSE COUNTRY HAS BEEN INVADED CAN BE EXPECTED TO APPROACH THE WAR FROM A WORLD POINT OF VIEW. . . ."

Before the conference broke up in Washington, Harry had a bulletin of his own to deliver, to the delight of the PM and my parent. He was going to be married to Mrs. Louise Macy, a New York hospital aide introduced to him only a few weeks earlier by friends who knew them both. Nothing would satisfy my parent but Harry's agreeing to have him as best man at the wedding, which was held in the Oval Room soon after Hopkins' return, and to bring the bride to live under the White House roof. Mother was allowed no say in the matter, possibly because Father had no misconceptions about her changed attitude toward the bridegroom.

The taste Harry had developed for high living disillusioned her. She made allowances, she thought, for his chronic ill-health and the demands he made on Henrietta Nesbitt, running to oysters on the half shell, avocado and grapefruit with French dressing. Nevertheless, she found him "often unreasonable." He had "lost some of his values," and he had a nasty habit of burning cigarette holes in tablecloths. Her implacable conscience bothered her, too. Harry lived at government expense, as she pointed out to Father, though he had never been elected to any office. It would have been rude, however, not to attend the wedding, for which she ordered the cake. "I think it should be fruitcake," said her note to Mrs. Nesbitt.

If the Roosevelt-haters detested anyone more than FDR, it was Harry. They made his honeymoon an occasion for venting their spleen. They had half the country believing that he ordered the Coast Guard to requisition a yacht owned by Roy Fruehauf, the Detroit truck-trailer maker, for himself and Louise. The newlyweds were, in fact, spending a few days at a farm in Connecticut. Another story told how the third and most attractive Mrs. Hopkins had been given emeralds worth $500,000 by Beaverbrook, eased out by Churchill on pretext of illness because he was as eager as Stalin for the second front. There were no emeralds for Louise.

However, the Hopkinses were given a fresh paint job for Harry's White House quarters, consisting of a bathroom, a little room used before as his secretary's office, and the best guest room in the house, boasting a four-poster bed and a fireplace with a commemorative plaque over it, saying that here Lincoln had signed the Proclamation of Emancipation on January 1, 1863.

That last room became a growing source of aggravation for Mother. Louise, chic and brisk, was up early and out of the house every working day, with a hospital job to keep her busy in Washington. When she came home, she and Harry made a practice of relaxing over cocktails, ordering up ice from the kitchen, inviting friends and colleagues to join them, not forgetting Anna, who moved in with her children after John Boettiger volunteered for the Army. The Hopkins' happy hour ended when they came downstairs for Father's evening ritual of mixing drinks before dinner.

Mother had not complained about Louis or Missy, two other nonpaying tenants who had never run in any election, but she did not hide her dissatisfaction with the Hopkins arrangement, convenient as it was to him and Father. "They really are quite *high* sometimes before they sit down to dinner," she would say. She was "careful not to develop intimacy" with Louise.

Mother was glad to get away to London. I heard from Father that "some member of the family" was coming over after Winston had casually asked if I might like to say hello when he called Washington from Chequers. My outfit was stationed at Steeple Morton, not far from Cambridge, engaged in photographic reconnaissance of Normandy and Brittany—but only as training for Africa. That weekend with the PM happened to include my birthday. To talk with Father was the most welcome gift Winston could have given me. I was mildly intrigued to discover that it took something over two hours for the call to go through. I was no more and no less intrigued to discover in London that Averell Harriman had made enough impression on Winston's daughter-in-law, Pamela, that she was acting now as hostess in his apartment: They became man and wife in 1971.

King George and Queen Elizabeth met Mother at Paddington Station with a royal Daimler. Gil Winant was with her, but

Harry had advised her in advance to pay little attention to him. Harriman, said Hopkins, was the man to consult on everything in London. She demonstrated her independence of spirit by ignoring Averell. Her first two nights were spent at Buckingham Palace, where I joined her to dine with her host and hostess.

English winters were one subject on which she and Harry agreed. She was uncomfortable from the cold that bleak October night. Unlike him, she preferred the King to his Prime Minister, whom she respected for his courage but certainly not for his opinions, which struck her as antediluvian. She clashed openly with Winston only once on that trip. When she dined with the Churchills, the conversation turned to Spain. He explained away his antagonism toward the Loyalists in the civil war there on the curious grounds that if they had been allowed to win, he and Father "would have been the first to lose their heads." Mother replied, with a little internal heat, that the loss of her own head would not concern her much.

Winston grunted. "I don't want you to lose your head and neither do I want to lose mine," he said, in what must have qualified as one of the more futile conversations of the season.

In her palace bedroom she sat up until all hours, teeth chattering, carefully avoiding mention of one secret that each of us had learned independently: Torch was about to burn. North Africa would be invaded next month, with Ike Eisenhower running the Allied effort.

Of all the thousands of hands she shook with genuine fondness in England—American and British, royalty and munitions workers—some were those of my photographic reconnaissance unit on a sullen, wet day at Steeple Morton. Her driver got lost on the way from London. Reverting to the code name pinned on her by Father, he had to telephone the embassy for directions, after announcing his predicament in a line that acquired a brief measure of renown: "Rover has lost her pup."

She arrived an hour late, in the hands of a committee of British escorts, to the cheers of every one of us who was waiting. After she had gone down the ranks, chatting with as many of the men as she could, we hurried her inside for a steaming cup of tea. When her guides let us know that they would prefer whiskey, we served it in tea mugs for Mother's sake.

16

Shangri-La, which was Father's name for the place, bore no resemblance at all to a "hidden paradise," which is a Webster's definition of the idyllic scene pictured by James Hilton in his novel *Lost Horizon*. The Presidential retreat, established the previous summer in the Catoctin Mountains of Maryland, sixty miles north of Washington, looked more like a Marine training camp, which is precisely what it had been, made up of rough pine cabins, most of them with two or three spartan rooms apiece. The rugs on the plank floors were of even older vintage than the secondhand furniture, drawn from a Navy warehouse.

It suited Father down to the ground—metal bed, bathroom door that refused to shut tight, bare walls ornamented only with some of his favorite cartoons. Hyde Park was too far from the nerve centers of the capital for him to spend much time there. From Shangri-La, he could be back at his desk within two hours, and he had a direct line to the White House. So he tried to get there on weekends, to sit working on the screened stone porch with Hopkins and others, glancing out at a beautiful view of the Catoctin Valley, keeping a logbook record of each visit as though these were the old days aboard the *Larooco*. With the *Potomac* assigned to combat duty, the Filipino mess hands took care of the catering here, which meant better food than at home, with a chance of sampling oyster crabs with whitebait or peach cobbler with thick cream like Granny used to serve. Either for want of desire or an invitation, Mother never set foot in his hideaway.

He was still wearing a mourning band on his sleeve for Granny on Saturday, November 7, when a late-night call came in from the War Department. His hands were trembling as Grace Tully handed him the telephone. "Thank God," he repeated, listening. Then: "Congratulations!" He turned in his chair. "We have landed in North Africa," he announced. "We are striking back."

All through the summer, the same telephone had brought news of catastrophe. When Sevastapol fell, the Panzers pushed ahead into the northern suburbs of Stalingrad. Russian dead were counted by the tens of thousands as the battle boiled from street to street. In the opinion of Allied staff chiefs, the city was as good as lost. The road seemed open for the Nazis to roll into Iran and the Middle East. Where was the promised second front, Stalin repeated, that would drain off perhaps forty of the 208 Wehrmacht divisions that were devastating the USSR?

He had been asking the same question in August, when Churchill and Harriman found heavy going in Moscow. As Stalin summarized the situation then, "We are of the opinion . . . that it is particularly in 1942 that the creation of a second front in Europe is possible and should be effected. I was, however, unfortunately unsuccessful in convincing Mr. Prime Minister of Great Britain thereof, while Mr. Harriman, the representative of the President of the United States, fully supported Mr. Prime Minister."

In the southwest Pacific, American troops clung to their hard-won toeholds in the Solomon Islands, which pointed like an arrow aimed at the Philippines, under bombardment by air and sea. The Marines on Guadalcanal and the citizens and soldiers of Stalingrad had much in common in the matter of courage. One summer afternoon at Shangri-La, Father learned of the loss of three of our heavy cruisers together with an Australian ship of similar class. There were moments when the prospect had to be considered of putting Germany second, not first, in order of priority.

His hope had been for Torch to be successfully lit before the midterm elections. The voters needed something to bolster morale. A confidential sampling commissioned from Dr. George Gallup in New York indicated national sluggishness. "I am a bit appalled," Father said, "by the percentage of people who have no clear idea of what the war is about." He had no time to see crowds or make speeches, and his Dutch got up whenever anyone accused him of playing politics in 1942.

He refused to distinguish between "home front" and "fighting front," and party politicking had no place on either. "There is just one front," he told Sam Rosenman. "It is all part of the picture of trying to win the war. Whoever is engaged on the home front is as much a part of it as any fighter."

Ed Flynn, picked as national chairman of the Democrats when Farley quit, could not make head or tail of this campaign. When he ventured what he considered to be a perfectly proper remark that the election of a hostile Congress would be tantamount to a major military disaster, Father jumped on him. "When a country is at war, we want Congressmen, regardless of party—get that?—to back up the government of the United States, and who have a record of backing up the government of the United States in an emergency, regardless of party."

Since Willkie, still nominal leader of the opposition, followed much the same line, the America-Firsters consoled one another with "I told you so." Instead of going out to belabor Democrats, he took off around the world, with Father's grateful cooperation, to "accomplish certain things for the President," as he explained. My parent notified Stalin: "I am delighted that you will receive him and I think it will be of real benefit to both of our countries if he can get a firsthand impression of the splendid unity of Russian and the great defense you are conducting."

There were some fleeting second thoughts when Willkie, who prided himself on speaking "as I damned please," denounced the Allies in Moscow for delaying the invasion of France and then, in Chungking, blamed them for failing to extend all-out aid to China. "You can't have it both ways," snapped Father.

The stoutest hearts had cause to be downcast. The toll of dead and wounded on Guadalcanal mounted by the day. The cost of living was up by 15 percent in a year. The country had to learn that fatter pay packets and a skimpier life-style went together when ration stamps became a new kind of currency, required to buy food, gasoline, shoes, and clothing. Together with the draftees, millions of men and women were uprooted from their homes to work in war factories, and the Great Depression was finally laid to rest. Houses, including the one at 1600 Pennsylvania Avenue, were cold, with thermostats turned down and cellar furnaces banked to conserve fuel.

Not the least of the national aggravations was the mess in Washington resulting from the mushrooming of new agencies, set up in hope of streamlining productivity and coordinating activities previously performed separately by departments of government. The price of the war was skipping toward $300,000,000 every twenty-four hours, and conservative economists were flashing their warning signals. The alarmist talk makes fascinating reading today, when one-third of America's gross income goes to support the federal government and its employees in the style to which they have grown accustomed.

Bureaucrats battled bureaucrats in a tornado of red tape. Vice President Wallace, now also chairman of the Board of Economic Warfare, was involved in two of the most spectacular of the endless feuds, with Hull at the State Department and with Jesse Jones, who had added Hopkins' old job as Commerce Secretary to his tenure at the Reconstruction Finance Corporation. Wallace could not break himself of the habit of speaking out of turn in public. He talked about postwar stablization overseas, which nettled Hull, who considered that to be his business; he blasted Jones for obstructing his board's efforts to stockpile strategic supplies.

Father's confidence in both men was limited. He distrusted his latest Commerce Secretary to the degree that he once set one of his adminstrative assistants, Jim Rowe, to filing confidential reports on the old banker. He kept Wallace completely in the dark about invading North Africa, which led to more friction with Hull when the Board of Economic Warfare started cutting back shipments required in advance for Torch.

The landings were made not before but four days after the election. On the drive up to Shangri-La that weekend, Father mulled over the results of the voting. They were disheartening. The Republicans had come within fifteen seats of taking over the House. They had picked up nine Senate places and governorships in major states, including New York, where Dewey had won his way to the executive mansion in Albany. It had been a black day for the Democrats. Even in 1918, when America was visibly tiring of Wilson and *his* war, a President had done better for his party at the polls.

There could be nothing more welcome to Father than Saturday night's advisory that 90,000 American and British fighting men were going ashore at a dozen points from Casablanca to Algiers. Admittedly, French were exchanging fire with French, but that would end halfway through the coming week, when the Nazis occupied all of France, and her admirals scuttled the rest of the French fleet at Toulon in retaliation. It looked that night as though a forecast of Eisenhower's was well-founded and Torch would succeed within six weeks, as planned.

Fighting was still going strong toward the middle of January when I received orders one morning to fly from Algiers to Casablanca. The colonel in charge of the field told me on arrival I had to stay out of sight for thirty-six hours. The town had recently been cleared of Germans, and it was riddled with French Fascist spies. If I was recognized on the streets, it would be a tip that Father was on his way. The last full-dress air raid was only three weeks past.

I went nosing around the compound which had been staked out with barbed wire and guarded by an armored division under General George Patton within an outer ring of extra antiaircraft batteries. With his party, Father was at that time in Brazil, the first President to leave the United States in wartime, the first since Lincoln to visit a battle zone, the first to use a plane—Uncle Ted took a hop, but that was after he left the White House. Hap Arnold personally piloted the Clipper that flew my parent from Miami. "I'm not crazy about flying, though it does save time if you have very little," said the man who had not been in a plane since we bumped along through headwinds from Albany to Chicago when he accepted the nomination in 1932.

Security was tight as a drum. The names of the Pullman cars were painted out when the Presidential Special left its secret Washington siding of tracks close by the Bureau of Engraving and Printing, with the conductors replaced by Filipino mess boys from Shangri-La. Aboard the Clipper, one agent in the Secret Service detail was picked for his endurance as a swimmer; if they were shot down at sea, his duty would be to stay afloat with Father for as long as possible. One plane preceded theirs and another tailed it. At a fueling stop in Trinidad, they had to leave Bill Leahy behind. He had been pulled out of his ambassadorship in Vichy when Pétain refused to give assurances that no French ships or French troops would be deployed to aid the Axis. Now Bill, with an unprecedented new title as Chief of Staff to the President, had caught the flu. He did not seem especially sorry.

At Bathurst in British Gambia, Father absorbed the fact that the prevailing wage for the ragged natives was less than fifty cents a day, and he and the rest transferred to a Douglas C-54. They flew at 13,000 feet over the Atlas Mountains, higher than Ross McIntire liked in view of his patient's fluttery heart condition, diagnosed in a previous year's checkup, and skirted Spanish territory for fear that a forced landing there might see FDR interned.

The Douglas transport touched down right on schedule at Casablanca's Medouina airport. An old, mud-encrusted French limousine carried us to his quarters within the compound, a grandiose villa named Dar-es-Saada. Outside stood an improvised air-raid shelter and a sunken swimming pool next to the handsome garden. His downstairs bedroom was all frills and froufrou, with an adjoining black marble bathtub. He whistled. "All we need is the madam of the house."

Hopkins brought Winston over from his private villa, Mirador, for dinner, along with a retinue of brass. Topic number one was the desirability of removing the entire conference to Marrakesh to avoid the danger of German bombers sneaking over as soon as Berlin discovered what was going on here. The British liked to get their own way in such affairs, but Father was against it. He had chosen Africa for this meeting because he wanted to take a trip and he was fed up with being confined. The Army rated Casablanca as safe enough, which satisfied him. He went on saying so when the sirens moaned toward the close of the party, the lights went off, and the talk ended by candlelight.

The conspicuously absent guest was Stalin. After Arcadia,

Winston had confessed to being baffled by the Kremlin's silence. Father reassured him. "Having come to the conclusion that the Russians do not use speech for the same purposes that we do, I am not unduly disturbed." Neither one of them shared the fantasy, spun in some circles in Washington and London, that Stalin was secretly negotiating peace with Hitler. The non-appearance of the Russians at Casablanca had a simple enough explanation. Twice before, Stalin had excused himself from meeting Father on grounds that it was impossible for him to leave Kremlin headquarters. This time, every Russian was celebrating the rout of the German armies at Stalingrad. The tide had turned for the Soviets, though 7,500,000 would be dead before victory. For the time being, Moscow pressure for a second front slackened. Torch and the Allied moves to follow would have Stalin's cool-headed approval.

Most of the omens were good at Casablanca. Japan's final bid to knock us out of the Solomons had exploded in a sea battle off Guadalcanal. Twenty-four minutes of incessant fire broke the backbone of enemy naval power. MacArthur's forces could begin the torturous job of herding the Japanese back toward their home islands.

Egypt was secured for the British after General Bernard Montgomery, biding his time until he had overwhelming advantages in men and armor, pushed Rommel's Afrika Korps into retreat and captured El Alamein. Before we left Casablanca, Montgomery's Eighth Army would begin moving against Tripoli as a prelude to advancing into Tunisia.

The principal purpose of these conferences was to have been agreeing or future strategy once Torch achieved the success that was within sight. It took the brass four days to decide on Husky, which made Sicily next. The Italian island was no more than a jump away from Tunisia. Seizing it would provide the Allies with a much-wanted base in the eastern Mediterranean. There was the possibility of eliminating Italy from the war by this strike at what Winston picturesquely called "the soft underbelly of the Axis." Once again, to the elation of the British, Roundup was put off without a date being set, and once again Stalin appeared to have been justified in a remark he had barked at Harriman: "Wars are not won with *plans*."

French politics intervened to take up chunks of Father's and

Winston's time. Somehow, they must reconcile two rival generals, Churchill's De Gaulle and ramrod-straight Henri Giraud, the pet of the United States, who had escaped from German captivity after the fall of France. He had been spirited out of France by submarine the previous year as part of the preparations for Torch, scheduled to be produced on the scene as the landings began at Algiers and take charge of French forces on the spot. But he turned up late, and Vichy's Admiral Darlan, as senior officer present in the city, assumed Giraud's intended role. Neither Father nor the PM had grieved when Darlan, sly as a mongoose, was assassinated the previous Christmas Eve.

Casablanca seemed an ideal place for bringing Giraud and De Gaulle together so that they could thrash out a working agreement on who should lead the fighting French. Father introduced the subject before dinner that first night. "You've got to get your problem child down here," he told Winston.

"De Gaulle is on his high horse," came the answer. "I can't move him from London. Jeanne d'Arc complex. And of course now that Ike has set Giraud in charge down here. . . ."

I sat with Father as he got into bed sometime toward three o'clock the next morning, then kept him up while he smoked two or three more cigarettes. "I have a strong, sneaking suspicion that our friend de Gaulle hasn't come to Africa yet because our friend Winston hasn't chosen to bid him come yet," he said.

Why? "Interests coincide. The English mean to maintain their hold on their colonies. They mean to help the French maintain *their* hold on *their* colonies. Winnie is a great man for the status quo. He even *looks* like the status quo, doesn't he?" As for de Gaulle? "Out to achieve one-man government in France. I can't imagine a man I would distrust more."

In the command ship, superbly equipped as a communications center, which the British had docked in the harbor overlooked by the gaily colored villas of wealthy French colonials, the British chiefs were busy concocting Operation Anakim to reopen the Burma Road, straddled by the Japanese.

"The British want to recapture Burma," Father commented. "It's the first time they've shown any real interest in the Pacific war. Burma—that affects India and French Indochina and Indonesia—they're all interrelated. If one gets its freedom, the others will get ideas."

I quoted Churchill's words after Montgomery's victory at El Alamein: "I have not become the King's First Minister in order to preside over the liquidation of the British Empire."

He replaced the stub in his holder with a fresh cigarette. "The thing is, the colonial system means war. Exploit the resources of an India, a Burma, a Java. Take all the wealth out of those countries, but never put anything back into them. . . . All you're doing is negating the value of any kind of organizational structure for peace before it begins." There was scorn in his voice.

By leaving the conduct of the war to the triumvirate of Marshall, King, and Arnold, he cleared his mind to concentrate on drawing plans "for the victorious peace which will surely come." In the White House the previous New Year's Eve, after his traditional toast, "To the United States of America," he had raised his glass to his brainchild, "And the United Nations!" He could set down the broad shape of his thinking in a single sentence: "I dream dreams but am, at the same time, an intensely practical person, and I am convinced that disarmament of the aggressor nations is an essential first step, followed up for a good many years to come by a day and night inspection of that disarmament and a police power to stop at its source any attempted evasion of the rules."

Our talk turned to India. "Should be made a commonwealth at once," said Father, then after five or ten years should be able to choose between remaining in the British Empire or having full independence. "As a commonwealth, she would be entitled to a modern form of government, an adequate health and educational standard," instead of having only one thing to look forward to every year. "Sure as shooting, they have a famine."

He paused to reflect for a moment. "I must tell Churchill what I found out about his British Gambia today. . . . Dirt. Disease. Very high mortality rate." Life expectancy was twenty-six years. "Those people are treated worse than the livestock. Their cattle live longer."

I told him that I had seen much the same in Algeria. He went on to say that what should be done there was to restore France as a world power, then make her trustee of her former colonies, obliged to file an annual report on her stewardship to the United Nations. "The Big Four—ourselves, Britain, China, the Soviet Union. We'll be responsible for the peace of the world," he said, "*when* we've won the war. . . . These great powers will have to assume the task of bringing education, raising the standards of living, improving the health conditions—of all the backward, depressed colonial areas of the world." When the United Nations decided that those areas had reached maturity, they must be given the opportunity of independence. "If this isn't done, we might as well agree that we're in for another war."

During each of the ten days that followed, I usually had a few private minutes with him. I slept upstairs in the villa in a room next to Harry Hopkins'. Franklin Jr. moved in the next evening—he'd been executive officer on the destroyer *Mayrant*, in action during the storming of this town.

Sometimes, Father's imagination raced as he speculated on what intelligent planning could do for this part of the world. A great irrigation canal to bring in water could transform the Sahara and "make the Imperial Valley in California look like a cabbage patch." That thought set him off denouncing the ways of colonial powers. "Wealth?" he cried. "Imperialists don't realize what they can do, what they can create. They've robbed this continent of billions, and all because they were too shortsighted to understand that their billions were pennies compared to the possibilities."

He was worried about Soviet reactions to the Combined Chiefs' decision to focus on Sicily next. "If Uncle Joe had only been able to get here himself—see for himself the difficulties we face in shipping, the problems of production. . . ." His voice trailed away. He complained, philosophically and in private, about British insistence on striking Europe in its "soft underbelly" instead of from the west.

"Wars are uncertain affairs. To win this one, we must maintain a difficult unity with one ally by apparently letting another down. . . . We have been forced into a strategic compromise which will most certainly offend the Russians so that later we will be able to force a compromise which will most certainly offend the British."

He had a startling prevision of what lay in wait little more than three years ahead. "The unity we have made for war is nothing to the unity we will have to build for peace. After the war—that's when the cry will come that our unity is no longer necessary. That's when the job will begin—in earnest!"

After working hours, he would lie in bed, reading magazines and, on one night, a paperback edition of George Kaufman's *The Man Who Came to Dinner*—Missy had once joked that Harry Hopkins, not Alexander Woollcott, was the playwright's inspiration. Looking for souvenirs, he picked through a selection of rugs which Harry, George Patton, and I arranged to have sent up from the downtown bazaars to the villa. He grudgingly accepted the word of Marshall and Eisenhower that a front-line inspection tour would be unduly hazardous, so he settled for a drive to Rabat, to take a look at the Second Armored, the Third Infantry, and the Ninth Infantry.

"Once in a jeep," he commented that evening, "is enough to last quite a time." He had come back carrying a memento in the form of the GI mess kit in which he had eaten an alfresco luncheon of ham and sweet potatoes while a regimental band honored its Commander in chief by playing "Chattanooga Choo-Choo," "Alexander's Ragtime Band," and "Deep in the Heart of Texas."

By then, he had reached his own conclusions about Giraud. The man entrusted with command of the French in North Africa sat like a West Point plebe in a chair facing Father, emitting no sign that he appreciated the political problems which outweighed his demands for weapons of war. The French would rally around Giraud? As soon as he had left, Father threw up his hands. "I'm afraid we're leaning on a very slender reed. He's a dud as an administrator. He'll be a dud as a leader." But Giraud was needed to balance off against de Gaulle.

On the evening that Father came back from his jeep ride, he was making his way to change clothes for dinner when Winston bounced in. "Wanted to tell you"—he beamed—"de Gaulle. It begins to look as though we'll be successful in persuading him to come down and join our talks."

Father said nothing for a moment, then moved on toward his bedroom door. "Congratulations, Winston," he said drily. "I always knew you'd be able to swing it."

Churchill's problem child arrived from London on the day my parent had the ninety-year-old Grand Vizier of Morocco to dinner along with the nine-year-old Sultan, Sidi Mohammed.

The son of the true faith, clad in flowing white silk, presented himself twenty minutes early, bearing gifts—a gold dagger for Father, two gold bracelets and a towering tiara for Mother, which produced a sidelong wink for my benefit from my parent. We could both picture her presiding at the White House with that doodad on her head. All these tokens of esteem finished up in the Hyde Park Library.

Out of deference to the Moslem guests, there was no "little sippy" before the meal and no wine served at the table, which may have had something to do with the gloom that enshrouded Winston, seated at Father's left, as the conversation proceeded. The host and the Grand Vizier were chatting in animated French about the possibilities of developing the natural resources of French Morocco—phosphates, cobalt, manganese ore, and oil—and retaining an important part of the cash proceeds to raise local standards of living. Winston tried unsuccessfully to change the subject.

The Grand Vizier pounced on the idea. But how could it be achieved when his country lacked the trained scientists and technicians capable of developing such industries unaided? No problem, said Father. They could take courses at American universities under some sort of reciprocal educational program. American firms could be hired on a fee or percentage basis to start the development projects. At least one Briton within earshot, a future Prime Minister named Harold Macmillan, wondered whether the President was deliberately baiting Winston.

As we rose, the Grand Vizier assured Father that he would petition the United States for development aid as soon as the war was over. "A new future for my country!" he said glowingly. He left with what seemed to be a meager return for the presents he had brought—a framed photograph of FDR. Winston followed him out, gnawing at his cigar.

He had suggested putting off the session with de Gaulle until ten thirty the next morning, but Father was feeling in form to see *le bon Charlie* right away. He stalked in ten minutes afterward, giving us the impression that thunder clouds were billowing around his narrow skull, and stayed for half an hour.

"I am sure that we will be able to assist your great country in reestablishing her destiny," said Father, all charm. His visitor merely grunted. "And I assure you it will be an honor for my country to participate in the undertaking."

"It is nice of you to say so," said the Frenchman icily, and that was roughly all there was to it. He marched out without a backward glance. Churchill popped in again to compare notes for another hour. Then Father cut across the debating. Equal rank for de Gaulle and Giraud, with equal responsibility for setting up a provisional assembly as a first step toward democracy for the French, who could then decide for themselves what leadership they desired. "The past is the past, and it's done," said Father, and I helped him to bed, to talk some more about Winston's problem child.

"He made it quite clear that he expects the Allies to return all French colonies to French control immediately upon their liberation," Father noted, but he was not sure that those colonies should ever be handed back without a pledge of progress for each of them.

"*How* do they belong to France? Why does Morocco, inhabited by Moroccans, belong to France? Or take Indochina. The Japanese control that colony now. Why was it a cinch for the Japanese to control that land? The native Indochinese have been so flagrantly downtrodden that they thought to themselves, 'Anything must be better than to live under French colonial rule!' "

Those same Indochinese were identified by different names in the 1970's. Their territory had been divided into three after the French, struggling to reestablish colonial control with the United States paying half their costs, were defeated by Ho Chi Minh's guerrillas in 1954's battle at Dienbienphu. Now they were Vietnamese, Laotians, Cambodians, which made no difference when four successive Presidents of the United States followed the French example and in the name of "democracy" tried to impose American control. The bill for that abortive effort ran high: 45,940 Americans dead and more than 300,000 wounded; more than 2,000,000 of the people once called Indochinese killed; close to $150 *billion* of American money gone; land poisoned with plane-spread chemicals so that it could not produce food in the next century.

"I'm talking about another war, Elliott," Father said in the small hours of Saturday morning, January 23, 1942. "I'm talking about what will happen to our world if after this war we allow millions of people to slide back into the same semislavery. . . . Don't think that Americans would be dying in the Pacific tonight if it hadn't been for the shortsighted greed of the French and the British and the Dutch. . . . One sentence, then I'm going to kick you out of here—I'm tired. When we've won the war, I will work with all my might and main to see to it that the United States is not wheedled into the position of accepting any plan that will further France's imperialistic ambitions or that will aid or abet the British Empire in *its* imperial ambitions." He pointed a finger to the light switch by the door.

There were four of us to lunch in the villa the next day—Father, who had slept late, the Prime Minister, Harry, and I. "Unconditional surrender" was born at the table, to be announced at the next day's press conference. It was my parent's phrase. Hopkins liked it at first hearing, though he felt that accomplishments so far were "a pretty feeble effort," in that Roundup had been set aside in favor of Overlord, which was to be a 1944 edition of the languishing cross-Channel invasion.

Winston chewed on for a while, frowned, then finally announced his verdict: "Perfect!" Half a decade later, he told Robert Sherwood, "I would not myself have used these words, but I immediately stood by the President and have frequently defended the decision. It is false to suggest that it prolonged the war."

With his phrase accorded the seal of approval, Father speculated about its impact elsewhere. He sucked a tooth. "Of course, it's just the thing for the Russians. 'Unconditional surrender.' Uncle Joe might have made it up himself." There would be no soft peace for the Germans or the Japanese or the Italians, though their populations would not be destroyed, or any peace at all until the philosophy of conquest had been erased.

The windup on Sunday was anticlimactic. A long explanatory cablegram to Stalin, underlining the importance of the Mediterranean in funneling supplies into the USSR, and a briefer one to Chiang Kai-shek. De Gaulle and Giraud, brought together at the villa, examining each other like two inquisitive dogs before they exchanged reluctant handshakes on the back terrace for the cameramen, then obliged once more because some photographers missed the shot. Father, with hollows under his eyes, sitting there in the early-spring sunshine that brought the scent of bougainvillea and oleanders, telling reporters about the terms of surrender, while Churchill, wearing a jaunty homburg, expounded on strategy. President and Prime Minister, he said, would see the war through together.

Father arrived back in Washington with a hacking cough and with what he kiddingly described as "Gambia fever," worn out by ten days of negotiating and, as he told Mother, "too much plane." He worked in bed for the better part of a week, and took himself off to Hyde Park for a spell. But he was still feeling the aftereffects of Casablanca in early March. His indifferent health at the time prevented his seeing as much of the current star guest of the White House as he would have liked. Mother, conversely, would not have been sorry to see the lady off the premises as soon as possible.

Madame Chiang Kai-shek, cold as ice and groomed to a hair, had flown into Mitchel Field from Chungking a month before Christmas. Hopkins met her at Father's request and escorted her to the Harkness Pavilion, New York, where she was booked into the entire twelfth floor for "medical treatment and rest"; she had been involved in a car accident on her home territory. She felt well enough to respin two of her favorite fantasies en route to the hospital. The first alleged that only the intervention of Hopkins and a few other dependables saved China from being sold down the river prior to Pearl Harbor because the United States sought to appease Tokyo. The second would have Harry believe that the way to win the war was to switch priorities to "Japan first" and concentrate American strength behind her husband. Harry confined himself to remarking that this was "unfeasible."

Mother paid some sympathy calls on her at the pavilion and found that tiny, delicate Madame Chiang was as much a propagandist as a patient, active in expounding her opinions in influential company, including that of publisher Henry Luce, a "Japan first" man himself, who was happy to open the pages of his *Life* magazine for her use as a platform. She was outraged that her husband had not been asked to Casablanca. From the medical center, Madame Chiang moved with her traveling court into a series of suites in the Waldorf Towers, where she proceeded to become one of the very best customers of the most expensive stores in Manhattan. As a gesture of harmony with Nationalist China's cause, it was agreed that the United States government would pick up all the bills, which exceeded $1,000,000 before she had finished.

In the middle of February, she was invited to stay in the White House. Mother was piqued when an advance guard of Chinese attendants showed up, bringing explicit directions for the care and feeding of their mistress, together with her own silk sheets for her bed. She spent a great part of the time there during her ten-day stay. Whenever she left it, even for a few minutes, top and bottom sheets, two pillowcases, and the silk, lace-trimmed blanket spread had to be changed. Two nurses sat on duty around the clock in a little next-door room, with a maid assigned to wait on them. Mrs. Nesbitt, hard-pressed to stretch the family's ration points to provide enough meals, wondered in her innocence how this fine lady had managed "while she was campaigning with the general in China."

The truth of the matter was that Chiang's campaigns existed mostly on paper. He was a figurehead for the Chinese warlords, who ruled as dictators in their private fiefdoms. Corruption was the name of the game in Chungking. Japan's puppet regime, set up in Nanking under Wang Ching-wei, controlled vast expanses of the country unchallenged. In the mountains of the northwest, Mao Tse-tung's Communists ran an independent guerrilla state, skirmishing with the Japanese, constantly angling for concessions from Chiang, who devoted as much effort to resisting them as to coming to grips with the invaders.

In Chiang, Father backed the wrong horse. There was never a period throughout the conflict when he could obtain an accurate, objective account of what the Generalissimo was doing with the 300 divisions he claimed to command. Beanpole-lean General Stilwell, in command of American forces in China, Burma, and India, yearned to expand the fighting. That made "Vinegar Joe" a burden to both the Chiangs, though he was officially the Generalissimo's Chief of Staff as well as local lend-lease administrator. Their darling was Claire Chennault, ex–United States Army, "air adviser" to Chiang, dashing commander of the Flying Tiger volunteers. Stilwell and Chennault were doomed to collide with each other, one insisting that only infantry could win in the long run, the other imagining that mass bombing could drive out the Japanese.

Father's hope was that Chennault was right in his dreaming. Allied strategists were appalled at the prospect of committing troops by the hundreds of thousands into battle against a skilled and resourceful enemy. The policy of "Germany first" left the Chinese short of supplies in all categories, but that could be corrected, once Hitler was beaten. If planes could perform the job in the East, the saving in lives would be incalculable. One question overhanging the talks at Casablanca, however, had been, How much longer will Chiang stay in the war?

Mother rewarded her housekeeper with a ticket to hear her guest sweep a special audience of the Senate and the House off its collective feet with her passionate persuasions for more help, speaking in the cause of "freedom" and "democracy" with calculated effect and, as Henrietta noted, "using some words I'd never heard before." Sentiment was strong in Congress for making Japan the number-one target.

The Chinese visitor was a mistress of flattery as well as rhetoric. She dismissed Willkie, whom she had seen in Chungking, as "an adolescent, after all," while Father—"Ah, Mr. President, you are *sophisticated.*" She could also be arrogant or forgetful, depending on the viewpoint. "Please do not bother to get up," she remarked once as she was about to leave the room.

Father's eyes gleamed. "Thank you for the compliment," he said.

He was never "soft" on Communism, but he was soft on the Chiangs, telling himself that they meant their promises about democracy for postwar China. In this instance, Mother was less gullible. Her unspoken convictions about the nature of her guest were confirmed at dinner one evening. John L. Lewis was demanding two dollars a day more for the miners in defiance of Presidential wage and price controls, a move which Jimmy Byrnes, currently the so-called "Assistant President," stigmatized as deliberate sabotage. How would Lewis be dealt with in China? Father asked Madame Chiang. She answered him by raising an exquisitely manicured hand and drawing a long fingernail across her throat.

He teased Mother about that when the opportunity presented itself. "Well, how about your gentle and sweet character now?" But Mother had discerned the ruthlessness of the uncrowned Empress of Nationalist China long before he did.

The lady was in New York at the end of a triumphant speaking tour when Winston returned to Washington, accompanied by the biggest flock of counselors brought in to date. Father wondered if she might like to meet the PM. No, she replied. Let him come up to see her, if that was his wish. Churchill was not interested.

The vital purpose of Trident, as the two weeks of conferences were called, was to fix a date at least for the second front in Europe, which had been hanging fire for more than a year. A sustained attack by all arms at maximum force should bring victory by 1945. If bombing the Reich and more of the peripheral campaigns which Marshall deplored continued to be the Allies' strategy, the war could last into 1950, and that would be too late. The Germans were developing weapons designed to wipe out Britain and hold the world to ransom.

Aerial reconnaissance had revealed the existence of an enormous underground experimental center at Peenemünde on the Baltic coast. There, the destruction of Germany's enemies by means of new technologies was in advanced stages of planning: the pilotless plane called V-1; the stratospheric rocket known as V-2; and also the atomic bomb. On the heels of Trident, Hitler visited Peenemünde. What he saw inspired him to tell his military chiefs that, in spite of reverses on the Russian front and the loss of Tunisia, all that Germany need do was hold on. London would be leveled by the year's end, and Britain would capitulate.

Peenemünde was to be saturated by Allied bombers, but the work there went on just the same. Building the Bomb had developed into a race between German science and our own. Just before the previous Christmas, the halfway mark had been reached at Stagg Field, Chicago, with the first self-sustaining nuclear reaction. The necessity for total secrecy in the Manhattan Project was more acute than before. So was the need to spend astronomical sums of unauthorized money, which Father as good as stole from departmental budgets. The role of British scientists was phased out with Winston's eager consent. Only the United States had the capacity to make the Bomb in time, and, curiously enough, he refrained from direct questioning of Father on the progress that was made; he was content to use Hopkins as his source of information.

Trident seemed to have resolved two long-standing controversies. May 1, 1944, was established as the day for the European invasion, which was to be coded as Overlord. The overall commander of the operation would not be Churchill's candidate, General Sir Alan Brooke, Chief of the Imperial General Staff, who really did not want a second front anyway. Marshall was the man who could be counted on to hold his own against Winston and strike at Germany where the Nazis were strongest, not temporize, as the British would have preferred, and delay landings in France until the Reich had been brought to its knees.

Before she made her final departure in June, Madame Chiang urged Mother to visit Chungking "as soon as the cool weather sets in." Impossible for the present, said Father, who was already framing a proposal to meet Chiang himself at "some place midway between our two capitals" in a bid to beef up the languishing Chinese war effort. He agreed that Mother might take another overseas trip, this time, however, to the southwest Pacific. Since she would be fed and boarded by the Army and Navy on her travels, he felt that it must be a nonprofit excursion. Income from the *My Day* columns she wrote while she was away was to be divided between the Red Cross and the American Friends Service Committee.

She would go without a permanent escort, so she carried a portable typewriter when she left, dressed in blue-gray Red Cross uniform, since she could wear that anywhere and keep her luggage within the forty-four pound limit. The impression my mother's sympathetic face and words made on the fighting men of the Pacific differed in only one respect from that of her transatlantic tour. In hospitals and mess halls on Honolulu, the Cook Islands, the Fijis, New Zealand, and Australia, she would stop to talk like a deeply concerned aunt to hundreds of them, individually, every day, sometimes bringing tears of pleasure to their eyes. But not all the brass welcomed her presence. The least chivalrous among them was Douglas MacArthur, who passed down the word that he was too busy to see her and flatly turned her down when she asked to visit Port Moresby.

One pleasure she was not to be deterred from enjoying on

her 23,000-mile swing was a reunion with Joe Lash, a draftee whose application for officer training had been rejected. There were some of us in the family who suspected that a certain amount of back-door influence had been exercised to get him sent to the other end of the earth. His ultimate destination was a Godforsaken landing strip on Johnston Island, southwest of Pearl Harbor. At the time of her trip, Sergeant Lash would be on Guadalcanal, and, as she wrote in advance in one of her flow of letters to him, "If I see you that will be a joy." Permission was granted by Admiral Bill Halsey, Seventh Fleet commander. Joe fidgeted outside while she lunched with the brass on Guadalcanal. Then the waiting reporters were astonished to see "Army protocol crashed as we embraced one another," in the words of Joe's subsequent letter home to Trude. Toward the close of the afternoon, she introduced him to Halsey. "So this is the young man," sniffed the admiral as press cameras clicked. Mother and her substitute son ended the day hashing over the events it had brought before she retired at eleven thirty for four hours' sleep to prepare her for another round of hospital wards the next day. Joe hated to see her go "because for a little while I was back in the world of those I love."

The timetable set for Overlord would leave Stalin feeling that yet again he had been given the runaround while his country bled. Putting himself in the Russian's shoes, Father could see no other possible reaction. If he could talk face to face with Uncle Joe, Father was convinced that he could alleviate suspicions that Britain and the United States were ganging up against the USSR. My parent had a particularly horrendous piece of information from the British to digest. Churchill's gray eminence of science, Cherwell, had told him that Britain had no interest in nuclear energy for industry, that the Bomb's importance lay in counteracting Soviety dominance after the war. But Father had limitless faith in what could be accomplished by a meeting of minds if one of them was his. "Meet 'em halfway" was fundamental in his philosophy.

The circumstances for a Roosevelt-Stalin get-together were distinctly unfavorable. Our latest ambassador in Moscow, Admiral William H. Standley, former Chief of Naval Operations and an old friend of my parent's, had lived up to his reputation as a plain-spoken seadog by telling American newspapermen there that the Soviet government, hiding the truth about lend-lease, was deluding its people into the belief that they were fighting the Nazis unaided. Shock waves rolled through the Kremlin. The admiral's indiscretion evoked a revealing response from Harriman in London. "The feeling is growing here," he reported to Father, "that we will build trouble for the future if we allow ourselves to be kicked around by the Russians."

With Standley self-disqualified as a diplomat, Father sent Joe Davies to convey his suggestion for a Big Two conference to Stalin. The proposal appalled Churchill. The war so far had been conducted much along the lines that he wanted. By his eagerness to come to see Father, he had given the British people convincing evidence that the two leaders were blood brothers, united in all that was said or done. A perilous precedent would be set if Father saw Stalin without Winston.

After eleven hours of talking with Davies, Stalin agreed that he would like to meet Father in mid-July at Fairbanks, Alaska. Shortly afterward, the Trident plans and schedules were formally delivered to the Kremlin. Their impact was worse than Father had feared. The Russian cabled Winston what amounted to an accusation of broken promises.

The Prime Minister had confided to his own ambassador to Moscow, Sir Archibald Clark Kerr, that he was "getting rather tired of these repeated scoldings considering that they have never been actuated by anything but cold-blooded self-interest and total disdain of our lives and fortunes." Past messages to the Kremlin had usually been jointly agreed in advance by Churchill and FDR. This time, Winston fired off an angry answer without checking its phraseology with Father. The Big Two conference was indefinitely postponed. Instead, Former Naval Person and POTUS would forgather again in Quebec in August, where an ever enlarged British delegation would rehash each one of its objections to Overlord.

Progress in the Mediterranean theater delivered powerful fresh arguments into their hands. The fighting in Sicily had gone almost exactly to plan against the Italians, who begged in vain for Hitler's help. In little more than a month, Patton's Seventh Army and Montgomery's Eighth overran resistance, except for the corner of the island in the shadow of Mount Etna.

Georgie Patton received congratulations from the White House. "It was suggested . . . that after the war I should make you the Marquis of Mt. Etna. Don't fall into the crater!"

The Commander in Chief was occasionally left in the dark about the accelerating drive to victory, especially over the weekends, when a corporal's guard took over in most Washington departments. He was up at Shangri-La on Sunday, July 25, working on a speech with Sherwood and Rosenman, when Steve Early telephoned. He had just heard a radio news flash reporting the resignation of Mussolini. Father took it calmly. "I wonder how we could get any confirmation on that. . . ."

Taking a turn at the telephone, Sherwood found everyone he spoke with trying to check with somebody else. "Oh, we'll find out about it later," said Father, returning to the manuscript. In the White House the following day, when King Victor Emmanuel appointed Marshal Pietro Badoglio as his Prime Minister, extra words were added to the speech: "Our terms to Italy are still the same as our terms to Germany and Japan—'Unconditional Surrender.'"

On August 5, the day Winston embarked with his wife, Clementine, daughter Mary, and a staff of 200 in the *Queen Mary* for Quebec, he messaged Father that Rome was fishing for peace. Communist riots were threatening to overthrow the monarchy, by which Winston set great store for Italy and elsewhere in the world. "Rampant Bolshevism," in his words, would follow if the House of Savoy were allowed to tumble. "The sooner we land in Italy the better."

In the old stone fortress of the Citadel in the capital of French Canada, the Prime Minister got his way. Before he recrossed the Atlantic three weeks later, Montgomery's forces had streamed across the Straits of Messina, General Mark Clark's Fifth Army swarmed ashore on Salerno's beaches, and Badoglio's government signed an armistice, meaningless in military terms, because the Germans had moved in to rescue Mussolini and force the fight.

Father's team exacted a stiff price from the conferees on the other side. The Overlord invasion of Fortress Europe, fanning out from the beaches of Normandy, must go forward with no more if's or but's even though Marshall had yet to be confirmed as commander. There must be supplemental landings by

American and French forces around Toulon in southern France. And the British must get busy in Burma.

Winston made a show of somber acquiescence, but he had no more intention of succumbing to American arguments than of surrendering to Nazi terror. Contrary to expectations, the Red Army had survived the slaughter inflicted by the Germans in three mammoth campaigns. There was little doubt by now that the Soviets would emerge from the war as the strongest power in Europe. To his habit of thinking, the main thrust of the Anglo-American attack should be made in the eastern Mediterranean and up through the Balkans. That might not be the most effective route for conquering Hitler, but as a means of containing the Soviets it had everything over invading Normandy.

The Prime Minister had once been justified in treating the United States as his junior partner, but North Africa was the last battleground where British troops outnumbered Americans. These days lend-lease accounted for nearly three-quarters of Britain's munitions supplies. America's productive strength was still surging toward its peak, while Britain's flagged. In this year of 1943, 260 United States destroyers were at sea on convoy duties, and for the first time in history America's merchant fleet surpassed theirs.

Father's parting words to me at Casablanca recognized the turnabout. Down the centuries, he said, the British chose their allies wisely and well. "They've always been able to come out on top, with the same reactionary grip on the peoples of the world and the markets of the world through every war they've ever been in. This time, we're Britain's allies. . . . I hope they realize they're not senior partner; that we're not going to sit by, after we've won, and watch their system stultify the growth of every country in Asia and half the countries in Europe to boot."

Accompanying POTUS south from Quebec, Winston tried a new tack in forcing the prized Anglo-American friendship which he assumed would enable him to retain his once-magical hold on his people's affection—and ultimately stymie Overlord. Wearing a borrowed scarlet robe, he spoke at Harvard University. He checked out with Father in advance the thought which he wanted to test on the wind and was assured that American sentiment for the valor of his people was strong enough to

make it worth a try—Father's ideas of tomorrow included federation for Europe, with open markets, passport-free travel,
and interchangeable currencies for all member nations, and a
matching arrangement for linking the countries of North and
South America.

"This gift of a common tongue is a priceless inheritance,"
said Winston, accepting an honorary doctor of literature degree, "and it may well some day become the foundation of a
common citizenship. I like to think of British and Americans
moving about freely over each other's wide estates with hardly a
sense of being foreigners to one another." *Wide estates* when the
United Kingdom's 94,209 square miles made it smaller than the
state of Oregon? Winston had slipped in a quiet boost for the
Empire.

He was more than willing for a Big Three conference to be
held as soon as possible. For the moment Stalin, kept on the
outside looking in, would go no further than agreeing that the
Foreign Ministers—Hull, Eden, and Molotov—should gather
in Moscow. Father would have sent Sumner Welles, too, had
that been possible, but Hull's animosity toward his Undersecretary and the aftertaste of the Pullman-car scandal meant that
Welles had to quit the State Department. Into his place stepped
hard-driven Ed Stettinius, once top man at United States Steel
and lend-lease administrator for the past two years.

Another change in the White House circle was in the making,
of more intimate concern to Mother. Mr. and Mrs. Hopkins
rented a cheerful little house in Georgetown, into which they
would move with Diana before Christmas. None of us who
knew the background of the previous year believed that this
was any of Father's doing.

Making the first flight of his life at the age of seventy-four,
Hull had some challenging commissions to fulfill in the Soviet
capital. Stalin must be formally invited to meet with Father and
Churchill. The Russian, who had not left his country in thirty
years, would not consider going farther than a day's journey by
plane away, since he was the working commander of the Red
Army. This factor fixed the site as Teheran, the shabby capital
of neutral but friendly Iran. Hull had a more delicate item to
raise. Looking ahead to success in Europe after Germany had
been assailed from west and east, would the Soviet Union then

enter the war on Japan? That would mean an enormous saving in time and American lives. Without the Red Army, according to secret United States military estimates, operations against the Japanese "might become abortive."

At the farewell banquet in the Kremlin on the night of November 2, Hull was seated at Stalin's right. Before they left the table, Stalin turned to his guest of honor and asked him to tell Father personally that he would "get in and help to defeat the enemy in the Far East" once the Germans had been defeated. The news went winging to the White House the moment Hull got back to Spaso House.

17

There would have to be two meetings, one with Chìang and a second with Uncle Joe before the four powers could begin working toward common goals. At the end of the summer, when I spent two months in Washington on reorganizing reconnaissance operations, Father had outlined for me what he visualized as his particular role.

The United States will have to lead. Lead and use our good offices always to conciliate. Help to solve the differences which will arise between the others: between Russia and England in Europe, between the British Empire and China, and between China and Russia in the Far East. We will be able to do that because we're big, and we're strong, and we're self-sufficient. Britain is on the decline; China, still in the eighteenth century; Russia, suspicious of us and making us suspicious of her. America is the only great power that can make peace in the world stick. It's a tremendous responsibility, and the only way we can start living up to it is by getting to talk with these men, face to face.

Chiang came up first, and the place was Cairo. It was no accident that the meeting took place on what was then Union Jack

345

territory. Winston contrived that by coaxing Father like a travel agent, with word-pictures of the scenery that would delight the traveler to the Land of the Pharaohs.

Father and the Joint Chiefs sailed from Hampton Roads, Virginia, in the big new battleship *Iowa* with an escort of destroyers. Five days out, he got off a note to Mother. "All goes well and a very comfortable trip so far. . . . All our crowd are getting a real rest, mostly reading—though I have had 2 staff meetings. It looks as if I'll be away a little longer than I thought. . . . Love to Anna and the chicks and loads to you."

One subject discussed at those staff meetings was who should command Overlord. Father's automatic nominee was Marshall, even though he had confessed that he would sleep less easily if his Chief of Army Staff left Washington. But that was pure selfishness. "I want George to be the Pershing of the Second World War," he told Marshall's strongest advocate, Black Jack himself. Eisenhower would be called back from the Mediterranean theater to substitute for George, though that would certainly rile MacArthur. He could not get along with Ike, his assistant in the Philippines from 1935 until 1939, when the promotions began which would leapfrog him over the heads of 366 more senior officers.

Winston's ears tended to lay back at the prospect of General George exercising total authority in the European theater. If he could not wangle Brooke into supreme command, then he would settle for Field Marshal Sir John Dill, known and admired by his American colleagues as ranking British officer on the Combined Chiefs of Staff in Washington. Dill could be depended on to give Churchill more or less free rein in the Mediterranean.

So as not to alarm "Dearest Babs," Father's note did not mention that on the second day out the *Iowa* had come within seconds of being torpedoed. He was sitting on deck, with cotton stuffed in his ears against the thunder of five-inch guns engaged in antiaircraft drill, when the battleship heeled over in a 90-degree turn at 31 knots. A tin fish accidentally fired by the *Thompson*, one of the destroyer escorts, heading straight for the *Iowa*'s hull, missed by roughly twenty yards.

With Franklin Jr., General Ike, and an assortment of Anglo-American brass, I was down at Oran's naval base, Mers-el-Kebir, at eight thirty on Saturday morning, November 20, to welcome Father as he came ashore in a motor whaleboat, shouting "Roosevelt weather!" in the crisp, clear sunlight. That afternoon, he reviewed my outfit, the Northwest African Photo Reconnaissance Wing—250 planes and a mixture of 2,800 Americans, British, French, Canadians, South Africans, Australians, and New Zealanders on station—after I'd hustled back to base to get things into the best approximation to apple-pie order. Dinner was a party, with blond Kay Summersby, Ike's English chauffeur, gracing the table along with one other girl.

Security precautions kept Father in Tunis until Sunday night, when he could be flown along the Nile to Cairo without telltale fighter escort all the way. He spent the day with Ike as his guide, swapping military history as ancient as the Macedonians' and as up-to-date as the Afrika Korps' as they viewed the ruins of Carthage and the burned-out tanks that studded the Tunisian battle zones. That night we drove to El Aouina outside Tunis to see the Presidential group off in the Air Transport Command C-54, which bore the nickname The Sacred Cow.

Over his protests about needless expense, the plane had been remodeled to his use with a galley, leg rests, room for a worktable, and two berths, one of them reserved for Hopkins on this trip. A knockdown ramp had been built in, again contrary to Father's wishes, since the standard thirty-foot model which had to be pushed across the tarmac was conspicuous notice that the wheelchair President was due to land.

Before their takeoff, a little biplane ignored the red warning flares that were fired across its path and landed immediately ahead of The Sacred Cow. Ten hours and 1,500 miles later, on the approach to Cairo over the muddy blue waters of the Nile, three escorting fighters had to peel off to shoo away a French plane that was heading in uncomfortably close.

I flew in with Ike and some of his staff the following day. He was fretting about his future, worried that he was about to be kicked upstairs to a Pentagon desk job. Three or four times during the week he was to voice his concern. If he thought there was anything I could do about it, he was sadly mistaken. All I could reply was, "The Joint Chiefs will surely consult you, sir, before they take any final action." I was none too certain even of that.

I found Father, looking well and rested, breakfasting alone

in bed at Ambassador Alexander Kirk's big villa close by the
Pyramids of Giza, west of the city. Winston, who had arrived in
Cairo early like the Chiangs, had greeted him at the airport.
"I've met the Generalissimo, taken a trip out to look at the Pyra-
mids, gotten a radiogram from Uncle Joe, saying that he'd be at
Teheran on the twenty-eighth—next Sunday," my parent re-
ported contentedly.

The Generalissimo and Madame had dined with him the
night before. "I learned more just talking to the Chiangs than I
did from more than four hours of meeting with the Combined
Chiefs. . . . More about the war that *isn't* being fought and
why. Chiang's troops aren't fighting at all, despite the reports
that get printed in the papers. He claims his troops aren't
trained and have no equipment—and that's easy to believe. But
it doesn't explain why he's trying so hard to keep Stilwell from
training Chinese troops. And it doesn't explain why he keeps
thousands and thousands of his best men up in the northwest,
up on the borders of Red China."

The time came for him to shift his tray aside, swing himself
out of bed, and start dressing, ready for an eleven o'clock meeting with the Combined Chiefs. Just before we went in for
lunch, I had a chance to ask him how it looked for Overlord.
"Very 'iffy,' at least from the British point of view. . . .They've
introduced the idea of a smaller attack, perhaps on Norway,
with the weight continuing in the Mediterranean. But it's not
over yet. General George is still the best man at the conference
table. As far as he's concerned, the only question open for discussion is, Who will be in command of our invasion from the
west?"

That afternoon, I presented his excuses and substituted for
him at a cocktail party thrown by the Chiangs at the villa in
which they were staying. Almost at once, Madame was leading
me to two chairs and performing as expert a job of flattery and
charm as anybody had troubled to exert on me in years because, I concluded, it was second nature to her. I guessed I'd be
terrified if I ever saw her first nature at work.

"I don't know that I'd put it as strongly as you do," Father
said with a thoughtful frown when I filled him in on the party.
"She's an opportunist certainly, and I'd certainly not want to be
known as her enemy in her own country. But at the moment,
who is there in China who could take Chiang's place? There's

just no other leader. With all their shortcomings, we've got to depend on the Chiangs."

Before the week was over, he talked a lot about China. "Chiang would have us believe that the Chinese Communists are doing nothing against the Japanese. Again, we know differently." He knew all about it when I mentioned that all our aerial mapping of China was withheld from the British. "We worked out that arrangement with the Chinese quite some time ago. . . . They made us promise before we went ahead with the work. . . . They're aware that the British want to look at them for commercial, postwar reasons."

Father by then had registered complaints with the impassive, shaven-skulled Chinese leader in the unwrinkled khaki uniform about the monolithic character of his Kuomintang government in Chungking. "I'd told him he would have to form a unity government, while the war was still being fought, with the Communists in Yenan. He agreed . . . once he had our assurance that the Soviet Union would agree to respect the frontier in Manchuria. That part of it is on the agenda for Teheran. . . . Actually, as far as he's concerned, the only earnest of our good faith that he expects is that when Japan is on her knees, we make sure that no British warships come into Chinese ports. Only American warships. And I've given him my personal promise that that's what will happen."

What would Churchill say to that? "There can't be much argument, inasmuch as it's ninety-nine percent American matériel and American men bringing about the defeat of Japan." Most Chinese, said Father, thought more highly of Japanese colonial policies than those of the British, the French, or the Dutch.

Chiang's trump card was the fact that at present China was the only feasible staging point for an ultimate assault on the islands of Japan. But the sole overland route for bringing in Allied troops and arms lay northeast across Burma into the province of Yunnan, and that road was blocked by Japanese. "Burma," Chiang insisted through his interpreters, "is the key to the whole campaign in Asia," but he was prepared to commit Chinese divisions into the highlands there only on condition that the Allies staged a major land, sea, and air attack on the Burmese coast from the Bay of Bengal.

British enthusiasm was tepid. They put no stock whatever in

the notion that the Chinese could be whipped into shape as a fighting force. To Winston, Burma had little strategic importance. It was a piece of Empire real estate to be liberated one fine day, preferably, for the sake of keeping face, without American or Chinese assistance. What he wanted was to restore British rights over Hong Kong, Singapore, Shanghai, and Canton, moves which the United States would resist, as Father promised Chiang, *provided* that Communists were given a place in the Kuomintang. It was admittedly quite a deal, but FDR wanted the Generalissimo to go home in a mood to bolster the morale among his people. To the same end, my parent told him that, in the postwar world, China would be a full-fledged member of the Big Four, which was premature, since this was another topic for the Teheran agenda.

The Chiangs went off serenely enough after tea in the villa's garden on Thanksgiving Day. At dinner, Father staged a demonstration for his guests of the fine art of carving two turkeys that had been packed aboard The Sacred Cow. His exuberance was infectious. The prospects for Allied unity seemed bright. In the Pacific, the shattering battles for Tarawa, Makin, and the Gilberts were over. Air armadas had delivered their fifth saturation raid on Berlin. The Red Army had freed Kiev, and the old Polish border lay no more than fifty miles ahead.

"By next spring, the way things are going in Russia now, maybe a second front won't be necessary," he had said to me glowingly, which would be Churchill's line, sure as fate, next week.

Toward the end of the meal, Father raised his wineglass with his eyes on the Prime Minister. "With the peoples of the United Kingdom in our family, we are a large family, and more united than ever before. I propose a toast to this unity, and may it long continue!" The orchestra from nearby Camp Huckstep went into action. Winston's daughter Sarah had some turns around the floor with a variety of partners, and her father and Pa Watson executed a few stately steps together.

The date in the log of The Sacred Cow was November 27, and at 0435 hours, Greenwich Mean Time, she took off from Cairo for Teheran. "Arrived: 11.30. Elapsed time: 6.55, Mileage: 1,310." Seventy-six other Americans flew with Father into the seemingly modern city, clustered at the foot of a range of

small mountains, which until recently had been general headquarters for all Axis espionage in the Middle East. Besides being a hornet's nest of Nazi agents and sympathizers, it had
monumental problems of health and sanitation. Downtown's
drinking water carried uptown's refuse, offal, and the threat of
typhus and dysentery.

Out beyond the broad, paved streets, the university, the hospitals, and telephone exchange, there was not much but graz-
ing land, except to the south, where oil fields, a British concession, had padded the bank accounts of upper-class Iranians
and government officials. Inflation burned like smallpox. Five
dollars bought a pack of American cigarettes, a year's average
income a sack of flour.

On his second day there, Father yielded to a warning from
Stalin, relayed through Harriman, that the risk of assassination
was high and moved out of the American Legation, which was
blocks away, into the Soviet Embassy. Uncle Joe vacated his
quarters to provide space for his guest, taking himself into a
smaller house within the tightly shielded compound, patrolled
by plainclothesmen and Russian guards, not one of them under
six feet tall. Every servant in the embassy was a member of the
secret police, with a handgun bulging under his uniform. Father's Filipino cooks and stewards moved in with him to prepare
meals, as they had in Cairo.

He had been in his suite, which opened directly into the des-
ignated main conference room, no more than fifteen minutes
before Stalin came a-calling. In the solidly comfortable living
room, with a view of cheerful gardens, the visitor saw a sallow-
complexioned, beaming giant of a man, sitting in a wheelchair
because he had neither time nor desire to clamp the steel onto
his legs. He was alone. "The way I looked at it," Father told me
afterward, "it would be taken as a gesture of my confidence and
my lack of suspicion if *his* interpreter were the only one present. And, as a matter of fact, it simplifies matters a whole lot,
too. Saves time."

His gaze took in a squat, dignified figure in a well-cut gray-
beige dress uniform, gold star of a Red Army marshal on his
red-and-gold epaulets and a single decoration, Hero of Socialist
Labor, on the tunic.

Pavlov, who came with him, would do the translating. "I am

glad to see you," Father said with a smile, as each took the measure of the other. "I have tried for a long time to bring this
about." Stalin blamed himself for the delay. Military affairs had
kept him busy, he said, making himself comfortable on the
couch.

Delayed by engine trouble in the B-25 that I flew in, I sat on
the same spot some twenty-four hours afterward while Father
briefed me on their first encounter. Did they talk state secrets?
"Not a bit of it. Mostly, it was, How did I like my quarters? and,
Thank you very much for turning over the main house to me,
and, What is the news from the eastern front? It's very good, by
the way. Stalin's most pleased. He hopes the Red Army will
have crossed the Polish border before we leave."

My parent liked what he had seen. "He's got a kind of massive rumble, talks deliberately, seems very confident, very sure
of himself, moves slowly. Altogether quite impressive, I'd say."
He was sure that the two of them would hit it off. "A great deal
of the misunderstandings and the mistrusts of the past are going to get cleared up during the next few days—I hope once
and for all. As for Uncle Joe and Winston, well . . . I'll have
my work cut out for me, in between those two. They're *so* different. Ideas, temperaments."

The first plenary session of the Big Three was scheduled almost immediately after Stalin's call. With Churchill heading a
team of eight, including Eden, Dill, and Brooke, the British had
the largest delegation at the specially built, carved oak table, circular in shape so that all might rank as equals. Winston, who
usually favored civilian clothes, took to wearing RAF air marshal's blue at Teheran in order not to be outdone by Stalin. Father, who stuck to his workday business suit, would have had
eight men with him, too, if Marshall and Arnold had not got
their signals mixed and gone off sightseeing, but he did have
Hopkins, King, and Leahy to flank him. The Russians were in
the minority—just Stalin; his Chief of Staff, Marshal Kliment
Voroshilov; Molotov; lanky Pavlov; and a secretary.

On the ground that, at sixty-one, he was the youngest of the
three—Stalin was three years older and Winston's sixty-ninth
birthday loomed two days ahead—Father was asked to preside.
Pleasantries were brief. "Let us get down to business," rumbled
Stalin after a few painstakingly translated words of welcome.

He chain-smoked strong, black Russian cigarettes in their two-inch cardboard tubes and doodled on the pad in front of him as Father reviewed the war to date, beginning with the Pacific, since the Russians seemed underinformed on progress in that theater. Then he came to the subject which had promised to destroy Big Three unity before the leaders could meet together. "Stalin was shown a copy of our plan for Overlord," Father told me afterward. "He looked at it, asked a question or two, and then just asked, 'When?' "

Churchill answered for Britain and the United States. During the next May, June, and July, it was planned to land 1,000,000 troops in Europe, starting with nineteen American and sixteen British divisions, which would have to be the United Kingdom's full contribution of its limited manpower. The Soviets, who suffered nine-tenths of all Big Three casualties in the war, had 300 divisions in Europe against 260 of the Axis.

Then Winston began to procrastinate. Shortage of landing craft might enforce delays on Overlord, he said, but the Anglo-American armies should not be left idle. Fresh action in his beloved Mediterranean could fill the time gap; bribe neutral Turkey with lend-lease aid into fighting with the Allies; press forward over the Italian Alps; enlist the Yugoslav partisans of Josip Broz, known as Marshal Tito, for a thrust into Rumania.

Overlord must take precedence, Stalin replied, his voice barely audible. The "scattering" of forces in the eastern Mediterranean would be unwise. The Red Army had found that two-front offensives worked best against the Nazis. If there were Allied soldiers to spare in Italy, let them make an early landing in southern France. After nearly three and a half hours, when the session broke up, the roles of the three protagonists were clear: Stalin urging invasion of France, Churchill still bucking it, Father serving as Mr. Interlocutor with liberal applications of "meet 'em halfway."

They picked up their discussions at dinner and talked there "about everything we could think of," Father reported. He and the man who had yet to be called Uncle Joe to his face—that came forty-eight hours later—had already covered a sizable list of topics between themselves. The Americans and British would have a postwar merchant fleet big enough for some ships to be spared for the USSR, Father had said. In that event, Stalin responded, greatly increased supplies of raw materials could be shipped from his country to the United States.

He had been cautioned by Father against raising with Winston the problems of India, where Mahatma Gandhi, urging nonresistance against the Japanese, had recently survived a new hunger strike under British detention. Stalin appreciated the point but added a footnote to Father's remark that reform in that deprived subcontinent should begin from the bottom. That, said Stalin, could only mean revolution.

He shared Winston's disdain for the fighting quality of the Chinese and blamed that on their present leaders, but in the course of the afternoon he had spoken of reinforcing the Red Army in the east when Germany was defeated so that "we shall be able by our common front to beat Japan."

Father had put in a great deal of thinking about the actual operating machinery of the still nebulous United Nations. At Teheran, he took a small sheet of paper and drew three circles, the center one marked "Exec Comm," with "4 Police" on its right and "40 U.N." on its left—the Executive Committee, the Big Four and the future General Assembly. He returned to the concept that evening.

"And we agreed that the peace will be kept by force, if necessary," he explained to me. "Our principal job was to come to agreement as to what constitutes the area of general security in the postwar world for each of our countries. That job is still before us, but we've made a start on it."

They also agreed, he said, that peace would have to depend on the three powers acting in unison to the point where negative action by any one of them on a major question would veto the entire proposition. The details had not been thrashed out yet, but in general he favored the principle of a single veto in view of the hard-rock necessity of preserving Big Three unity.

Feeling queasy, he retired early, leaving Winston and Uncle Joe together and missing his amiable presence. Stalin had no high opinion of either Father's or Churchill's ideas for controlling a conquered Germany, and he let the PM know this. Obedience to discipline impressed the old Bolshevik as a German characteristic impossible to eradicate. He got to reminiscing about his early days as a revolutionary thirty-six years previously in Leipzig, when 200 German workers missed the train that was to bring them to a mass rally because nobody was on duty at the station to punch their tickets. "Unconditional surrender" struck him as a phrase so vague that it served only to prolong resistance. Specific terms, no matter how harsh, would speed the day of surrender.

There was no record of Winston's arguing the point on that occasion, but Mother as well as Father reached some early conclusions about his thinking. "Mr. Churchill always favored a less harsh attitude toward Germany," she remembered from her own observations, "and as fear of Russia increased, his feelings naturally intensified."

Whatever was said, he asked Father to lunch the following day in advance of the afternoon's full-dress sitting and was taken aback when he declined. The logic was simple enough. The servant-guards would have reported the tête-à-tête, and the last thing Father wanted was to feed Stalin's probable suspicions that his fellow conferees were scheming behind his back. To stress his good faith, Father spent forty-five minutes after lunch with him and Molotov, which gave me the opportunity to meet them. I was surprised by the Soviet leader's short stature—and by the twinkle in his eyes. There was a dynamism about him that, by contrast, made Molotov seem gray and colorless, a kind of faded print of Uncle Ted.

They went back to discussing the FDR concept of Big Four Policemen for the peace-keeping organization, in particular China's qualifications for the task and Chiang's anxiety about the Manchurian frontier. Since world recognition of Soviet sovereignty was a cardinal principle with him, Stalin replied, with an occasional nod as Pavlov translated, he most certainly would respect, in turn, the sovereignty of other countries, large or small. This was the only discussion of policy. For the rest, all was informal and relaxed until Pa Watson ushered us into the boardroom, lined with British and Soviet honor guards, where a Red Army band was working its way through the "Internationale" and "God Save the King."

On behalf of King George, the Prime Minister presented Stalin with a fifty-inch blade of tempered steel, the "Sword of Stalingrad." The old Bolshevik kissed its hilt, then offered it for Presidential inspection. "Truly they had hearts of steel," Father murmured as he drew the blade from its scabbard.

The room was cleared, and twenty-eight men, representing history's mightiest concentration of military power, got down to business again. Stalin introduced the big question: "Who will command Overlord?" He could not place much faith in the planning until its commander was named. Father must have been sorely tempted to name General George on the spot, but he restrained himself for Churchill's sake. "Marshall has got to the point where he just looks at the PM as though he can't believe his ears," he confided afterward. "If there's one American general that Winston can't abide, it's George Marshall."

This round lasted more than three hours. It closed with another question from Stalin: "Do the British really believe in Overlord, or are they only saying so to reassure the Soviet Union?"

Father came back to his apartment too tired and edgy to take a nap. He pushed his glasses off to rub his eyes as he stretched out on the sofa, refusing a drink just now because Stalin would be host at dinner, and my parent guessed that might mean a toast for every day of the year.

"He gets things done, that man," he murmured. "He really keeps his eye on the ball he's aiming at." He leaned up on an elbow. "Whenever the PM argued for our invasion through the Balkans, it was quite obvious to everyone in the room what he really meant . . . keep the Red Army out of Austria and Rumania, even Hungary, if possible. Stalin knew it, I knew it, everybody knew it . . . .

"And Uncle Joe . . . he was always conscious of the political implications, too, I'm sure. Never let on, though, by so much as a word. . . . Trouble is, the PM is thinking too much of the postwar and where England will be. He's scared of letting the Russians get too strong. Maybe the Russians will get strong in Europe. Whether that's bad depends on a whole lot of factors.

"The one thing I'm sure of is this. If the way to save American lives, the way to win as short a war as possible, is from the West and from the West alone, without wasting landing craft and men and matériel in the Balkan mountains, and our Chiefs are convinced it is, then that's *that*.

"I see no reason for putting the lives of American soldiers in jeopardy in order to protect real or fancied British interests on the European continent. We're at war, and our job is to win it as fast as possible and without adventures. I think—I *hope*—that he's learned we mean that once, finally and for all." He decided to sip a weak old-fashioned while his bathwater ran.

I was a guest at dinner only because Stalin spotted me in a doorway during serving of the first course and pulled me into the dining room, to sit between Eden and Harriman. I discovered that the only way to introduce a topic of conversation at a Russian banquet was by proposing a toast. Stalin stuck to vodka poured from his personal bottle, and there was no pretending it was water, as I learned when he filled my glass from it. Our first American defection was Harry Hopkins, who excused himself halfway through the meal.

Sometime later, Stalin rose for the umpteenth time, to say something along these lines: "I propose a salute to the swiftest possible justice for all Germany's war criminals—justice before a firing squad. I drink to our unity in dispatching them as fast as we capture them, all of them and there must be at least fifty thousand."

Winston, who had abided by brandy, jumped up, flushing crimson. "Any such attitude is wholly contrary to our British sense of justice. The British people will never stand for such mass murder. I take this opportunity to say that I feel most strongly that no one, Nazi or no, shall be summarily dealt with before a firing squad without proper legal trial, no matter what the known facts and proven evidence against him."

Stalin's dark eyes gleamed as he set about needling the Prime Minister, disregarding the fact that Winston's temper had gone beyond the breaking point. Father, amused at first, stepped in. "As usual," he said with a smile, "it seems to be my function to mediate this dispute." Couldn't they compromise and settle on a smaller number of war criminals due for execution? "Shall we say forty-nine thousand five hundred?"

Americans and Russians chuckled, with sense enough to realize that this was not a serious seminar. The British, uneasy at their Prime Minister's exploding fury, sat straight-faced. Stalin, pursuing his humor, asked around the table for fresh estimates. I was hoping he would change the subject before my turn came, but he did not.

It seemed to me that the whole thing was academic. "Russian, American, and British soldiers will settle the issue for most of those fifty thousand in battle. I hope that not only those fifty thousand war criminals will be taken care of, but many hundreds of thousands more Nazis as well." Before I could sit down, Stalin had walked around the table to put an arm across my shoulders. An excellent answer that deserved a toast to my health! Suddenly, a Churchillian finger was waving in my face. "Are you interested in damaging relations between the Allies? Do you know what you are saying? How can you dare say such a thing?" He started to stamp out of the room before Stalin led him back.

Happily, the dinner was soon over. Father roared with laughter when I followed him into his suite to apologize. "Winston just lost his head. . . . Forget it. Why, Winston will have forgotten all about it when he wakes up." But in all the months I was to be stationed in England, I was never again invited to Chequers.

The next day was Winston's birthday, so in the morning Father had himself taken to the United States Army post exchange which had been temporarily set up in the Soviet Embassy and chose a Kashan bowl from the display of knives, daggers, and carpets. Back in his suite, he received a new visitor, young Shah Mohammed Reza Pahlavi, "Light of the Aryans," who came with three of his Ministers and a little Persian rug as a gift for Mother. Seventeen years old and handsome as a hawk, the Shah had a reputation as a playboy, but there was no hint of that here. His eyes fixed on Father's as my parent dipped into the past, recalling those days, centuries ago, when this land had been heavily forested and fertile, watered by the flow of the Euphrates. Then, with the felling of the trees, Iran had gradually deteriorated into sand and dust.

Father warmed to the theme. Soil erosion had produced the dust bowl in America's Midwest; forestry had worked wonders for him at Hyde Park. He began to spin a vision of a future Iran, starting with reforestation—the United States would provide seedling trees—then the building of irrigation dams and hydroelectric projects, always with emphasis on the country's retaining its just share of profits from its oil and mineral wealth. The adolescent ruler frowned in concentration. It would take decades for the country to emerge as an independent power, said Father, but it could and should be done.

He was impressed by the potential he sensed in the Light of the Aryans. "He'll have a great future, if he survives," he said when his visitors had taken their leave. "Iran can serve as a buffer to any Soviet expansion, serve as a bridge between the Near and Far East, independent of the Arabs and India."

Mohammed Reza Pahlavi turned out to be a disciple who took an FDR plan and ran with it. Since the degree of help from the United States that Father had envisaged was not forthcoming, the Shah had to go it more or less alone in industrializing his country. It was the world's second-largest oil exporter in 1975, with its gross national product expanding by a staggering 50 percent a year, earning more than $20 billion from its oil wells. The Shah argued early on for price increases to meet the bills for modernization, but when the Arab world cut off oil exports in 1973, he kept shipments flowing. I liked to think that his morning with Father in Teheran had some influence in that, just as I sincerely trust that when Henry Kissinger drops cryptic hints of United States intervention with force in the Middle East to ensure that the flow continues, he is only shadowboxing.

Before Father went off for another Big Three Luncheon, he asked me to find Pat Hurley, the tall, overbearing Irishman who had been Hoover's Secretary of War from 1929 on and was due to be sent out to Chungking to try to make peace between Chiang, Stilwell, and Mao's Communists. Like Knox and Stimson, Major General Hurley was an unregenerate Republican whom FDR trusted, unlike some career diplomats in the State Department. "Half the time, I can't tell whether I should believe them or not," Father used to say.

Hurley's job that afternoon was to draft a memorandum, which the Soviets and British signed without demur, guaranteeing Iran's independence and self-determination of its economic interests. Pat, with his shock of snowy hair and matching mustache, was a man of many parts, but he had no more success than any other emissary in urging Chiang into battle with the Japanese.

Shortly after eight o'clock, wearing his dinner jacket and clutching the Kashan bowl, Father moved to the British Embassy, with its guard of turbaned Indian soldiers, for Winston's birthday party. "May we be together for many years," said Father, handing his gift to the PM, who was wreathed in good cheer and cigar smoke. We spent a good part of dinner with our glasses raised in toasts. "My fighting friend Churchill!" said Stalin, and later, "My fighting friend Roosevelt!" Winston responded in kind: "Stalin the mighty!" and "Roosevelt the President—my friend!" Father provided some variety with, "To our unity—war and peace!"

A frown crossed Stalin's face when General Brooke was on his feet, remarking that the British had suffered more, fought more, and done more to win the war. The grizzled old revolutionary rose after that. "The most important things in this war are machines. The United States has proven that it can turn out from eight to ten thousand planes a month. England turns out three thousand a month, principally heavy bombers. The United States, therefore, is a country of machines. Without the use of those machines, through lend-lease, we would lose this war."

Long past midnight, Father asked if he might say a final word to wind up the party. He was dog-tired after nearly three weeks of travel and tough negotiating. On top of that, he was compelled to cope with sheaves of official documents—state papers to study, memorandums and letters to write, bills which the law stipulated must be signed, or vetoed within ten days of their passage by Congress. These were flown in on a daily schedule, keeping the wheels turning within a system of government designed for homebody Presidents, not for international policymaking on the other side of the world from Washington.

He said: "We have differing customs and philosophies and ways of life. Each of us works out our scheme of things according to the desires and ideas of our own people. But we have proved here at Teheran that the varying ideals of our nations can come together in a harmonious whole, moving unitedly for the common good of ourselves and the world." Then it was time for goodnight.

He had planned to leave on Friday, but the weather forecasters detected a cold front passing over Cairo which would fill the mountain passes by that time, driving The Sacred Cow up to altitudes considered hazardous to his health. So tomorrow, Wednesday, he would sandwich in ten solid hours of work and depart at ten thirty P.M.

He got the day off to a good start after concluding that one way to defrost Stalin would be to keep up the banter about

Churchill. Buttonholing the PM before the morning session began, he said, "Winston, I hope you won't be sore at me for what I am going to do." A grunt was the only answer. Winston's throat was so sore that he could barely speak. In the boardroom, Father opened a brief, private talk with the Soviet leader by whispering, "Winston is cranky this morning; he got up on the wrong side of the bed."

A faint smile in response convinced him that he had found the right tactic. At the table, he teased the old Tory about his John Bull manner, his incessant cigar-smoking, and his flamboyant style. As Churchill's frown deepened, Stalin's chuckles increased, until a hearty guffaw signaled that enough was enough. "For the first time in three days, I saw light," my parent told Frances Perkins later. "It was then that I called him 'Uncle Joe.' . . . The ice was broken, and we talked like men and brothers."

Alone with Stalin, Molotov, and an aide or two, Father that afternoon brought up a subject which, sixteen months afterward, would be a pretext for demolishing his plans for peace and big-power cooperation. The primary purpose of his after-luncheon talk was to provide the Russians with a cram course in American politics. A Presidential election was coming along next year. He had shunned issuing any statement that he would run for a fourth term because, as he wrote one influential supporter, "I must ask you to believe me when I tell you that my one consideration now is to win this war." Defeating the Axis before November, 1944, was an obvious impossibility. He could not avoid seeking reelection, and he would have to make certain, if he could, of his own victory at the polls.

In the United States, he told Stalin, there were six or seven million Americans of Polish extraction whose opinions and votes must be respected. Personally, he saw the Soviets' need to regain Polish territory up to the 1939 frontier, which was more or less the Curzon Line of 1919. But couldn't both borders of postwar Poland be set farther west, taking a bit out of Germany? Stalin did not disagree. In the temporary euphoria that characterized Teheran, both men underestimated the reverence felt for every yard of their homeland by absentees, the Irish in Boston, the French in Canada, and in this case the Poles in Britain and the British armed forces.

Later in the day, Stalin gave Father his views about the Polish government in exile. It had a new Prime Minister in Stanislaw Mikolajczyk now that Sikorski had died in an air crash at Gibraltar, but it was no less adamant against surrendering acreage. So far as the Soviets were concerned, the London group was largely made up of Polish Fascists who had not changed their spots since 1939. Their followers behind the battle lines worked hand in glove with the Nazis to kill Communist partisans, said Stalin. What must be assured for security's sake was a postwar Poland friendly to the USSR.

Father spent Wednesday night at our Camp Amirabad at the foot of the Elburz Mountains. Before takeoff at six ten the next morning, he had a few words for our men there about the twin purposes of the Big Three conference: "winning the war just as fast as we possibly can . . . attempting to plan a world where war will cease to be a necessity." Shortly after three o'clock, he was back in Kirk's Cairo villa.

Five more punishing days had to be spent conferring with Winston, who flew in to join him, though he was in far worse physical shape than Father. Before this round of summitry was over, his doctor, Lord Moran, found him sitting in his bedroom, head in hands, muttering, "I have never felt like this before. Can't you give me something so that I won't feel so exhausted?" Ceaseless battling for the cause of Empire had sapped his strength. Before the end of the year, he suffered a heart attack, and Moran believed him to be dying. According to reports from Moscow, Stalin underwent similar trouble.

The job of closing my outfit's rear headquarters and flying it north to Italy kept me out of Cairo until Sunday, December 5. I found Father in bed, reading a detective story. His day so far had included President Ismet Inönü's visiting the villa for two hours and proving reluctant to drag Turkey into war. My parent still had to dine with Winston. Then, and on the following days, Father had a few things to tell me:

"You know, any number of times the men in the State Department have tried to conceal messages to me, delay them, hold them up somehow, just because some of those career diplomats aren't in accord with what they know I think. They should be working for Winston. As a matter of fact, a lot of the time, they *are*.

"The biggest thing was in making clear to Stalin that the

United States and Great Britain were not allied in one common bloc against the Soviet Union. I think we've got rid of that idea, once and for all. I hope so. The one thing that could upset the applecart after the war is if the world is divided again, Russia against England and us. That's our big job now, and it'll be our big job tomorrow, too: making sure that we continue to act as referee, as intermediary between Russia and England.

"People at home, Congressmen, editorial writers, talk about the United Nations as something that exists only on account of war. The tendency is to snipe at it by saying that only because we are forced into unity by war are we unified. But war isn't the real force to unity. *Peace* is the real force. After the war—then is when I'm going to be able to make sure the United Nations are really the *united* nations."

As the man in the middle of the Big Three, the final authority by reason of American productive power, he had now to restore the balance between Churchill and Stalin. At Teheran, he had conspicuously sided with Soviet points of view. Now Winston must be favored on two issues close to his heart. It took four days of the Prime Minister's locutions but then Father yielded and sent a succinct cable to Chiang, canceling the promised amphibious operation in the Bay of Bengal, which Churchill had consistently opposed. Stalin's promise to fight Japan downgraded the importance of the Generalissimo and an extended campaign in Burma, though this must be left unsaid in the cablegram. Chiang's objections to the turnabout were restrained. As balm, he asked for further American aid, notably $1 billion in gold.

The second decision in Winston's favor was the choice of a Supreme Commander in Europe—not General George, after all, but Ike Eisenhower. "Marshall. . . ." Father mused. "It's not that he's argued too often with the PM on military matters, it's just that he's won too often."

Along with Ike and a few others, I was on hand when The Sacred Cow flew into Tunis on December 7. Father had enjoyed a perfect aerial view of the battleground where Montgomery had driven Rommel into retreat, and he was as excited as though he had personally led the British Eighth Army. "Well, Ike, you'd better start packing" was all he chose to tell Eisenhower as yet about his new appointment. Formal notification must come from General George, who remained in Cairo. Ike misinterpreted those words as meaning that he was being put behind a desk in the Pentagon. Not until the next day's seven A.M. flight to Malta would he be briefed by Father on the prodigious job, and its attendant problems with the British, that awaited him in London.

Together with everybody else I knew in those days, I liked Ike, who struck everyone as being an unpretentious, simple-living soldier, lacking all interest in the material things of life. He told me that he had never once voted in a Presidential election because he felt that this would be out of place for a man devoted to serving his country as an Army officer. Otherwise, he said, his vote would have gone to FDR every time; he had great reverence for Father. In England, he was virtually unknown, though it was Ike who had planned the breakout in North Africa and drawn the blueprints for invading Sicily.

Troubles with his wife, Mamie, who stayed in a Washington apartment throughout his service overseas, were no secret, any more than his fondness for Kay Summersby, one-time actress and model. But those closest to him discounted rumors of romance—he had no time for drawn-out affairs. His quarters were no more sybaritic than a post exchange. The only visible vice might be a game of bridge, which he played with deadly skill. Patton, Carl Spaatz, and Ira Eaker were generals who liked to turn an officers' mess into a fair facsimile of a high-class club.

Yet Eisenhower gradually became carried away with his own importance. He became an obliging tool in the clasp of manipulators who worked to make him rich and President of the United States, in spite of his declaration that "the necessary and wise subordination of the military to civil power will be best sustained . . . when lifelong professional soldiers, in the absence of some obvious and overriding reasons, abstain from seeking high political office." When he said that, in 1948, he could not afford to run for the Presidency.

The hurdle was jumped when chubby-cheeked George Allen and a Wall Street colleague negotiated a publishing contract for Ike's war memoirs, *Crusade in Europe,* giving him $500,000, on which a special Internal Revenue Service ruling minimized the tax bite. Then these two applied their influence to making him president of Columbia University in New York City, while they set up an investment fund for him with borrowed money. It was easily repaid, since they built up the fund independently on his behalf when he was in the White House, criticizing his Vice President, Richard Nixon, for following the Presidential example and taking money from businessmen to finance his own disastrous career. A farm in Gettysburg, Pennsylvania, and a herd of prize Black Angus cattle worth a modest fortune on the hoof were perfectly proper gifts for President Eisenhower, it would seem, but poor, persnickety Sherman Adams, his right-hand man in Washington, got himself fired for accepting a New England industrialist's favors, none more lavish than a vicuna topcoat.

Ike, the war hero with the infectious grin, could be vindictive in the Presidency, as Mother learned. Four years before he was elected, Perle Mesta, the Washington party-giver whom Truman appointed ambassador to Luxembourg, carried a tale about Mother's asking her "whether General Eisenhower has any problems with his wife." Ike felt so affronted that from then on he was barely civil to Mother, whom he had previously put in the same category of near-angels as Father. When she resigned as our envoy to the United Nations, she received not a word of thanks from President Eisenhower.

After the flight with Ike to Malta, Father presented the islands with a scroll for standing "alone but unafraid in the center of the sea . . . a beacon for the clearer days which have come." He made his way back via Sicily, where he awarded an astounded Mark Clark with the Distinguished Service Cross. Then, after one more night in Tunis, he was off to Dakar, where the *Iowa* was waiting to carry him home. In all, he had been gone for five weeks from the White House.

Christmas, 1943, was the first he spent at Hyde Park in ten years. Mother and Anna were there, of course, as well as Franklin Jr. on leave and Johnny, who was soon to be shipped out in an aircraft carrier to the Pacific now that he had dismissed the idea of registering as a conscientious objector..That Christmas, Father had seven grandchildren as an audience for *A Christmas Carol* as he sat by the tree in the library, nursing what he imagined to be a dose of influenza. Two days earlier he had summed up his travels in a letter to Endicott Peabody, headmaster of Groton ever since my parent's schooldays there almost half a century ago: "I had the most interesting trip I have ever taken—and I am glad to get away from the poverty and disease and barrenness of North Africa and Egypt and Palestine and Iran. But we can help those countries in the days to come—and with proper management get our money back—if only we do not revert to the ostrich policy of 1920."

18

The influenza refused to let go. He felt perpetually tired these days. One trouble followed another—chronic indigestion compelled him to forgo combining business with eating; on occasion, he was drenched with sweat; a phlegmy cough racked his lungs. His state of mind was not improved when he heard that Ruth and I had decided on divorce.

"I'd like a shoulder to weep on," Mother wrote Joe Lash, but there would be no reunion with Joe on the trip she was about to undertake. The third of her overseas excursions took her roving to the Caribbean, then on to the Galapagos Islands, Brazil, Venezuela, Colombia, Ecuador, Panama, Guatemala, and Cuba. There was no suggestion that she should postpone leaving on account of Father's condition.

She was reconciled to the fact that he felt duty-bound to run for four more years in office, even if he recognized that this must inevitably shorten his life. He could see nobody else to take his place before victory, and she agreed with his assessment. However, she was totally opposed to his thinking, outlined to a press conference, that "old Dr. New Deal" had successfully treated America's internal ailments, but the "pretty bad smashup" which the patient suffered at Pearl Harbor called

367

for the services of his partner, "Dr. Win-the-War," a specialist
in orthopedics. "When the time comes," he promised, Dr. New
Deal could take charge again. The cheers of the opposition
over the hoped-for death of the New Deal lasted no longer than
two weeks. He was too ill to deliver his State of the Union message to Congress in person, but he spelled out every word in a
fireside chat on January 11. With Wehrmacht power in the
West as yet unchallenged by Overlord's invasion of Normandy,
he hit out at home-front complacency and "the whining demands of selfish pressure groups who seek to feather their
nests while young Americans are dying." He checked off what
he wanted from a Congress intent on exercising its prerogatives
and marching out of step with him: taxes on all "unreasonable"
profits; continuing price controls; stabilization of the dollar to
curb inflation; antistrike legislation for the duration of the war;
and plans to raise American standards of living "higher than
ever known before."

What the United States had achieved since 1933, he said, was
a second Bill of Rights: the right to a job paying enough to provide food, clothing, and recreation; the right of farmers to a decent living; the right of businessmen to freedom from unfair
competition; every family's right to a decent home, medical
care, and good health; the right to protection from the economic hazards of old age, sickness, accident, and unemployment; the right to a sound education.

"And after this war is won," he declared, "we must be prepared to move forward, in the implementation of these rights,
to new goals of human happiness and well-being." It seemed to
me, chewing over his words, that he had no cause to worry
about defeat next election day, even if he did literally ache for
retirement. "I would give a good deal personally," he said soon
afterward, "to return to Hyde Park and Georgia just as soon as
the Lord will let me."

He did not get to Georgia that spring, but he went as far as
South Carolina and Baruch's 23,000-acre estate of Hobcaw
Barony for the rest that his doctors prescribed. His health deteriorated in Mother's absence. Ross McIntire concluded, none
too soon, that Father needed a checkup at Bethesda Naval Hospital. On March 27, he was wheeled in, ashen-faced and breath-
less from any kind of exertion, still joking in spite of the rales
clearly audible in his chest.

A young Naval Medical Corps cardiologist, Dr. Howard G. Bruenn, ran the tests—electrocardiogram, fluoroscopy, chest X-rays. He conveyed his diagnosis to McIntire. Father was suffering from hypertension, hypertensive heart disease, cardiac failure in the left ventricle of his heart, and acute bronchitis. "These findings and their interpretation . . . had been completely unsuspected up to this time," Dr. Bruenn was to report twenty-five years after Father's death.

In the case of an average patient, the treatment would not have been difficult to apply: a week or two in bed with nursing care; a daily dose of digitalis to stimulate the heart; a light, salt-free diet; codeine for the cough and sedation for sound nights of sleep; and a weight-reducing regimen. The demands of the Presidency as the war approached its climax made these recommendations impossible to fulfill.

A compromise course had to be worked out with McIntire and a group of other physicians. These were the proposals which were discussed, though not in this sequence:

Limitation of daily activity, with swimming in the pool prohibited.

Curtailment of cigarettes.

Phenobarbitol three times a day, plus a trial of aminophylline.

One hour's rest after meals and a 2,600-calorie, low-fat diet.

Mild laxatives, if necessary, to avoid straining.

Light passive massage.

A minimum of ten hours' sleep.

And *avoid, if possible, irritation and tensions of office* (my italics).

Father knew nothing of these deliberations. He was content to be feeling and looking better. Dr. Bruenn examined him at the White House most days, usually between nine and nine thirty in the morning while he was still in bed after breakfast. On the last day of March, two additional doctors, James A. Paullin and Frank Lahey, took a close look at him and went into conference with their colleagues already on the case to decide what was to be done next.

Bruenn stuck to his diagnosis of congestive heart failure and recommendation of digitalis. Paullin argued that Father's heart condition did not warrant such medication, but he was won around. The group agreed to meet again two weeks later to reassess their patient's progress. Meanwhile, ought he to be told the full facts to induce him to cooperate in the treatment? According to medical courtesy, that commission could be left only to Ross McIntire.

By his own subsequent account, Father's personal physician interpreted the tests as evidencing "a moderate degree of arteriosclerosis, although no more than normal in a man of his age. . . ." Arteriosclerosis—hardening of the arteries? The group's conclusion had been that it was something considerably more serious. If Dr. McIntire relayed to Father the true findings of his fellow doctors, it was more than he did for Mother or any member of the family.

During the first week of April, Father's condition steadily improved. He cut his smoking to half-a-dozen cigarettes a day, though that abstinence was shortlived. He complained that he was growing too fat, so his daily diet was cut by a further 800 calories. He conscientiously swallowed the little green digitalis pills, whose dosage was reduced to one-tenth of a gram. By the time the medical men reconvened, the enlargement of his heart had decreased and his lungs were clearing up satisfactorily. For his progress, he was rewarded by being allowed to return to swimming, and he was thankful for that.

From then on, Bruenn saw Father three or four times a week at the White House, checking his heart, lungs, and blood pressure, remarking to himself that never did his patient pass any comment about the frequency of his visits or about the laboratory tests which were conducted as a routine. It was inconceivable that my parent, with his insatiable curiosity, did not care. The only conclusion I could ever reach was that he chose to stay uninformed, shielding himself from knowledge of his frailty in accordance with that ancient bit of workaday philosophy, "What you don't know can't harm you."

He went along with his doctors' advice that he should get away from Washington for a week or two of rest and relaxation as soon as possible. Contrary to the fancies of those who would having him flying off into the arms of Lucy Mercer Rutherfurd, his first thought was to enjoy the sun and perhaps get in a little fishing at Guantánamo Bay, Cuba. The war and his health made that inadvisable. He settled, instead, for Hobcaw and on April 19 traveled down there with Pa Watson, Bill Leahy, Ross McIntire, Howard Bruenn, and a few others, including a communications crew and a Secret Service detail.

He spent his first few mornings in bed, reading the newspapers and attending to the mail with his temporary secretary, Lieutenant William Rigdon. He would be up in time for lunch, moving always by wheelchair, since he had all but discarded the braces, which were reserved for public appearances. After a brief afternoon nap, he would set off to taste the joys of Hobcaw on these cool, sunlit days of spring.

Baruch's domain stood near the coast, where the Pee Wee River met the Waccamaw. Father could fish in a Coast Guard patrol boat, with Secret Servicemen tagging along in another, or go motoring along miles of secluded roadways, scented by magnolias, azaleas, and camellias in early bloom under canopies of Spanish moss trailing from the boughs of the live oaks. He had a variety of visitors—Mother and Anna, Washington emissaries on urgent business, Daisy Suckley, and Lucy.

Lucy drove over from her nearby home in Aiken to extend the care and love she had not lost for this lonely, ailing, cheerful man. Her visits were taken as a matter of course by the Hobcaw group, but Mother was not told a word. Part of Mother's anguish when she learned the truth immediately after Father's death came from the fact that her trusted counselor, Bernie Baruch, was an accomplice in keeping the secret.

In the early evening, Father would tackle the official documents in need of signature, which were flown in every day. One or two dry martinis preceded dinner, served at seven and lasting for the best part of two hours, spiced with brisk talk, led by himself, of past campaigns and current events at home and overseas. He felt fine, slept and ate well, complained of nothing but occasional indigestion. His blood pressure stayed high. He continued on digitalis, but was taken off the phenobarbitol which was given to relieve the abdominal pains.

On May 2, when the pangs were sharp, a heating pad and a shot of codeine gave him a fair night's sleep, though his blood pressure was up, his body throbbed, and the back of his neck felt sore. There were no cardiac symptoms to alarm the doctors. Two days in bed put him back into working shape. His heart remained enlarged, and there were suspicions about his gall bladder.

If nervous tension played a part in the temporary setback, the cause was not hard to find. May 1 had been set as D Day for Overlord, but the day had come and gone without action, thus breaking the pledge made at Teheran to Stalin. Tides and moon had been right for the cross-Channel armadas of war-ships and landing craft, but Winston squeezed in one last month of delay—until early June when sea and moon would be favorable again. He had used the borrowed time for a final fling in the Mediterranean theater, with American and British forces landed in January at Anzio, behind the German posi-tions in Italy. A Wehrmacht counterattack nearly pushed the invaders back into the sea, and the scheduled Allied landings in southern France, timed to coincide with Overlord, had to be postponed until August 15.

X-rays taken on his return to Washington indicated that Fa-ther had gallstones. A low-fat diet was prescribed to reduce his weight from its present 188 pounds, which was heavy in spite of his height, since his thighs and legs were thin. He was so proud of the results of self-denial at mealtimes that he stuck to dieting after his doctors urged him to eat more. He set his sights on hit-ting 170 pounds, not giving a hoot about the new, haggard look in his face resulting from rapid reducing or the gap between neck and shirt collar that set off a flurry of speculation about his well-being when it showed up in press photographs. He soon lost two or three more pounds than he had aimed for. Ciga-rettes tasted so awful that it was not hard to smoke less than half a pack a day.

What he missed more and more in Washington was a wom-an's warm, enspiriting companionship, which Mother by her very nature could not provide. She was more businesswoman than wife, respected by Father for her singlemindedness in pursuing her causes, but no kind of company when he wanted to relax without listening to her voice of conscience. Before his convalescence at Hobcaw, he had tried to bring Missy down from Massachusetts to spend a few days in Washington, but Mother had written to her, canceling the invitation because "I want to be here when you come."

The best solution seemed to be to ask Anna and her youngest child, Johnny, to stay now that her husband was serving in Eu-rope in military government. I had run across John Boettiger in Cairo, where it was he who brought Inönü in to see Father. Mother had some understandable reservations about her daughter taking over the reins in running the White House, but she did not make an issue of it. Anna moved into the redecorated Lincoln Suite, where Harry and Louise had stayed and their dog Susie had chewed the rugs. My sister would serve as chatelaine, confidante, and jealous protector of Father.

The prayer in which he led the nation in an evening broadcast on June 6, when D Day arrived at last, was written by Anna and her husband: "Give us faith in Thee; faith in our sons; faith in each other; faith in our united crusade." Stalin waited to see whether the mass landings in Normandy would take hold, then, in accordance with his promise to the Big Two he sent more than a million Red Army men smashing forward along a 450-mile front. Within a week, they had encircled Germans in the hundreds of thousands and captured Minsk. They would surge on into Poland, to take Lublin and Brest-Litovsk; into Rumania, Lithuania, and the eastern tip of Czechoslovakia. There was nothing to stop them from crossing the Danube to thrust across Bulgaria and Yugoslavia to the Greek and Turkish frontiers. From London, Winston sent a jittery cable, crying for another Big Three conference, to Hopkins, who was convalescing in his Georgetown house after seven more months in and out of hospitals.

Three weeks after D Day, the Republicans convened in Chicago, to nominate forty-two-year-old Tom Dewey on the first ballot. Willkie was out of the picture completely after getting trounced in the primaries. With the same precision that marked the cut of his suits and the trim of his brown mustache, Dewey selected a fellow governor, stolid John Bricker of Ohio, to run with him on the strongest ticket the party could produce.

Father left the impression on those around him that, as Pa Watson put it, "He doesn't seem to give a damn." Thirteen days elapsed before he announced his willingness to go for a fourth term if the Democrats chose him at their convention, also in Chicago, beginning July 19. Since the result was a foregone conclusion, the only flicker of suspense concerned his nominee for the Vice Presidency. Whispers about his health made his preference more significant than ever before, but he had no premonitions of mortality and no particular favorite, so long as it was someone who would not alienate major sections of the country and impede him in what he regarded as his prior commitment over the coming four years. Creating the United Nations would need both parties' cooperation.

That automatically ruled out Wallace, in spite of Mother's

fondness for him. Doubly damned as too callow and too radical, Hank would be made Commerce Secretary the following March. Meanwhile, he joined the doleful roster of envoys sent to Chungking in one more futile attempt to unite the Chinese. Half a dozen men might make satisfactory replacements for him as running mate: Speaker Rayburn; Alben Barkley, the old Senate wheelhorse; dynamic young Supreme Court Justice William O. Douglas, who stood very high in Father's esteem; Jimmy Byrnes, who was itching for the nomination but was altogether too devious in his ambitions; Harry Truman, conscientious, aggressive, well liked for having saved the taxpayers $15 billion in his probes of arms spending, who remained none the wiser about progress toward building the Bomb. Father resorted to his technique of neither discouraging nor commending any one of them.

The most pressing business was a meeting arranged for him to sit down with Nimitz and MacArthur at Pearl Harbor to work out strategy for victory in the Pacific. He left Washington six days before the convention opened in Chicago, to make a leisurely train trip to San Diego, there to board the heavy cruiser *Baltimore* for Hawaii. He was all set to enjoy himself, sleeping well again without medication, perhaps fitter than he had been for months.

The train stopped at Chicago, but he did not leave it. Coming aboard to huddle in the Presidential quarters, Bob Hannegan left with two penciled notes from Father. "You have written me about Bill Douglas and Harry Truman," said the first. "I should, of course, be very glad to run with either of them and believe that either one of them would bring real strength to the ticket." The second note was identical with the first, except that Truman's name came ahead of Douglas'. That was Hannegan's doing. The convention would accept Truman without making trouble. In Father's eyes, the prime qualification of the Senator from Missouri was his popularity with his colleagues on the Hill. He was just the man to help when the time came to ratify the peace.

The Presidential Special pulled out of the Chicago yards, leaving the party delegates to the ritual of nominating Father by 1,066 votes—Farley received exactly one—while half a dozen Vice Presidential hopefuls waited with their lightning rods up for a strike.

Sitting in a specially equipped railroad car in San Diego, FDR broadcast his acceptance speech to the Chicago Stadium. The first job, he said, was to win the war; the second, "to form worldwide international organizations"; the third, "to build an economy for our returning veterans and for all Americans— which will provide employment and decent standards of living."

He had one more piece of convention business to take care of before he sailed. Bob Hannegan telephoned from the Blackstone Hotel. He had Truman in the room with him, and he had just told him that he was Father's choice. But the spicy-tongued man from Missouri, who made stubbornness a cardinal virtue, refused the role. He had gone to Chicago to nominate his good friend Jimmy Byrnes, and that was what he still planned to do.

"Have you got that fellow lined up yet?" Father asked Bob.

"No. He is the contrariest Missouri mule I've ever dealt with."

"Well, tell the Senator that if he wants to break up the Democratic Party by staying out, he can. But he knows as well as I do what that might mean at this dangerous time in the world. If he wants to do it anyway, tell him to go ahead."

Listening in to the browbeating, Truman yielded grudgingly. "I guess I'll have to take it. Why the hell didn't he tell me in the first place?" He disliked nothing worse than the feeling that he was being pushed around, but he could come to instantaneous decisions if he had to. "I did not hesitate a second" was a standard boast of his.

On the face of it, Father's reference to "this dangerous time" appeared to be an exaggeration. One and a half million men and as many tons of matériel had been put ashore in France. Montgomery was dragging his feet on the left flank, but the Americans were roaring ahead. In the Pacific, the Japanese mainland was starting to feel the weight of American bombing; the enemy navy was penned in; Tojo and his entire Cabinet had resigned the previous day, shamed by the loss of Saipan. Lord Mountbatten's Allied troops had beaten back a Japanese thrust through Burma at India, and the enemy was in full retreat. The most electrifying news of all filtered in from Berlin, where a bomb planted in a briefcase by dissident generals almost killed Der Führer.

A note from San Diego to "Dearest Babs" said, "I might have to hurry back earlier if this German revolt gets worse! I fear though that it won't."

This was a truly dangerous time because of reasons unmentioned by Father. Hitler had launched the first of his secret weapons against Britain a week after D Day. Around the clock, the V-1, the pilotless flying bomb, droned in by the thousand toward London. Ten thousand were fired, more than 6,000 people died. Supersonic V-2, the second secret, started to hurtle down two months later, a total of 1,115 of them taking 2,754 lives. And according to some reports to my parent, the Germans were racing ahead of us in developing the Bomb.

Father took tremendous interest in the activities and results of my 325th Reconnaissance Wing. This Allied reconnaissance command had the responsibility of checking the progress of the Germans at their Peenemünde research center. Daily missions had to be flown over this intensively guarded target. The assessments of the resulting photos kept the Allied military and political leaders fully aware of the accelerating activity of this site. Clearly, Hitler would have his big atomic weapon before long. American and British bomber commands launched a desperate series of bombing raids that were successful in slowing down completion of the final product. It was a tense race, with Father urging on the Manhattan Project and, at the same time, reading the assessments that my planes returned with after each bombing raid. Actually, we broke the back of German resistance in Europe only weeks ahead of the time that Hitler would have had his ultimate weapon.

Against that background, the latest flareup of trouble with the Poles seemed inconsequential. Father had Mikolajczyk over from London to talk about the problem of new borders. My parent had done some homework, studying three centuries of maps of the country whose frontiers had fluctuated east and west. "It is rather difficult to untangle the map of Poland," he had told his guest. He had another thought to relay. "In all our dealings with Stalin, we must keep our fingers crossed."

The Marshal was in process of recognizing a provisional ruling group of his own coloration in the territory that the Red Army had just cleared of Nazis. The Lublin "committee of national liberation" would be more malleable than the London Poles, and it had the indisputable advantage of being on the site of operations.

On the eve of embarking for Honolulu, Father watched the

Fifth Marine Division, whose intelligence officer was my brother Jimmy, stage a practice landing at Camp Pendleton. Jimmy saw a spasm of pain strike—caused by gallbladder stones, in all probability—but Dr. Bruenn was not told, and Father dismissed it as "the collywobbles." He showed no other signs of trouble. Aboard the *Baltimore,* only Pa Watson needed medical attention, this for fluid on the lungs.

Just before the dawn sailing on July 22, Father sent congratulations to Harry Truman, chosen by 1,031 votes over Wallace's 105 on the second ballot: I AM, OF COURSE, VERY HAPPY TO HAVE YOU RUN WITH ME. LET ME KNOW YOUR PLANS. I SHALL SEE YOU SOON. Perhaps the telegram sounded patronizing, but then he knew the second man on the ticket only as an able hometown politician, not in any sense as an intimate.

The white-clad crews of the flattops, battleships, and assorted vessels of war that filled Pearl Harbor cheered as the *Baltimore* approached her moorings. Father spent three hectic days inspecting Navy, Marine, and Army installations, dining with the brass, playing mediator once more as MacArthur pressed for liberation of the Philippines as the next step and Nimitz urged landings on Formosa. Overhanging all their words was the cheerless estimate that conquering the Japanese home islands one by one would cost a minimum of 500,000 American casualties.

When Father decided for MacArthur's plans to recapture Leyte, there were embittered Navy men who smelled election-year politics at work. They were mistaken. Father had boasted repeatedly in Big Three sessions about American timetables for extending self-rule to the Filipinos. The islands occupied a special place in his thinking as a model for imperialist powers to follow.

From Pearl, the *Baltimore* steamed north on a four-day crossing through fog, rain, and cold to Alaska, for another round of inspections and receptions. Halfway through the voyage, he received the news which he had accepted as inevitable in advance. Missy was dead of cerebral thrombosis. Father left no record of his feelings about the loss of the woman who had served him with her life, yet an act of his carried echoes of the days and weeks aboard the *Larooco,* when they swam and fished and lazed in southern sunshine together. One Alaska evening after dinner, when a driving crosswind kept the *Baltimore* at her berth, he had himself wheeled forward to drop a hook and line over the side from the forecastle. Missy would have been delighted that, in spite of the weather, he reeled in some Dolly Varden trout.

At Kodiak Island, the party transferred to the destroyer *Cummings* and sailed for Bremerton, Washington, by way of the Inland Passage. After months off-stage, he wanted to limber up and face an audience in person again, so the braces were locked on his shaky legs. Thousands of shipyard workers crammed the dockside at Bremerton as he pulled himself upright to rest his arms on the speakers' stand erected on the destroyer's fantail with canvas-covered guns as the backdrop.

The chatty account of his travels went out over a nationwide radio hookup. During the first fifteen minutes, he felt an oppressive sensation in his chest, spreading into both shoulders. He ignored it and continued to talk for a further twenty minutes, holding himself upright by gripping the edge of the stand with one hand, struggling with the other to turn the pages of the hastily prepared text as they fluttered in a stiff wind. Now and then he missed his place, and his voice momentarily faltered.

When he had finished, he mentioned the discomfort he had experienced to Dr. Bruenn, who was traveling with him. Within the hour, a white blood count was taken and an electrocardiogram tracing made. They revealed nothing unusual. Blood pressure was no higher than had come to be expected.

One biographer magnified this incident out of proportion and claimed that Father "was suffering his first and only attack of angina pectoris he had ever had, or would have." Bruenn's findings gave no support to that opinion. This heart specialist, who attended Father from March, 1944, through the day of his death, seeing him almost daily and accompanying him on every trip, had this to report:

"I should also like to comment on the allegations that the President had suffered several 'small strokes' before his death. Clinically, there was no evidence of strokes. His memory for both recent and past events was good. His behavior toward his friends and intimates was unchanged and his speech unaltered."

In their efforts to drive him out of power in 1944, the Roosevelt-abusers concocted an altogether different story. He returned to Washington to find the country flooded with campaign propaganda featuring a blown-up press photograph, taken as he broadcast his acceptance speech in San Diego. It pictured him slack-jawed and harassed, with the results of dieting evident in his shadowed cheeks and oddly sharper nose—a dramatic contrast with the beaming face that the world had come to recognize.

That chance photographic shot was manna for the Republicans, who wanted to highlight Dewey's appeal as the virile young nemesis of crime, corruption, and "tired old men" in high office. The rumor mills were put on overtime: Father had undergone secret surgery at Hobcaw; he was so sick that the Pearl Harbor trip had come close to cancellation; his stumbling words at Bremerton Navy Yard were proof that he was losing his mind. On Capitol Hill, volunteers in both parties circulated the hearsay. Public opinion polls disclosed an ominous decline in his popularity, and almost until election eve Dr. Gallup's figures indicated a win for Dewey. *Time* forecast a margin so narrow that weeks might go by before the soldier vote was counted to determine the victor.

Father's alleged senility was the only real weapon in his opponents' arsenal. Eisenhower in France, MacArthur and Nimitz in the Pacific, provided the answers to charges that this administration was fumbling the war. Lend-lease had obviously made America the "arsenal of democracy," as Father had anticipated and not the "end to free government in the United States," as Dewey had predicted. One question on my parent's mind was "the scope and scale of mutual lend-lease aid between the United States and the British Empire after the defeat of Germany and during the war with Japan," in the words of a memorandum he wrote to Cordell Hull. The British counted on making this concluding stage of the Allied war effort last as long as possible to ease their transition to a peacetime economy.

As for the home-front situation, Dewey could only cry "Me, too" to the bulk of New Deal legislation. Otherwise, he risked alienating a majority of voters, who found it hard to remember just how grim living had been for millions of them before the "second Bill of Rights" came into being. Father had already

added the "GI Bill of Rights" to that, providing servicemen on
their return home with opportunities for education and career
training, loans, unemployment pay and reemployment rights,
life insurance, medical care and more hospitals, dependents'
allowance and job-hunting facilities. "The American people,"
he said, "do not intend to let them down," as had happened in
1918.

Patterns for weaving prosperity and peace were being tested
on the looms of diplomacy. At Bretton Woods, New Hamp-
shire, top-flight economists of the United States, Britain, the
Soviet Union, and France agreed to contribute quotas of cash
and credit for an international bank which would provide
working capital and loans to rebuild war-shattered industries
and develop new sources of wealth in countries victimized by
the Axis. "Commerce is the lifeblood of a free society," Father's
greeting to the conferees declared. "We must see to it that the
arteries which carry the bloodstream are not clogged again."

Closer to home, in the Georgetown mansion known as Dumbarton Oaks, envoys of the great powers raised the framework
of the United Nations as an international police headquarters.
Among the Big Three, there was total agreement that on matters affecting world peace, decisions must be unanimous. Any
one of them, together with China, could exercise a veto within
the Security Council, which Father's rough sketch at Teheran
had identified as "4 Police."

The principle of veto suited the United States, Britain, and
the Soviet Union equally. It would ensure that under no circumstances could American servicemen be ordered into action
by the United Nations Council. It satisfied the British that the
Empire could be shielded from encroachment. It guaranteed
the USSR that no anti-Bolshevik adventures could be waged
against it.

Not the principle as such, but its application divided the Soviet delegation's leader, wry-lipped Andrei Gromyko, and Ed
Stettinius. The American position was that no country named
in a complaint should be allowed to vote on the subject of contention. Gromyko stuck to the Kremlin argument that no limits
must be set on the policemen's powers. At Father's request, he
was escorted into his White House bedroom at nine-thirty one
morning in early September by Stettinius. My parent wanted to
try his hand at winning over the obdurate Russian.

As usual, he opened with a few minutes of chatter, then firmly and clearly presented the United States case. "So deadlock had been reached on preserving the peace even as Soviet and Anglo-American troops were winning it," wrote one American historian, gifted with his craft's 20-20 hindsight. Once again, an eyewitness took an opposing view. Stettinius, the capitalist millionaire, was "convinced that the FDR discussion was an important step in winning the cooperation of the Soviet Union for a world organization . . . only one example of the way he could work with the Russians in a spirit of patience and calmness."

Father nursed a startling strategy for consolidating support in America for his dream of reshaping the world. He credited Willkie with the concept in the first place. Father called Sam Rosenman into his office to outline what might be done. "I think," he said, "the time has come for the Democratic Party to get rid of its reactionary elements in the South and to attract to it the liberals in the Republican Party." Willkie, as bitter a foe of the rightists as FDR himself these days, visualized a coalition between progressives of both parties. "I agree with him one hundred percent," said Father, "and the time is now—right after the election. We ought to have two real parties—one liberal and the other conservative. As it is now, each party is split by dissenters. Of course, I'm talking about long-range politics—something that we can't accomplish this year. But we can do it in 1948, and we can start building it up right after the election this fall. From the liberals of both parties, Willkie and I together can form a new, really liberal party in America."

Sam was dispatched to a secret meeting with Wendell in a suite at the Hotel St. Regis on East Fifty-fifth Street, Manhattan. He brought back precisely the response Father was looking for from Willkie: "You tell the President that I'm ready to devote almost full time to this." Perhaps the most promising start, Father thought, would be for his old adversary to take on the appointment of Chief Executive of the United Nations. That would keep the spotlight on him as a star performer, rallying public opinion behind him. But these were more fond hopes that came to nothing then and have languished ever since. Nothing concrete had been worked out when Willkie died on October 8.

All through the summer and into early fall, Dewey had the

campaign trails to himself, presenting a picture of moderation, sweet reason, and expensive tailoring, coaxing the electorate in his honeyed baritone, leaving the undercover men to spread a different kind of bait—about Communist infiltration into the White House, Mother's cloudland radicalism, and her sons' featherbed assignments in uniform. Father held his fire. He had more important matters to attend to. On both the eastern and western fronts, the Germans were in retreat. They were fighting now inside the borders of the Fatherland. There was a slim chance that the year and the war might end together, though my parent remained skeptical of these rosy military estimates.

It was time for the Big Three to meet again, as he cabled the Kremlin. "Stalin replied in a very nice tone," he told Ickes, "that he could not possibly leave his army, which is now on the offensive, at this time, but that he did want to meet with Churchill and me as soon as he could." Dosed with penicillin to ward off threatened pneumonia, Winston was already fishing for another twosome talk with Father, preferably in Scotland. In London, the word was out that the two of them would be in Paris to watch the liberating armies march on the Champs-Elysées. Father had heard nothing of this. He had no thought of going overseas for a meeting that deliberately excluded the Soviets.

The Prime Minister was raging because the Red Army advance had halted outside Warsaw to wait for essential reinforcements. With shortened lines of communications, the Germans could not be budged. Churchill was convinced that Stalin had ordered the standstill only to give the Nazis a free hand in massacring Poles in the ravaged city, where Hitler's soldiers slew the wounded in hospital beds and protected their tanks with shields of shuffling women and children. Two hundred thousand inhabitants were killed, according to the final count. The Prime Minister seriously debated cutting off convoys of war supplies to the USSR in protest. The stalemate outside Warsaw lasted five more months. In that interval, other Soviet armies conquered Rumania and Hungary in attacks principally designed to draw the Wehrmacht away from the deadlocked Polish front.

Father finally consented to go back to Quebec to talk with Churchill on topics relating to "Anglo-American operations in the near future that do not concern Russia." Winston arrived a sick man, looking old and depressed, with a new habit of holding his head in his hands to clarify his thinking. Father's doctor rated FDR in good trim. A curious incident was noted in his medical records: His blood pressure rose as he watched a screening of the current Hollywood hit, *Wilson,* a partly fictionalized biography of the President whose own bid to reform the world with the League of Nations met with disaster in the Senate. My parent was determined not to repeat the mistakes of the man he had idolized a quarter of a century previously.

One transaction concluded at Quebec certainly held little concern for the Soviets. Against Ernie King's wishes, Father accepted Churchill's offer to send the British fleet into the Pacific war, which the experts calculated would not be over for at least another eighteen months. Another deal clinched there did have vital implications for the USSR—Morgenthau's scheme to dismantle postwar Germany.

Father's views were clear-cut. "I think that both here and in England there are two schools of thought," he wrote to Queen Wilhelmina, "those who would be altruistic in regard to the Germans, hoping by loving kindness to make them Christians again—and those who would adopt a much 'tougher' attitude. Most decidedly I belong to the latter school, for though I am not bloodthirsty, I want the Germans to know that this time they have definitely lost the war."

The subject entered this latest conference through the back door. Henry the Morgue was summoned to discuss the extent of lend-lease aid Britain would receive during the process of battering down the Japanese—$3.5 billion of it, plus another $3 billion for reconstruction at home. Henry went on to outline his personal proposals for breaking the back of German industrial power and reducing the Reich to a country "primarily agricultural and pastoral in character."

Winston glared as he spoke and drenched him with scorn after he finished. "I never had such a verbal lashing in my life," Morgenthau complained later. The Prime Minister's objections to leveling Germany were summed up in a single, baleful sentence: "What are we going to have between the white snows of Russia and the white cliffs of Dover?"

Hull thought Morgenthau's scheme was "a plan of blind vengeance." Father did not entirely agree. He let Churchill wear himself out on Henry and was intrigued to discover before the conference ended that the inscrutable Lord Cherwell had turned his master around by citing the benefits to British exporters if German competition were erased. It was Churchill who dictated the memorandum which he and Father initialed, stating in part: "The Germans have devastated a large portion of the industries of Russia and other neighboring Allies, and it is only in accordance with justice that these injured countries should be entitled to remove the machinery they require to repair the losses they have suffered."

A final item waited to be dealt with in the three days Winston spent at Hyde Park before he sailed home. There, the two men reviewed the Manhattan Project, which the British habitually referred to as "tube alloys." The PM's hand was plain in the aide-memoire that emerged: "The suggestion that the world should be informed regarding tube alloys, with a view to an international agreement regarding its control and use, is not accepted. The matter should continue to be regarded as of the utmost secrecy, but when a 'bomb' is finally available, it might perhaps, after mature consideration, be used against the Japanese, who should be warned that this bombardment will be repeated until they surrender. . . ."

Among the American team at Quebec, Leahy doubted whether the Bomb would work, anyway. As he saw it, Japan would fall of its own weight under air bombardment and sea blockade without help from the Soviets. The Army, MacArthur in particular, thought otherwise. My parent, who paid little heed to his Chief of Staff, sided with the Army.

Winston left for London, to go on from there to Moscow, where he and Stalin took no more than a few minutes to share out intended "spheres of influence" in Eastern Europe. The Prime Minister jotted the figures down on half a sheet of paper: "Roumania, Russia 90 percent, the others ten percent; Greece, Great Britain (in accord with the USA) 90 percent, Russia ten percent; Yugoslavia, 50-50 percent; Hungary 50-50 percent; Bulgaria, Russia 75 percent, the others 25 percent."

He pushed the sheet across the felt-covered table. Stalin glanced at it in silence, then penciled a blue checkmark on the page before he tossed it back. The Prime Minister felt a pang of conscience about deciding the fate of millions in a matter of moments. "Let us burn the paper," he suggested.

"No. You keep it," Stalin replied.

Winston had no trouble, either, in persuading the Marshal that Mikolajczyk and his London compatriots should be invited to join these Big Two discussions. Bowing to British pressure, the Polish leader had already expressed his willingness to accept a coalition government in which Communists could have 20 percent of the seats.

Churchill's conscience pricked him again with regard to Father. Contrary to what had been arranged, Harriman was being left out of some of the Moscow meetings. In a private message to POTUS, Winston justified that on the grounds that everything would be provisional and subject to "melting down with you. I am sure you will not mind our trying to have a full meeting of minds with the Russians." He returned to Downing Street, to tell Parliament, "Our relations with Soviet Russia were never more close, intimate and cordial. . . ."

With Quebec and Winston out of the way, Father buckled down to the business of beating Dewey. Every rule for rest and relaxation laid down by the doctors would have to be ignored for the time being. The only concession he would make was to deliver his speeches sitting down. He was spoiling for a fight with an opponent for whom he felt only contempt.

"You ought to hear him," he said with a chuckle to Bob Sherwood. "He plays the part of the heroic racket-buster in one of those gangster movies. He talks to the people as if they were the jury and I were the villain on trial for his life."

With that quadrennial neurosis that afflicts some party chieftains, Hannegan and his colleagues feared to the end that overconfidence among the Democrats would keep them home on election day and enable the Republicans to steal the victory. My own feelings were that Father was the surefire winner from September 23 on, the night he opened his campaign with a speech at a Teamsters Union banquet in the gleaming new Hotel Statler, Washington. Of all his partisans there—including the union's boss, Dan Tobin; William Green of the American Federation of Labor; and Henry Kaiser, whose West Coast yards produced Liberty ships with sausage-factory speed—Anna seemed the most apprehensive that our parent might flop for want of practice.

"Well, here we are again," he began cheerfully and proceed-

ed to annihilate the GOP to guffaws of laughter and the thump
of heavy hands on tabletops. Then he came to the personal gem
that he had dictated to Grace Tully a few days earlier. He spoke
in pretended sorrow, with a look of innocence on his actor's face.

"These Republican leaders have not been content to make
personal attacks upon me—or my wife—or my sons. They now
include my little dog, Fala. Unlike the members of my family,
Fala resents this. When he learned that the Republican fiction
writers had concocted a story that I had left him behind on an
Aleutian Island and had sent a destroyer back to find him—at a
cost to the taxpayer of two or three or twenty million dollars—
his Scotch soul was furious. He has not been the same dog
since. I am accustomed to hearing malicious falsehoods about
myself"—here he ad-libbed—"such as that old, worm-eaten
chestnut that I have represented myself as indispensable."
Then resuming, "But I think I have a right to object to libelous
statements about my *dog.*"

Sherwood recalled someone saying, "From now on the
American people will consider this as a contest of Dewey versus
Fala." The prediction proved to be one hundred percent correct. Father dug out his dark-blue Navy cape and beat-up gray
fedora—his "good luck hat"—and set out to let the voters see
for themslves that the planted whispers about his health were
largely lies. He rode with his automobile's top down through
whatever weather the day might bring, bitter cold or driving
rain. To his doctors' astonishment, his blood pressure actually
decreased. His appetite picked up. He silenced the doubt that
he would ever stand again by performing leg exercises just as
he had twenty-three years previously, so that he could snap the
braces on again and remain on his feet for as long as half an
hour. He came through without so much as a sniffle in the nose.

After fifty-six miles in an open car in a cavalcade that wound
through all five boroughs of New York City, he had this to say
to the Foreign Policy Association in the Waldorf-Astoria's
grand ballroom: "The power which this nation has attained—
the moral, the political, the economic, and the military power—
has brought to us the responsibility, and with it the opportunity, for leadership in the community of nations. In our own best
interest, this nation cannot, must not, and will not shirk the
responsibility."

Quadrennial neurosis found another victim in Tom Dewey, and Father saw the Bolshevik bogey dragged out of the cellar for the fourth time in his White House career. He had begun the betrayal of his country at Teheran, it was alleged, and as soon as the war was over he would deliver the United States to the control of Communism. Mrs. Nesbitt was not alone in saying, "Big money didn't want him to stay on."

He responded in his windup speech in Boston. "When any political candidate stands up and says, solemnly, that the government of the United States—your government—could be sold out to the Communists—then I say that candidate reveals shocking lack of trust in America. He reveals a shocking lack of faith in Democracy—in the spiritual strength of our people."

In the final week, betting in the five-dollars-apiece White House pool on his electoral college vote went like this: Sherwood 484, Early 449, Hopkins 440, Rosenman 431, Watson 400. The candidate himself settled on a modest 335. They were all there at Hyde Park on election night, Father with his tally sheets on the dining-room table, Mother moving around, taking care of the guests. The only difference from other years was the emptiness in Granny's little sitting room. Soon after ten o'clock, Bill Leahy, another overnight visitor, went to bed on Father's word that they were over the bridge. An hour later, the marchers arrived from the village with torches, fife, and drum in their traditional victory celebration. At two o'clock Leahy was on his way downstairs for a glass of milk when he met Father being carried up.

"I've been waiting four hours for that son of a bitch in New York to make up his mind and admit that he's defeated," snapped the four-time winner.

Four hundred and thirty two electoral votes gave the pool to Rosenman, who had been holding the stakes, anyway. Father carried thirty-six states, but his popular vote was down. The 3,591,840 majority was the smallest any President had picked up since 1916. Dewey's quarterbacks figured that a switch of roughly 300,000 votes in a few key states would have put their man in. The answer was that 282,000 more Democrats in the states he did not carry would have given Father all forty-eight of them. As for Congress, there was no appreciable change. The immovable coalition of conservatives still prevailed. One question remained dangling: How many Americans had fallen for the Red scare?

"The little man made me pretty mad," Father confessed, in what he branded (his own capitals) THE DIRTIEST CAMPAIGN IN ALL HISTORY. He reflected on the reasons for the outcome. "They voted, I think, for a faith in the confidence that we would carry that faith forward to full victory for freedom on this earth and to the use of our full powers for plenty here at home. We can be proud of the manner in which we have advanced the stakes of human dignity and security in the past. We must recognize the imperative in the continuing advance to which the people have assigned us."

He suspected the war's end might bring a resurgence of isolationist sentiment in America, as it had in 1919. That made the telegram from his new Vice President almost incomprehensible: ISOLATIONISM IS DEAD. HOPE TO SEE YOU SOON. Father's reply was enigmatic: I AM VERY HAPPY THAT THINGS HAVE GONE SO WELL . . . I WILL SEE YOU VERY SOON IN WASHINGTON. Churchill, Stalin, Mao Tse-tung, and 100,000 others added their congratulations. Truman squeezed in with Wallace to sit beside Father in the open limousine which met him at Union Station, when he returned in a downpour to the music of seven bands and the cheers of 300,000 Washingtonians who lined the streets.

From January until now, I had been serving under Carl Spaatz in England, occupied first with reorganizing American Reconnaissance Air Forces units, then after D Day with photographic reconnaissance over France, Germany, and the Lowlands. A trip to Moscow and the Soviets' southern front to inspect airfields assigned for shuttle-bombing was thrown in for good measure before I was sent back on a technical mission in the Pentagon. Anna was the first of the family to meet me in the White House. She warned me to expect some change in Father's appearance, but what I saw was scarcely surprising. He looked older, tired and thinner, but that was all.

"What did you expect?" he asked, sticking out his hand. "These campaign trips get a little tougher, but I thrive on them." He wanted to talk not about the election but about what was happening to Big Three unity. The next conference had been agreed on, but Yalta had not yet been chosen as the site.

"Stalin is anxious that it be somewhere in Russia. . . . It's hard to refuse. He is in charge of the Red Army, and the Red Army *is* on the go." The mighty winter offensive was starting on the eastern front.

The chance to talk over one series of events in Europe came two or three mornings later when I caught him early in his bedroom, scowling over some dispatches, his newspapers flung down in irritation on to the floor. "Greece," he barked. "British troops. Fighting against the guerrillas who fought the Nazis for the last four years."

The Germans had pulled out. The underground resistance movement, EAM, under Communist control, had moved into the vacuum, parading through Athens with shouts of "Long Live Roosevelt!" Churchill instantly sent 60,000 British troops in, under orders to shoot to kill if necessary. In the name of democracy and liberation, he was after restoring the Greek monarchy, with its blood ties to the British crown. Stalin made no protest and no move to help the guerrillas. Winston's penciled memorandum gave the British top hand in Greece, and the Marshal accepted that. His silence continued when the Prime Minister flew into Athens on Christmas Day and imposed a temporary regency under Archbishop Damaskinos, "a scheming mediaeval prelate," in Winston's private judgment. Possibly, the Communist leader believed that the figures on the half sheet of paper meant that he in turn would receive similar forbearance if trouble arose in his newly acquired zones of influence.

"How the British can dare such a thing!" Father exclaimed that morning as we shared a pot of coffee that he had brewed. "The lengths to which they will go to hang onto the past! I wouldn't have been surprised if Winston had simply made it clear that he was backing the Greek royalists. That would be only in character. But killing Greek guerrillas. . . . I don't suppose there's much I can do about it. . . . Time enough to raise it when I see Winston in February."

He turned abruptly to a different, less abrasive subject. Queen Wilhelmina had promised him, he said, that immediately after victory in Japan her government would announce the granting of dominion status with the right of self-rule to the Dutch East Indies. The next step then would be to allow the people to decide in a free, binding vote whether they wanted complete independence.

"Just as we are granting it in the Philippines," he said. "That's a commitment. And it means a sharp break away from the leadership of the British. Think what that will mean to Stalin. How it will show him what the Western nations can and will accomplish in the postwar! . . . We're going to be able to make this the twentieth century after all. You watch and see."

I left Washington for Arizona, where Faye Emerson and I were to be married on December 3, and he made his way by train to Warm Springs for rest, recuperation, and the intermittent company of Lucy. He also had a loose right molar extracted without any difficulty. He took a dip in the heated pool, but that caused such a steep rise in blood pressure that swimming was discouraged from then on. He reverted to exercises, lying on the edge of his bed and lowering his heels to the floor to strengthen the muscles of his thighs.

His appetite faded, possibly as a consequence of daily doses of digitalis. "I cannot taste food," he grumbled, and his weight went down again, close to 160 pounds. "His general condition remained essentially unchanged," Dr. Bruenn reported. Seventy-two hours before the three-week break ended, Hitler launched an offensive in the Ardennes, the weakest point in the Allied line that stretched from Antwerp to the frontier of Switzerland. On December 19, the day Father returned to the White House, the Germans had advanced forty-five miles. For a while, it seemed that something akin to another Dunkirk might be in the making. The Battle of the Bulge began. On the eastern front, the Red Army would run into no such problems. A thrust up the valley of the Danube carried them past Budapest and on toward Vienna.

Once more that Christmas we were together as a family. In the living room-library, the long center table was pushed back to make room for the glistening, candlelit tree, and a separate chair held each pile of presents. We all found places around Father as he took to his accustomed rocking chair beside the fireplace and opened the well-thumbed book. Stretched out on the rug, I let my thoughts wander as the tale of the salvation of Ebenezer Scrooge rose and fell in my ears.

Faye's elbow in my ribs woke me. "You were snoring. Sit up!"

My sheepish look brought a grave wink from Father, who continued with his reading. A second interruption came from three-year-old Chris, Franklin Jr.'s boy. "Grandpère, you've lost a tooth! Did you swallow it?" For some reason, the front gold tooth that he screwed in for public occasions and always for *A Christmas Carol* had been dispensed with this year.

"There's too much competition in this family for reading aloud." He laughed, laying the book aside.

"Next year," said Faye, "it'll be a peacetime Christmas, and we'll all listen as good as gold."

"Next year," said Mother, knitting needles clicking, "we'll all be home again."

On Christmas Day, he was carefully inserting one of his most gratefully received gifts in a stamp album when we talked again. The Big Three would meet next month, he said, "as definite as anything in this life. I'm looking forward to it. Change will do me good."

He was seriously thinking of making a trip to England in the late spring. There was a standing invitation from Former Naval Person, who had promised Parliament a general election after Germany's defeat. As the mood of the disillusioned, war-weary British drifted leftward, his Conservative-dominated "national" government was coming apart at the seams. Continuance of special treatment by the United States and his vaunted bloodbrother relationship with Father were the essence of Winston's plans to retain high office. If Father could put in a few kind words for him, his chances with the electorate would be vastly improved. Mother did not care to see Franklin employed as a cat's-paw. She hoped he would not lend himself to the scheme.

He had more cogent reasons for going. "I think that might well be the best way to sell the British people and the British Parliament on the need for Britain to put its hopes for the future in the United Nations and not just in the British Empire and British ability to get other countries to combine in some sort of bloc against the Soviet Union."

Was there actual danger of that? "It's what we've got to expect. It's what we've got to plan now to contend against." A pause, and then, "This is no talk for Christmas."

"Just what I was going to say," murmured Mother, coming up behind us.

19

The Fourth Inaugural was the simplest of them all—no parades, no ball, no crowds to clog traffic. He was tickled pink that it could be done for something less than $2,000 instead of the $25,000 that had been appropriated. He had asked for chicken à la king for his luncheon guests, but Mrs. Nesbitt anticipated problems in keeping that warm, so he settled for chicken salad, butterless rolls, and cake without frosting.

He found that there were precedents for passing up the Capitol as the site for the ceremony, so he chose instead the South Portico of the White House. On Saturday morning, January 22, 1945, he stood out there without hat or topcoat under the cold gray sky, wearing a two-piece lightweight suit as he gazed down at the guests, who could be counted in hundreds only, gathered on the snow-covered lawn. It seemed that once again he might be testing his ability to endure.

He spoke for perhaps five minutes, but he had worked harder on those words than on any he had delivered for the past two years. Bob Sherwood, listening, thought that Father was summing up the essence of his belief as he quoted Ralph Waldo Emerson: "The only way to have a friend is to be one." To which, he added a warning: "We can have no lasting peace if we approach it with suspicion and mistrust—or with fear."

His sixty-third birthday waited eight days ahead, but in forty-eight hours he would be leaving for Yalta, so the family celebrated that night with the first rib roast served in months. Roosevelts didn't buy black market, as Mrs. Nesbitt proudly noted, splurging all their meat ration points.

Anna was the only one of us who took the train with him to Norfolk to board the *Baltimore*'s sister ship, the heavy cruiser *Quincy*. Stirrings of concern for Father's health prompted Mother to ask to go along. He let her know that she might only be in the way. At my headquarters in England I had hoped that the pattern of Argentia, Casablanca, Cairo, and Teheran might be repeated, but he hesitated to put in a request to the War Department for my services.

The Republicans on the Hill were already screaming to the skies over the affairs of a dog named Blaze, which had been flown over from England for Faye, now in Hollywood. The gale of publicity over that blew stronger when, with diabolical timing, my name appeared on the roster of men nominated for general officer's grade which arrived on his desk, with approval from Doolittle, Spaatz, and Eisenhower.

My parent was subjected to exhortations from various quarters that this Roosevelt should be discreetly omitted from the list before he passed it on to Congress. He mulled that over two or three times before he said, "Elliott on his record has earned promotion. He did not ask that the dog be put on the plane or given high priority. And I'm not going to have him punished for something he did not do." But no Yalta for me. It was good that Anna would be with him.

The fact that during the last years of the war, up to the time of Father's death, Anna lived at the White House, gave her the same opportunity to achieve a close relationship with him that Jimmy and I had had on previous occasions. She was a great comfort to him during that period of utmost strain. As he gradually felt his vitality ebbing, he needed more and more the comforting affections of someone close to him. I think Mother would have liked to slip into this role, but the barriers erected years before could not be put aside. Anna served as confidante and sounding board for an increasingly tired and beleaguered man. It must have been with deep sadness that she, more than anyone, watched the slow ebbing of Father.

Unfortunately, neither Franklin Jr. nor John ever had the

opportunities the three oldest children had to achieve a communion of spirit with our father. He was to remain forever in
our minds a generous, loving, understanding and, above all,
forgiving parent.

As usual, he reveled in his ten days at sea, which were rough
at first, but that was part of the pleasure. Yalta would be the
place where the foundations of a new world order were to be
laid. He had the supreme confidence of believing that there was
never a problem that human effort could not resolve, and he
had committed himself to contribute whatever effort might be
necessary. Face to face, he could bring the other two around to
his point of view. When the war was over, he would continue
regular summit meetings with Stalin and Churchill or whoever
their successors might be.

Just before leaving, he had said, "I am inclined to think that
at the meeting with Marshal Stalin and the Prime Minister I can
put things on a somewhat higher level than they have been for
the past two or three months."

He had sent Hopkins on ahead in The Sacred Cow to spend a
few days in London, working on Winston, whose forebodings
of disaster darkened with every Red Army advance. Making a
steady sixteen miles a day, the Soviets would be within eighty
miles of Berlin by the end of the month. Father had made his
feelings about imperialistic land-grabbing plain to the PM in
advance. "Winston, this is something which you are just not
able to understand. You have four hundred years of acquisitive
instinct in your blood, and you just don't understand how a
country might not want to acquire land somewhere if they can
get it. A new period has opened in the world's history, and you
will have to adjust yourself to it."

The same sense of history governed his thinking about Stalin. Any brand of dictatorship was repugnant to Father, but
change in men and nations was as inexorable as birth and
death. No country stood still. Firm patience in dealing with the
USSR would speed its evolution from tyranny toward a free,
more tolerant society. As he saw his own position after the previous year's election, "I am going down the whole line a little
left of center." That had held true for almost a dozen years.

The stance took him closer to Stalin than to "dear old Winston." One noteworthy conversation between the American

President and the Soviet Marshal had touched on a likely outcome. "So much depends in the future on how we learn to get along together," Father said. "Do you think it will be possible for the United States and the USSR to see things in similar ways?"

"You have come a long way in the United States from your original concept of government and its responsibilities and your original way of life," Stalin replied. "I think it is quite possible that we in the USSR, as our resources develop and people can have an easier life, will find ourselves growing nearer to some of your concepts, and you may find yourselves accepting some of ours."

The timetable called for the *Quincy* to dock in Valletta harbor, Malta, on February 2, then for Father and his party to drive to Luqa airfield for the flight to the Crimean airport of Saki. From there, they would cover the last eighty miles by automobile to Yalta, on the coast of the Black Sea. Messages from Winston, all discouraging, began arriving for Father as soon as the Prime Minister reached Malta on the last day of January with a raging temperature that put him to bed for the first day.

"If we spent ten years on research we could not have found a worse place in the world than Yalta. . . . It is good for typhus and deadly lice which thrive in those parts." He gave POTUS warning that the ride from Saki took six hours, not two, as Harriman had calculated, and it ran across frightening mountains, impassable at times. It was permissible to speculate that, even at this late date, Winston yearned to find some pretext for calling the whole thing off.

When Harriman came aboard at Valletta, he put the situation back into perspective. The mountain road from Saki would not be too tiring in daylight. A high-class debugging job had been done at Yalta by Navy medical officers of the communications ship *Catoctin*, moored at Sevastapol for fear of unswept German mines in Yalta waters. Soviet preparations included setting 1,000 Red Army soldiers to work repairing roads, patching bomb damage, and planting flowerbeds. Trainloads of furniture, food, and domestic staff had been brought in from Moscow, not forgetting a mammoth double bed at Winston's explicit request.

Harriman was a familiar figure at these conferences, like

those others on the 135-strong team of Very Important Persons—Hopkins, Leahy, Marshall, and Pa Watson. Pa had filled in time on the crossing by organizing bets on whether the Americans would get to Manila before the Red Army entered Berlin. There were also some newcomers, such as the first man up the gangway from the dock, Ed Stettinius, Secretary of State since Hull, truly a tired old man, resigned straight after the election. Jimmy Byrnes, in his capacity as War Mobilization Director, went to Yalta, too.

The British had planned to get Father working as soon as the *Quincy* docked, but he took the afternoon off for a drive around Malta in cool sunshine with Anna. He spent an evening hour with Winston, but avoided dining with him, which increased the Prime Minister's uneasiness. "The President was so unpredictable," Eden complained later.

At eleven o'clock, Father was lifted into The Sacred Cow by the built-in elevator, a fitful device which did not always function, and he was asleep in his bunk before the 1,400-mile flight began, with six P-38 fighters flying escort. At ten- and fifteen-minute intervals through the night, thirty more big transports roared up and across the Aegan and the Black Sea to Saki, while American and Soviet warships prowled the waters below as insurance against forced landings.

The Presidential armored limousine was shipped to Yalta, but its 8,000 pounds made it too heavy for these winding, rutted roads. From Saki, a Soviet car and driver took Father and Anna along in the motorcade that wound over the ravaged, snow-blanketed countryside, dotted with ruined buildings and abandoned Nazi tanks, then up over Red Crag, while our parent catnapped in the back seat. Red Army men—and women— guarded the entire route with submachine guns nestled in their arms.

He slept soundly that night in the czar's bedroom in the Livadia Palace, once an imperial summer home, then a sanitorium for tubercular comrades, lately staff headquarters for the local Wehrmacht. The Grand Ballroom would serve for formal sessions. Ernie King was allotted the czarina's boudoir, Hopkins another upstairs room, where he passed most days in bed, living principally on coffee, cigarettes, and paregoric. Space in general was so tight that sixteen Army colonels found themselves sharing the same *Lebensraum*. Stalin's villa lay six miles away. Winston was quartered in splendor in the Vorontov Palace, with terraced gardens descending to the beach and its bathrooms equipped with imported British toilet tissue.

On Sunday morning, Father woke and breakfasted early, with scarcely a moment to glance out his windows at the mountains that overshadowed the shore or at the two small pictures on a bedroom wall, which were all that the Nazis left behind when they were driven from the palace.

For the next nine days, he forced himself to the limits, often compelled to miss his mandatory afternoon rest to cope with the constant stream of visitors arriving from the time he awakened. At first, a cough disturbed his sleep, but codeine and terpin hydrate took care of that. He denied feeling any particular pains. His lungs were clear, heart and blood pressure unchanged. Russian cuisine appealed to him, and it suited his digestion.

After he died, there was no shortage of observers to proclaim their discovery of his faltering health at Yalta, Ernie King and Churchill's Lord Moran among them. The record spoke otherwise. Eden thought Father was "in particular fine shape," but obviously in need of more sleep. Harriman judged that "He carried on the negotiations with his usual skill and perception. Any suggestion to the contrary is utterly without foundation in fact." Stettinius concluded that it was Winston who showed signs of physical and mental deterioration. "The Prime Minister seems to be going through some sort of menopause," he said.

Shortly after his valet, Arthur Prettyman, had helped Father dress on that Sunday morning, a black Packard brought Stalin over on a social call from his quarters in Koreis Villa, owned once by Prince Yupusov, the assassin of Rasputin. Guest and host sat together in Livadia's paneled study. My parent remarked that what he had seen of German devastation in the Crimea made him more bloodthirsty than he had been a year ago. He should see the Ukraine, replied the Marshal, where everything had been wantonly destroyed. He left in time to pay his respects to Winston at three P.M. before returning for the first plenary session in the Grand Ballroom early that evening.

The days fell into a set pattern. The ballroom would be filled by four P.M. for formal meetings lasting three to four hours, followed by dinner some sixty minutes later. Cablegrams, carried over specially laid land lines to the *Cactoctin*, streamed to and from Washington, 5,700 miles away; London, 3,000 miles distant; Moscow, a mere 900 miles to the north. White House couriers sliced their travel time from five to three days each way before the conference ended.

Yalta, in Stettinius' opinion, marked the high tide of Big Three cooperation in the war and on proposed settlements for the peace. At the first night's dinner in the palace—caviar, sturgeon, beef, sweet cake, vodka, and five varieties of Russian wine served by the Filipino mess crew—Winston went so far as to propose a toast to the world's proletarian masses.

In the sessions ahead, they returned to the question of dismantling Germany in spite of some reluctance on the part of the Prime Minister, who had written earlier to Eden: "It is much too soon to decide these enormous questions. . . . It is a mistake to try to write out on little pieces of paper what the vast emotions of an outraged and quivering world will be. . . ." The subsequent claim that Father, too, wanted to temporize on eliminating or controlling all German industry was utterly false. The night before he died, he left Henry Morgenthau convinced that he was determined "not to allow any sentimental consideration to modify the conditions necessary to prevent Germany and the German people from becoming aggressors again."

Estimates by the United States Office of Strategic Services produced at Yalta set Soviet war losses at $16 billion in fixed capital—25 percent of all prewar industry—plus another $4 billion in inventories and personal property. When Stalin suggested extracting a total of $20 billion in reparations from the battered Reich, with 50 percent of that earmarked for the USSR, Winston objected. Hopkins slipped a note to Father: "The Russians have given in so much at this conference that I don't think we should let them down." Father as chairman left the door open for future debate between the Foreign Ministers of the three powers. Stettinius promised Molotov that he was ready at any time to discuss long-term American credits to help Soviet reconstruction.

They talked interminably about how to defeat Japan. The chief of the Manhattan Project, iron-faced General Leslie

Groves, enjoyed enough confidence in the outcome to have ordered air crews into training for the drop, though testing of a prototype in the desert of New Mexico would not be undertaken until July 16. None of the handful of Britons and Americans at Yalta who knew of the work in progress had such faith as Groves. If the Germans had perfected the Bomb, Hitler would surely have used it by now. Leahy, for one, felt sure that "The Bomb will never go off, and I speak as an expert in explosives."

MacArthur's views were repeated to James Forrestal, former investment banker, Navy Secretary since Frank Knox's fatal heart attack almost a year previously. Meeting with Forrestal in liberated Manila at the end of the present month, the pipe-puffing general dismissed as "negligible" the help that the Chinese could provide in conquering Japan. What was essential therefore, he said, was for Stalin to prosecute a campaign in Manchuria "of such proportions as to pin down a very large part of the Japanese army."

Father's principal military objective was to obtain a firm commitment from the Soviets to fight Japan within three months after Germany's defeat. That would allow enough time to redeploy United States forces from Europe to the Pacific and move twenty-five Red Army divisions as promised from the eastern front. With Stalin's help, a minimum of 500,000 American servicemen could be spared death or battle wounds. This was the overriding consideration, not Winston's barely suppressed anti-Bolshevism.

Stalin agreed. He also agreed to recognize Chiang Kai-shek's graft-ridden government as the rightful rulers of China and Manchuria, and to supply Chiang with soldiers to oust the Japanese. The conditions set by the Soviets struck nobody in key positions on the scene as unreasonable. Outer Mongolia must remain a Communist people's republic. Russian territory lost to Japan in the humiliating war of 1904 (which Uncle Ted arbitrated) must be restored and the Kuril Islands ceded to the USSR. For the time being, nothing of this could be disclosed to Chiang, since whatever was known in Chungking was passed to the Japanese. Stalin could not risk countermoves by Tokyo until reinforcements had reached his armies in Siberia. Father undertook to use his persuasions on Chiang when the time was ripe.

This was one of Yalta's alleged secrets employed afterward

by his detractors to tarnish Father. The agreement encompassing these points was signed by the Big Three on February 11. On August 10, after Stalin carried out his part of the bargain, a Treaty of Friendship and Alliance was signed between China and the Soviet Union with no complaint from the Chinese that the Yalta compact had handicapped them in their negotiations.

In the topsy-turvy climate that developed in what could be called the post-Roosevelt era, appearances were reversed as in a looking glass. Father, as deft a bargainer at Yalta as at every other conference, was supposedly Stalin's dupe, Stalin emerged as a sinister puppet-master, Churchill as the folk hero of Western democracy. On the testimony of Stettinius, "The Soviet Union made more concessions to the US and the UK than were made to the Soviet Union by either the US or Britain."

It was our State Department that drafted the Declaration on Liberated Europe which was signed without changes, reaffirming the Atlantic Charter, setting down the belief that, "Only with the continuing and growing cooperation and understanding among our three countries and among all peace-loving nations can . . . be realized a secure and lasting peace." It was Winston who procrastinated when Father pushed for the United Nations to be born in the United States within the next four weeks.

"There is something behind this talk that we do not know of its basis," said another note that Hopkins slipped to Father in the middle of the Prime Minister's rhetoric. "All this is local politics," said my parent's scribbled reply. Churchill was afraid of how the United Nations might impinge on the Empire when his best hope of reelection resided in his appeal to the voters as the sturdiest of British patriots. He sought to get both my parents to England in May, before any peace-keeping organization saw the light of day.

As he said with a chuckle to Sam Rosenman, "The British people would not resent—and of course I would particularly welcome—any word that he might want to say in favor of my candidacy."

Stettinius felt the weight of Winston's lash when he brought up the subject of establishing United Nations trusteeships for colonial territories along the lines that Father advocated so warmly. "I will never agree," stormed the Prime Minister, "to the fumbling fingers of forty or fifty nations prying into the life's existence of the British Empire." He swung on Stalin. How would *he* like to see the Crimea turned into an international summer resort? The Russian growled that he would be happy to give it over as a permanent site for Big Three meetings.

One member of the Presidential entourage who sided wholeheartedly with Churchill was Bill Leahy. He was secretly delighted to hear Winston declaim, "While there is life in my body, no transfer of British sovereignty will be permitted." This was real, old-fashioned courage, Leahy decided; he had little sympathy with his Commander in Chief's fancies about trusteeships.

Churchill had to concede on the United Nations' birthday. April 25 was chosen as the date, San Francisco as the place. Father and Mother would be there to see his greatest hope for tomorrow's world emerge into tangible shape.

Only one agreement entered into by my parent at Yalta deserved to be labeled a secret. His error—and it was a serious miscalculation—lay in withholding all reference to it when, two days after his return to Washington, he sat on a red plush chair in the well of the House of Representatives' chamber, making his report on Yalta to a joint session of the Congress and the people of the United States. He begged pardon for "an unusual posture of sitting down," but he saw no reason to explain or apologize for the bargain struck in the Livadia Palace, granting the USSR three votes in the United Nations.

Gromyko had blazed the trail at Dumbarton Oaks by suggesting that each of the sixteen republics which constituted the Union of Soviet Socialist Republics should be seated in the United Nations. Father's instant reaction was that he would demand a vote for each of the forty-eight states if the Soviets insisted, but he felt sure he could get Stalin to see the light. He could also detect a certain logic in the Russians seeking extra voting strength when the British looked forward to obtaining a seat for each of their five Dominions, which would amount to a ready-made anti-Soviet block in Winston's long-term calculations. On top of that, London's influence in Western Europe would probably ensure support from two or three other countries for Britain's imperial policies.

As early as the previous December, Stalin had backed off

from the sixteen-votes proposition. At Yalta, he asked only one apiece for the Soviet Union itself, the Ukraine, and Byelorussia. Father's inclination was still to refuse, but Winston favored the idea. After twenty-four hours of internal debate, Father yielded in a prime example of diplomatic horse-trading. He would support the Soviet claim not as a fait accompli, but subject to a free vote at the San Francisco conference. He also wanted an "insurance clause." If a tempest blew up on Capitol Hill, the Russians and the British would endorse him in securing two extra votes for the United States. Stalin and Churchill both gave him their pledge.

The Soviets made a further concession, which neither of the other Big Two regarded as inconsequential: No major Security Council power could veto consideration of any complaint lodged against it. Father's maneuvering had cleared the way for his brainchild to be welcomed into the world as a lusty adult, with a minimum of prenatal problems in need of doctoring.

In the middle of the day-and-night haggling at Yalta, on Thursday, February 8, Father came close to cracking under the strain. Three days had passed since he told his two fellow bargainers, "I should like to bring up Poland. . . . It would make it easier for me at home if the Soviet Government could give something to Poland." The talking had swung to and fro ever since. What he asked for was a government of national unity in Warsaw, not the Lublin regime of Communists which Stalin had adroitly recognized a month previously to maintain "peace and quiet" in the Red Army's wake. Winston echoed Father. "This is what we went to war against Germany for—that Poland should be free and sovereign. . . . It nearly cost us our life as a nation."

The Marshal was host at dinner that Thursday night, when, as usual, the tensions of the conference table were soothed in round after round of toasts. From Stalin to Churchill "as the bravest governmental figure in the world." From Winston to Stalin "as the mighty leader of a mighty country," which had broken the back of the Wehrmacht. From the Marshal to the President of the United States and lend-lease together. From Father to the Big Three's objectives in giving "to every man, woman, and child on this earth the possibility of security and well-being."

He needed rest. Brave words hid his mounting anxiety about

the day's discussions, which had failed to soften Stalin's stance on Poland. Father's face was gray when Dr. Bruenn examined him before bedtime, and his blood pressure was fluttering. This time, the physician's orders prevailed. Working hours must be cut. Visitors were barred before noon. An hour to relax must be fitted in every afternoon before he returned to the ballroom to continue the struggle.

Within forty-eight hours, his heartbeat had steadied and his spirits were soaring. Before the conference wound up on Sunday afternoon, Stalin consented to a free, secret ballot for the Poles to reorganize the Lublin government "on a broader democratic basis." The details of how that election might be monitored were left unresolved. Whatever happened, Stalin, in exactly the same manner as Father and Winston, would not be maneuvered into ignoring what he interpreted to be the best interests of his country. The frontiers of the USSR had to be secure.

On the eve of departure, dinner was on Winston. Father repeated one of his stories, telling how Mother, on a visit to a country schoolhouse in the New Deal's early days, found a history class of ten-year-olds gazing at a wall map on which the Soviet Union was represented by blank white space. The local school board had decided that the children were not to be contaminated by information about Russia.

He left Winston flabbergasted with the news that he was going to fly to Egypt for prearranged meetings with three feudal kings—Farouk of Egypt, Ibn Saud of Saudi Arabia, and Haile Selassie of Abyssinia. The Prime Minister smelled a plot to undermine the Empire. The following morning, a smug Winston told Father that he, too, would shortly be in Egypt to see each of the monarchs for himself *after* they had talked with my parent.

The drive to Sevastapol, then the flight to Egypt, put an exhausted man aboard the *Quincy* again, at anchorage in Great Bitter Lake, south of Ismailia. Anna thought that he was surviving principally on nerve, but medically he was symptom-free. His first royal visitor was fat Farouk; their conversation centered on the thousands of American tourists who would someday flock to the Valley of the Nile. Next came Haile Selassie, nervously endorsing Father's hopes for closer contacts between their countries.

The next day brought Ibn Saud, in bejeweled white robes,

from Jidda, where a United States destroyer had collected him
for his first trip away from his kingdom. Father's plan was to
talk him into allowing tens of thousands of Jewish refugees into
Palestine. Of all the men he met in his life, he said afterward, he
made the least progress with this hawk of an Arab, whose only
answer was no. Nonetheless, he received three marks of my
parent's regard: his personal wheelchair, a private plane, and a
promise that Father would sanction no American move hostile
to Arab peoples.

On Sunday, February 18, the *Quincy* finally set off for home,
with his staunchest companion of the good old days missing
from Father's side. Bluff, big-hearted Pa Watson, who had suffered congestive heart failure on the automobile ride over the
mountains from Yalta, lay dying in his cabin. Just before a cerebral hemorrhage ended his life at eight o'clock on Tuesday
morning, Father took part in the rites of confirming Pa into the
Catholic faith. To preserve security on the voyage, news of the
death was withheld until the *Quincy* docked at Newport News a
week later.

He had concealed his feelings about the loss of Louis and
Missy, but that was impossible to repeat now. He felt disinclined
to do any more work than glance at a book or a document that
must be attended to, yet he had to draft his report to Congress,
and this without the help of Hopkins, who was too ill to make
the ocean crossing. Father could not control his grief as he
spoke with the closest of those remaining in his circle or sat
puffing cigarettes in the afternoon sun with Anna beside him.
But when he and Mother met again, he could say with a return
of his old warmth, "It's been a global war, and we've already
started making it a global peace."

When Churchill related his version of the events of the following weeks, he wrote: "Actually, though I did not realize it,
the President's health was now so feeble that it was General
Marshall who had to deal with these grave questions." Strange
words when Moran, in constant attendance on the Prime Minister, reported that at Yalta he gave Father "only a few months
to live." Winston was planting excuses for his inability to obtain
White House backing in his mounting quarrel with Eisenhower. Curbing the Red Army had become a Churchillian obses-
sion. Eastern Europe must be preserved from the Soviets. He

inundated Ike with what amounted always to the same exhortation: "We should march as far east into Germany as possible . . . should Berlin be in our grasp, we should certainly take it."

Eisenhower refused to be drawn into any improvised race against the Russians to see who could be first into the shattered German capital, where Hitler was holed up in the maze of bunkers beneath the Chancellory. Strictly according to plan, Ike thrust farther south, to link up there with the Red Army and split the Reich in half, knowing that Berlin, a target of limited military importance, would lie deep within the Soviet zone of occupation on the provisional map which had been hastily drawn at Quebec a year ago. By pretending that his old antagonist, General George, was to blame for the lack of response from Washington, Churchill could still foster the illusion that Father would have reacted differently. None of this was true. Father was content as always to let Marshall mastermind the European war.

My parent shrugged off his doctors' advice, skipped rest periods, and labored long into the nights. His appetite suffered and his weight dropped again. Yet his cough cleared up, blood pressure fell, and his heartbeat sounded clear and steady, though a murmur remained. All that troubled him was the tastelessness of his food.

It was not General Marshall who wrote to me on March 3: "Dear Bunny, It is grand to be able to address you as Brigadier General. . . . " Or to Jimmy Byrnes, who resigned on March 23: "I was, of course, knocked off my feet. . . I am distressd but I, in part, appreciate your reasons. . . . " Or the bubbling note to Harold Ickes on March 27: "I, too, have an invitation to the Gridiron Club on April fourteenth and I am told they have at last abandoned white weskits, white ties, and full-dress suits. This is a great moral victory for me. It has taken twelve years to attain it. Unfortunately, I shall be away on April fourteenth. . . ." In forty-eight hours, he would be leaving for Warm Springs.

The going was rough all through the month of March. Complaints from Winston about Eisenhower and the Russians rained in on Father. The old war-horse, who had personally celebrated the capture of Hitler's Siegfried Line by flying to the scene and urinating on it, gave hints of regret for besetting my parent in this fashion after it was too late to matter. "I did what I could," he wrote, "in personal telegrams to relieve the strain of the divergencies which Soviet anatonism brought into our official correspondence, but I had not realized how serious the President's condition had become."

Communications from Moscow grew suddenly terse. Early in the month, General Karl Wolff appeared in Berne, Switzerland, with a provisional offer to surrender the German army in Italy to the Allies. General Sir Harold Alexander's response was to send a British and an American officer from his staff to check out the proposition. Four days elapsed before the Kremlin was notified of what was in hand. Stalin's resurgent suspicions surfaced in a spate of icy messages. Soviet representatives, he said, "were barred" from the Berne negotiations. "This circumstance irritates the Soviet Command and engenders distrust."

The harshness of the exchanges between the Kremlin and Washington increased. Stalin told Father that he could not account "for the reticence of the British, who have left it to you to carry on a correspondence with me on this unpleasant matter, while they themselves maintain silence, although it is known that the initiative in the matter of the Berne negotiations belongs to the British. . . . A momentary advantage, no matter how great, is overshadowed by the fundamental advantage of preserving and promoting trust between Allies."

Father reported back his "astonishment" at receiving such words. "It would be one of the great tragedies of history," he replied, "if at the very moment of victory, now within our grasp, such lack of faith should prejudice the entire undertaking after the colossal losses of life, material and treasure involved."

The Marshal was not yet satisfied. "I still consider the Russian point of view to be the correct one, because it precludes mutual suspicions and gives the enemy no chance to sow distrust between us." My parent had the final word: "Thank you for your frank explanation. . . . There must not be mutual distrust, and minor misunderstandings of this character should not arise in the future." That postscript was received in Moscow the day after he died.

In the middle of this fracas—on March 16—Father held a Cabinet meeting. Assistant Navy Secretary H. Struve Hensel attended in place of Forrestal. Hensel's notes read: "The President indicated considerable difficulty with British relations. . . . He stated that the British were perfectly willing for the United States to have a war with Russia at any time and that, in his opinion, to follow the British program would be to proceed toward that end."

Poland was a major bone of contention. Instead of permitting the promised election, the Soviets were planning to seat a Lublin government representative at San Francisco. Kremlinologists in Washington pored over the tea leaves and decided that Stalin had run into trouble with the Politburo for agreeing that the Poles might elect their own leaders when it was a certainty that the outcome would be an anti-Communist regime in Warsaw. As a mark of irritation, he delegated Gromyko, a second-stringer compared with Molotov, for San Francisco. Father protested. "I am afraid that Mr. Molotov's absence will be construed all over the world as a lack of comparable interest on the part of the Soviet government in the great objectives of this Conference."

Steve Early suggested that perhaps he should change his mind about opening the conference in case it failed. "But I'm going to be there at the start and the finish, too," my parent told Bob Sherwood. "All those people from all over the world are paying this country a great honor by coming here, and I want to tell them how much we appreciate it."

His elbow was being tugged from one other quarter. His new Vice President kept up a steady flow of requests, inviting Father to attend meetings with him and pressing the claims of fellow Missourians for federal jobs. He received no personal response from Father. To the innermost circle, Truman remained a stranger. There was a commanding reason for telling him nothing about the Manhattan Project when his own probes of arms factories had failed to unearth a single clue to its existence. The penny-conscious Vice President would have been overwhelmed to learn that $2 billion had been spirited away. That was unquestionably an impeachable offense under the terms of the Constitution, and impeachment proceedings which would open his way to succession could not be risked at this time.

On March 23, Father called into the White House the bipartisan delegation he had chosen for San Francisco: Senator Tom Connolly and Representative Sol Bloom, Democrats; Senator Arthur Vandenburg and Representative Charles Eaton, Republicans. These four were let in on the secret that the United States and Britain would urge three votes for the USSR. In his doctor's words, Father by now "began to look bad." A period of total rest was ordered for him. The Republican New York *Herald Tribune* which he read at breakfast on March 29, the day he left for Warm Springs, carried an exclusive story of the three-votes deal, which presumably only one of the four could have revealed. Washington was thrown into a frenzy as reporters laid siege to the White House and the Roosevelt-haters trumpeted the news that here was final, conclusive proof of treachery.

His accommodations at Warm Springs were little changed from the time he bought the place. The little clapboard cottage bore a family resemblance to Shangri-La, not San Clemente. The kitchen had an old-fashioned icebox, not even a refrigerator. A week there in the Georgia hills seemed to restore him. He started to eat well again, adding a bowl of gruel between meals. "Roosevelt weather" enticed him out into the sun every afternoon on brief automobile rides, sometimes with Lucy for company, inspecting the new tree-planting that he was forever ordering, relishing the pink and white clouds of the dogwoods. By April 10, the pallor was gone from his gaunt cheeks, and he was asking for "second helps" at mealtimes. He was looking forward to a weekend barbecue—two hogs, a lamb, and a side of beef—at his favorite picnic spot, with a hillbilly concert to follow.

The next day, Wednesday, he dictated what were probably his last words to Winston: "I would minimize the general Soviet problem as much as possible, because these problems, in one form or another, seem to arise every day, and most of them straighten out. . . . We must be firm, however, and our course thus far is correct."

Father had just waked up from a good night's sleep when Dr. Bruenn saw him on Thursday morning, April 12, at nine twenty. He had a slight headache and a stiff neck, which gentle massage relieved. He passed the morning in his leather chair in the living room, which served as dining room, too, with Lucy, Daisy

Suckley, and Aunt Polly. As usual, he combined two jobs at once. In what promised to be the toughest term of all in relations with Congress, he had to plan for fending off inflation while making 60,000,000 jobs available when reconversion got into its stride. The mail and the daily delivery of documents of state were heavy as he sat, in a Harvard-crimson tie and his old Navy cape, posing for a portrait by Elizabeth Shumatoff which Lucy had commissioned as a gift for her daughter Barbara. Lucy agreed with the others on how well he looked. In the kitchen, Daisy Bonner, the cook, prepared lunch for one o'clock.

What followed has been told too many times to bear repeating. The tossing away of his World War I draft card into a wastebasket. The circling of his left hand over his temple. The murmur, "I have a terrific headache." Aunt Polly running for the nearest Secret Serviceman. Arthur Prettyman and a Filipino houseman carrying him, unconscious, from his chair into bed.

A telephone call brought Bruenn racing by car from the swimming pool, two miles off. Cleaned up and put into pajamas, Father was was pale, cold, and bathed in sweat, breathing stertorously. His heart was beating steadily at 96 to the minute, blood pressure way up, legs totally numb. The immediate task was to apply blankets and hot-water bottles and inject a grain of papaverine and some amyl nitrate. Close to an hour went by before there was a minute for Bruenn to contact Ross McIntire on the private line to Washington and report a massive cerebral hemorrhage. McIntire promised an immediate call to Dr. Paullin in Atlanta, eighty miles away.

In the years ahead, Bruenn was to speculate time and again what turn history might have taken if modern methods for controlling hypertension had been available to Father. Dieting was the principal treatment for hypertensives until the end of World War II. Then an armory of new drugs began to be developed, which today are the therapy of choice: pentaquine, originally devised to combat malaria; hexamethonium and chlorisondamine, which block the constricting of blood vessels; hydralazine to dilate the arteries and thus lower pressure; guanethidine and reserpine, which cause a change in body chemistry; diuretics to cut the kidneys' retention of salt.

Father's hypertension was diagnosed in 1937, when he was fifty-five years old. Insurance company tables nowadays show that, properly treated, a man of that age has a life expectancy of seventeen more years. That would have meant he might well have lived until 1954. Had that single life been spared, the countless deaths of the Cold War might have been saved, too.

As it was, Bruenn watched and waited. By two forty-five, color had returned to Father's face. Blood pressure had fallen, and the heartbeat was down to 90. Lucy led Elizabeth Shumatoff from the cottage. Half an hour later, his breathing began to slow. In a corner, Grace Tully murmured prayers. Fala sat in the bedroom. Shortly after three o'clock, Aunt Polly telephoned Mother in her White House sitting room, saying only that Father had fainted and been put to bed. She checked with McIntire. He did not wish to alarm her, but they should fly down to Warm Springs together later in the day, he said.

At twenty-nine minutes to four, breathing ceased. There was no audible beat in the heart. Bruenn had injected an intramuscular shot of caffeine sodium benzoate and started artificial respiration when Dr. Paullin arrived. A final injection of adrenalin directly into the heart had no effect. At three thirty-five, Bruenn pronounced Father dead. Fala crashed through a screen door and ran, barking, into the hills.

The time in London was eight thirty-five. I had driven in from Mount Farm, my air base south of Oxford, for a dinner party in a West End restaurant. The hostess was Lady Sylvia Ashley, a future wife of Clark Gable's. I had no sooner been seated when she took me aside and said that an officer from General Doolittle's headquarters in High Wycombe was waiting to see me. When I heard the news, I was too benumbed to realize that it could be true. It seemed impossible, that was all.

I left straightway for Mount Farm. A cablegram from Mother was waiting there, sent from the White House, where the thirty-third President of the United States was sworn in before she left for Warm Springs. HE DID HIS JOB TO THE END AS HE WOULD WANT YOU TO DO, her message said. I made contact with Doolittle's headquarters and was told that if I was ready early next morning, I could join Sam Rosenman, Bernie Baruch, and Ed Flynn, who was over in London on a mission for Father, on a flight to Washington, to be there in time for the funeral.

Looking back on that night, there was a mystery that haunted me concerning Former Naval Person, who stayed up working until all hours as a matter of habit and enjoyed a superb communications system. "When I received these tidings early in the morning of Friday, the 13th," he was to write in his memoirs, "I felt as if I had been struck a physical blow." I could never discover how it was that many other people in London learned so many hours before the Prime Minister of my father's passing.

20

A fresh batch of those fables of leadership in which all peoples, in democracies and under dictatorships alike, are taught to believe had already started to form when I rode with Mother in the seventeen-car funeral train from Washington to Hyde Park. The old enemies within were circulating rumors that Father had fallen over a cliff, been shot—or was it that he shot himself? From the Kremlin an urgent request came for an autopsy, refused by Mother, to ascertain whether there had been foul play at Warm Springs.

Legends were building regarding the new President's "average-man" modesty, stemming from his startled comment to reporters after Mother broke the news to him in her White House sitting room: "Boys, if you ever pray, pray for me now." When he walked down the long red carpet between the banks of lilies in the East Room, where the coffin lay, nobody stood up. The succession was forgotten. The thought among the mourners was that *the* President was dead.

That was dispelled in less than forty-eight hours. The thirty-third President telephoned an official to inform him of a new Presidential appointment. Had the President made it before he died, he was asked. "No," snapped Truman. "He made it just now."

He had his own set of intimates with him in a separate car of the train rolling north. Harry Hopkins, Henry Morgenthau, and others of Father's team shared the car with Mother and me. It was there that Mother was told that Truman intended to make Byrnes his Secretary of State, which in those days, before passage of the twenty-fifth amendment to the Constitution, put him next in line for the White House. She was horrified. "This is the worst mistake in the world," she said softly, knowing that Father had placed little trust in Byrnes and gave him missions to perform only because of his proven competence in handling them.

Byrnes was the first to tell Truman something of the Manhattan Project and the Bomb, whose test day was approaching. There was no record of his reacton to the discovery that he had been hoodwinked for half a decade, but Missouri skepticism was rooted in his nature. Leahy reaffirmed his assurance that the Bomb would never work, and Truman possibly accepted that assessment. Leahy was asked to stay on as Chief of Staff, a profound believer in America first, last, and always, who preferred to call Russians "Bolshies." From Churchill, Truman was to hear welcome criticism of Father for not unveiling the whole story to his Vice President. "This proved of grave disadvantage to our affairs," Winston commented.

A flurry of telephone calls and cablegrams crisscrossed the Atlantic. The battle-scarred Prime Minister wished to fly over for the funeral and a simultaneous introducton to the new President; Eden ultimately came instead and stayed on for the San Francisco Conference. Winston kept up his prodding for the capture of Berlin, venturing to sound the anti-Bolshevik alarm louder than before. A phrase designed to tingle the spine made its initial appearance in one message: "An iron curtain is drawn down behind the front . . . it would be open to the Russians in a very short time to advance if they chose to the waters of the North Sea and the Atlantic." He sought to have Eisenhower ordered to preserve the Luftwaffe as well as all captured German weapons. "He may have great need of these some day." And Churchill referred explicitly to the possibility of a third world war. He was all for drawing the Russians into battle with the Japanese as soon as possible in order to drain the strength of the Red Army.

This was the trump card. Problems with the Soviets must be

magnified to this extent in the hope of convincing an' underinformed American leader that Winston, not Father, knew the
truth and should shape the future. Hitler had forced the
United States and Britain into a wartime partnership. Common
peril from Bolshevism must be acknowledged—or invented—
to keep them as partners in Churchill's last fling at preserving
the *ancien régime.*

Father had been dead for six days when Winston messaged
Truman: "I do not wish our Allied troops or your American
troops to be hustled back at any point by some crude assertion
of a local Russian general." Summoned from Moscow to the
White House, Harriman spoke in much the same vein as the
Prime Minister, forecasting that "we might well have to face an
ideological warfare just as vigorous and dangerous as Fascism
or Nazism.'

Just as he was warming to his theme that "a barbarian invasion of Europe" was on its way, Truman interrupted him to say
(Truman's words) that "I was not afraid of the Russians and
that I intended to be firm." The United States, said the President, "should be able to get eighty-five per cent" in any international dealing.

Harriman, who was quick to see both sides of any question,
recalled, "I had talked with Mr. Truman for only a few minutes
when I began to realize that the man had a real grasp of the situation. What a surprise and relief this was!" Among the numer-
ous advisers the President consulted in this crash course in
statesmanship, only Stimson, soon to be allowed into retirement, spoke up strongly for the Russians. They had performed
faithfully in battle according to their promises, said the Army
Secretary, often, in fact, exceeding what they promised. One
incident, the thwarted Polish elections, would not justify a rift
between the United States and the USSR, in his frank opinion.

Old, honorable Henry, who sometimes dozed off at Cabinet
meetings, equated the Soviet desire for amicable neighbors
with America's strategy of extending overseas defenses
through bases built on trusteeship territories. One great power
achieved its goal by the stark pressure of its troops, the other by
employing the United Nations as its tool. Stalin had already
changed his mind about Gromyko as a result of Father's protest
and was sending Molotov first to Washington and then on to

San Francisco. The conference would be Stettinius' last big job as Secretary of State before he was replaced by Byrnes and given a more limited appointment as first United States delegate to the United Nations. This was the post that Gil Winant set his heart on obtaining. The turndown he received added to the melancholy which eventually drove him to suicide.

Eleven days after Father's death, Truman had an afternoon appointment scheduled with Molotov and Gromyko. At a morning meeting with his senior counselors, he brushed aside Leahy's thought that perhaps the Yalta agreement on Poland was susceptible of two interpretations. Agreements with the Soviets, the President declared, were a one-way street. "It is now or never," Stettinius' assistant, Charles Bohlen, quoted him as saying. Again Stimson interposed the thought that perhaps the Russians were "being more realistic than we were in regard to their own security."

That afternoon, the breeze of the Cold War began to blow. Truman delivered a tongue-lashing to Molotov on the subject of Poland. The prim, frosty commissar bridled. "I have never been talked to in my life like that," he said.

"Carry out your agreements and you won't get talked to like that," retorted the peppery Chief Executive. He intimated that he would press ahead in the United Nations with or without Soviet participation, and Leahy applauded his "strong American stand." The Chief of Staff was overjoyed by the attitude of his new boss. "I believed it would have a beneficial effect on the Soviet outlook on the rest of the world," he reported. "The Russians had always known that we had the power."

Stalin bent a little, though his reply irritated the President because he "used the 'Big I Am.'" The Red Army had been in full possession of Vienna for the past week and promised to take over Prague. Hungary, Rumania, Yugoslavia—one by one the countries of Eastern Europe were being drawn into the Soviet orbit. Winston had nightmares of Stalin's troops marching into Denmark. But Moscow agreed to take a few exiled Poles into the Warsaw government as a condition of Poland's being seated in the United Nations.

For a month now, Nazi leaders had been probing for openings to deal with the British to escape capture by the avenging Russians. The Kremlin smelled a plot to arrange a unilateral armistice on the western front to release German troops to fight the Red Army in the East. The Prime Minister began begging Truman to visit London with the dual purpose of indoctrinating him with his point of view and bolstering the Prime Minister's election chances.

Before his April 25 welcome—by radio—to the delegates from around the world assembling in San Francisco, Truman received another telephone call from Winston. He had sensational developments to report. Heinrich Himmler, Gestapo chief and number-two man in Germany, had met with Count Bernadotte of the Swedish Foreign Office in Lübeck, northwest of Hamburg, offering surrender on the western front. The British Cabinet, Churchill said, felt that this should be kept secret from Stalin. Truman wanted no part in such chicanery. The message that went from London to Moscow read, "There can be no question . . . of anything less than unconditional surrender to the three Major Powers." For the moment, Stalin's doubts were allayed. "I consider your proposal the only correct one," said his instantaneous reply. "Knowing you, I had no doubt that you would act in this way."

The next twelve days brought total victory in Europe—and further disintegration among the Big Three. On April 28, Communist partisans shot Mussolini and his mistress, Signorina Petacci, and hung their corpses upside down on meathooks at a gas station on the Piazzale Loreto in Milan. On April 29, the Germans in Italy surrendered unconditionally to Alexander. On April 30, Hitler and Eva Braun, his bride for twenty-four hours, committed suicide in the lamplit Berlin bunker. On that same Monday, Churchill cabled Truman, pressing for "your forces" to liberate Prague, but Eisenhower was holding his troops on Czechoslovakia's 1937 frontier. General Sir Henry Maitland Wilson, head of the British joint staff mission in Washington, sent a top-secret signal to London: "The Americans propose to drop a Bomb sometime in August. . . . Do we agree that the weapon should be used against the Japanese?" The question went unanswered by the Prime Minister for three weeks.

On May 4, remnants of the Wehrmacht in northwest Germany surrendered unconditionally to Montgomery. Admiral Karl Doenitz, nominated by Hitler as his successor, made a futile attempt to haggle and continue fighting the Soviets. Three more days passed before the Germans signed a surrender on all fronts at Eisenhower's headquarters. Ike would not meet the defeated enemy, whom he left to the attentions of his staff officers. As a gesture of amity, the surrender terms were to be ratified at Red Army headquarters in Berlin the next day. Until that had been done, Ike meant to keep the news secret, to allow simultaneous announcements by the Big Three, again according to previous agreement.

An American reporter broke the ban, which sowed fresh discord. Truman had Leahy take Winston's telephone call. The PM argued that peace should be proclaimed in London and Washington without waiting for Stalin. "It is an idiotic position. . . .You know my difficulties." When Truman stuck by the arrangement made with the Soviets, Winston grew petulant. "Just because the Russians have an absolute control over the presses and such, under tyrannical conditions, we really can't wait for them."

He surmised that the Soviets were out to steal more territory in the next twenty-four hours, so a stratagem was devised to thwart them. His Ministry of Information whipped out an urgent bulletin to be broadcast around the world: "It is understood that in accordance with arrangements between the Three Great Powers an official announcement will be broadcast by the Prime Minister at three P.M. tomorrow, Tuesday, May 8. In view of this fact tomorrow, Tuesday, will be treated as Victory in Europe Day." Which is why Britain and the United States celebrated peace twenty-four hours before the USSR.

In less than a week after its opening, the San Francisco conference was foundering on the rocks. Molotov was heading home, and so was Eden. Harriman proposed to Truman that Hopkins, in retirement and confined to bed, should fly to Moscow to talk with Stalin. The vital question was whether the Marshal would abide by his word and commit the Red Army into Manchuria while the United States, with British and Commonwealth forces reluctantly assigned to overall American command, essayed a direct invasion of Japan.

The President wanted time to think over the proposition. Soviet cooperation was indispensable, but Stalin must not be allowed any hand in postwar control of the Japanese. "The

Russians are planning world conquest" was the thought that haunted Truman.

Without notifying Churchill, he had Hopkins leave on May 23, taking along Louise. Harry would be gone for twenty days. The nub of his mission was to convince the Kremlin leadership that the new President was a man of like mind to Father and to set up another meeting of the Big Three, possibly in Berlin. Hopkins had come around to sharing my Father's estimation of Winston. Just before he took off, he confided to Forrestal that he thought it was of vital importance that we not be maneuvered into a position where Great Britain had us lined up with them as a bloc versus Russia to implement England's European policy. The Socialist opposition was clearly gaining ground in Britain. Forrestal, who would head the unified Department of Defense when Truman abolished Navy and Army as separate entities in 1947, could see little difference between Socialism and Communism.

Hopkins returned buoyed with hope that his parting words to the Marshal, "Our countries have so much in common that they can find a way to work out their problems," would be realized. Stalin had acceded to the United States stand on United Nations voting procedures, which saved that organization from death in the cradle. He looked forward to another summit, where such problems as the Polish question could be reexamined in the spirit of the Roosevelt era. He confirmed that the Soviet Army would be fully deployed in Manchuria by August 8. In general, he had done little but reaffirm the Russian positions on everything ironed out in previous Big Three encounters, but the official record contained one ominous sentence: "The Marshal expects that Russia will share in the actual occupation of Japan."

Churchill was peevish because Hopkins had not gone to see him in London. To appease him, the President sent Joe Davies there in advance of the Potsdam Conference, scheduled for July 17. Davies found Winston tired, nervous, and devoting hours to violent denunciations of the USSR. "How much influence the new President might be able to exert on Churchill was problematical," Leahy concluded.

On the eve of the first plenary session in the Cecilienhof Palace, Potsdam, which had been the rural estate of Crown Prince

Wilhelm, Truman received word that the Bomb had fulfilled all expectations in the Alamogordo test. At Stalin's suggestion, he chaired the next day's meeting at five P.M and postponed giving Winston a full account of the dawning of the atomic age until the day after that. The Marshal had to wait one more week to hear any mention of it.

Cecilienhof, the Russians' choice, was an oasis of green parkland, with freshly planted red roses, geraniums, and hydrangeas blooming in the courtyard. Around the conference table, an immediate drought set in. Winston had called for the British election on July 5 and formed a caretaker government until the results were tallied. That would take three weeks because of the time needed to count the votes of servicemen overseas. He would be "only half a man" at Potsdam until that had been done, he grumbled.

He had set the tone of his campaign against the Labor Party in a nationwide radio speech: "No socialist system can be established without a political police . . . some form of Gestapo." Stalin imagined that a leader so resourceful as Churchill could not fail to be reelected. Hopkins felt otherwise. He had told Forrestal, who turned up at Potsdam uninvited, that the British people craved for new government housing to replace Victorian slums, nationalized industries to guarantee full employment, and a welfare state, none of which Churchill had any thought of delivering.

Hopkins excused himself from going to Potsdam on grounds that he might overshadow Secretary of State Byrnes and Stettinius. The one man available who might have exercised Father's kind of calm and applied some of his techniques of mediation was absent from the conference. Without someone to supply the necessary lubrication, there was no way in the world for empathy to develop between a suspicious Russian, an embittered Englishman, and an unpracticed American leader.

Initially, Truman was impressed by Stalin, and he took an instant liking to Churchill. "There was something very open and genuine about the way he greeted me," the sometimes ingenuous President remembered. "Churchill and I never had a serious disagreement about anything." Even Winston was astonished by Truman's take-it-or-leave-it approach to the Marshal.

The talks had barely begun before Chairman Truman announced that unless they got to the major issues, "I was going
to pack up and go home. I meant just that." Stalin broke into
throaty laughter. "I want to go home, too." Winston, who had
taken a week off beforehand to rest in the south of France, had
promised, "I shall keep in the background of the conference."
He was no more capable of that than of voting Labor. He wanted to discuss the Western powers' rights to their prewar property in Rumania, he told his fellow conferees, but "an iron curtain has come down around the British mission in Bucharest."

"All fairy tales!" growled Stalin.

They left the resolution of those rights unsettled, along with
the matter of reconstruction in Poland. One of the few agenda
items on which they finished in accord was the program for war
on Japan. As they all were aware, the last of the Axis powers
had started putting out peace feelers four days before they met
in Potsdam.

In Moscow on July 13, Ambassador Sato had received orders
from Foreign Minister Shigemitsu in Tokyo to see Molotov and
lay before him "the Emperor's strong desire to secure a ter-
mination of the war." Sato made no pretense to Molotov. Japan
was "thoroughly and completely defeated." The only course
left was "quick and definite action" in recognition of that fact.
Magic's code-cracking gave our State Department knowledge
of this turn of events.

In the three-handed poker game played in the Cecilienhof
Palace with the peace and security of the world for stakes, Stalin
said nothing about Tojo's overtures for two weeks. On the second day of the conference, a request from Tokyo was relayed
to him, specifically asking for his mediation with the others of
the Big Three to end the war. A Japanese prince would be sent
to Moscow to head the negotiating mission. The Marshal rejected the proposal as too vague and relayed no word of it either to
Truman or Churchill. The following day, the military chiefs
gathered in supplementary meetings at Potsdam to set November 15, 1946, as "the date for the end of organized resistance by
Japan," contemplating another sixteen months of battle.

Winston had already been told the full story of the device
whose heat had fused the desert sands and sent an enormous
cloud unfolding in the sky like an umbrella. He felt overwhelm-

ing relief. "We should not need the Russians. The end of the
Japanese war no longer depended on the pouring in of their
armies for the final and perhaps protracted slaughter. We had
no need to ask favors of them."

He urged Truman to total secrecy: tell Stalin nothing until
the conference was over, then simply pass on the fact and refuse to divulge details. With only forty-eight hours left in office,
the Prime Minister was host at a banquet on Tuesday, July 24.
As the guests left the table, the President drew Stalin aside and
mentioned as casually as the buyer of a new kitchen stove that
the United States had "a new weapon of unusual destructive
power." By Truman's later account, the Marshal was not especially interested. He was glad to hear it, he said; he hoped it
would be put to good use against the Japanese. Churchill hov-
ered close by, straining to catch every word of the conversation.

"How did it go?" he asked Truman.

"He never asked a question." His fellow conspirator grinned.

On Wednesday morning, Winston left for London to await
the election results. Labor came in on a landslide—393 seats to
the Conservatives' 213. In the matter of the Bomb, he left its
employment for Truman to decide, issuing what amounted to a
blank check without consulting the British Cabinet. On Thursday, July 26, the day that the colorlessly competent Clement
Attlee took over as Prime Minister, a Big Three proclamation
gave solemn warning to Tokyo: "The time has come for Japan
to decide." Choose to surrender unconditionally or face the unspecified consequences.

On Saturday, Stalin had a further message from Tokyo, out-
lining the working program which the proposed Japanese
peace mission would follow and offering to collaborate with the
Soviets. He proceeded to fill in Truman and Attlee, who had
hurried to Potsdam, with details of this and the previous communications. The latest feeler was still too vague for his liking,
said the Marshal.

Whether and where and when to drop the Bomb was Truman's decision alone. Two of the men he relied on most gave
him their counsel. Byrnes was "most anxious to get the Japanese affair over with before the Russians got in." Leahy felt the
same way. "Some of us indulged in a hope," he recalled, "that
Japan might get out of the war before the Soviet Union came

in." Truman himself professed that he "never had any doubt that it should be used." In that, he had the concurrence of a committee of distinguished American citizens whom he hand-picked to study the potentials as soon as he learned of the Manhattan Project.

I can only guess what Father would have done in the circumstances. I know that he conjectured ordering a demonstration drop on a purely military target, remote from any city. Would he have sanctioned that much in the face of hard evidence of Japanese desire to seek peace? Again, I can only speculate.

He felt certain that, possessing this new instrument for good or evil in addition to the greatest productive capacity on earth, the United States could enlist other countries in a program of international self-development, with gradual liberalization of the Communist dictatorships and controlled evolution of capitalism to the point where both systems could join in the peaceful pursuit of better living conditions for all peoples. I believe that he would have moved to put the Bomb's deterrent power and the development of atomic fission as an energy source into the hands of his chosen instrument for the creation of a world governed by law and reason—the United Nations.

The USS *Augusta* was plowing westward across the Atlantic, bringing the Presidential party home, when the map room officer handed Truman a top-priority signal from the Secretary of War: BIG BOMB DROPPED ON HIROSHIMA AUGUST 5 AT 7:15 P.M. WASHINGTON TIME. FIRST REPORTS INDICATE COMPLETE SUCCESS WHICH WAS EVEN MORE CONSPICUOUS THAN EARLIER TEST. "This is the greatest thing in history!" exclaimed the beaming President. He had the crew assembled in the mess hall to hear the news. It was greeted with deafening cheers.

Two days later, the Soviet Union declared war on Japan, and the toll of the dead in the city of Hiroshima stood at 100,000. The following morning, Nagasaki was obliterated, a prelude to Japanese surrender twenty-four hours afterward. The war went on, though it was labeled "cold" now, and the list of the defeated contained some surprises, accompanying the switching of sides.

Before the month was over, Truman terminated lend-lease to Britain and the Soviet Union. "I am merely living up to a promise I made as Vice-President," he said opaquely. "It is no longer necessary." Prospects of a reconstruction loan to Moscow died simultaneously. He recognized that Britain was propelled into an immediate crisis, faced with bankruptcy in what some economists termed "a financial Dunkirk."

The British owed more than $16 billion around the world. Their exports were down by more than half. Government spending overseas stood at five times the prewar figures. The Empire, for which Winston had fought like a bull mastiff, was falling to pieces. Every timetable for postwar recovery had to be jettisoned. Despite the contributions of their scientists, all further information on the Bomb and the potentials of atomic energy were cut off until new arrangements could be worked out in Washington. Forrestal held that the Bomb and the knowledge it produced were "the property of the American people." Leahy went farther than that. At least for the present, "the United States must have more and better atom bombs than any potential enemy."

When a stream of emissaries came begging from London, they found that Truman drove stern bargains. It took the best part of a year to persuade him to grant a little more than half the loan they had been seeking. "When it became apparent that we would go no higher," as he put it, they signed on his terms for $3,750 million over fifty years, starting July 15, 1946.

Winston played an unrecognized role in tying down American aid and turning Truman's sharp eyes toward world affairs when he would rather have turned his back. Anti-Bolshevism worked the trick. The turnabout in American policies that followed instantly on Father's death clinched Stalin's suspicions of the West. A *cordon sanitaire* of friendly governments in Eastern Europe was as imperative as the Kremlin's frantic effort to perfect its own Bomb, which was produced in August, 1949, three years ahead of our Defense Department's expectations, setting off the race to construct weapons of infinitely greater destructive capacity, utilizing hydrogen as their core.

In the middle of the beating down that the British loan negotiators were submitting to in Washington, Truman and Churchill were in close contact. At the President's invitation, Winston turned up at Westminster College in Fulton, Missouri, to be awarded an honorary doctorate. The President rode with him on the train. The new POTUS, in cap and gown, introduced the cherubic Former Naval Person, similarly clad, who was to deliver an address entitled, "The Sinews of Peace." The phrase that made the headlines was one that Churchill had been bandying around for the past year.

"From Stettin to the Baltic, to Trieste in the Adriatic, an iron curtain has descended across the Continent." He had a solution to propose. "Let no one underestimate the abiding power of the British Empire and Commonwealth. . . . If the population of the English-speaking Commonwealth be added to that of the United States, with all that such cooperation implies in the air, on the sea, all over the globe, and in science and in industry, and in moral force, there will be no quivering, precarious balance of power to offer its temptation to ambition or adventure. . . . The high roads of the future will be clear, not only for us but for all, not only for our time but for a century to come."

The date was March 5, 1946. This was the official, sponsored declaration of cold war. Across the world, with words and deeds and weapons, West would battle East as one side lumped together all its supposed enemies as Communists and the other denounced capitalism as the implacable foe. West and East alike drove other nations of all sizes to pick between them, though the smart ones made a practice of playing one side against the other.

The milestones on the "high roads of the future" would be death and deprivation, brought on in part by the United States as the biggest arms dealer in the world, with sales of $29.7 billion from 1963 to 1973, followed by Soviet deals of $15.6 billion in the same period. In that decade—the most recent for which the U.S. Arms Control and Disarmament Agency has figures—the nations of the world spent $2.5 *trillion* for military purposes, Americans $765 billion, Soviets $674 billion.

Each side escalated the contest for fear of what the other might do. After the Fulton speech, Stalin immediately denounced Churchill as "a firebrand of war" and anticipated an invasion of Eastern Europe on Churchillian lines. "A peaceful international order" was impossible, the old Bolshevik concluded, "under the present capitalist development of the world economy." A five-year expansion of the Soviet arms industry was ordered "to guarantee our country against any eventuality."

Truman saw the situation in looking-glass terms. "The fundamental design of the Soviet Union is a world dominated by the will of the Kremlin. Whether we like it or not, this makes the United States the principal target of the Kremlin and the enemy that must be destroyed or subverted before the Soviets can achieve their goal."

Father intended to leave the people of all nations a legacy of peace and well-being. Instead, they have lived in fear of annihilation by bigger and better Bombs, quarreling with each other in the madhouse world where law and reason are as scarce as enlightened leadership. What he did achieve by April 12, 1945, was crystallized by a British historian: "The British and the Americans sat back, though not of malice aforethought, while the Russians defeated Germany for them. Of the three great men at the top, Roosevelt was the only one who knew what he was doing; he made the United States the greatest power in the world at virtually no cost."

A Fireside Reflection

The other night, after completing this account of the twelve turbulent years of Father's Presidency and the carefully laid plans which he envisaged for the postwar world, I fell to reading news of the deterioration of American world leadership and the rising confrontations appearing all over the globe. The populations of the countries on our planet's surface have little realization of the cataclysmic destruction which their leaders are thrusting upon them.

I remembered Father talking to me about the shifts of power through the ages. He said, "Bunny, when you look back over history, you recognize that the center of world power has followed a pattern of westward movement since thousands of years before the birth of Christ down to the present day. The Chinese, Persian, Egyptian, Greek, Roman, Western European, British, and finally United States emergence as world leaders, directing the destinies of other nations, is there in the record. How long our country remains a leader depends on what we do in the last half of this century. Ours is probably the most difficult challenge of all. All other powers created their eras of leadership through conquest and domination of other nations. We must lead the world away from conquest toward the goal of a peaceful solution of our mutual problems.

"Peace on earth through an end to armed conflict will elude our grasp unless we can overcome some basic faults of humanity. First and foremost of these is the innate greed of the individual man. Second is man's animal instinct to reduce the surplus population through wars of attrition. Third is the basic lack of understanding of each other by the haves and the have-nots, compounded by differences in language and ethnic backgrounds.

"To these basic obstacles must be added the problems of overpopulation, with resultant starvation of countless millions; drainage of the earth's natural resources; pollution of our air and water; and, lastly, our failure to utilize the scientific research of all humanity to seek and find the solution to all these seemingly insoluble problems.

"I hope to point the efforts of our countrymen and, by their example, the rest of the peoples of this earth on the high road to accomplishing the solutions. But it will remain for others to follow who have the will and ability to complete the task. Their failure can only mean the extinction of mankind."

Now, thirty years after he told me this, I look at the intervening decades and realize that three-quarters of the twentieth century has passed. The world continues on a mad course toward destruction. FDR died without setting our country and the world on the path of which he dreamed.

Like all other humans, I have been feeling more and more discouraged and frustrated by events taking place daily in the United States and throughout the world. A voice in the back of my mind keeps saying, "There is still time! There is still hope! Mankind will find the leadership of unselfish men to give us the answers before it is too late. God did not create man to have him destroy himself by holocaust."

The other night I went to bed with these thoughts tumbling through my head. When I fell asleep, a dream emerged.

I saw before me a great round table and around this table were gathered men of many tongues, colors, and religions. I realized, as they talked, that I was witnessing a summit meeting of the leaders of nations from all parts of the globe. The solemnity of the discussion was heightened by the fact that this meeting was being televised and broadcast to every living person on our planet. The statements of these men were being translated into all tongues. The world was seeing and hearing whether their leaders could evolve a global method for man to coexist with his neighbor and accept the responsibilities incumbent upon him for his neighbor's welfare.

One man started to speak, and the others fell silent. The cameras and microphones concentrated on him and the words that came from his lips made me feel as I had forty-odd years before, when, with most of a nation, I had listened to a fireside chat by the man who restored for all of us our dignity, our faith, our consciences, our will to work and survive.

In my dream the speaker said:

"My fellow citizens of the world, we are gathered here as your representataives and servants and for one purpose. We are faced with the fact that self-destruction may overcome us all. Since the last global conflict, which ended in 1945, we have created a body designed by its founders to meditate disputes among nations and bring equal dignity, liberty, and opportunity to all peoples.

"The man who conceived the creation of this body, the thirty-second President of the United States of America, died a few days before it came into being in the city of San Francisco. But he had prepared, the day before he died, a speech which he planned to deliver to that convention. In it he had this to say:

"'Today we are faced with the preeminent fact that, if civilization is to survive, we must cultivate the science of human relations—the ability of all peoples, of all kinds, to live together and work together, in the same world, at peace.

"'Let me assure you that my hand is the steadier for the work that is to be done, that I move more firmly into the task, knowing that you—millions and millions of you—are joined with me in the resolve to make this work endure.

"'The work, my friends, is peace. More than an end to war—an end to the beginnings of all wars. Yes, an end, forever, to this impractical, unrealistic settlement of the differences between governments by the mass killing of peoples.

"'Today, as we move against the terrible scourge of war—as we go forward toward the greatest contribution that any generation of human beings can make in this world—the contribution of lasting peace—I ask that you keep up your faith. I measure the sound, solid achievement that can be made at this time by the straight edge of your own confidence and your resolve. And to you, and to all Americans who dedicate themselves with us to the making of an abiding peace, I say: The only limit to our realization of tomorrow will be our doubts of today. Let us move forward with strong and active faith.'

"Those words were written thirty years ago and, alas, no one listened to their message. Nuclear fission as a mass weapon of destruction came into being. The United States decided to keep this discovery to itself, and not turn control of it over to a peace-keeping United Nations police force. Soon the Soviet Union developed the same destructive ability. China, England, and France developed similar lethal weapons. Now India, South Africa, Israel, Japan, Australia, Germany, and others have the same capabilities.

"During this past thirty years new regional conflicts have developed. In Southeast Asia millions have been killed, maimed, and made homeless. In the Middle East a senseless conflict has raged, heightened by religious bigotry. In Africa millions have died by starvation, tribal warfare, and racial hatreds. All over the world corrupt governments, dictators, and inept leaders have brought on civil wars that have proven disastrously costly in lives and well-being.

"The United States and the Soviet Union have jointly aided and abetted this series of events. To a lesser extent China, England, France, and the rest of Europe have contributed to the carnage.

"At the same time, all the industrial powers have competed with one another to win economic supremacy. A huge proportion of the world's productive capability is today spent in the creation of more and more armaments.

"The Communist world has endeavored to export its social and ideological formulas to the rest of the world, to help the Soviet Union in establishing a new worldwide empire. Already, cracks are appearing in this Communist solidarity, with the rising challenge to Soviet leadership by the People's Republic of China.

"Today, the United Nations is a body made up of many nations. Unfortunately these nations, many of them, are not represented by men capable of governing for the greatest good of their people. Many more use the United Nations solely to further their own self-serving aims. In short, the body, founded for the noblest aims, has rapidly deteriorated into a sounding board for self-serving blocs, each intent on military or economic domination of others.

"At this point in time, we are witnessing the disintegration of the world, brought on by military and economic wars and by the irresponsible leadership extant throughout most of the nations of the world.

"With sadness in my heart, my fellow world-citizens, I note that little has been done in the last thirty years to tackle the problems that sooner or later must overwhelm us all.

"First, the threat of nuclear warfare can effectively wipe us all from the face of the earth. This threat can be solved in only one way. A United Nations peace-keeping police force must be set up. All nuclear arms must be turned over to this body. All armed forces of all nations must be cut back to policing organizations for domestic duties, and conventional armed forces will be contributed, proportionately, to the UN police force, for their control and use to keep peace throughout the world.

"Second, the increase of the population of this earth must be effectively controlled to ensure the survival and well-being of every inhabitant. This can only be accomplished with the support of ethnic and religious leaders, who will recognize the inevitable need of this decision.

"Realization by these leaders that without control through education and health benefits the people of this planet will rapidly outgrow the productive capacity of the earth is all-important. The only final result can be cannibalism and internecine warfare.

"Third, the natural resources of this earth must be developed and preserved for the greatest good of all our people. This demands a common development and marketing plan for all resources, no matter in what nation they are located. It further entails, especially in the energy field, the rapid development of other sources of energy, such as solar and nuclear, on a worldwide basis.

"Fourth, there must be created a worldwide agricultural production plan, which will ensure the adequate feeding of all people, without the ever-present threat of starvation confronting so many millions.

"Fifth, a pollution program on a worldwide basis must be inaugurated to protect the air which we breathe and the water and food which are necessary for our existence.

"Sixth, a universal code of law must be created, with world courts to administer it. These courts must be superior to, and obeyed by, those of every nation, large or small.

"Seventh, many other administrative and policymaking bodies must be set up and given global authority within the framework of a reorganized and revitalized United Nations. I refer to international trade, transportation, health, education, scientific research, and the further development of outer space with its tremendous potentiality to further man's attainments.

"My fellow human beings, none of this can come to pass without the wholehearted support of all the nations of the world.

"Failure by any segment of the earth's population to work in support of this effort toward a peaceful world of joint effort for survival can have only one result: world economic chaos, followed by extinction through nuclear holocaust.

"A man died in 1945. The day before his death he expressed the conviction that we all wanted to live in peace and to prosper. For thirty years we have denied his faith. Let us today agree to reaffirm his creed, and, unselfishly, forget our own personal, nationalistic or ideological aims and join together in forging a world of peace and hope for mankind."

When the speaker in my dream stopped talking and settled back in his chair, I awoke. I felt that a new presence had stepped forward to pick up the torch and lead the peoples of this world to unexplored summits of achievement. I felt that Franklin Delano Roosevelt had not lived and dreamed in vain.

I still believe that this will come to pass.

Index